SEEKING WORLD ORDER

SEEKING
WORLD
ORDER

The
United States and
International Organization
to 1920

Warren F. Kuehl

Vanderbilt
University Press
Nashville

To Olga

179786

This is an account of more than a century of effort in the United States to achieve an international organization. It begins with a brief introduction to the earliest known plans for world co-operation and ends with the defeat of the Treaty of Versailles in the Senate on March 19, 1920. It is a study of an idea and an ideal, the history of a movement and the men and societies which made it. Other writers have touched upon parts of the story, but no full picture has ever been presented of internationalism in American life during these years. Scholars have long discussed its counterpart, isolationism, without fully appreciating the continuous efforts, particularly between 1890 and 1920, to create an international organization. Yet historians of the future may eventually record this movement as one of the most notable products of the twentieth century.

While this work concentrates upon events within the United States, it also explores activities elsewhere, since it would be impossible to treat the subject of international organization from the perspective of one nation. No claim for inclusiveness, however, can be made for developments in other lands. Likewise, this study confines itself primarily to attempts to achieve a politically organized world. Social, humanitarian, and economic aspects have not been ignored, but they have been examined only to discover what impact they had upon political concepts. Thus, the word "internationalist" has been used to describe any person who thought in terms of an organic functioning body.

A variety of views existed among the internationalists. Generalists endorsed an ideal without elaborating upon their beliefs. Arbitrationists hoped that some society could be developed through a network of arbitral treaties binding nations to the pacific settlement of disputes. Legalists or judicial advocates added to that dream their desire for a court of justice which would serve as the core of any body and achieve peace through law. Such men were usually conservative in their programs, believing in a gradual approach toward their goal, and highly sensitive to the concept of sovereignty and the attitudes of governments.

Some internationalists, however, called for a more radical approach. Federationists emphasized a need for a more complete union in which nations would combine under a form of government comparable to that of the United States. Most of them would have limited the powers conferred, but a few of them believed in extensive grants of authority. World government exponents emphasized that sovereignty had to be subordinated to the will of an international organization, and they often called for a supranational agency to maintain peace. Woven into the picture were the sanctionists. The more radical thinkers insisted upon an international army and navy; the more cautious ones spoke only of economic pressures. Between these two extremes existed a wide variety of sanctionists, each insisting that some force would be required to make a world society effective but unable to agree upon the degree of power needed or how it should be applied.

Such diversity of ideas and exponents should indicate that no exact definition can be given for many of the terms used. Indeed, change was one of the major features of a movement covering many decades and lands. The phrase "League of Nations," for instance, had a meaning in 1919 that was different from its meaning in 1907 or 1914. Thus, words did not change, but men's thinking about them did.

Reference appears throughout this study to the modern movement for an international organization. This began around the turn of the twentieth century when a new group of internationalists appeared whose attitudes toward the subject were distinctly different from those of peace advocates who had emphasized the brotherhood of man in their discussions. The latter had also campaigned primarily against armaments and militarism by preaching a philosophy of nonresistance and relying upon ethical and moral arguments in attacking the idea of war. A few of them had departed from this essentially negative posture to support some type of world society, but they were still pacifists first and internationalists second. The modern advocates of a politically organized world, however, were internationalists first and pacifists only incidentally. They were converts to the ideal of an organized world and were not limited in their thinking, their plans, or their efforts. While they usually co-operated with peace societies, they introduced a new type of thinker to the American scene.

Some comment should be made regarding the terminal date of this study. Most scholars viewing the struggle in the United States for membership in the League of Nations carry their discussion through the election of 1920. While this has often seemed logical for their purposes, the arguments and issues raised in the campaign that year are more in keeping with developments in the 1920s and 1930s than with previous efforts. They have been left, therefore, for what is projected as a companion volume to cover the endeavors of American internationalists in those two decades.

This work has relied heavily upon contemporary sources in the form of ephemeral printed materials and manuscript collections. It was not possible to locate all of the pamphlets and leaflets published, and the papers of a few of the important figures were of little value. It is doubtful, however, that additional information from these sources would have altered the patterns described or the conclusions reached.

I am indebted to many persons who have aided me, especially Professors Don R. Gerlach and David C. Riede of the University of Akron. My obligation is also great to Professor Richard W. Leopold of Northwestern University whose perceptive suggestions contributed greatly to the form and accuracy of this study. Professors Martin D. Dubin of Northern Illinois University, Calvin D. Davis of Duke University, and Roland N. Stromberg of the University of Wisconsin at Milwaukee also read the manuscript and shared with me their specialized knowledge of the subject. Any omissions and shortcomings, however, are still mine alone.

To my wife, Olga, and my sons, Marshall and Paul, I wish to make amends for the many hours I have spent away from them both in research in diverse places and in my study at home. They have been more than understanding and patient.

W. F. K.

T A B L E   O F   C O N T E N T S

The internationalists who care for the human future and enjoy some world citizenship have no precedents, no technique, no common tradition or understood procedure to guide them. The science of international relations is for them like the first stumbling of a child. They live at the very dawn of new ways and thinking, and they are certain to meet many failures before their minds have clarified their task. Our own generation may thus see no great discovery, no telling formulation of principles. It will suffer in experiments which are blind, and accumulate a little wisdom in suffering. The more naïve will build high hopes and fall into disappointment. They will grow impatient with those who end every affirmation with a question mark and surround every plan with a disturbing doubt. But the more critical will know that peace is a long adventure, which would be crushing in its difficulties if it were not sustained by the finest hope that lures the mind of man.

New Republic, May 1, 1915.

SEEKING WORLD ORDER

An Idea
Evolves

On the nineteenth of March 1920, according to a Senate vote, the United States refused to join the newly formed League of Nations. The American people had debated that issue for several months as they weighed alternatives; now the decision had been made. The events that day marked the culmination of centuries of effort on the part of men to create an international organization, and they also revealed a striking paradox. The nation which rejected membership in the League had been the one which had seen more agitation and planning toward that end than any other. Indeed, Americans for more than eighty years had led the world in discussing the subject. What, then, had led to this contradictory situation? Why were those very people who had been the ideal's greatest exponents unable to agree on a satisfactory compromise which would have taken their country into the League? Only a study of evolving ideas, some of them centuries old, concerning an international organization can provide the answers.

Even in Grecian times, men realized that by uniting their states in confederations and amphictyonic councils they could achieve stability and peace.[1] Later, as thinkers looked back at the peace of the Roman Empire

---

1. Elizabeth York, *Leagues of Nations: Ancient, Mediaeval, and Modern*, pp. 2–8, 25–36; A. C. F. Beales, *The History of Peace*, p. 20; "A League of Nations, B.C.," *Living Age*, CCXCVIII (July 13, 1918), 113–115.

and the equilibrium achieved by the Roman Catholic Church in medieval times, they pondered conditions and suggested a federation under either the Pope or the Holy Roman Emperor.[2]

Among these planners, the proposals of Pierre Dubois, a Norman lawyer, and George Poděbrad, a king of Bohemia, merit attention. In 1306 Dubois suggested an assembly of princes, a permanent court of arbitration, and the use of economic and military sanctions to uphold decisions and thus keep the peace.[3] In 1460 Poděbrad called for a congress, a court, sanctions, and an executive agency in the form of a secretariat. As a permanently functioning body, it would maintain an army, coin money, and impose and collect taxes.[4]

The appearance of nations, however, had a greater impact upon concepts of an international organization than did unitary states. As large, purely centralized territorial entities appeared, organized in accordance with the new idea of sovereignty, wars engulfed Europe. Men thus had reason to desire peace and to suggest that countries might attain a degree of stability by uniting. They faced a difficult task, however, for the very existence of the new nation-state, jealous of its powers and suspicious of others, stood as an obstacle to their dream. Most of the early planners, therefore, realized that governments could never be compelled to join an association and that all action would have to be on a voluntary basis.

Not until 1623, therefore, did anyone present a plan of merit which considered the changed realities of international life. Émeric Crucé, a French scholar, in the "New Cyneas," suggested a permanent congress of ambassadors, not princes, who would represent nations. He thought in terms of a world-wide league, since he included Ethiopia, Persia, the Indies, and China. A tribunal would hear disputes between states, enforce the assembly's laws, and "pursue with arms those who would wish to oppose it." Crucé also

2. August C. Krey, "The International State of the Middle Ages: Some Reasons for Its Failure," *American Historical Review*, XXVIII (October 1922), 1–12; Beales, *History of Peace*, pp. 21–22; Sylvester J. Hemleben, *Plans for World Peace through Six Centuries*, pp. 1–21; York, *Leagues of Nations*, pp. 52–69; Edward Krehbiel, *Nationalism, War and Society*, pp. 151–152.

3. C. Delisle Burns, "A Medieval Internationalist," *Monist*, XXVII (January 1917), 105–113; Charles H. Levermore, "Synopsis of Plans for International Organization," *Advocate of Peace*, LXXXI (August 1919), 266; Margaret Robinson, *Arbitration and the Hague Peace Conferences, 1899 and 1907*, p. 9; Robert Jones and S. S. Sherman, *The League of Nations from Idea to Reality*, p. 43.

4. Hemleben, *Plans for World Peace*, pp. 14–17; Levermore, "Synopsis of Plans," p. 266.

realized that a union should do more than adjudicate questions; it should anticipate conflicts and allay conditions which might lead to war.[5]

Crucé included no provision for an executive, and he saw no danger in leaving national forces intact, a view quite different from the proposals for disarmament of internationalists who followed him. He did, however, perceive that internal domestic conditions could affect peace. Therefore, he recommended trade and educational programs to promote feelings of fraternity, and many later writers, especially William Penn and William Ladd, borrowed this idea.[6] In Crucé, one finds an unusual blend of the old and the new concepts of his day. He believed in the divine-right theory of monarchy and thus would maintain rulers on their throne. Yet at the same time he recognized that the world would not remain static and that territorial changes would occur. Hence, rather than resort to war, princes should refer the legitimacy of their claims to the congress.[7] In this appeal to logic, Crucé also anticipated the arguments of later American advocates.

A contemporary of Crucé, Maximilien de Béthune, duc de Sully, also presented a plan that influenced later thinkers.[8] This friend and admirer of Henry IV of France suggested that Europe be divided equally among fifteen nations so that none of them would envy or fear the other. A "general council" with commissioners from each state would then sit continuously as a senate with power to legislate and resolve disputes. Sully also provided for lesser bodies to act as courts with the council serving as an appeals body. Decrees would be binding and would be upheld by the military arm of the commonwealth. Members would contribute to the force on a quota basis, and since the contingents would be larger than those of any country, they could keep the peace. Sully, however, also planned to use this army and

5. Émeric Crucé, *The New Cyneas*, trans. and ed. Thomas W. Balch, pp. 104, 120–122; John A. R. Marriott, *Commonwealth or Anarchy?*, p. 58.

6. Crucé, *New Cyneas*, pp. 130, 294, 60–76.

7. *Ibid.*, pp. 124, 130, 168–178. Since Crucé thought that Protestants were not members of the Christian church, his inclusion of pagan states is all the more remarkable. *Ibid.*, p. xv.

8. It has long been debated whether Sully, Henry IV of France, or Queen Elizabeth of England formulated his plan. Most authorities agree that Sully wrote it, probably after the death of Henry in 1610. Elizabeth V. Souleyman, *The Vision of World Peace in Seventeenth and Eighteenth-Century France*, p. 28; Beales, *History of Peace*, p. 28; James Westphall Thompson, "The Great Design of Henry IV," *School Review*, XVIII (February 1910), 146–147; Edwin D. Mead, "Reply . . . ," *ibid.*, (June 1910), pp. 424–425; William Ladd, *An Essay on a Congress of Nations*, p. xv; Hemleben, *Plans for World Peace*, pp. 34–35.

navy to push back the Turks in Europe and even to regain North Africa.[9]

Sully's Great Design possessed shortcomings. He referred only to Europe and never thought in terms of Crucé's more universal association. He also omitted a detail which became important to later internationalists. The Great Design contained no definitive provisions for arbitration, although an arbitral process was implicit in Sully's idea that disputes should be settled peacefully. Sully did, however, suggest one unusual thing—the sentiment of nationality should be considered in territorial adjustments. Thus the principle of self-determination found its first advocate.[10]

Although the Great Design may have been little more than a scheme to revamp the power structure in Europe, it served as a model for many later planners and subsequently influenced their projects. By the twentieth century, most of the internationalists in the United States knew of the man and his work and often praised him.

In 1625, a book written by a Dutch jurisconsult, Hugo Grotius, appeared. *De Jure Belli ac Pacis* also reflected the eddying currents of Europe in the seventeenth century. It revealed a reaction against the international anarchy of the age and the unscrupulous political methods which Niccolò Machiavelli had described in *The Prince*.[11] It also disclosed a growing rational approach to problems which the *philosophes* of the late eighteenth century developed. Finally, it showed the extent to which the infant study of international law had developed.

Building upon the labors of certain predecessors, Grotius introduced into the subject of international law two basic ideas. First, he injected ethical and moral principles into a discussion of war. Second, he employed reason to argue that a body of rulers which could be applied to governments actually existed. Agreeing with Aristotle that man is essentially a political animal, Grotius reasoned that men organized first into tribal communities and then into states. As they did so, they accepted a system of law. He saw a society of nations as a natural fact (*jus naturale*), already operating under regulations which merely awaited codification. By recognizing the exuberant nationalism of the age and applying his codes, Grotius hoped to find a way to peace and order.[12]

9. Béthune, *The Great Design of Henry IV . . .* , pp. 33–36; 23–25.
10. *Ibid.*, pp. 26–34, 36–43.
11. Andrew D. White, *Seven Great Statesmen*, pp. 72–87.
12. Hemleben, *Plans for World Peace*, pp. 42–44; Ladd, *Essay*, p. xiv; Beales, *History of Peace*, pp. 29–30; Marriott, *Commonwealth or Anarchy?*, pp. 61–62; Amos S. Hershey, "History of International Law Since the Peace of Westphalia," *American Journal of International Law* (hereafter cited as *AJIL*), VI (January 1912), 30–32.

Grotius never developed a plan for a genuine international organization, but he did suggest the creation of a congress of Christian powers. It should meet, decide upon controversies submitted to it, and force parties to accept its decisions. While his assembly would have convened only periodically, it still opened a way for the peaceful settlement of disputes.[13]

De Jure Belli ac Pacis had a widespread impact. Grotius has been praised as the "Father of Arbitration" and of international law, and as the "founder of the science of international law." Some of these titles are not wholly justified in that Crucé advanced the idea of arbitration and that the codification of law had been a topic of discussion for many years.[14] Grotius's real contribution lay in the area of morality, for he indicated that in international relations governments could rely upon the ideal of right rather than force to settle differences. For the first time, men began to think in terms of peace through law. They finally recognized that nations might be regulated by rules comparable to those which governed people.[15]

Near the end of the seventeenth century, William Penn presented his views in an *Essay Towards the Present and Future Peace of Europe*. Later American internationalists considered Penn their spiritual forefather because of his relationship with the colony of Pennsylvania and because of his philosophy that peace could be maintained only "by justice, which is a fruit of government."[16] Penn suggested a new European order built around a congress to which all kings should send deputies. It would meet yearly or at least once every two years or on occasion. All disputes which nations could not solve should be referred to this body. Any country refusing to abide by the provisions or ignoring decisions or embarking upon war would face "all the other sovereignties, united as one strength." These powers would "compel the submission and performance of the sentence, with damages" assessed for the party harmed and for the cost of enforcement. No government in Europe, said Penn, could defy such an authority.[17]

Some ninety diplomats would constitute the assembly, with wealth determining the number from each state. Penn suggested a rotating presidency

13. Hugo Grotius, *De Jure Belli ac Pacis Libri Tres*, trans. F. W. Kelsey, II, 560–563; Marriott, *Commonwealth or Anarchy?*, pp. 59–62.

14. Beales, *History of Peace*, p. 30. The names of St. Thomas Aquinas, Francisco de Victoria, Francisco Suárez, Balthazar de Ayala, and Alberico Gentili are often listed as predecessors to Grotius.

15. Marriott, *Commonwealth or Anarchy?*, p. 61, citing C. Van Vollenhoven, *The Law of Peace*, p. 192.

16. William Penn, *The Fruits of Solitude and Other Writings*, pp. 3–8.

17. *Ibid.*, p. 8.

to allay jealousies. He also worried about corruption, and to circumvent it he outlined a system of balloting which required a three-fourths vote on measures.[18]

Penn considered possible objections to his plan. To the argument that the powerful and wealthy nations would not co-operate, Penn replied that they should be compelled to join. He faced the charge of an increasing effeminacy as armies declined with a proposal for a greater emphasis upon "mechanical knowledge and in natural philosophy." To counteract a claim that unemployment would increase, Penn responded along the same lines— develop education in trade, farming, and science. In these proposals, Penn re-echoed Crucé, but he failed to propose direct education for peace. To a final argument that the project would weaken the power of princes, he answered that their rule would not be affected at home. If any change occurred, it would be that the more powerful kings would be unable to dominate the scene so easily. Penn noted many benefits from his program and ended by acknowledging the sources for his ideas. He attributed the federal principle to the Republic of the United Netherlands and his general scheme to the Great Design.[19]

In the next one hundred years plans appeared in increasing numbers. Charles Irénée Castel de Saint-Pierre presented an elaborate one between 1712 and 1714 in his *Project for Settling an Everlasting Peace in Europe.* He proposed a "perpetual Union" of the Christian rulers of Europe. Each deputy from the major powers could cast one vote in the congress, while smaller states would be grouped to render a collective ballot. A court would render decisions without right of appeal, and sovereigns would be expected to honor and uphold the decrees.[20]

Additional clauses provided for mediation and arbitration. Any nation which failed to respect the process or the award would face the combined forces of the league, be threatened with a loss of territory, and be assessed the costs of the war if it refused to acquiesce. The plan suggested that governments reduce their armies and have the organization maintain their constitutions and defend their rulers against sedition and rebellion. The congress could borrow troops from the members and raise money by a direct levy.[21]

The Abbé de Saint-Pierre had a limited concept of an international society, for he confined his association to European and Christian states. He

18. *Ibid.*, pp. 10–12.

19. *Ibid.*, pp. 13–21.

20. Hemleben, *Plans for World Peace*, p. 56; Carl J. Friedrich, *Inevitable Peace,* p. 29; York, *Leagues of Nations*, p. 170; W. Evans Darby, *International Tribunals: A Collection of the Various Schemes . . .* , pp. 20, 32, 26, 22, 24.

21. Darby, *International Tribunals*, pp. 24, 30, 28, 26, 32.

also thought in terms of a repressive agency which would maintain the status quo. Yet he showed foresight in suggesting compulsory arbitration, in asking countries to renounce war, and in proposing a police force to maintain peace. Most important of all, Saint-Pierre's scheme did not die. It circulated widely and eventually influenced both Jean Jacques Rousseau and Immanuel Kant in their views on a world organization.

Rousseau's interest appeared in 1761 when he published an abridgement of Saint-Pierre's plan and added ideas of his own. He argued that the process of federation should be followed in forming a union, and he cited the Greek, Germanic, and Swiss systems as examples. The union should be perpetual, be allowed to settle all disputes through judicial or arbitral processes, be empowered to impose its will upon violators of any treaty provisions, be a legislative body, and the guarantor of the governments and territories of all members.[22]

In a later publication in 1782, Rousseau criticized some of Saint-Pierre's suggestions and in so doing reflected emerging concepts of self-government. Rulers would not act nobly as Saint-Pierre thought; real gains would come only from people expressing their "general will."[23] Thus Rousseau perceived a need for a representative type of federation, and later planners have re-echoed his belief that any organization had to be voluntary and that it had to be a co-operative union of governments rather than a league of monarchs.

Other political theorists of the eighteenth century also discussed a society of nations. Jeremy Bentham recorded his views between 1786 and 1789 by referring extensively to the American, Swiss, and Germanic federations. In his comments on justice and in a section decrying secret diplomacy, he revealed how far his age had shifted from concepts of monarchy to those of democracy.[24] Bentham was the first internationalist to emphasize public opinion as world force, and William Ladd developed this idea later. The information bureaus of twentieth-century international bodies have confirmed Bentham's belief that an educated people can be a powerful agency in an association of states. Bentham, in noting the new confederation in North America, also became the first planner to see it as an important contribution toward a broader union. But Bentham filed his notes away, an act which may disclose his belief that such dreams could not succeed in his lifetime.

One of Bentham's fellow-philosophers, Immanuel Kant, however, re-

---

22. York, *Leagues of Nations*, pp. 196–214. York contains Rousseau's *A Lasting Peace Through the Federation of Europe*, translated by C. E. Vaughan, pp. 195–247.
23. *Ibid.*, pp. 220–221; Friedrich, *Inevitable Peace*, pp. 170–177.
24. Jeremy Bentham, *The Works of Jeremy Bentham. . .* , II, 546–547, 552–557.

vealed greater optimism when he published the essay *Perpetual Peace* in 1795. He disclosed a knowledge of earlier advocates, especially of Saint-Pierre and Rousseau. The instability nations faced, said Kant, would eventually lead them to unity. While they could never achieve a natural state of permanent peace, they could try to establish rules and build an organized society upon principles of law and right. A "world republic" would materialize, but it would not come easily or in a short time.[25]

Kant's proposal called for a federation which nations could enter or withdraw from at will. It would be a constitutional republic, not a pure democracy. He believed in mankind but wanted rational action which could best be attained under a republican system.[26] Kant referred to a world citizenship and, in elaborations upon his original plan, he expanded upon his theory of nature upon which his ideas were based. In doing so, he emphasized that peace was not only desirable but practical. Kant has been called the father of the Hague Conferences, and at least one authority has argued that if states had followed his proposals in regard to absolutism, war loans, disarmament, secret diplomacy, intervention, self-determination, and a league, there would have been no war in 1914.[27]

Of all the early planners for an international organization, Kant had the greatest influence upon American thinkers. His ideal of a society built upon republican principles matched perfectly the experiment in government pursued by the United States. Moreover, Kant raised the discussion of peace above that of the political arena. It became a rational, an ethical, and a moral question with which the mind and conscience of men had to deal. Nineteenth-century American proponents echoed this theme above all others.

A number of other men gave some thought to the idea of an association of states late in the eighteenth century, including more and more Americans. Benjamin Franklin explored the subject through the writings of a Frenchman, Pierre-André Gargaz of Thèze. This schoolmaster, a former galley slave, sent his project to Franklin in 1779 when Franklin lived in Paris, and in 1782 Franklin published it with an introduction. It suggested a permanent European union with a congress, president, and judicial structure in the form of mediators. It called for a rigid imposition of a status quo which could be changed only by the league, free trade, and equality of states in voting.

25. Friedrich, *Inevitable Peace*, pp. 160, 164–165, 59–60; Marriott, *Commonwealth or Anarchy?*, pp. 95–96, 98.

26. Immanuel Kant, *Perpetual Peace*, pp. 14–21.

27. Ladd, *Essay*, p. xxxvii; Jessie W. Hughan, *A Study of International Government*, pp. 155–156.

Elaborate provisions sought to curtail militarism while keeping armies intact. Gargaz later approached Thomas Jefferson, Franklin's successor in Paris, who showed no interest in the subject.[28]

Several of Franklin's remarks reveal how Gargaz influenced him. In 1780 he uttered his oft-quoted plea for "the discovery of a plan that would induce and oblige nations to settle their disputes without first cutting one another's throats." Three years later, he pondered the possibility of "a compact between England, France, and America," and Franklin often called for the creation and application of a "law of nations" and the arbitration of disputes.[29]

The third notable American to discuss a world body presented his views in 1791 in his famous essay *Rights of Man*. Thomas Paine had served in the Revolutionary Army and as secretary to the Committee on Foreign Affairs of the Continental Congress from 1777 to 1779. He thus knew well the ravages of war and the difficulties of diplomacy. Paine had examined earlier projects, for he referred to the Great Design and commented on its advantages. He concluded that negotiation and arbitration would replace the sword in relations between states, that a league would bring disarmament, and that the old system of diplomatic intrigue would be replaced by "a different system of Government." A "confederation of Nations" and a "European Congress," he predicted, would come. Indeed, he saw it "nearer in probability, than once were the revolutions and alliance of France and America."[30]

One other development of importance in the history of international organization which, like Kant's proposal, played a role in influencing later American thinkers and their plans, occurred in the eighteenth century. This was the creation of the United States, both as it existed under the Articles of Confederation and under the Constitution of 1789. In fact, the evolution of the system seemed to illustrate how nations could first combine in a loose association and eventually develop a more perfect union.

Internationalists had long argued that earlier experiments in confederation, notably the Hanseatic League from the thirteenth to the seventeenth century and the Swiss and Dutch arrangements dating from the thirteenth and fourteenth centuries, provided men with a clue to the organization of

28. George S. Eddy, *A Project of Universal and Perpetual Peace*, pp. 3–5, 11–22; Gerald Stourzh, *Benjamin Franklin and American Foreign Policy*, pp. 222–224; Benjamin Franklin, "On War and Peace," *Old South Leaflets*, VII (No. 162), 234–235.

29. *Ibid.*, pp. 226, 233, 229, 232, 238–239.

30. Thomas Paine, *Rights of Man*, pp. 141–143; R. C. Roper, "Thomas Paine First to Urge League of Nations," *The Public*, XXII (May 10, 1919), 488–489.

nations. In North America, the New England Confederation, the Albany
Plan of 1754, a suggestion by Franklin in 1775, the League of the Iroquois
Indians after the sixteenth century, and the almost federal relationship of the
British colonies to their mother country all seemed to substantiate claims
that it could be done.[31] But the ideal remained a dream, tried as it had been
on so small a scale and without formal constitutions.

The establishment of the United States seemed to prove that the political
theory could be successfully applied on a large geographical basis. Moreover, the American experiment contributed in other ways to emerging concepts. Men like Saint-Pierre had envisaged a federation but only in terms of
a semicompulsory arrangement. The achievement of a *voluntary* association in an age of rampant nationalism revealed how far mankind had moved
from the concept of a world unitary state. Even more, it showed the transition
toward the democratic-republican ideal for which Kant had pleaded shortly
after the creation of the United States. It was no league of princes; it was a
republic of self-governing states.

Finally, the Constitution of 1789 in provision after provision met structural problems which stood as a challenge to internationalists. Matters of
representation, voting, equality of states, financing, allocation of powers, defense, and operation all seemed to be solved. It is not surprising, therefore,
to find that men saw in the events of 1776 and 1789 the "great rehearsal"
for experiments in world co-operation of the twentieth century.[32]

Much education and effort, however, had to precede concrete achievements; hence the advocates continued their labors into the nineteenth century. The years 1814 and 1815 began auspiciously with four proposals.
Plans by Claude Henri, comte de Saint-Simon, a Frenchman; Karl C. F.
Krause, a German; Noah Worcester, an American; and the Tsar of Russia,
Alexander I, reveal a widespread interest in the subject of an association of
nations. None of these projects, however, contained original ideas. They revealed an already stereotyped concept of a representative congress with
some executive and judicial functions. Worcester, a Congregational minister,
reflected their generalities in a peace tract, *A Solemn Review of the Custom*

31. Albert B. Hart, "Washington as an Internationalist," *Bulletin of the Pan
American Union*, LXVI (July 1932), 477–478.
32. Carl Van Doren, *The Great Rehearsal*, pp. vii–x. A number of writers have
discovered in the works of Washington, Hamilton, and Jefferson statements which
indicate an interest in the subject of a union of nations. Such claims, based upon isolated remarks which were never amplified, seem dubious. Hart, "Washington as an
Internationalist," pp. 477, 491; Edwin D. Mead, *The Principles of the Founders*, pp.
23–27; Foster Rhea Dulles, *America's Rise to World Power, 1898–1954*, p. 4.

of War, in which he emphasized a court but failed to elaborate upon the jurisdiction, structure, or authority.[33]

Alexander's scheme appeared at the Congress of Vienna, one of the first genuine international conferences. It not only acted in traditional fashion in seeking satisfactory peace terms but also sought to resolve many problems by planning for their future solution through the co-operative action of European governments.[34] Alexander proclaimed all nations as a family under God and suggested that a Holy Alliance be formed in which the signatories guaranteed each other their support. It contained no reference to executive, legislative, or judicial bodies or to provisions on ways to settle disputes between states.[35]

Although several countries signed the treaty, the statesmen at Vienna recognized its weaknesses. On November 15, 1815, they signed a more conventional agreement in the form of a renewed Quadruple Alliance. Yet they did not abandon the principle of consultation which Alexander considered basic to his plan. The document provided for meetings "at fixed intervals" to discuss common problems which threatened the peace.[36] In ensuing years, the powers of Europe acted under it several times. There has been a tendency to associate their efforts with the Holy Alliance, but the two operations were separate. Indeed, one might question whether the Holy Alliance ever functioned save in the form of the treaty arrangement which followed it.

The agreements beginning with the Congress of Vienna and ending with the concert system did, nevertheless, contribute to the evolution of international organization. The Vienna conference was one of the first to formulate rules for the welfare of Europe, the world, and peace. Its efforts to

33. Hemleben, *Plans for World Peace*, pp. 96–97; Clay MacCauley, *Krause's League for Human Right and Thereby World Peace*, pp. 1–32; MacCauley, "Krause's Proposition for a European League of States," *Advocate of Peace*, LXXIX (December 1917), 337–339; Noah Worcester, *A Solemn Review of the Custom of War*, pp. 6–7, 20–23.

34. Many accounts speculate upon the origin of Alexander's views on a league. He knew of early plans, especially of Rousseau, and he had been introduced to Penn through literature of the Society of Friends. He had also read Worcester's *Solemn Review*. York, *Leagues of Nations*, pp. 307–309; [Walter A. Phillips], "The Peace Movement and the Holy Alliance," *Edinburgh Review*, CCXV (April 1912), 413–414; Devere Allen, *The Fight for Peace*, pp. 101–102; Phillips, *The Confederation of Europe*, pp. 49–57, 141–142. Napoleon claimed while in exile that he had hoped to unite the people of Europe "by unity of codes, principles, opinions, feelings, and interests." He insisted that a congress, modeled after the American or amphictyonic, would be sound. Phillips, *Confederation*, p. 24.

35. Phillips, *Confederation*, pp. 142–144, 305–306.

36. *Ibid.*, pp. 144–147.

abolish the slave trade, to classify diplomatic agents, and to provide for the free navigation of international rivers all fall within the scope of a league's activities. Furthermore, the arrangement stimulated the idea of a European commonwealth, promoted the concept of collective responsibility on the part of European states, and introduced multilateral treaties regulatory or legislative in their effect. It gave impetus to the study of international law, fostered thought about an executive agency, and through periodic meetings injected the principle of united action into European diplomacy. In these ways, the concert system has been judged to be a forerunner of the Hague Conferences and the League of Nations.[37]

On the other hand, not too much should be read into the agreements. In the first place, the statesmen at Vienna had no intention of creating a new order; they sought primarily to restore and to reconstruct. Moreover, from the perspective of the United States, they created an international structure which Americans abhorred. The United States did not act upon suggestions by the Tsar that the nation co-operate with the Holy Alliance, and in 1819 Secretary of State John Quincy Adams refused to consider membership in the Concert of Europe.[38] Americans could favor a system which had noble aspirations but not one which suppressed revolutions or threatened to intervene in the New World to aid Spain in the recovery of her colonies.

At the same time that Europe's statesmen were building their alliance system, American pacifists were laying the foundation for another development in the history of international organization. They created peace societies, beginning in 1815 on local and state levels and finally in 1828 organizing the American Peace Society on a national scale. While these groups attracted little popular support, the men who led them in their first decades—Noah Worcester, William Ellery Channing, William Ladd, and Elihu Burritt—proved to be able and enthusiastic spokesmen for their cause.[39]

37. Edmund C. Mower, *International Government*, pp. 181–182, 283, 152, 156, 169–170, 220–221, 270–271; Albert F. Pollard, *The League of Nations in History*, p. 9; Phillips, *Confederation*, pp. 275, 282–287, 298–299; Charles E. Hughes, "Some Aspects of the Work of the Department of State," *AJIL*, XVI (July 1922), 359; Rose Sidgwick, "The League of Nations," *Rice Institute Pamphlets*, VI (April 1919), 62; Charles Hodges, *The Background of International Relations*, pp. 259–260. The provisions for the navigation of the Danube River led eventually to the creation of a Danube Commission in 1856, "the first International Executive" agency. Beales, *History of Peace*, pp. 39–40.

38. J. Fred Rippy, *America and the Strife of Europe*, pp. 45–46; Dexter Perkins, *Hands Off! A History of the Monroe Doctrine*, pp. 23–24.

39. Benjamin Trueblood, "The Historic Development of the Peace Idea," *Advocate of Peace*, LXVII (November 1905), 228; Merle Curti, *Peace or War, The American Struggle, 1636–1936*, pp. 37–40.

The pacifists of the nineteenth century, in seeking to abolish armed strife, described it as inhuman, un-Christian, futile, and horrible. In spreading this gospel they contributed to the evolution of world organization because men had to be awakened to the evils of war before they would plan for or support a league of nations.

Peace societies, however, did more than propagandize against warfare. Many of them endorsed the ideal of a congress of nations, and they sought to introduce that proposition to the people. The American Peace Society promoted it with such vigor that by the 1840s Europeans were already referring to the concept of a congress as the "American plan."[40]

In the light of twentieth-century developments, the peace leaders of that day viewed the world from a narrow spectrum. Until the 1830s and even after in the minds of many of them, they had thought of world unity built upon moral principles and the universal brotherhood of man. They envisaged a fraternal union of peoples rather than a politically organized body representing governments. While some Americans had heard of Grotius, Rousseau, Penn, Saint-Pierre, and others, they had generally ignored the ideas of these pioneer internationalists. In 1829, however, this situation changed. That year the American Peace Society, under the leadership of William Ladd, offered for the first time a prize for the best essay on a congress of nations.[41]

Either because of the unorthodoxy of the subject or the limited award of only fifty dollars, few writers responded. Moreover, the contributions received had to be rejected because of their inferior quality. The prize was then increased to five hundred and finally to one thousand dollars, a sizable amount for that day. Thus by 1834 several men had submitted worthy projects. Two committees, including former President John Quincy Adams, Senators John C. Calhoun and Daniel Webster, and justices James Kent and Joseph Story, could not agree upon a winner. After considerable delay, the Society finally decided in 1840 to publish the five best essays and add a composite review in which William Ladd condensed the ideas embodied in the thirty-five papers deemed less worthy.[42]

40. Curti, *The American Peace Crusade, 1815–1860*, p. 55; Christina Phelps, *The Anglo-American Peace Movement in the Mid-Nineteenth Century*, pp. 103–104. The American Peace Society endorsed arbitration procedures and the idea of a congress four years before English pacifists did so. Beales, *History of Peace*, pp. 53–54.

41. W. Evans Darby, "Origin of Peace Societies, Principles and Purposes of Their Formation," *Official Report of the Fifth Universal Peace Congress, 1893*, p. 55; Ladd, ed., *Prize Essays on a Congress of Nations*, pp. iii–iv.

42. *Prize Essays*, pp. iii–vi; "History of the Seventy-Five Years' Work of the American Peace Society," *Advocate of Peace*, LXV (June 1903), 114.

The five essays were not strikingly original or fully detailed. All set the scene with the stereotyped pacifist protest against war to show the need for a new program. All discussed the beneficial results which would accrue from an association of nations. Nearly all noted the evolutionary trend toward greater world unity by referring to ties of commerce, to the growing co-operation in science and learning, and to the development of international law. All suggested a court as an essential function of a congress, all hailed the latter as an immensely practical and wise step, and all emphasized the need for a codified standard of behavior. Finally, all the plans relied primarily upon moral sanction to enforce laws and decisions.

In content, the first two essays reflected more mature and thorough thought than the other three. They spelled out in greater detail the structure and operation of their league, and some of their ideas merit examination. John Bolles, a Boston lawyer, devoted an entire chapter to the subject of organization and powers. He believed in a congress with authority to negotiate with states, to operate as a permanent court, and to prepare and draft a code of international law. Bolles feared a body with excessive power to maintain peace and argued that a "natural respect for justice" would generally be sufficient to unite mankind in supporting its actions. He realized, however, that sanctions could not be dismissed, for he suggested that nonintercourse be applied against those governments which embarked upon war without first submitting a dispute to debate and decision. His congress could not impose such action, however; it could only recommend it. Bolles did not want any state to fear an international society. He concluded with a suggestion that men could either establish a limited-type association or move in the direction of additional sanctions.[43]

The second essayist, writing under the pseudonym "Hamilton," showed even more concern for the structure of a congress. He assumed it would play a role as a court and base its actions on wisdom and justice. Delegates should serve as representatives of people rather than of governments. He revealed some concern about the problem of force, advocating limited action in the form of outlawry, censure, blockade, and nonintercourse as long as any action fell "short of war." He proposed a union of Great Britain, the United States, and France as a beginning step, leaving nations to enter or withdraw from the league at will.[44]

Ladd wrote the sixth essay and the explanatory "advertisement" of the book. He had been born in New Hampshire in 1778, had attended Harvard, had lived most of his life as a seaman and farmer, and had been converted

43. *Prize Essays*, pp. 64–76.
44. *Ibid.*, pp. 158–194.

to the peace movement in 1823 after reading Worcester's *Solemn Review*. Ladd henceforth devoted his life to the cause, and in 1828 he had led in the formation of the American Peace Society.[45]

That organization, perhaps because of Ladd's interest, injected the idea of a congress of nations into its early literature. It printed a rudimentary proposal in the first issue of its journal, the *Harbinger of Peace*.[46] Ladd had read widely and knew of the early internationalists; yet in 1832 when he published a twenty-eight-page pamphlet, "A Dissertation on A Congress of Nations," he reflected the standard pacifist thinking of the time rather than the advanced views of the earlier planners. Ladd devoted most of his space to the argument that a union was a worthwhile and workable ideal. He included few details on its structure or operation.[47] This was understandable since most of his readers knew little about the subject. Before they would heed details, they first had to be convinced of the soundness of the proposition.

This realization prompted Ladd's subsequent campaign for a congress of nations. Discussions in the American Peace Society had resulted in the essay contest, and the thought it stimulated led to one of the most important developments in the internationalist movement in the nineteenth century— Ladd's essay. In digesting the forty contributions and in his appointed task of summarizing the thirty-five unprinted ones, Ladd became familiar with every current idea. As a result, he emerged with an original concept. He divided "the subject into two distinct parts." First, governments should form a congress; next, they should create a court as a separate agency within the league. Ladd noted that he had never found this division in any proposals he had read.[48]

Ladd's plan of separating the functions of court and congress, although unique in its application to an international organization, actually existed in the political structures of his day. He acknowledged that the Swiss Diet and Court of Judges influenced him, but he must have realized that the pattern of his own government provided a perfect model.[49] It seems remarkable that nearly fifty years had to elapse from the inauguration of the Con-

---

45. Ladd, *Essay*, p. vii; Curti, *American Peace Crusade*, pp. 34–35, 42–43, 55–56, 58; Georg Schwarzenberger, *William Ladd: An Examination of an American Proposal for an International Equity Tribunal*, p. x.

46. Ladd, *Essay*, pp. 64–65; Curti, *American Peace Crusade*, p. 56.

47. Ladd wrote under the name "Philanthropos," *A Dissertation on a Congress of Nations*, pp. 1–28.

48. Ladd, *Essay*, pp. xlix–l. Bentham had expressed this idea, but his views did not appear in print until 1843. Frederick C. Hicks, *The New World Order*, p. 74.

49. Ladd, *Essay*, p. 44.

stitution before someone applied its structure to that of an association of nations. Aside from this point, Ladd thought as Grotius did. If individuals unite, why not states? Men should cultivate a "spirit of peace" and devise methods to settle their disputes.[50]

In Ladd's organization, each civilized nation would have one vote. All action would be valid only after unanimous approval and ratification by the members. The congress could enact a code of law; establish a court; promote trade, transportation, and communication; and seek uniformity in such standards as weights and measures. It could not intervene in the internal matters of states. Ladd believed that public opinion could be exerted to uphold the acts passed; hence he did not include provisions for an executive.[51]

Ladd explored the subject of a congress fully, but he showed less concern for particulars in discussing the structure and procedure of his court. Each country, he suggested, should name two judges. The tribunal could hear cases referred to it by governments, settle boundary disputes, suggest laws for enactment, and render decisions by majority vote. Ladd probably favored the compulsory arbitration of differences, but he did not include clauses for such. He did, however, suggest that states resort to mediation whenever they could not agree to submit issues to the tribunal. His judges, therefore, seemed authorized to deal with legal or justiciable questions as well as with nonjusticiable matters.[52] By this ambiguity, Ladd avoided a pitfall which disturbed many later advocates of a judicial system.

Although Ladd empowered his court to render decisions, he left enforcement to public opinion, "the queen of the world." His refusal to include sanctions in any form reveals the strength of his pacifist convictions. Arbitrators, said Ladd, had never had to rely upon arms to support their decisions. Men did not obey the law because they feared the results; they acquiesced because they were concerned about what their neighbors might say. No nation, he believed, could stand against the power of public opinion.[53]

Ladd has been cited and acclaimed as a prophet, with scholars seeing in his ideas a direct lineage to the International Court of Justice recommended by the Hague Conferences and to the peace settlement of 1919.[54] His claim to

50. *Ibid.*, pp. 4–5.
51. *Ibid.*, pp. 8–33.
52. *Ibid.*, pp. 34–37; Schwarzenberger, *William Ladd,* pp. 20–22.
53. Ladd, *Essay*, pp. 1, 6, 77.
54. *Ibid.*, pp. xxxviii–xxxix, lxiii, xlv; Schwarzenberger, *William Ladd*, pp. xi, xv, 34–37; Curti, *American Peace Crusade,* p. 59. Two studies compare and contrast Ladd's essay with twentieth-century plans for an international organization. Christina Phelps, in her *Anglo-American Peace Movement,* added an appendix, pp. 193–206, in

fame, however, did not rest solely upon his essay, for he labored in other ways to advance his dream of a union. He often spoke on the subject, and he arranged for the widespread distribution of the *Prize Essays*. Political figures and foreign statesmen in the United States received copies. Ladd also reprinted his plan, and it went to readers on both sides of the Atlantic.[55]

Ladd also utilized another favorite device of the nineteenth-century pacifist—the petition. Largely through his efforts, the Massachusetts senate in 1835 approved a resolution favoring the amicable settlement of international disputes. Then, in 1837 and again in 1838, the Massachusetts legislature in both houses adopted measures in response to an appeal. Its action in 1837 stated "that the institution of a Congress or a Court of Nations appears to be, at present, the best practical method by which disputes between nations can be adjusted, and the appeal to arms avoided."[56]

The crusade carried to Capitol Hill where late in 1837 a petition for a congress gained a hearing. Bearing 1,427 signatures, including 135 names of Massachusetts legislators, this document ended in the House Committee on Foreign Affairs, which suggested that the idea seemed premature and impossible. The pacifists, however, continued their labors. They returned each year from 1838 through 1841 with their entreaties. In 1839, Ladd personally appealed to congressmen as he had previously done with President Martin Van Buren, but without success.[57] Hence, little headway had been made on the national level when Ladd died in 1841.

With Ladd's death, America lost its foremost internationalist, but Elihu Burritt soon appeared to continue Ladd's quest. This modest self-educated

---

which she collated Ladd's ideas with provisions in the Covenant of the League of Nations. Schwarzenberger relates them to the legal problems of the twentieth century and the need in the 1930s for a revised international structure, pp. 53–76.

55. Curti, *American Peace Crusade,* pp. 59–60; Phelps, *Anglo-American Peace Movement,* pp. 48, 74–75.

56. Curti, *American Peace Crusade,* p. 56; Ladd, *Essay,* pp. 67–68. The latter source reprints the petitions and resolutions, pp. 112–129.

57. Curti, *American Peace Crusade,* p. 57; Phelps, *Anglo-American Peace Movement,* p. 126*n*; Ladd, *Essay,* pp. 69–73, 129–161. The *Advocate of Peace* contained many references to the idea of a congress in the late 1830s. "A Congress of Nations," II (November 1838), 122–123; T. C. Upham, "Circumstances Favorable to an International Congress," II (January 1839), 174–181. In the British Parliament during debates over the Webster-Ashburton treaty, the subject of a congress appeared. The legislatures of Massachusetts and Vermont in 1844 and 1852 approved resolutions for a congress. Beales, *History of Peace,* p. 63; John Bassett Moore, *History and Digest of the International Arbitrations to Which the United States Has Been a Party . . . ,* II, 2109.

blacksmith had read the *Prize Essays* and accepted their arguments. He proclaimed himself as Ladd's disciple and became the spokesman for the "American idea." Burritt's mode of operation, however, differed from that of Ladd, for Burritt not only wrote and spoke but also promoted peace conferences where he continually introduced the proposal for a congress of nations.[58]

The first international assembly of pacifists met in London in 1843. The delegates spent little time discussing a league, but they did endorse the wider use of arbitration and the idea of a congress of nations.[59] Burritt had not been present at London, but he laid the foundations for an ensuing series of meetings between 1848 and 1851. At Brussels, in 1848, Burritt called for consideration of a congress to draft a code of law. Only an international body could do this work, he argued. Its enactments, referred to national legislatures for ratification, could result in a set of rules which would be honored. The delegates responded with a resolution of approval.[60]

The next year at Paris, Burritt again introduced Ladd's suggestion, and it initially appeared that enthusiasm for the proposal had grown. The president of the assembly, the noted author Victor Hugo, devoted a substantial part of his address to the subject. He envisaged a day when bullets and bombs would "be replaced by votes, by the universal suffrage of nations, by the venerable arbitration of a great Sovereign Senate, which will be to Europe what the Parliament is to England, what the Diet is to Germany, what the Legislative Assembly is to France." Burritt hoped that Hugo's remarks would stimulate wider support for the idea, but the delegates proved to be cautious. Only after Francis Amasa Walker, a banker and legislator from Massachusetts, and the Abbé Deguerry of Madeleine supported the resolution could Burritt persuade the assembly to retain the endorsement of 1848.[61]

At the meeting in Frankfurt in 1850, Burritt again called for a congress to draft a code. He seemed embarrassed that the proposal was commonly "denominated *American*," argued that it was hundreds of years old, and observed that many Europeans had contributed towards its development.

58. Merle Curti, ed. *The Learned Blacksmith: The Letters and Journals of Elihu Burritt,* pp. 3–7, 28; Ladd, *Essay,* p. iv; J. B. Scott, "Elihu Burritt," *Advocate of Peace,* LXXII (June 1910), 131–132.

59. Beales, *History of Peace,* p. 67; Curti, *American Peace Crusade,* pp. 138–139.

60. Elihu Burritt, "A Congress of Nations," *Old South Leaflets,* VI (No. 146), 441–447.

61. *Ibid.,* pp. 447–456; Victor Hugo, "The United States of Europe," *World Peace Foundation Pamphlets,* IV (October 1914), 5; Curti, *American Peace Crusade,* p. 175.

He claimed that with a growing spirit of co-operation between nations the world seemed ready to accept an international organization.[62]

Not even the peace conferences, though, were to live. Enthusiasm dwindled, and many pacifists turned to other causes. In the United States, the slavery controversy and the Civil War distracted them, and even Burritt ended his campaign. The gains had been slight. Few Europeans adopted the "American idea" with enthusiasm; even in the United States projects for an international organization aroused only limited support. While pacifists embraced it, they showed more interest in disarmament and general co-operation.[63] A few political leaders may have favored the idea, but they spoke in generalities. In 1849, former President John Tyler referred to a "community of nations," and Senator Charles Sumner of Massachusetts endorsed a league similar to that suggested by Ladd.[64]

The poet Ralph Waldo Emerson provided insight into attitudes in an address to the American Peace Society in 1838 when he observed that "the proposition of the Congress of Nations is undoubtedly that at which the present course of events do point. But the mind, once prepared for the reign of principles, will easily find modes of expressing its will."[65] The mind of America by the 1850s could not yet accept the "principles" of the internationalists. Their crusade had only carried them to an outpost from which they often chanted the words of another poet, Alfred Lord Tennyson, who expressed their dream of that day:

> Till the war drum throbbed no longer
> and the battle flags were furled
> In the Parliament of Man, the Federation
> of the World.

62. Burritt, "Congress of Nations," pp. 456–462.

63. Curti, *American Peace Crusade,* pp. 133–135, 169–188; Phelps, *Anglo-American Peace Movement,* pp. 58–60, 125–128.

64. New York *Times,* December 7, 1958; Charles Sumner, *Works of Charles Sumner,* II, 223–277; David Donald, *Charles Sumner and the Coming of the Civil War,* p. 118.

65. *Advocate of Peace,* LXXII (September 1910), 204.

The Foundations of Modern International Organization

The internationalists before 1850 had labored to introduce their ideas and plans of a congress and court to mankind. In the last half of the nineteenth century, they were aided by developments in two areas where men had long sought attainments. These were arbitration and international law. Without these two subjects, which came to be widely discussed, there could have been but little progress toward the creation of the League of Nations in 1919 because they advanced the idea of an ordered society among states.

Arbitration appeared far back in the pages of history. Biblical references as well as archeological and historical evidence indicate an ancient heritage.[1] Men perceived quite early that disputes between groups might profitably be referred to a third party for settlement. The Greeks and Romans utilized this principle, and after the fall of Rome the Roman Catholic Church settled many controversies through negotiations of an arbitral nature.[2]

The rampant nationalism in Europe, however, adversely affected rational efforts to avert strife. It became virtually impossible to settle disputes by

---

1. W. L. Westermann, "Interstate Arbitration in Antiquity," *Classical Journal,* II (March 1907), 197–198; Jackson H. Ralston, *International Arbitration from Athens to Locarno,* pp. 153–154.

2. Ralston, *International Arbitration,* pp. 153–189; William L. Penfield, "International Arbitration," *AJIL,* I (April 1907), 335–339; J. B. Scott, *The Hague Peace Conferences of 1899 and 1907,* I, 188–210.

pacific means. Hence, not until the Jay treaty of 1794 did arbitration re-emerge as an important element in diplomacy. Even then, governments had few rules to guide them. Arbitral processes remained in scope and application basically as they had been in ancient times. Arbitration was a rudimentary form of judicial procedure, a level above mediation and the diplomatic settlement of differences because it relied upon a judge or judges who rendered a decision which the parties to a dispute had previously agreed to accept. While the arrangement was judicial in process, it usually lacked essential foundations which would have given it a legalistic or genuine judicial character.[3]

First, there was no one body of judges, no fixed court to which nations could turn in time of need. In each case, the third parties had to be found when controversies arose. Second, arbitral judges rarely decided a case upon legal or judicial grounds or even upon the facts in a particular dispute. They tended to split monetary or territorial differences without regard to the question of right. Limited concepts of international law, a desire to avert bloodshed through compromise settlements, and the absence of obligatory agreements between nations had all combined to restrict the arbitral process. Action on the part of any government was largely voluntary, and where clauses to arbitrate appeared in treaties the area of operation was often rigidly prescribed. Usually only questions involving the interpretation of the compact itself could be considered.

These shortcomings in the arbitral system go far to explain the suggestions of Dubois, Crucé, Penn, and other internationalists for some formal agency to settle disputes. Ladd perceived the need when he proposed a court as a separate body free from the political influence of a congress. Grotius had called attention to the need for concrete rules on which nations could rely, but men had made little headway on that task. Hence, by the middle of the nineteenth century this entire area remained a fruitful field of endeavor, and into it the pacifists and internationalists plunged.

The Jay treaty had revived interest in the principle of arbitration because of its provisions for mixed commissions to settle outstanding controversies, and in subsequent years the United States and Great Britain had resolved several differences amicably. The processes were not always arbitral, but the fact that potential disputes had been allayed by peaceful means stimulated demands for a wider acceptance and use of arbitration. A resolution in the Massachusetts Senate in 1835 proposed the submission

3. Scott, *Hague Peace Conferences*, I, 210–224.

of *all* international controversies, a radical idea which insisted that important as well as insignificant questions should be arbitrated.[4] Judge William Jay, the son of John Jay of treaty fame, in 1841 and again in an essay on *War and Peace* in 1843, argued that point and called for agreements among nations on the subject. Jay suggested the insertion of an arbitral clause in all treaties, even commercial ones, a proposal carried to Europe and enthusiastically endorsed by the peace congresses of the mid-nineteenth century.[5]

All through the 1840s and 1850s, the American pacifists campaigned to commit Congress to accords which stipulated that arbitration be followed in resolving difficult problems. If enough treaties could be negotiated with this proviso, nations would be bound by a web and commitment which in time might compel them to establish some formal tribunal to decide upon disputes. Horace Bushnell, educator and theologian, expressed this desire clearly in 1843 in a call for universal arbitration so that "all law shall come into unity, and a kind of virtual oneness embrace all nations." The Senate, however, remained unresponsive to these pressures, and administrations ignored them. During the Oregon controversy, President James K. Polk refused to consider British arbitration proposals.[6]

Article XXI in the treaty of Guadalupe Hidalgo in 1848, which provided for the peaceful settlement of issues by arbitration between the United States and Mexico, greatly encouraged the peace advocates. They expended great energy in seeking further official commitment of the principle on the part of their government. Ladd's proposal for a congress and court virtually disappeared in the 1850s. It had initially gained support because of its imaginative nature, but Ladd sought a virtually unattainable end. It seemed far better to seek a simpler, more practical goal, namely, arbitration. Precedent favored that method over a league since foundations had already been laid. It seemed a more rational approach which could engender support from many persons who had seen in the congress scheme implausible, if not dan-

4. Ladd, *Essay,* pp. 112–116.

5. Benjamin F. Trueblood, "History and Work of Peace Societies in America," *Report, Fifth Peace Congress,* p. 70; William Jay, *War and Peace,* p. 55; Curti, *Peace or War,* p. 41; David Low Dodge, *War Inconsistent with the Religion of Jesus Christ,* pp. xxii–xxiii.

6. Edwin D. Mead, *Horace Bushnell the Citizen,* p. 18; "Arbitration and the United States," *World Peace Foundation Pamphlets* (League of Nations Series), IX (1926), 487–492; Robert N. Margrave, "The Policy of the United States Respecting the Development of International Adjudication," pp. 42–47; Frederick Merk, *The Oregon Question: Essays in Anglo-American Diplomacy and Politics,* pp. 219–233.

gerous, ideas. Finally, any advances in the area of arbitration would be in line with Ladd's goal. A network of arbitral treaties and a possible tribunal would bring greater international co-operation and thus point the way toward an eventual association of states.[7]

The pacifists, however, failed to obtain even the endorsement of governments to general treaties of arbitration or to the principle of stipulated arbitration, a setback which cooled their ardor in the late 1850s and throughout the 1860s. Yet they could point to modest gains. Nations did resort to arbitration in a number of instances, led by the United States, Great Britain, France, the Netherlands, and Spain, but no government officially or formally accepted the system as a declared policy.[8] This unhappy situation for the pacifists changed, however, in 1871, when Great Britain agreed to arbitrate the *Alabama* claims.

Thereafter, pacifists on both sides of the Atlantic sought to develop arbitration as their chief weapon against war. In England, Randal Cremer, the secretary of the Workingmen's Peace Association, and Henry Richard, the leader of the London Peace Society, led the revived crusade to obtain official endorsement by introducing resolutions into Parliament and by organizing to arouse public opinion.[9]

In the United States, Philadelphia attorney Thomas W. Balch, Senator Charles Sumner, and the leaders of the American Peace Society assumed the initiative. Sumner believed that an evolutionary process would result in the growing organization of mankind, and he had studied the earlier confederations by which men had sought to avoid war. He found nothing to show that governments could not agree to the pacific settlement of disputes. On May 31, 1872, he reflected this philosophy when he introduced a resolution calling for the arbitration of "any question or grievance which might be the occasion of war or of misunderstanding between nations." It failed, however, to surmount the machinery of Congress. In December of the following year, Sumner returned to the quest with a measure which a few months later, shortly after his death, received the approval of the Senate Committee

7. Phelps, *Anglo-American Peace Movement,* pp. 126–127, 150–152.

8. *Ibid.,* pp. 153–164; Edward Lindsey, *The International Court,* pp. 39–41. As late as 1866, the American Peace Society sent a deputation to Washington with a petition for a court and congress and for stipulated arbitration. Arthur D. Call, "The War Has Not Destroyed," *Advocate of Peace,* LXXXII (August 1920), 272.

9. Irwin M. Abrams, "A History of European Peace Societies, 1867–1899," pp. 81–82; "Anglo-American Arbitration: Facts of History," *Advocate of Peace,* LXVI (February 1904), 30–32.

on Foreign Relations. Its report, by Senator Hannibal Hamlin of Maine, mildly endorsed arbitration as "just and practical." On June 17, 1874, the House acted more vigorously by unanimously passing two resolutions. One authorized the president "to enter into such negotiation for the establishment of an international system whereby matters in dispute between different governments agreeing thereto may be adjusted by arbitration." The other approved the negotiation of treaties "to adjust all alleged cause of difference by impartial arbitration." The Senate, in less sweeping terms, merely approved the report of its Foreign Relations Committee on June 23.[10]

In ensuing years, Presidents Grant, Hayes, Arthur, and Harrison added the weight of their endorsements to the campaign. Most of these men, however, qualified their statements. Only in specified or "proper" instances, they noted, should arbitration be used. But one of them, Arthur, favored the settlement of "all international difference" by this process.[11]

Yet despite such resolutions and verbal support, no general treaty appeared, and no nation seemed ready to assume any initiative. Tense and complicated conditions in Europe deterred governments from action there; hence, French and British pacifists increasingly turned to the United States for leadership. The Swiss-born leader of the League for Peace and Freedom, Charles Lemonnier, began a futile quest in 1879 to prod the United States into action. He found receptive listeners in Presidents Hayes and Arthur and in Secretary of State Theodore Frelinghuysen, but the Department of State failed to act upon a model treaty submitted to it and endorsed by American pacifists. Richard, in England, embarked upon a similar unsuccessful venture in 1881, and Cremer assumed charge of the crusade in 1887. Subsequently, both Parliament and Congress passed resolutions in favor of the ideal, but they would not move beyond that point.[12]

Public response to these efforts appeared in several ways prior to 1890. An ambitious reformer named Robert McMurdy helped form a National Arbitration League, which in 1882 elected as its president a former governor of Kansas, Fred P. Stanton. That year and again in 1883, it sponsored national conventions in Washington and Philadelphia which received consider-

---

10. Curti, *Peace or War*, pp. 94–96; *Congressional Globe*, 42 Cong., 2d sess., 45, pt. 5:4106–4107; *Congressional Record*, 43 Cong., 1st sess., 2, pt. 1:3; pt. 6:5114, 5124, 5407.

11. Samuel J. Barrows, "Peace on Earth," *The Independent*, LVII (December 22, 1904), 1413.

12. Abrams, "European Peace Societies," pp. 229–241; Curti, *Peace or War*, pp. 149–158; "Arbitration and the United States," pp. 496–500.

able publicity. In 1884 the Republican party, in convention, approved a plank endorsing arbitration, and both major parties thereafter expressed this need in their platforms.[13]

When the Pan-American Conference met in Washington in 1889, arbitration attracted the interest of the delegates who negotiated a treaty embodying the idea. Many of the petitions received in Congress had suggested that the Latin American area would be a suitable one in which to begin an experiment in the pacific settlement of disputes, and the resulting document was one of the first multilateral agreements to arbitrate differences. "Article V of the Committee on General Well-Being" included a qualification, however, which limited action to a number of specified diplomatic questions and to "all other disputes of whatever nature" save matters relating to national independence. Opposition arose when some of the Latin American states, led by Chile, voiced doubts as well as a fear that the arrangement might result in a permanent arbitral body dominated by the United States. This objection apparently carried weight, for only seven of the seventeen nations represented at the conference signed the accord. The friends of peace celebrated this action, but their hope proved to be premature. None of the signatory governments ever approved the treaty within the time allotted for ratification.[14]

Only a few days before the signing of the Pan-American treaty, Congress reflected the mounting sentiment for arbitration in another way. On April 3, the House approved a concurrent resolution presented by Republican Senator John Sherman of Ohio. This measure, previously passed by the Senate, requested the President to open negotiations with nations "to the end that *any* differences or disputes" be settled by arbitration.[15] Although the administration did not respond, pacifists and internationalists viewed all of the limited results with optimism. It would only be a matter of time, they believed, before an arbitral body would be needed. The latter, in turn, would

13. Curti, *Peace or War,* pp. 81, 137, 148–149; Margrave, "The Policy of . . . Adjudication," pp. 53–54.

14. David S. Muzzey, *James G. Blaine,* p. 434; Helen M. Cory, *Compulsory Arbitration of International Disputes,* pp. 15–19. Margrave, "The Policy of . . . Adjudication," p. 429, in citing State Department files, claims that seven of the signatories gave "favorable responses" to an extension of time proposal, but nothing was done. One writer claims that Simon Bolívar should be credited as an internationalist because of his interests which led to the Panama meeting in 1826. R. Rivas, "Bolívar as Internationalist," *Bulletin of the Pan American Union,* LXIV (December 1930), 1266–1267, 1279, 1283–1286.

15. *Congressional Record,* 51 Cong., 1st sess., 21, pt. 2:1325; pt. 3:2986. Italics added.

require some formal rules upon which to base decisions, and men had also been busy on this subject.

International law had never been universally applied by governments, even though rules among ancient peoples, agreements between Greek city-states, Roman law, church canons, treaties determining relations with other nations, and a few generally accepted standards of behavior had been a reality of life for centuries.[16] No systematic effort had been made to compile these eclectic customs into a body of law based upon philosophical assumptions until Grotius wrote his treatise in 1623 and 1624. The Grotian concept of an existing standard of behavior within a community of nations that could be expressed in form of a code introduced an idea closely related to international organization. While critics have challenged Grotius's "state of nature" theory, there has been a general acceptance of the belief that modern states do actually subscribe to certain standards of morality and action.

Grotius perceived two sources for these rules—natural moral principles, which applied to countries as well as to men, and the enactments of governments, which reflected the institutions and ideas of mankind. Through a systematic examination of these factors, men could, Grotius argued, compile a set of acceptable statutes called the "law of nations."[17]

From the time of Grotius to the nineteenth century, however, only limited progress had been made toward such a compilation. Legal scholars had utilized treaty provisions in seeking commonly accepted practices, and they had also discovered a way to simplify their task when they began to divide laws into two categories, public and private. The first applied to relations between states; the second to international contacts between individuals or companies.[18] Even then, governments showed but little interest in the subject.

In the nineteenth century the situation changed. A "new era" marked by trends toward a written law and a study and classification of diplomatic procedures appeared. Two factors stimulated this development. First, business, commercial, and communication needs demanded specific provisions in agreements which could be easily compiled. Second, nations grew increasingly open in their negotiations as their governments shifted from au-

16. York, *Leagues of Nations*, pp. 8–11; Arthur Nussbaum, *A Concise History of the Law of Nations,* pp. 2–71; George G. Wilson and George F. Tucker, *International Law,* pp. 13–19.

17. White, *Seven Great Statesmen*, p. 88; Nussbaum, *Law of Nations*, pp. 102–114; George B. Davis, *Outlines of International Law*, p. 15.

18. Simeon E. Baldwin, "International Law as a Factor in the Establishment of Peace," *Advocate of Peace*, LXXII (July and August 1910), 163–164.

thoritarian to democratic systems in western Europe. This "trend toward the new form of cooperation originated as though ordered by a higher directive," and it "marked the start of a most powerful and auspicious historical movement."[19]

A third factor also encouraged the awakening interest in a law of nations. The proposals for a congress and court plus the agitation for a wider use of arbitration made men realize that formal statutes on both procedure and fact would be needed. As legal scholars began to search for a practical way to approach their problem, they accepted the word "international," which Bentham had coined in 1770. It was

calculated to express, in a more significant way, the branch of law which goes commonly under the name of the *law of nations*: an appellation so uncharacteristic, that, were it not for the force of custom, it would seem rather to refer to internal jurisprudence. The chancellor D'Auguesseau has already made, I find, a similar remark: he says, that what is commonly called *droit* des *gens* ought rather to be termed *droit* entre *les gens*.

There remain, then, the mutual transactions between sovereigns as such, for the subject of that branch of jurisprudence which may be properly and exclusively termed *international*.[20]

Governments did little to follow Bentham's advice that they seek agreement on a set of practices, but legal scholars did try to compile statutes based on usage and fact. Domin-Petrushevecz, an Austrian official, has been credited with drafting one of the first codes of international law in 1861. A German-American, Francis Lieber, followed closely in time with his rules for northern armies during the Civil War. Lieber, in turn, influenced the thinking of a Swiss-born jurist J. C. Bluntschli, who produced his work *Das moderne Völkerrecht* in 1868. At approximately the same time, David Dudley Field, an American clergyman and legalist, prepared a study which he published in 1872.[21] Finally, the labors of these men culminated in 1873 in one of the most notable achievements of the age. At two separate congresses, jurists formed the first societies devoted to the scientific study of international law.

This development reflected the increasing interest in the subject. Only four years before, a journal, the *Revue de droit international et de législation*

19. Nussbaum, *Law of Nations,* pp. 196–211.
20. *Ibid.*, p. 136; York, *Leagues of Nations,* p. 278; Bentham, *Works,* I, 149. John C. Faries, *The Rise of Internationalism*, explores the origin and use of the word "international," pp. 11–16.
21. Abrams, "European Peace Societies," p. 98; Curti, *Peace or War,* p. 97.

comparée, had appeared. Then, the Franco-Prussian War, the arbitral achievements in the *Alabama* claims controversy, the emerging number of nations, and the threatening competitive rivalry of governments further stimulated the trend toward organization which came in 1873. The first congress of thirty-three men from twelve nations assembled in Brussels in October. They appeared to be of both pacifist and legalist temperament, which caused significant differences of opinion. They agreed on the aims of their proposed association—to promote, to study, and to prepare a code of international law—but not on how to proceed. The more idealistic pacifists wished to begin immediately. They could see no problem in incorporating into the law principles, like the arbitration of all questions, which had not yet been universally accepted. The legalists warned that they should move more cautiously and realistically.[22]

As a result of their differing views, the men at Brussels decided to postpone action on a code. They did, however, organize as the Association for the Reform and Codification of the Law of Nations, which after 1895 they renamed the International Law Association. They realized that before they could compile a set of statutes it would be necessary to lay foundations. Hence, they sought to awaken popular support for their cause, to have important principles incorporated into treaties, to stimulate interest in arbitration, and to hold annual conferences where they might move slowly toward their goal of an accepted international code. They thus sought "to advance the science by an appeal to reason."[23]

The second group to organize that fall assembled at Ghent where the delegates founded the Institute of International Law. This was a more exclusive society of trained legalists who had to be nominated for membership. One American, Field, participated in the Ghent meeting, and he became president of the Institute at its first annual assembly in 1874. The conservative nature of this body became apparent immediately. It sought to avoid controversial questions, and it devoted most of its attention in ensuing years to the development of a private code.[24]

22. Abrams, "European Peace Societies," pp. 107–109.

23. *Ibid.*, pp. 109–112; Curti, *Peace or War,* pp. 97–100; "The Twenty-first Conference of the International Law Association," *Advocate of Peace,* LXV (November 1903), 207; J. B. Scott, "The Work of the Second Hague Peace Conference," *AJIL,* II (January 1908), 8.

24. Theodore Baty, "The International Law Association," *Review of Internationalism,* I (June 1907), 181–182; Beales, *History of Peace,* p. 151; Abrams, "European Peace Societies," pp. 107–112; J. B. Scott, "Preface," *Resolutions of the Institute of International Law, 1916,* pp. vii–viii; Ralston, *International Arbitration,* p. 139; F. S. Lyons, *Internationalism in Europe, 1815–1914,* pp. 218–221.

In the formation of both bodies, citizens of the United States played roles of paramount importance. Ladd and Burritt, with their proposal for a congress and court, had publicized the need for formal rules. Lieber, in letters from 1866 to 1872, had suggested the assembly which founded the Institute of International Law. Burritt, likewise, had pursued a similar goal through correspondence and trips abroad; and Dr. James B. Miles, the secretary of the American Peace Society, along with Field, laid the foundation for the International Law Association.[25]

Despite these new organizations, co-operative codification efforts made little headway. For one thing, governments showed only limited interest in the subject. Also, despite energetic efforts, the two societies could not agree on a program. As late as 1890, they did not know where to begin or what they should include in their statutes. This left the field open to individuals, who compiled drafts of treaties, listed the results of arbitral decisions, and recorded the general rules under which nations seemed to operate.[26]

The nineteenth-century activities in international law, nonetheless, had a considerable impact on the movement for world organization. When men discussed formal standards of behavior, they presumed that an association of nations already existed. Attorney John Westlake of England reiterated that assumption of Grotius. A body of rules presupposed an informal union. "When we assert that there is such a thing as International Law, we assert that there is a society of States; when we recognize that there is a society of States, we recognize that there is International Law."[27]

Such a belief led to another assumption—that as nations gradually accepted such rules, they moved more and more toward a community with identical interests. Internationalists took advantage of this evolutionary hypothesis to argue that governments should meet in conferences. They could then consider laws, obtain common accord on them, erect formal machinery to systematize the process, and finally create agencies to ad-

25. Beales, *History of Peace*, pp. 143–144, 151; Curti, *Peace or War*, p. 100; Scott, *Resolutions*, pp. vi–viii; Baty, "The International Law Association," p. 182; Baty, "International Law Association," *Advocate of Peace*, LXXII (July and August 1910), 173.

26. Nussbaum, *Law of Nations*, pp. 243–249, and Hershey, "History of International Law Since the Peace of Westphalia," pp. 65–67, describe many of these authors and their works.

27. Charles G. Fenwick, *International Law*, p. 61; John Macdonell, "Seven Postulates of International Law," *Living Age*, CCLXXXVIII (March 4, 1916), 582–583, citing John Westlake, *Collected Papers*, pp. 3, 81.

minister and uphold the accepted principles. Their point seemed to be confirmed in 1889 when the Pan-American Conference met. Although the agreements reached there proved to be meaningless, the fact that nations had united to discuss common problems confirmed the community theory. Hence the Pan-American meeting contributed in an indirect way to the development of an international organization.

Acute observers found other evidence to show that men and governments recognized the need for greater co-operation. Throughout the nineteenth century more than 350 international conferences, both public and private, considered various problems, with the number growing toward the end of the century. The most famous of these took place in Europe at Vienna (1814–1815), Troppau (1820), Verona (1822), London (1831), Paris (1856), London (1871), Berlin (1878 and 1884), and The Hague (1899). The New World kept pace with the Panama meeting in 1826 and the Pan-American Conference in 1889.

Governments and private organizations also sponsored assemblies which discussed an ever-widening variety of topics such as sanitation, police regulations, money, patents, copyrights, standardization of weights and measures, international law, the Red Cross, communications, commerce, agriculture, and peace. These meetings engendered a spirit of co-operation which further advanced thinking about a world organization.[28] In the planning and calling of such sessions, the United States and Britain usually led.

The formal participation of the United States government in these gatherings, however, was not as extensive as some of its citizens wished. Yet their nation did adhere to the Red Cross agreement in 1882; it co-operated in a session to explore the subject of an International Prime Meridian in which delegates from twenty-six nations assembled in Washington in 1885; and it sent representatives to the Berlin Conference of 1884–1885 where the great powers explored the problems of West Africa. After 1890, the United States participated more and more in such meetings, especially those dealing with nonpolitical matters.[29]

---

28. Faries, *Rise of Internationalism,* pp. 43–98; Simeon E. Baldwin, "International Congresses and Conferences of the Last Century," *AJIL,* I (July 1907), 565–578; Raymond L. Bridgman, *The First Book of World Law,* pp. 18–282; Douglas Maynard, "Reform and the Origin of the International Organization Movement," *Proceedings,* American Philosophical Society, CVII (June 1963), 230–231; Lyons, *Internationalism in Europe,* p. 370.

29. Bridgman, *First Book of World Law,* pp. 147–282. Faries, *Rise of Internationalism,* pp. 180–202, contains an index listing various official and unofficial conferences on nonpolitical matters.

The expansion of this type of co-operation along with the advances in arbitration and developments in law may explain why so few plans for an international organization appeared between the time of Ladd's death and 1890. Most men interested seemed content to follow indirect paths. Those proponents of a league, however, who did exist in the three decades prior to 1890 can be divided into four groups: the arbitrationists and legalists who sought a congress of nations to formulate a code and establish a court; the advocates of an English-Speaking Union; a group which proclaimed the advantages of a European league; and the more imaginative internationalists who envisioned a world-wide society.

The arbitrationists and legalists were quite numerous, and it is possible to mention only a few of the men who proposed a congress to establish laws and an arbitral court. Leone Levi, a professor at King's College, presented his ideas in a *Draft Project of a Council and High Court of Arbitration* in 1886. Europeans like Émile de Laveleye, a Belgian economist, also saw an assembly of "diplomatic representatives aided by jurists" as a vital need. Laveleye revealed the influence of American planners from Penn through Ladd and Burritt, and he suggested the formation of a judicial body modeled after that of the Supreme Court of the United States. The most notable Spanish internationalist, Arturo de Marcoartu, wrote a small book *Internationalism* in 1876, and he became known for his sponsorship of an essay contest on "The Best Means of Establishing a Representative European Arbitral Assembly." David Dudley Field revealed American thinking in his "A High Tribunal of Arbitration," first published in 1872 as part of his proposed code. Field suggested that existing treaties be combed for all provisions which nations might accept as law. Governments should then adopt and maintain rules and settle their disputes through established procedures. If any state violated the provisions, it should face the coercive power of the "High Tribunal" or a "Joint High Commission."[30] Thus Field hinted at a compulsive feature but did not elaborate upon that point.

The idea of an English-Speaking Union undoubtedly arose as a result of a growing Anglo-American rapprochement. Some men spoke of a league of Anglo-Saxon peoples, but the aim remained the same regardless of the scope. Some of the earliest suggestions for such a step appeared in the United

---

30. Darby, *International Tribunals,* pp. 122–130; Abrams, "European Peace Societies," pp. 93–94, 153; Bertha von Suttner, *Memoirs of Bertha von Suttner,* II, 30; Beales, *History of Peace,* pp. 141–142; Émile de Laveleye, "On the Causes of War and the Means of Reducing their Number," *Cobden Club Essays,* pp. 28–36; Field, *Outlines of an International Code,* pp. 369–373.

States. As early as 1868, a Delaware newspaper owner and editor, Francis Vincent, recommended an association under a federal constitution. Other states should then be allowed to join, thus forming "the Final Union of the World into One Great Nation." The Union League Club of New York City in 1874 discussed a similar plan involving an alliance with Great Britain in which the two powers would combine their navies on behalf of peace.[31]

Proposals for a European society received great impetus in the nine-teenth century as a result of the unification movements in Italy and Germany. The trend seemed inevitable, and a few men looked toward the day when all Europe would be united. Giuseppe Garibaldi of Italian unification fame favored such a course, as did Dr. Eduard Loewenthal, a German pacifist of Dresden, and Dr. Adolphe Fischof of Austria. The Geneva League of Peace and Liberty began publishing a journal, *The United States of Europe*, which endorsed a plan written by its treasurer, Marie Georgg. The editor of that magazine, Charles Lemonnier, also presented a call for a federal struc-ture along Swiss and American lines. At first he thought the mere act of federation would advance the cause of peace, but he later grew discouraged and turned to arbitration. By 1889 he had decided that a European union was impossible, and the *Ligue International de la Paix et de la Liberté* echoed his conclusion in a resolution that year which admitted that "the formation of a European Federation and the creation of an International High Court are not immediately realizable."[32]

Two English proponents of a congress of Europe spelled out their views in 1871. Professor John R. Seeley of Cambridge, in arguing that the states of Europe "must constitute themselves into some sort of federation," urged that the United States be used as a model with executive, legislative, and judiciary systems comparable to those in the United States Constitution. He believed not only in a powerful executive but also in a police force. Only in this way could justice replace the anarchistic conditions of Europe.[33]

John Russell, Viscount Amberly, came to essentially the same con-

31. Vincent, *Essay Recommending the Union of Great Britain and her Colonies and the United States* . . . , pp. 5–6, 12–13; E. W. Cole, comp., *Cyclopaedia of Short Prize Essays on the Federation of the Whole World*, p. 197. An interesting European view can be found in the proposal of G. R. Drysdale, a physician and writer, *Home Rule and Federation* . . . , pp. 33–36.

32. Suttner, *Memoirs*, II, 112–114; Merze Tate, *The Disarmament Illusion: The Movement for a Limitation of Armaments to 1907*, p. 158; Beales, *History of Peace*, p. 225; Abrams, "European Peace Societies," pp. 33–37, 55, 136–139, 150–152, 229.

33. Seeley, "The United States of Europe," *Macmillan's Magazine*, XXIII (March 1871), 439–448.

clusion. England should lead the way to "a common authority" with power "to enforce its decrees." A voluntary association could operate through a "Federal Council" made up of six delegates from each state. Both large and small nations should have an equal vote, said Amberly, because the lesser ones might well need their voice to protect them from the larger powers. Amberly seemed unfamiliar with Ladd's proposal to separate agencies within a league, for his council would function both in a legislative and judicial capacity. Amberly agreed that laws should be upheld, but he did not stand as firmly for military action as Professor Seeley did.[34]

The most detailed plan for a European federation came from Professor Bluntschli. He suggested a two-house assembly to prepare a code, preserve peace, and administer justice. A permanent administrative bureau would function at all times. Bluntschli discussed many details but emphasized legal procedures. A special College of Great Powers would execute the decisions of the federation after special votes in both houses. In this way, there would be no injustice, since all action would presumably be based on law after open hearing. The impact of the United States appeared in Bluntschli's call for a government with executive, legislative, and judicial powers.[35]

The more radical internationalists who spoke and wrote in the three decades prior to 1890 were largely eclipsed by the previous three groups. Few notable plans appeared, and only a handful of citizens in the United States seemed interested. George C. Beckwith, who had aided Ladd in compiling his volume of *Essays*, continued to publish a revision of a plan he had first presented in 1847. It suggested nothing that Ladd's scheme did not contain, but at least Beckwith kept that proposal alive. Francis Vincent only glimpsed in elementary fashion a world-wide union. Andrew Carnegie vaguely perceived the need of a "league of peace to which each continent will send delegates to decide international differences" in the "not quite so far" future. It was to be several years, however, before Carnegie did much to popularize his dream.[36]

In England, a well-known peace advocate, John Noble of Brighton, around 1865 prepared a plan in which he advocated a Supreme Court of

34. Amberly, "Can War be Avoided?," *Fortnightly Review,* n.s., IX (May 1, 1871), 616–624.

35. J. C. Bluntschli, "The Organisation of European Federation," appears in Darby, *International Tribunals,* pp. 102–120. Bluntschli showed the influence of the United States in his suggestion that the American structure of government be adopted. Bluntschli, *Gesammelte kleine Schriften,* II, 302–312.

36. Beckwith, *The Peace Manual,* pp. 230–238; Carnegie, *Triumphant Democracy,* p. 396.

Nations. He called for a periodic assembly empowered to set its own rules, "revise international law," and "declare war and conclude peace." Nations should share expenses and decide matters by majority vote. A similar plan by James Lorimer, professor of the Law of Nature and of Nations at Edinburgh University, discussed a government with legislative, executive, and judicial authority and an army to impose sanctions against lawbreakers. Two other men also speculated on the use of force. Prince Peter von Oldenburg of the Russian royal family suggested that governments guarantee each other's territories and establish an arbitral body to settle disputes. Another Russian, Count L. A. Kamarowski, a professor of international law at the University of Moscow, also spoke of a collective arrangement to preserve peace.[37]

Two other planners merit attention, an Australian, Edward C. Cole, and an Italian, Pasquale Fiore. Cole, a publisher from Melbourne, revealed great interest in all reforms and believed firmly in the unity of the world. He referred to a "supreme federal government" which would promote education, seek standardization of coinage and language, and maintain peace through an army. Cole showed little interest in structural matters, but he revealed considerable imagination in publicizing his views.[38]

Fiore served in the Italian senate and taught international law at the Royal University. He published his plan, based on earlier study and writings, in 1890. His congress would meet periodically, enact and codify statutes, and enforce its actions by a "collective guaranty." People as well as governments should have a voice; hence Fiore suggested the election of delegates by popular vote. Unlike Ladd, he saw no need for a separate court and congress, yet the drafting of law and the compulsory submission of disputes to arbitral hearing dominated his thinking.[39]

Thus, by 1890 internationalists could perceive several encouraging signs. First, groundwork had been laid for the more legalistic settlement of disputes through advances in arbitration and the codification of law. Second, the creation of unofficial international associations and the participation of governments in the conferences of the age had stimulated a growing spirit of co-operation. Third, proposals for a European league revealed how the

37. *Report, Fifth Peace Congress*, p. 89; Lorimer, *The Institutes of the Law of Nations*, II, 279–299; Edith Wynner and Georgia Lloyd, *Searchlights on Peace Plans*, pp. 78–79; Suttner, *Memoirs*, II, 44–45; Tate, *Disarmament Illusion*, p. 117.
38. *The Life of E. W. Cole*, pp. 89–94; Cole, *Cyclopaedia of Short Prize Essays*, pp. 3–5.
39. Pasquale Fiore, *International Law Codified*, pp. 55–62.

"American plan" and the United States system of government had affected planners in the Old World.

A fourth factor, previously unmentioned, also aided the movement in the nineteenth century. The growth of free-trade concepts tended to unite nations because lower tariffs and open economic intercourse fostered a spirit of interdependence. The Cobden Club, founded in England in 1866 to promote the unfettered exchange of goods, soon had chapters throughout the world, and Francis Vincent responded to an essay contest sponsored by the Philadelphia branch when he wrote his treatise on a British-American union. The Club in England also published a series of pamphlets which included Laveleye's proposal for a congress.

The role of Americans between 1850 and 1890 could be described as vital in the arbitration movement and in the development of international law but unimportant in direct planning for an organization. Indirectly, however, Americans did affect thinking because European advocates often referred to the United States as an important model for federation.[40] This may at first glance appear startling in the face of the Civil War, which posed a real challenge to that system, yet the United States had weathered that crisis. In so doing, it had strengthened rather than weakened the idea that a republic of nations could be established and endure.

40. Drysdale, *Home Rule and Federation,* pp. 38, 40, 44–47; Laveleye, "On the Causes of War," pp. 35–36; Seeley, "The United States of Europe," pp. 440, 443, 445; Abrams, "European Peace Societies," p. 138.

A Decade
of Progress,
1890-1899

Throughout the 1890s, pacifists and internationalists in the United
States continued their endeavors as charted in the previous three
decades. They encouraged a more widespread use of arbitration, sought
acceptance for it in treaties, and labored to advance international law. They
also formulated new proposals for world organization as they tried to
educate mankind to the benefits of some type of union. Even more important,
they gained a wider hearing for their views than ever before. Thus, the
period proved to be one of progress.

Much of the effort and success can be traced to an awakened pacifist
movement. The American Peace Society experienced a revival under its
president, Robert Treat Paine, and its secretary, Benjamin Trueblood, who
assumed that position in 1892. Alfred H. Love organized the Universal
Peace Union in 1866 and aggressively led it for forty years until his death
in 1913. Another Quaker body, the Peace Association of Friends, had appeared in 1867.[1]

In Europe, the activities of pacifists also quickened. According to the
International Peace Bureau in 1897, there may have been as many as 425
peace groups in the world that year. These agencies, however, had neither
political influence nor impressive rosters of members. They also tended to

---

1. Curti, *Peace or War,* pp. 123, 136–137.

be divided despite efforts to federate into some effective and efficient force.[2] Their labors, nevertheless, contributed to the development of an international organization. Before men would devote their talents and energies to achieve a world union, they first had to be informed about the horrors of war and convinced that it should be abolished. The peace societies had long propagandized with this idea in mind, but they came to realize that their old negative antiwar doctrines could no longer be effective in a world which saw increasing rivalry among nations and an ominous emphasis upon military preparedness. Pacifists thus re-evaluated their programs and turned more and more from negative moralistic and religious arguments to positive programs of action. In the 1890s, they seized especially upon arbitration and an international court as a panacea to pursue.[3]

In their endeavors, they built stairs which the later internationalists could use. This was especially true of arbitration. It provided nations with an opportunity to explore possible areas of co-operation, thereby preparing governments, statesmen, and people for future steps toward international accord. It introduced, in rudimentary form, many of the technical and emotional questions which such ventures entailed, and governments in seeking answers to such obstacles moved closer to the day when they might unite in a more comprehensive endeavor. Finally, the arbitral crusade contributed to the atmosphere which in 1899 resulted in the first genuine world-wide political assembly at The Hague. The progress was slow, but the developments in arbitration in the 1890s greatly hastened the movement for an international organization.

Throughout the decade, interest in arbitration increased, especially at annual international peace congresses held between 1889 and 1897. At nearly every conference, the delegates endorsed this method of adjudicating disputes. At the 1893 session, which met in Chicago in conjunction with the world's fair, three New York lawyers, Cephas Brainerd, William Allen Butler, and Dorman B. Eaton, presented a detailed plan "for the Organization of an International Tribunal of Arbitration." Nations should sign a

2. Abrams, "European Peace Societies," pp. 23–32, 182–211, 255–271, 283, 310–323, 335–363, 448–453; Frédéric Passy, "Peace Movement in Europe," *American Journal of Sociology,* II (July 1896), 1–12; Madeleine Z. Doty, *The Central Organisation for a Durable Peace (1915–1919), Its History, Work and Ideas,* p. 10.

3. "The Purpose of the Peace Societies," *Advocate of Peace,* LX (April 1898), 78. Examination of printed materials in the Swarthmore College Peace Collection substantiates the point that the religious and moral antiwar approach underwent considerable change in the 1890s, with a notable shift to arbitration. Curti, *Peace or War,* pp. 136, 144–146, 166–167, also notes the change.

treaty under which all disputes would be submitted to a court save those dealing with "the independence or sovereignty of a nation, or its equality with other nations, or its form of government or its internal affairs." The delegates at Turin in 1898 approved a resolution calling for the creation of an international code and the signing of general treaties of arbitration despite warnings of some of the speakers that such proposals were premature.[4]

In addition to peace societies, a number of other groups promoted the arbitral ideal. The Woman's Christian Temperance Union established in 1889 a department on peace and arbitration which distributed large quantities of literature. By 1896, sentiment for the cause and concern over the recent Venezuelan crisis prompted a group of Chicago citizens to unite, and their efforts led to a national gathering of nearly three hundred delegates in Washington, D.C., on April 22 and 23 in a National Arbitration Conference. There, some of the most influential citizens of the nation, including James Cardinal Gibbons, Chauncey M. Depew, David J. Brewer, John W. Foster, Simeon E. Baldwin, and Carl Schurz, spoke boldly for arbitral agreements, especially between the United States and Great Britain.[5]

The Lake Mohonk Conferences on International Arbitration, however, became the most active means of promoting the idea. Each spring from 1895 through 1916, businessmen, politicians, clergymen, journalists, reformers, pacifists, lawyers, educators, and other persons of prominence united to explore lines of action. Quaker pacifists, the genial Smiley brothers Alfred and Albert, originated the meetings, served as hosts at their New York mountain resort, and acted as a cohesive and unifying factor in planning and directing the work of the conferences.

At the first meeting, in 1895, the delegates reached a decision from which they rarely wavered as the years passed. Arbitration would take precedence over other subjects in discussions, speeches, and resolutions. Related topics would be largely ignored. Eventually general agreement appeared on four points. First, arbitration offered nations the best systematic way to settle disputes and avoid war. Second, an extensive campaign of education should

4. Abrams, "European Peace Societies," pp. 334–349; Benjamin Trueblood, "Greatness and Permanence of the Arbitration Cause," *Report,* Fourth Annual Conference on International Arbitration, 1898, pp. 8–9. These volumes will hereafter be cited as *Mohonk Report* along with the proper date. T. J. Lawrence, "The Tsar's Rescript," *International Journal of Ethics,* IX (January 1899), 141; W. Stull Holt, *Treaties Defeated by the Senate,* pp. 154–162.

5. Edwin D. Mead, "The International Duty of the United States and Great Britain," *World Peace Foundation Pamphlets,* I (April 1911), 3–13. *The Independent,* XLVIII (May 7, 1896) devoted most of this issue to arbitration.

be conducted to inform the public in general and statesmen in particular of this fact. Third, the United States should sign a treaty with Great Britain to arbitrate certain types of disputes. Fourth, a permanent international arbitral court should be established to hear and decide questions.[6]

The delegates to the Mohonk conferences, while idealistic and optimistic, cannot be described as totally impractical men. In their discussions they often warned of precipitate action, and they filled their speeches with words of caution to proceed toward their goal gradually. Proposals had to be realistic. The Senate would never approve an arbitral agreement which did not exempt questions of national honor, vital interests, and independence. Nations, especially the United States, would not entrust important domestic or foreign policies to any international body regardless of its nature. As former congressman and diplomat John A. Kasson noted in 1896, "Experienced statesmen will have nothing to do with sweeping generalities, binding their nations for an unlimited time and unknown future."[7] What governments might accept by the 1890s were clauses in treaties which provided for the arbitration of misunderstandings arising over the terms of the accords. This was a step forward, since it advanced the idea of obligatory arbitration. It was an improvement over the earlier procedure of voluntary action in which states agreed to arbitrate only after a dispute arose.

In the 1890s several nations, especially those in the New World, negotiated treaties, some of unlimited scope. Officials in the United States, however, showed great reluctance to sign any paper which might obligate their land even though they appeared ready to study the subject. Indeed, a congressional appropriation in 1893 led to a major compilation of the arbitral settlements to which the United States had been a part, but that was as far as the government would move until 1895.[8]

That year, the threat of war over the Venezuelan boundary awakened interest in an accord with Britain. After prolonged discussions, Secretary of State Richard Olney and British Ambassador Sir Julian Pauncefote reached agreement early in 1897 on a general obligatory treaty to arbitrate pecuniary and territorial disputes for a five-year period. Senators, however, in con-

6. This summary is based upon a careful reading of the *Mohonk Reports.* Resolutions on the four points listed appear in: *1895,* pp. 81–82; *1896,* pp. 129–130; *1897,* pp. 130–131; *1898,* pp. 100–101; *1899,* pp. 91–92.

7. *Mohonk Report, 1896,* p. 92. For references revealing a cautious approach, see the various *Reports: 1896,* pp. 51–53, 55–56, 58, 90–92; *1897,* pp. 81–82.

8. This study resulted in John Bassett Moore's massive *History and Digest of the International Arbitrations.* For a list of treaties concluded, 1890–1899, see "Arbitration and the United States," pp. 589–590.

sidering this document, suggested substantial changes. They added clauses exempting matters affecting national honor, territorial integrity, or vital interests; called for a Senate voice in the nomination of arbitrators; and insisted that it also approve by a two-thirds vote the submission of each question. Despite this and other drastic suggestions, the Senate then failed by three votes to reach the necessary two-thirds majority.[9]

Public response to the treaty had always been favorable, and many persons expressed dismay at the outcome. In searching for answers, they concluded that Anglophobia, the Irish question, the silver controversy, and the Senate's concern for its prerogative had determined the outcome.[10] The rejection of the Olney-Pauncefote compact should have revealed to proponents of international organization that senators were more sensitive about departures from traditional ways than they had suspected. They should have learned a lesson, but time was to reveal some amazing blind spots.

The events in the Senate in 1897, however, did disclose some willingness on the part of the United States to participate in world affairs. The treaty, even though rejected, had been an advance over the bland congressional resolutions of approval which had been common for some sixty years but which had produced no results. Moreover, in the Senate debate over the Olney-Pauncefote agreement, virtually no one voiced opposition to the theory of arbitration, only to the form in which it should be applied; and when the vote is analyzed it is evident that rejection came at the hands of a "controlling minority."[11]

Thus the supporters of arbitration, although disappointed, did not consider the action on the Olney-Pauncefote accord as more than a temporary setback. They continued to plan, and in their thinking they took advantage of one weakness that the negotiations between Olney and Pauncefote had revealed. This was the problem of how to obtain an impartial tribunal. A permanent international court seemed to be the solution, and many men

9. Nelson M. Blake, "The Olney-Pauncefote Treaty of 1897," *American Historical Review,* L (January 1945), 230–240.

10. *Ibid.,* pp. 231–234, 237–241; George F. Edmunds, "Opening Address," *Mohonk Report, 1897,* pp. 5–9; Benjamin Trueblood, "Address . . . ," *ibid.,* pp. 14–15; Edwin D. Mead, "Address . . . ," *ibid.,* p. 23; Edmunds, "Remarks," *ibid.,* pp. 44–45; B. F. Mills, "Remarks," *ibid.,* p. 66; Theodore L. Cuyler, "Address . . . ," *ibid.,* p. 72; Theodore Woolsey, "The Arbitration Proposals at The Hague," *The Independent,* LI (June 15, 1899), 1608; "An Anglo-American Arbitration Treaty," *Advocate of Peace,* LXVI (April 1904), 71–72.

11. Edwin D. Mead, "Address . . . ," *Mohonk Report, 1897,* p. 23; H. K. Carroll, "Address . . . ," *ibid.,* p. 53.

accepted it, as the Lake Mohonk Arbitration *Reports* revealed. The preface to the volume on the 1895 conference described the contents as "addresses and discussions on the special subject of International Arbitration and related matters." That of 1896 noted that the delegates would also consider the "subject of a permanent international tribunal and related matters."[12]

A flurry of proposals for a court had appeared by the mid-1890s. The author, clergyman, and editor Edward Everett Hale argued that men had discovered a more practical goal than a congress of nations. "What we are after here is not a Parliament of Peace; it is a Supreme Court of the Nations; it is a Permanent Tribunal." Justice David J. Brewer of the United States Supreme Court, who studied law under his uncle David Dudley Field, agreed. In an address to the American Bar Association in Detroit in August of 1895, he observed that while a parliament remained a dream, a world supreme court was not.[13]

The Interparliamentary Union also favored the creation of an arbitral tribunal. This body, consisting of legislators from the congresses of various nations, had met first in 1888 to explore avenues of peace. It soon found arbitration an attractive possibility, and at its meeting in Brussels in 1895 the assembled representatives drafted a plan for a permanent court. The International Law Association shortly thereafter did the same. In October of that year, Chauncey M. Depew, attorney and industrialist, introduced the subject to the New York Bar Association, which appointed a special committee to explore the matter. Its report suggested that no arbitral board could be considered a court unless it was permanent and consisted of more than two powers, that such an agency should be created with judges chosen from the highest judicial bodies of nine co-operating states, and that it should hear disputes and decide questions submitted to it in impartial fashion. Each nation would pay its own judges, no treaty would be necessary to create the court, and once it was established the governments would then discuss its powers and jurisdiction and incorporate agreements into treaties.[14]

Strangely, no parallel movement for a tribunal can be found in the field of international law. The only important gains of the 1890s came in the area of private law, with conferences in 1889–1890, 1893, 1894, and 1900. To those legalists who thought in terms of a code to restrain governments

12. *Mohonk Report, 1895,* p. 3; *ibid., 1896,* p. 3.
13. Edward Everett Hale, *A Permanent Tribunal*; Hale, "Address . . . ," *Mohonk Report, 1896,* p. 19; Lyman Abbott, "Opening Address," *ibid.,* p. 7.
14. Suttner, *Memoirs,* II, 55–58; W. M. Jones, "The Plan of the New York State Bar Association," *Mohonk Report, 1899,* pp. 43–44; Walter S. Logan, "A Working Plan . . . ," *ibid., 1896,* pp. 60–64; Alden Chester, "Address . . . ," *ibid., 1897,* p. 34.

and provide statutes for a court, the advances were discouraging. English pacifist W. Evans Darby voiced a common concern as early as 1893 when he decried the fact that the International Law Association had been drawn from its main goal of reform and codification by "aspects of international law" other than those related to peace.[15]

This reluctance to act reflected a prevailing belief that law had no real meaning to governments. It did not exist in any universally acceptable form despite the work of codifiers; it had no agency to apply it; and no power existed to uphold it. Moreover, the existence of some body to administer a code could threaten the sovereignty of nations. States would then no longer be free to act with impunity. Hence, any significant acceptance of law would constitute a genuine revolution in international relations.[16]

Thus, in terms of progress, the decade saw little advance toward a law of nations. As the Hague Conference approached, a widespread hope emerged that some breakthrough might be achieved at the sessions, but the delegates there devoted more time to rules of war rather than peace. They did, however, decide to establish a Permanent Court of Arbitration.

Various motives have been attributed to Tsar Nicholas II of Russia, who issued the initial call for the gathering; but regardless of the reasons his action was both unusual and significant.[17] A rescript of August 24 introduced the idea of a meeting with little reference to specific subjects to be considered, but the Tsar followed that note on January 11, 1899, with a suggestion that the powers discuss limitation on armaments, consider the rules of war, and examine how they might best advance the pacific settlement of disputes.[18]

Comment in the United States on the Tsar's notes and the conference was highly favorable. Elsewhere, response outside of pacifist circles did not rise to notable heights despite considerable propaganda effort on the part of peace advocates. The latter showed understandable jubilation. To them, the assembly at The Hague was a dream come true. A virtually unattainable goal had been suddenly thrust within their grasp.[19]

The official response of governments to the Tsar's notes, however, can

15. *Report, Fifth Peace Congress*, p. 209.

16. Austin Abbott, "Address . . . ," *Mohonk Report, 1895*, p. 78.

17. Calvin D. Davis, *The United States and the First Hague Peace Conference*, pp. 43–46; Robinson, *Arbitration*, pp. 20–21.

18. Scott, *Hague Peace Conferences*, II, 1–5.

19. Abrams, "European Peace Societies," pp. 418–423, 429–430, 440–445; Andrew D. White, *Autobiography of Andrew Dickson White*, II, 251–252; Suttner, *Memoirs*, II, 272–273; Curti, *Peace or War*, pp. 187–188.

only be described as cool. The statesmen of the world suspected the Tsar's motives, and even as they gathered at The Hague they felt that little could be achieved. In the United States, President William McKinley and Secretary of State John Hay had read the messages with interest but without enthusiasm. Hay seemed ready to follow other nations rather than assume any initiative on submitting proposals.[20]

This attitude changed, however, when President McKinley appointed a relatively strong commission to represent the United States. Andrew D. White, at the time ambassador to Germany and the former president of Cornell University, headed the group. Frederick W. Holls, a prominent New York lawyer and German-American, received appointment as secretary. Seth Low, president of Columbia, Stanford Newell, the United States minister to the Netherlands, Captain William Crozier, an ordnance officer, and Captain Alfred Thayer Mahan, the noted naval authority and strategist, completed the list of delegates. Assistant Secretary of State David Jayne Hill, in collaboration with Hay, drafted their instructions. These counseled the delegates to avoid participation in disarmament discussions on the ground that the subject could hardly apply to the United States. On arbitration and mediation, however, the instructions specifically authorized action, and they included detailed proposals for the establishment of an international court modeled, in part, after that of the New York Bar Association plan.[21]

After the Americans arrived at The Hague and examined the situation and attitudes, they concluded that their most important role would be in the area of arbitration. Because of the failure of the Olney-Pauncefote treaty, nations had to be shown that the United States still favored this method of settling disputes. No other group of nationals came as well prepared on the subject as the Americans.[22]

At The Hague, the delegates agreed to create three commissions, one on the difficult question of armaments, one on the rules of war, and a third on arbitration, mediation, and good offices. Virtually no decisions could be reached on the first topic, and only limited agreement proved to be possible on the second. Hence, the achievements of the Hague Conference resulted

20. Davis, *U.S. and First Hague Conference,* pp. 38–42, 63; Robinson, *Arbitration,* pp. 21–23; N. M. Butler to F. W. Holls, February 18, 1899, Holls Papers, Columbia University.

21. Scott, *Hague Peace Conferences,* II, 6–9, 15–16; Beales, *History of Peace,* p. 236.

22. Scott, *Hague Peace Conferences,* II, 8; Davis, *U.S. and First Hague Conference,* pp. 77–80, 90; Robinson, *Arbitration,* pp. 24–29, 98.

from the work of the third group, in which Holls, White, and Low represented the United States. They had hoped to present their plan for a tribunal, but other nations acted first and hence have received the credit for introducing that important subject. Yet many European delegates viewed a court with suspicion. Indeed, it soon became obvious that none could be created unless its functions and jurisdiction were narrowly prescribed.[23] Thus, as finally approved, the convention eliminated obligatory clauses which would have required the submission of disputes, and it exempted questions of national honor and vital interests. It also called for a separate *compromis* or agreement every time two or more states wished to submit issues to the tribunal. Any other provisions in 1899 would have carried nations farther than they were willing to go.[24] Although the delegates called their creation a Permanent Court of Arbitration, it was not a court in the usual sense but a list of names of judges from which powers could select a panel when needed.

The Americans, who had abandoned their position on obligatory arbitration, contributed only one important clause to the convention. This allowed review of arbitral decisions and thus strengthened the judicial quality of the proceedings. In signing the Hague agreements, however, they accepted the provisions for a court with the following reservations.

Nothing contained in this convention shall be so construed as to require the United States of America to depart from its traditional policy of not intruding upon, interfering with, or entangling itself in the political questions or policy or internal administration of any foreign State; nor shall anything contained in the said Convention be construed to imply a relinquishment by the United States of America of its traditional attitude toward purely American questions.[25]

Even with such a safeguard, critics who attacked the provisions for a court and mediation appeared during public discussions over the Hague agreements. They condemned the United States for participating in the conference and predicted dire results. Rumors that the Senate might reject the whole thing circulated, but on February 5, 1900, it gave its advice and consent.[26]

23. Davis, *U.S. and First Hague Conference,* pp. 138–141, 147–161; Scott, *Hague Peace Conferences,* II, 54–60.

24. Davis, *U.S. and First Hague Conference,* p. 165; Robinson, *Arbitration,* p. 131.

25. Davis, *U.S. and First Hague Conference,* pp. 137–138, 163; "Revision of Arbitral Decisions," *The Outlook,* LXII (July 29, 1899), 693–694; Scott, *Hague Peace Conferences,* II, 59.

26. Davis, *U.S. and First Hague Conference,* pp. 196–199.

The Senate's approval simply reflected the fact that the treaty did not obligate the United States to act under any part of the machinery of peace—arbitration, mediation, inquiry, or good offices. Even if the government chose to refer a dispute to arbitration, nothing required its submission to the so-called court at The Hague. Furthermore, no one had to obey the decisions, a point which did not disturb pacifists or internationalists. In virtually every instance in which nations had referred their differences to arbitration, they had honored the award and its terms. Thus men could proclaim that no direct force would be needed by a tribunal. The moral weight of public opinion would compel acceptance.[27]

For the scholar interested in world organization, the Hague Conference of 1899 contributed substantially to the movement. Skeptics argued at the time and later that little had been achieved and that the machinery of peace erected proved to be weak, yet the assembly left its mark. In the first place, a genuine international gathering had taken place, representing twenty-six states, including two from North America and five from Asiatic areas. It proved that nations could unite on a broad scale to discuss their problems. Second, it showed that governments could reach accord on certain subjects even when they had agreed that all decisions should be reached unanimously. Obstacles could be overcome. The one positive gain, the Permanent Court of Arbitration, emerged as a pioneer venture, an agency with specified rules of procedure, with a designated meeting place, and with an administrative council always in session.[28]

While it could be argued that the court rarely functioned and made but little mark on the world, it did contribute modestly to developments in international law, especially in establishing procedures and legal precedents. Furthermore, the court and arbitral agreements at The Hague led to the extension of arbitration through the signing of treaties as recommended under Article 19 of the Convention. Once nations took this step, men could look ahead to plan for a tribunal subject to judicial hearing and procedure. It could become an agency of justice rather than of arbitration.

Elihu Root later perceived as secretary of state that the real significance of the First Hague assembly lay not in its achievements but in its promise for the future. He said,

27. George F. Edmunds, "Address . . . ," *Mohonk Report, 1896*, pp. 5–6; George F. Seward, "Address . . . ," *ibid., 1897*, p. 81; Herbert Welch, "The Vital Principle of Arbitration," *ibid., 1899*, p. 18; William L. Scruggs, "The Progress of Arbitration," *ibid., 1898*, pp. 57–58; Lord Russell, "International Law and Arbitration," *The Forum*, XXII (October 1896), 212.

28. White, *Autobiography*, II, 351–354.

The most valuable result of the Conference of 1899 was that it made the work of the Conference of 1907 possible. The achievements of the conferences justify the belief that the world has entered upon an orderly process through which, step by step, in successive conferences, each taking the work of its predecessor as its point of departure, there may be continual progress toward making the practice of civilized nations conform to their peaceful professions.[29]

Thus the meeting at The Hague proved to be both a beginning and an end. Especially noteworthy was the fact that it marked the close of a century of effort on the part of peace workers and internationalists and revealed how far they had come.

Developments in arbitration and the creation of a court were not the only evidence of the trend toward international organization in the 1890s. The usual activities which tended to unite peoples continued, including the creation of new world-wide associations. A federation of peace societies began operating in Berne, Switzerland, in 1892, under the direction of Albert Gobat. Originally called the Interparliamentary Conference for International Arbitration, later the International Peace Bureau, its aim was to co-ordinate the work of the various national groups and to compile factual and statistical evidence to use in the struggle against war. Its members became interested in establishing a court in 1891 and may have influenced the plan of the Hague Conference through its proposals.[30]

The Interparliamentary Union continued its labors after its formation in 1889, concentrating upon resolutions favoring arbitration. It met annually and by 1895 claimed a membership of over twelve hundred representatives. Not until 1894, however, did anyone in the United States show interest. That year a group of congressmen, including Democrats James B. McCreary of Kentucky and Andrew Price of Louisiana and Republican Henry H. Bingham of Pennsylvania raised the question of co-operation. In 1896, the Union extended a formal invitation to the United States requesting active participation, and the following year congressman, clergyman, and editor Samuel J. Barrows attended a session. In 1899, Republicans Barrows and Richard Bartholdt of St. Louis met with the group.[31]

Interest in international co-operation appeared in other ways. At the Columbian Exposition of 1893, Charles Carroll Bonney, a Chicago lawyer, served as president of a "World's Congress Auxiliary," which sponsored a

29. Scott, *Hague Peace Conferences*, I, 143.

30. Beales, *History of Peace*, p. 225; Abrams, "European Peace Societies," pp. 244, 329; Davis, *U.S. and First Hague Conference*, p. 148n.

31. Benjamin Trueblood, "Address . . . ," *Mohonk Report, 1895*, p. 7; "Notes and Comments," *Advocate of Peace*, LVI (March 1894), 62–63; J. L. Tryon, *The Interparliamentary Union and its Work*, pp. 3–5.

"World's Parliament of Religions." Bonney realized that the promotion of good will and understanding could not be left to chance; hence, he organized the World's Unity League. While it sought to develop a spirit of brotherhood and love, it also played a role in educating citizens about arbitration.[32]

A Human Freedom League also appeared in 1891 with attorney William O. McDowell of Newark, New Jersey, as its president. It proclaimed the advantages of internationalism in the form of a broad federation of peoples devoted to the advancement of free institutions everywhere. Such a fraternity could result in a world-wide republic with a court to legislate as well as to adjudicate disputes. A Committee of Three Hundred assembled at Independence Hall in Philadelphia that year to formulate a program of action. Such notable citizens as Edward Everett Hale, former Governor John W. Hoyt of Wyoming, suffragette Lucy Stone, and Mayor Champion S. Chase of Omaha agreed that as men of the eighteenth century left the United States to the world, they hoped to leave to the twentieth century "a legacy as far-sighted, as human, and hopeful."[33]

Further evidence of the broadening thought on international organization can be found in the views of Rev. George Dana Boardman of Philadelphia. Throughout the 1890s, he pleaded for men to apply Christian doctrines toward people and nations and suggested "a covenant of everlasting amity" with "a peace league that shall be not only Pan-American but also Pan-Human." The United States, he declared, should lead in calling a congress to establish "The Parliament of Man." Boardman even considered the possibility that it might need a police agency.[34]

One factor which prompted such attitudes can be found in the industrial developments of the late nineteenth century which carried the nation into the arena of international trade. As economist John Bates Clark observed as early as 1897, "there is evolving, as we all know, a world-state," united by economic and commercial activities, ideas, and systems. That same conclusion appeared in a statement from the United States Bureau of Foreign Commerce when it noted that industrially and commercially the nation was no longer isolated and would henceforth have to engage in universal trade.[35]

---

32. B. O. Flower, "The World's Unity League," *The Arena*, XXIV (November 1900), 529–533.

33. E. P. Powell, "World-Wide Republic," *ibid.*, V (January 1892), 212–216.

34. Boardman, *Disarmament of Nations*, p. 10; Boardman, "Nationalism and Internationalism; or Mankind One Body," *Advocate of Peace*, LVII (July 1895), 152; *Report, Fifth Peace Congress*, p. 223.

35. Clark, "Address . . . ," *Mohonk Report, 1897*, p. 74; Arthur M. Schlesinger, *The Rise of the City*, p. 418; "The President's Message," *Advocate of Peace*, LX (January 1898), 7.

The human, moral, and economic factors uniting people eventually contributed to a growing sense of cosmopolitanism. Americans felt they had become part of the world, that they had obligations, and that peace could depend upon what they did to promote brotherhood and co-operation. Benjamin Trueblood and the editor of the *New England Magazine*, Edwin D. Mead, realized that this spirit went far to explain the willingness of states to conclude treaties of commerce and arbitration. Other men saw it ushering in unlimited opportunities for friendship, which could result in a fuller political solidarity.[36]

An increasing number of men believed that they should plan actively for some type of international union, and a number of proposals appeared in the 1890s. The trends of the earlier years continued with a mounting interest in an English-Speaking Union or a federation of Anglo-Saxon peoples. Most of the discussion, however, occurred in England rather than in the United States, for there the idea was interwoven with the emerging dream of a vast imperial federation. William T. Stead, Cecil Rhodes, Sir George Grey, and Lord Rosebery led in the discussions, but occasionally an American endorsed the proposal. Andrew Carnegie did so; and in 1895 at a conference of peace workers in Chicago a resolution carried which suggested that Washington's birthday that year mark a movement "for cementing all the English-speaking people of the world in peace and fraternal unity." By 1898 the leading pacifist organ, the *Advocate of Peace*, showed a mounting interest in this ideal.[37]

Suggestions for a federation of European states also continued to appear, again with the impetus provided by Europeans. The English journalist Stead especially proclaimed this scheme, and in Great Britain the proposal gained momentum when Lord Salisbury on November 10, 1897, speaking as Prime Minister, noted that only a "Federation of Europe" could "save civilization

36. Trueblood, "Address . . . ," *Mohonk Report, 1895*, p. 8; [Edwin D. Mead], "Editor's Table," *New England Magazine*, XIV (March 1896), 126–128; James H. Mays, "Internationalism," *Advocate of Peace*, LVII (July 1895), 153–154.

37. F. J. Wylie, "Cecil Rhodes and His Scholars as Factors in International Conciliation," *International Conciliation*, No. 25 (December 1909), p. 7; Mead, "The International Duty of the United States and Great Britain," p. 4; E. P. Powell, "International Arbitration," *The Arena*, XVII (December 1896), 111; Sir George Grey, "The Federation of the Anglo-Saxon Race," *Public Opinion*, XVII (August 30, 1894), 521–522; R. R. Meredith, "A Concert or a Congress," *Mohonk Report, 1898*, p. 31; W. T. Stead to Carnegie, July 6, 1892, Carnegie Papers, Library of Congress; Scott F. Hershey, "Peace Among The Nations," *Advocate of Peace*, LX (February 1898), 40–42; "Editorial Notes," *ibid.*, (July 1898), pp. 155–156; "Editorial Notes," *ibid.*, (October 1898), p. 203.

from the desolating effects of a disaster of war." The Baroness von Suttner, E. T. Moneta, Baron d'Estournelles de Constant, Jacques Novicow, and similar pacifist leaders sought to advance the idea on the continent. At the peace congresses it became increasingly possible to pass resolutions favoring the proposal, but the delegates endorsed no specific plan.[38]

It was certainly logical that such men and women would also look beyond a regional arrangement. General expressions of approval of an international organization became somewhat commonplace. The Baroness von Suttner referred to a vague and undefined union, and the Swedish industrialist Alfred Nobel grasped the idea with a fuller awareness of what was involved. Lord Russell of Killowen observed as early as 1896 that there could be no real peace "until the Great Powers of the World, in League, bind themselves to coerce a recalcitrant member of the Family of Nations," but he observed that little headway had been made in that direction. James Stansfeld, in Commons, felt compelled to inquire whether it would not be wise for governments to unite "into a civilized society of nations" to create and enforce international law.[39]

In the United States, such prominent men as William H. P. Faunce, minister and educator, noted the need for a confederation, and Andrew Carnegie continued to speak of a "league of peace." The child is already born, declared Amory H. Bradford, an associate editor of *The Outlook*, who "will live to see a United States of the World, as there is now a United States of America." A remark typical of such broad and undefined expressions, however, was that of John W. Hoyt. There should be, he said,

special organizations in different countries, and then there should be a great international association established somewhere, at some point convenient of access for the world in general so that its representatives from time to time may assemble and measures can be taken to bring about this glorious result.[40]

Some men did speak with more certainty. Raymond Bridgman, a Boston journalist, presented his views in an article in 1899. He described the Hague

38. W. T. Stead, *The United States of Europe on the Eve of the Parliament of Peace*, pp. 26, 60–81, 467; Francis W. Fox, "The Federation of European States and a Permanent International Federation Tribunal," *Review of Internationalism*, I (April 1907), 29; Suttner, *Memoirs*, I, 426–427, II, 295–296; Abrams, "European Peace Societies," pp. 363–364; John R. Mez, "Jacques Novicow," *World Unity Magazine*, XIII (January 1934), 220, 225–226.

39. Suttner, *Memoirs*, II, 400–404, I, 337, 438–439; Russell, "International Law and Arbitration," p. 212; *Report, Fifth Peace Congress*, p. 300.

40. A. H. Bradford, "The Unity of the World," *Mohonk Report, 1898*, p. 79; W. H. P. Faunce, "Signs of Promise," *ibid.*, p. 27; *Report, Fifth Peace Congress*, p. 229.

Conference as a "step toward the attainment of the constitution of the re-public of nations." The growing conscience of governments and the progress toward co-operation revealed a trend which would soon result in "a congress of nations." While Bridgman provided few details about this organization, he did refer to judicial, executive, and legislative agencies which would evolve according to needs and conditions.[41]

Another American, the dedicated secretary of the American Peace So-ciety, Benjamin F. Trueblood, also examined the subject. Trueblood pre-sented his views in 1899 in a small book, *The Federation of the World*. He sought to convince his readers not only that a "federation of the race ought to exist" but also that events were moving men in that direction. "The social and political unity of the world," he declared, "is a consummation rationally to be expected in the not remote future." Trueblood sought to reveal the dependence of men and nations upon each other and to show the oneness of mankind.[42]

In a lengthy exposition on the destructive qualities of warfare, True-blood observed that men had already challenged the "war system." The arbitration movement reflected this.[43] Wise men, however could already see a step beyond to a "higher state" of co-operation. If headway could be made in reducing armaments and international tensions, nations could move to-ward this next stage—federation. All developments in travel, communica-tion, law, diplomacy, conferences, and arbitration "foreshadow a complete political unity of the world, a great international world state, built up some-what on the pattern of our union of States, with supreme legislative, judicial and executive functions touching those interests which the nations have in common."[44]

Men needed such an agency to settle their problems, argued Trueblood, and a federation could come in various ways. Other nations might join the United States to form an association in the Western Hemisphere, or Europe might unite, or some racial merger might occur along the lines of an Anglo-Saxon union. The "federative forces" at work, however, would someday culminate in an international citizenship. The world, Trueblood declared, would see a court evolve from the arbitral agreements which nations were already concluding; a legislature would grow from that; and someday there

41. Bridgman, "The Body Politic of Mankind," *New England Magazine*, XXI (Sep-tember 1899), 23–31.
42. Trueblood, *The Federation of the World*, pp. vi–vii, 7–55.
43. *Ibid.*, pp. 80–117.
44. *Ibid.*, pp. 124–125.

would even be an executive agency with a police force at its disposal. Trueblood did not believe in a strong government, however. Its functions would be "legislative and judicial and its executive duties will be largely those of simple direction and guidance rather than of compulsion."[45]

This idea sounded so logical to some men that a few of them attacked the basic policy of isolationism that prevented the United States from participating in a league. E. P. Powell, an editor of *The Independent* magazine, had been an enthusiastic supporter of "a completer Internationalism—organic and fraternal," and as early as 1896 his journal challenged the famous warning of George Washington to beware of permanent alliances. It noted that in his statement Washington "did not mean to prevent us taking our fair part in the policing of the world and in putting down inhuman outrages." Historian and philosopher John Fiske likewise reviewed Washington's words in 1897 and reached a similar conclusion. Once European union could be achieved, said Fiske, the United States could not stand aloof. The time would come when in the interest of peace "a policy of isolation will not always be possible, nor will it be desirable."[46]

Once the Hague Conference ended, many men seemed gifted with prophetic vision. Such pacifists as Robert Treat Paine saw it as "the first step towards the federation of the world," a statement which Stead in England and Trueblood echoed. The venerable Edward Everett Hale, who had prophesied the coming of a court and a European union, now foresaw periodic meetings which would culminate in an "international system of the civilized world." Hale organized a series of meetings in Boston in the spring of 1899 to awaken popular interest through a number of lectures under the lofty heading "The Organization of the World." Editors quoted Tennyson's lines so often that the phrase "the federation of the world" must have been known to every schoolboy, and some writers even began to discuss an international capital as within the grasp of men.[47]

In the general expressions endorsing the ideal of an organization, two themes appeared. In one, the United States was hailed, both in Europe and

45. *Ibid.*, pp. 127–144.
46. Powell, "International Arbitration," p. 111; "Washington's Doctrine and Arbitration," *The Independent*, XLVIII (February 20, 1896), 247; Fiske, "The Arbitration Treaty," *Atlantic Monthly*, LXXIX (March 1897), 407–408.
47. Paine, "Remarks . . . ," *Mohonk Report, 1899*, p. 23; Hale, "The Possibilities at the Hague," *ibid.*, pp. 11–12; Jones, "Plan of the New York State Bar Association," *ibid.*, p. 46; W. T. Stead, "The Conference at The Hague," *The Forum*, XXVIII (September 1899), 1; *The Independent*, LI (September 28, 1899), 2638; Curti, *Peace or War*, p. 190.

America, as a federal model to be followed in the process of union. As Edwin D. Mead argued in 1898, the interdependence of the world had grown to such a degree that countries were closer in nearly every respect than the American colonies had been in Washington's time. Governments should combine as the states had done in 1776 "into a family of nations, into a federation and fraternity, with a comprehensive law, an efficient police and a purposeful economy."[48] The Supreme Court of the United States also received attention as a model to be followed in erecting a judicial body. One cannot underestimate the influence of this idea, for the Supreme Court enjoyed unique powers not only to decide national questions but also to rule on issues between states or between states and the federal government. Moreover, it had been vested with the authority to determine its own jurisdiction in cases. It was a working illustration that invited examination and emulation.[49]

The theme second in popularity appeared in a revival of Kant as the philosopher of internationalism. Mead played a major role in this renewed interest, for in articles and speeches he reminded men that the German philosopher had clearly reflected the ambitions and ideals of mankind in his call for a federation.[50] Trueblood also contributed by translating Kant's *Eternal Peace*, which appeared in the *Advocate of Peace* and in book form in 1897. Both themes fit in perfectly with the ambiguous but ambitious and hopeful dreams of the age. The United States had evolved without great upheaval toward a more perfect union, and it provided the world with an example of Kant's federation in which sovereignty would be retained by the members at the same time that the international organization appeared.

The growth of democracy in the nineteenth century, with its emphasis upon representative governments, also seemed to indicate that Kant had been right in his political reasoning. Men could, perhaps, adopt this system in creating a congress.[51] Moreover, the unification movements in Italy and Germany resulted in governments based upon federal principles. Thus Kant's goal of an international society built upon democracy and federalism marked him as a prophet worth remembering in the 1890s.

48. "Editor's Table," *New England Magazine*, XIX (December 1898), 514–520.

49. Curti, *Peace or War*, p. 123; W. T. Stead, "The Influence of the New World Upon the Old," *The Independent*, LI (June 29, 1899), 1727–1729; Stead, *The United States of Europe*, pp. 1–3; E. R. Moneta to William O. McDowell, March 17, 1893, McDowell Papers, New York Public Library; *Report, Fifth Peace Congress*, pp. 24–25; Philip C. Garrett, "Address . . . ," *Mohonk Report, 1895*, p. 20.

50. Mead's views are best expressed in *Organize the World*, pp. 1–9, and in an "Address . . . ," *Mohonk Report, 1896*, pp. 85–86.

51. Phelps, *Anglo-American Peace Movement*, p. 103.

Another subject, the application of force by an association of nations, also revealed how far discussions had proceeded. As long as a league remained a remote dream, men had felt no need to consider the rather academic question of its powers. But once a union appeared to be possible, this knotty problem had to be considered. Most of the views expressed in the 1890s reveal naivete and superficiality. Most thinkers believed that military force would not be needed nor should be applied. If countries agreed to arbitrate disputes, if they accepted a court as a fair method of settlement, would they not abide by its decisions? The only *posse comitatus* needed already existed in the form of the moral weight of mankind. This would be sufficient to compel obedience.[52]

A few observers, however, did perceive some need for a military establishment. Justice Robert Earl of the Court of Appeals of New York noted in 1895 that any nation rejecting an arbitral award should have its property seized "if necessary, by force of arms." He further observed that such action by a combined agency acting under the authority of a tribunal would not constitute an act of war even though military sanctions be employed. Another legalist, former Vermont Senator George F. Edmunds of Philadelphia, also perceived that unless a court could uphold its decisions and sustain its jurisdiction, its action might be meaningless. John Brisben Walker, the editor of *Cosmopolitan Magazine*, suggested in 1896 that the worrisome problem of the Cuban revolution could be easily resolved. Cuba should be wrested from Spain and made the military headquarters for an international police force under a combination of the major powers.[53]

Only a few such radical views appeared in the 1890s. Most internationalists accepted a philosophy of gradualism and referred to it as a "rational" approach.[54] They rejected detailed and unattainable schemes; they called for evolution rather than revolution. Thus, they subordinated dreams to practical programs. They joined the exponents of arbitration, the advocates of a court, the propagandists for world conferences, and the spokesmen for the rational settlement of disputes.

The experience of the decade largely supported this evolutionary hy-

52. A. T. Mahan, "The Peace Conference and the Moral Aspect of War," *North American Review*, CLXIX (October 1899), 438, 441; J. H. Stiness, "Address . . . ," *Mohonk Report, 1896*, pp. 34–37; Edmunds, "Remarks . . . ," *ibid.*, p. 42; James M. Ludlow, "Remarks . . . ," *ibid., 1899*, p. 25; White, *Autobiography*, II, 353; Abrams, "European Peace Societies," pp. 343–345.

53. Earl, "Address . . . ," *Mohonk Report, 1895*, p. 28; Edmunds, "Remarks," *ibid., 1897*, p. 45; Walker, "International Arbitration," *Cosmopolitan Magazine*, XXI (May 1896), pp. 103–104.

54. Trueblood, *Federation*, p. vii; E. D. Mead, "The International Peace Congress," *Mohonk Report, 1904*, p. 147.

pothesis. The 1890s began with considerable interest in arbitration but with little hope that a court could be attained within the lifespan of men then living. It ended not only with a tribunal but also with a world-wide assembly. Thus, without elaborate plans and even without formal constitutions, the nations and peoples of the world moved closer to an international organization. The arbitral body and the Hague Conference represented an achievement of real consequence in the evolutionary process that men had come to accept. With a court, with arbitration agreements concluded, with one assembly as a precedent, men could turn to the "next step" in constructing and perfecting the machinery needed.

The Modern
Movement for an
International
Organization

For nearly four years following the First Hague Conference, American internationalists remained unusually quiet. The meeting at The Hague had apparently caught up with their ideas and plans; hence men paused to assess where they had been and where they should go.

Events, indeed, had been rapid. The United States had entered a new era not only by participating in the conference, but also because of its expanding economy and its involvement in the Spanish-American War. The latter experience had thrust the United States into the world arena where henceforth it would play the role of a major nation. Naval authorities had recognized as early as 1890 that in the shifting balance of power the United States would not be able to live apart much longer, and President William McKinley expressed the realities of the economic change in September of 1901 when he noted that "isolationism is no longer possible or desirable."[1] McKinley did not conclude that an international organization was needed, but some of his countrymen did. They perceived that in participating in world affairs their country would move inevitably toward that goal.

This realization stimulated discussion about an association of nations and especially its related subject, the Hague court of arbitration. No clear pattern of thought, however, emerged for a few years. Men tended to be

1. Dulles, *America's Rise*, p. 28; "President M'Kinley's Address . . . ," *Review of Reviews*, XXIV (October 1901), 433.

ambiguous, with broad prophecies that evolutionary trends would lead inexorably to an international arrangement and with passing references to a congress of nations. An editorial in *The Independent* in 1901 revealed such thoughts when it proclaimed that the new century would "doubtless see the smaller States absorbed or confederated with the larger ones the world over." Another observer, economist John Bates Clark, perceived the evolutionary movement as substantial as a "rock in the process of making, and well advanced in the process." He saw economic laws drawing the nations toward a federation of the world as "through the action of cosmic force."[2]

A Chicago businessman, E. S. Wicklin, also noted commercial ties as tending to unite mankind. He suggested a concert of powers, modeled after the British empire, wherein "all present governments may be superseded by one civil government of the world." Wicklin seemed unconcerned about the structure of the organization other than to suggest that it have a court and a written constitution.[3]

The growing interdependence of states prompted other observations that an inevitable trend toward internationalism had begun. Philosopher and pacifist Robert Treat Paine noted in 1900 that the decade of the 1890s had seen the development of an "international conscience." The most active spokesman of this view was still Benjamin Trueblood, but a number of other prominent persons expressed a similar thought.[4]

Some men refused to sit passively talking and writing while time brought their goal to reality. W. T. Stead sought to form a European International Union, but its program to compel nations to submit their quarrels to the Hague peace machinery placed its emphasis on that body rather than on a more complex structure. Edwin D. Mead appealed to pacifists in 1902 to dedicate themselves to the cause of a legislative congress and to move beyond the purely judicial functions of the Hague court, but only a few men followed him.[5]

2. "South America's Future," *The Independent*, LIII (January 31, 1901), 287; Clark, "Address . . . ," *Mohonk Report, 1901*, p. 49.

3. Wicklin, "Prepare the World for Peace," *The Arena*, XXV (February 1901), 164, 166–167.

4. Trueblood's opinions can be found in *The American Friends' Peace Conference*, pp. 154–159. Other statements appear on pages 119–121, 124–125, 160–161. Edwin R. A. Seligman, "The Growth of International Unity," *Advocate of Peace*, LXV (January 1903), 16.

5. Stead to Andrew Carnegie, September 21, 1900, Carnegie Papers; Mead, "The Education of Public Opinion," *Mohonk Report, 1902*, pp. 48–49; Homer B. Sprague, "Address," *The Peacemaker*, XXI (October 1902), 236; Nathaniel Schmidt, "Address . . . ," *Mohonk Report, 1901*, p. 40.

Most of the internationalists as well as peace workers in those early years chose a less ambitious course. They looked to the perfection of the Hague structure. The first step seemed to be to accept the final recommendations in the declarations of 1899, which suggested that individual governments conclude treaties to arbitrate their differences. Virtually no one could quarrel with such a noble aim, and few voices protested such action. Discussions, therefore, centered upon which nations could be approached, what type of pact should be negotiated, and how inclusive the agreements should be in regard to the type of dispute submitted.

On the first question, sentiment favored a treaty with Britain, although a few men cautioned that it might be strategically sounder to begin elsewhere. On the second point, discussion moved more and more to favor obligatory arbitration. A special distinction had appeared between the words "compulsory" and "obligatory." The former seemed to imply a use of physical force to compel nations to submit their differences to settlement, whereas the latter implied a moral obligation on the part of the signatories to abide by the terms of the treaty.[6] Nearly everyone believed that the "compulsory" formula could not be accepted by governments.

On the question of what type of dispute to include or omit, men could not agree. The bolder advocates favored accords to submit all issues of whatever nature to the Hague tribunal. The more cautious leaders recognized that questions of national honor and vital interests should be excluded largely because any treaties would have to be approved by the Senate. In the light of the Olney-Pauncefote experience, a realist would conclude that any new compacts should be drafted in accord with the wishes of the Senate.

The arbitrationists campaigned vigorously. They sought to awaken and to educate the American people and to obtain expressions of support from prominent citizens and leading journals. They then moved to direct these voices of public opinion toward responsible government leaders. Several events indicate not only the degree to which they succeeded but also how each achievement stimulated further interest in arbitration.

President Theodore Roosevelt, for instance, in 1902 turned a receptive ear to the voice of a visiting pacifist, the French senator Baron Paul H. D. d'Estournelles de Constant. The latter argued in a conversation with Roosevelt that the Hague court was dying of inertia. Not a single case had been

6. William Hayes Ward, "Address . . . ," *Mohonk Report, 1900*, pp. 45–48; E. M. Gallaudet, "Address . . . ," *ibid.*, pp. 54–56; Trueblood, "Address . . . ," *ibid.*, *1902*, pp. 12–14; "Obligatory Arbitration," *The Independent*, LV (May 7, 1903), 1108; "The Armed Allies of Arbitration," *The Outlook*, LXXIV (June 13, 1903), 395–396; "A Year of Arbitration," *The Independent*, LV (June 4, 1903), 1353.

carried to it and governments were beginning to question whether the court had any role to play in international life. Roosevelt took the hint. He asked Secretary of State Hay to find some issue which the United States could submit to the tribunal. Hay responded with the Pious Funds case, an ancient dispute with Mexico which both countries agreed to hand to the judges. This modest gesture thrust both Roosevelt and the United States into the world's limelight, with both receiving applause as the savior of the Hague structure. Roosevelt further endeared himself to pacifists and internationalists that year. He succeeded as an intermediary when Venezuela and her European creditors agreed to submit a controversy over debts to the Hague court.[7]

The growing interest in arbitration led, by 1904, to renewed demands for treaties which committed the United States to that goal. Public resolutions, demonstrations, articles, and speeches all sought action despite an absence of consensus upon the provisions. Petitions poured into Congress in such numbers that the Senate Foreign Relations Committee formed a subcommittee to consider them. In January of 1904, the movement culminated in a national conference on arbitration in Washington similar to that of 1896. Some two hundred prominent citizens attended, while many others endorsed the meeting and its goals as stated in a set of final resolutions. These favored a treaty with Britain in which "all differences" should be submitted to arbitration.[8]

A special delegation from the conference called upon President Roosevelt and Secretary Hay to submit the proposals, and its members received a warm welcome and promises of co-operation. When a similar group appeared at the door of the Senate Committee on Foreign Relations, however, its members sensed an ominous coolness in the cursory hearing granted. The Senate, as in 1897, still remained a stumbling block.[9] It felt pressures

7. Curti, *Peace or War*, pp. 190–191; Suttner, *Memoirs*, II, 390–391; William S. Penfield, "The First Session of the Hague Tribunal," *The Independent*, LIV (November 27, 1902), 2808–2811; Howard K. Beale, *Theodore Roosevelt and the Rise of America to World Power*, pp. 395–398.

8. John W. Foster, "The Year's Progress in Peace," *The Independent*, LV (July 2, 1903), 1553; "The Stated Congress," *Advocate of Peace*, LXVI (March 1904), 47; *The Second American Conference on International Arbitration*, (1904), p. 12. Resolutions and other expressions of popular support can be found on pages 97–131 and in "Brevities," *Advocate of Peace*, LXVI (January 1904), 10–11; "Resolutions of the Boston Chamber of Commerce," *ibid.*, (February 1904), p. 37; "Brevities," *ibid.*, (March 1904), p. 48.

9. John W. Foster, "The Status at Washington of International Arbitration," *The Independent*, LVI (May 26, 1904), 1186–1187; "The Senate and Arbitration," *ibid.*, (March 10, 1904), p. 572.

to act, however, from more than domestic agitators. Abroad, nations began to break barriers as twenty governments signed arbitral agreements between 1899 and 1903, and in 1904 some twenty-six treaties were concluded. As French Minister of Foreign Affairs Théophile Delcassé observed, a revolution had begun.[10]

Theodore Roosevelt saw these developments. In his annual message to Congress in December of 1903, he had expressed an interest in the pacific settlement of disputes, recommending recourse to arbitration and the Hague court. He noted, however, it was not yet possible to include questions of national honor and vital interest. Certainly he had no intention of drafting any all-inclusive treaties which the Senate would not approve. His administration waited, therefore, until it could negotiate an accord which the senators would receive with favor.[11] Hay finally completed the first of a series of agreements late in 1904 in which the provisions recognized the Senate's views as expressed in 1897.

The Foreign Relations Committee, however, did not adopt Hay's handiwork as presented nor did the Senate. One clause in the accords seemed particularly unacceptable. This called for a "special agreement" to be concluded between the signatories whenever they had resort to the treaty to determine issues, powers, and procedures. Many senators wished to change the words "special agreement" to "treaty," thus assuring their body the right to review every dispute before it could be submitted to arbitration.[12]

The President fully recognized the implications in this revision. As he wrote Senator Henry Cabot Lodge, who favored the amendment, it "cuts the heart out of the treaty." It made the transaction a "sham," Roosevelt declared, and he threatened to "abandon the whole business." On the day before the Senate vote, Roosevelt again unburdened himself as he sought to influence the outcome. The amended form, he insisted, actually amounted "to a specific pronouncement against the whole principle of a general arbitration treaty." It would block settlements similar to those the government

10. Denys P. Myers, comp., "Revised List of Arbitration Treaties," *World Peace Foundation Pamphlets*, II (July 1912), 18; Trueblood, "Another Year's Progress in Arbitration," *Mohonk Report, 1903*, p. 10. A full record of the trend in arbitration can be found in M. Stuyt, *Survey of International Arbitrations, 1794–1938*, pp. 241–298.

11. *Papers Relating to the Foreign Relations of the United States with the Annual Message of the President . . .* (1904), p. xix; John Hay to Benjamin Trueblood, March 1, 1904, Trueblood Papers.

12. *Congressional Record*, 58 Cong., 3d sess., 39, pt. 3:2477; Holt, *Treaties Defeated*, pp. 204–207.

had been concluding for years through executive action, would provide no benefits whatever, and might be insulting to the other signatories.[13]

The Senate, however, approved the amended version. Roosevelt castigated its action by noting that it had in a treaty merely agreed that at some future time it might possibly agree to another treaty, a right it already had. Hence, he withdrew Hay's work, thus closing the subject officially. But publicly, the matter did not end. With a feeling of shock and regret, the arbitrationists sought to analyze the outcome.[14] The treaties had conformed to the Senate's views as outlined in the debates in 1897. They were modest in scope and intent. Nearly everyone claimed to favor them, including those senators who had supported the amendment. Yet the result had been failure, in part because Roosevelt did not exert himself to the fullest and also because of a controversy between the President and the Senate involving the Dominican Republic. This concerned the question of an executive agreement, the issue which largely prompted the amendment to Hay's arbitration treaties.[15] The complex picture should have caused the advocates of a world organization to think seriously about their proposals. The Senate could be an obstacle of significant proportions. Interestingly, few of them seemed aware of this, or else they chose to ignore it; for at the same time the internationalists were busy on a proposition for a world congress which called upon their government to play a major role in its creation.

The agitation began in 1903, a date which may mark the beginning of the modern movement for an international organization. That year two men began identical quests. They did not know each other, but both began chain reactions which have never stopped. One of these men, Raymond L. Bridgman, had been active in the cause; the other, Hayne Davis, entered the ranks for the first time.

Bridgman was born in South Amherst, Massachusetts, in 1849, was

13. Holt, *Treaties Defeated*, pp. 207–208; Roosevelt to H. C. Lodge, January 6; to Shelby M. Cullom, February 10, 1905, Elting E. Morison, ed., *The Letters of Theodore Roosevelt*, IV, 1093–1095, 1118–1119.

14. Roosevelt to Silas McBee, *ibid.*, pp. 1121–1122; "The Senate and Arbitration," and "Is the Constitution Involved?," *The Outlook*, LXXIX (February 18, 1905), 405–406; "The Arbitration Treaties," *ibid.*, (March 11, 1905), pp. 622–625; "The Arbitration Treaties," *Advocate of Peace*, LXVII (February 1905), 25–26; "The Arbitration Treaties Dead," *ibid.*, (March 1905), pp. 50–52; [Gaillard Hunt], "The Real Facts about Arbitration," *The Nation*, LXXX (March 9, 1905), 184; Hayne Davis, "The Progress of Peace," *Harper's Weekly*, XLIX (March 25, 1905), 435, 440; George W. Taylor, "A Regularly Organized International Court Needed," *Mohonk Report, 1905*, p. 49; H. B. F. Macfarland, "The Arbitration Treaties . . . ," *ibid.*, p. 61.

15. Holt, *Treaties Defeated*, pp. 209–218.

graduated from Amherst College in 1871, and had attended Yale as a graduate student from 1874 to 1876. He then became a journalist, serving as a reporter on the Boston *Daily Advertiser* from 1876 to 1884. That year he became the Boston correspondent of the Springfield *Republican*, a job which required his presence at the state capital to report on the work of the legislature and the executive department. There Bridgman developed an interest in the political scene which he expressed in various books, including *Ten Years of Massachusetts* (1888) and *Biennial Elections* (1896). He also lent support to such societies as the Massachusetts Civil Service Reform Association and the American Anti-Imperialist League. He also broadened his journalistic endeavors by serving as an editor or owner-editor of a number of small newspapers, most of them in the Boston area.[16]

No evidence reveals when or how Bridgman became a convert to the cause of internationalism. His first article of importance on the subject appeared in 1899, and thereafter he wrote regularly for national journals, publishing a collection of essays in 1905 in a small volume entitled *World Organization*. Bridgman's real contribution, however, came in 1902 and 1903 when he began a movement for a congress of nations. It started with a petition to the Massachusetts assembly which he wrote and which Edwin D. Mead joined him in promoting. It requested the state legislature to ask Congress to call a conference to set "in motion . . . a world legislature." Apparently Bridgman did not know when he drafted his request that a similar measure had been approved by the same body in 1837. This time, however, the assembly merely referred the suggestion to the next session, which convened early in 1903.[17]

Meanwhile the American Peace Society, which then had its headquarters in Boston, became interested. Bridgman recognized the Hague Conference as an important development and believed that some action should be taken to strengthen the machinery created in 1899. But where most pacifists saw arbitration treaties as the means toward that end, Bridgman advocated further meetings which could bring progress in the form of concrete agreements. This idea appealed to Benjamin Trueblood who, as secretary of the peace society, redrafted Bridgman's petition, circulated it

---

16. B. N. and J. C. Bridgman, comps., *A Genealogy of the Bridgman Family*, p. 108; *Who's Who in America*, 1924.

17. Lucia Ames Mead, "The Next Step a World Congress," *The Union Signal*, XXX (August 11, 1904), 5; L. A. Mead, "What Are We to Do?," *Advocate of Peace*, LXV (August 1903), 143; "A Stated International Congress," *ibid.*, (March 1903), p. 37. The petitions appear in Raymond L. Bridgman, *World Organization*, pp. 159–163.

for signatures, and presented it to the legislature in 1903 with a supporting memorial signed by 750 citizens.[18]

At a hearing before the Federal Relations Committee of the Massachusetts Assembly, several prominent persons testified in support of the measure. It was reported to the floor, and on February 12 and 25 the House and Senate voted unanimously to send the following to Congress.

Resolved, That the Congress of the United States be requested to authorize the President of the United States to invite the governments of the world to join in establishing, in whatever way they may judge expedient, a regular international congress to meet at stated periods to deliberate upon the various questions of common interest to the nations and to make recommendations thereon to the governments.[19]

The American Peace Society and Bridgman, while agreeing upon the idea of a congress and the fact that it was an evolving reality, did not see eye to eye on what such a body should do or what its powers should be. The former saw it as an essential corollary to the growing interdependence of the world and perceived it not so much as a policy-making agency but as a periodic assembly where representatives of nations, meeting every five to seven years, could more or less catch up with developments.[20]

Bridgman possessed more imagination. He envisaged a congress as the beginning of a functioning organization which would eventually have clearly defined departments of a legislature, a court, and an executive. The congress should come first, said Bridgman, since the need here was greatest. It should be modeled after the United States, "which foreshadows the form of world government which will exist when all mankind are brought into organic political connection." States would delegate power, enjoy equality regardless of size or strength, send their best citizens to represent them, and approve any statutes which the assembly passed. Bridgman failed to elaborate on this point, but he apparently agreed that unanimous ratification would be necessary for the law to be in effect. To Bridgman, his proposals were no "new departure." International conferences had already acted in a legislative capacity by creating various bodies like the Postal Union and the Hague court. The process should now be carried further by a call from the United States in which nations were requested to accept this idea and relinquish

18. Bridgman, *World Organization*, pp. 160–163.
19. *Ibid.*, p. 163.
20. "A Stated International Congress," *Advocate of Peace*, LXV (February 1903),
21.

a degree of sovereignty to the legislature in specified areas of trade, coinage, sanitary matters, patents and copyrights, exploration, "and regulation of world monopolies."[21]

Once governments agreed to a congress, they should consider the creation of a genuine court, said Bridgman. The arbitral body created at The Hague in 1899 was generally unrelated to international law and should be transformed into a "supreme court of the world." A judicial system should be evolved with lesser agencies for minor questions to promote "justice on a higher plan than would be covered by the law of any single nation." The benefits, according to Bridgman, would be limitless. Men would see the elimination of evils, of force, of brutality, and of international anarchy. As in his plan for a legislature, Bridgman suggested that this structure should not be created suddenly but that it should evolve "one stage at a time."[22]

Bridgman also called for an executive. The congress and court already existed in rudimentary form, and he discovered that to a lesser degree the third department had also begun. He found the germ of it in the bureaus functioning under multilateral conventions. These agencies, similar to those for the Postal Union, could be considered as executive bodies. There would be evolution here, too, declared Bridgman, to "some higher official to coördinate the work of these separate offices and to subordinate all disjointed work to the orderly good of the whole." Eventually some "commissioner in chief" would emerge as a president. He would, however, never be a ruler. He would be a responsible servant to supervise and "to execute the will of the world for the harmonious administration of the different departments."[23]

In elaborating upon his ideas, Bridgman provided few specific details, but he did reveal the attitudes and arguments common to the internationalists of his generation. He displayed an unalterable conviction that the political organization of the world was inevitable, that processess already at work would lead inexorably toward unity, and that this evolutionary trend could not be reversed. He also relied, in building his case, upon the United States as the perfect illustration of the type of structure needed, and he continually referred to its evolution toward a more centralized government.[24]

Bridgman viewed the concept of absolute sovereignty of individual states as a formidable obstacle, and he attacked it as unrealistic. Mankind should realize that a community of men and nations existed, that the

21. Bridgman, *World Organization*, pp. 34–54.
22. *Ibid.*, pp. 55–62.
23. *Ibid.*, pp. 63–70.
24. *Ibid.*, pp. 14, 145, 157–158, 15–19, 110–112, 134–142.

"sovereignty of mankind" was real, and that a country's authority was not absolute. He presented no suggestions regarding a division of powers between nations and his world body, but he indicated that the internal matters of states would not be affected save in one possible area. Bridgman would allow some action by his international organization where individual and human rights had to be guaranteed. Some balance could be found, however, between the two groups.[25]

The proposal for a periodic congress awakened considerable interest, and one writer soon described it as "the demand of the hour." This remark, while exaggerated, reflected a widespread response to Bridgman's proposition. A number of influential newspapers and national magazines expressed their approval, including the Boston *Transcript, Christian Intelligencer, Congregationalist, Leslie's Weekly,* and *The Independent.*[26]

Such publicity combined with a propaganda campaign by the American Peace Society brought additional endorsements from civic groups, religious bodies, and public citizens. The mayor and city council of La Crosse, Wisconsin, submitted an unsolicited resolution of approval; a national woman suffrage convention voted favorably on the proposal; a commission on International and Industrial Peace of the Methodist General Conference recorded its endorsement; the governors of Massachusetts and Pennsylvania, John L. Bates and Samuel W. Pennypacker, wrote letters of support; and a document from the Peace Association of Friends in Philadelphia bore the signatures of many prominent men including seven judges of the Pennsylvania Supreme Court.[27]

In the spring of 1904, the Lake Mohonk Conference departed from its prescribed program of arbitration to include in its platform a statement of approval. The two ideas had become intimately related. At the same meeting, a special committee of businessmen likewise supported the call for an international congress. The capstone of this wave of endorsements, however, came with a petition campaign waged by the *Christian Endeavor*

25. *Ibid.*, pp. 7–13, 88–91, 119–120.

26. "A World-Parliament," *The Peacemaker,* XXII (April 1903), 77; "Favorable Reception of the Proposition for a Regular International Congress," *Advocate of Peace,* LXV (March 1903), 38; "Full of Promise," *ibid.,* (April 1903), p. 66; "International Congress," *ibid.,* (June 1903), pp. 100–101; "Seventy-Sixth Annual Report . . . ," *ibid.,* (June 1904), p. 108; "A World's Congress," *The Independent,* LXVI (July 14, 1904), 111–112.

27. "The Stated International Advisory Congress," *Advocate of Peace,* LXV (December 1903), 214; "National Woman Suffrage Convention," *The Peacemaker,* XXIII (March 1904), 72; "Methodist Conference," *Advocate of Peace,* LXVI (June 1904), 100–101; "The Stated International Congress," *ibid.,* (May 1904), pp. 91–93; *Mohonk Report, 1903,* p. 138.

World. That journal entreated its youthful readers to sign memorials in their Christian Endeavor societies and send these to Senator Lodge in the Senate and Samuel W. McCall in the House. A total of 1,642 such documents, supposedly representing the views of 100,000 persons, reached the desks of these men.[28]

The proposal even awakened some interest in Europe, where Trueblood presented the idea at the International Law Association in Antwerp and at the Interparliamentary Union meeting in Vienna in 1903. Noting that some thirty-three world conferences had been held in the nineteenth century, only six of which met before 1865, he argued that nations should see what was evident and act in a definite, orderly manner by holding stated congresses. Trueblood also noted an interesting anomaly which most observers had missed. Peace workers who had supported the "American plan" of Ladd and Burritt had turned things around. The latter had called for a legislature which would then establish a court. The world now had a tribunal but no assembly. Logic demanded a body to formulate the laws which the judges would apply.[29]

The agitation for a periodic congress resulted in 1904 in a concerted effort to have President Roosevelt call for a Second Hague Conference. This campaign gathered momentum as Bridgman's proposal gained popular support, but the real agitation to have Roosevelt act came from another direction and another group. This movement originated in 1903 when one of the most important internationalists the United States has produced entered the picture. This was Hayne Davis, an attorney of New York City, who had had no contact with Bridgman or established pacifist groups.

Davis was born near Statesville, North Carolina, in 1868, had attended the University of North Carolina, been graduated from its law school, and for a short time had practiced law in Knoxville, Tennessee. As in Bridgman's case, no evidence exists to indicate how Davis became an internationalist, but his ideas developed during or after a European trip early in 1901.[30]

He first presented his views in an article in *The Independent* early in

28. *Mohonk Report, 1904*, pp. 110, 115; "World's Congress Memorials," *Advocate of Peace*, LXVII (March 1905), 53. A table indicated national distribution of the petitions: Massachusetts, 130; Illinois, 104; Ohio, 127; Iowa, 62; Kansas, 57; Minnesota, 46; Alabama, 12; Florida, 8; Mississippi, 1.

29. Trueblood, "A Regular International Advisory Congress," *Advocate of Peace*, LXV (November 1903), 194–197. At least two Europeans, Arturo de Marcoartu and Alfred H. Fried, urged the idea's acceptance. "For An International Assembly," *The Peacemaker*, XXII (October 1903), 222; "The Stated International Congress," *Advocate of Peace*, LXV (April 1903), 57.

30. Davis, Travel Notes, 1900–1901; Davis to Frank P. Graham, May 2, 1939 (copy), Davis Papers, Southern Historical Collection, Chapel Hill, N.C.

1903. Inspired by the creation of the Hague tribunal, Davis noted the vast area yet to be included within its jurisdiction. Many questions lay outside the ambiguous field of arbitration; international law needed development so that nations could have recourse to judicial proceedings rather than to war. Davis compared the situation to England where even though courts had been established in the twelfth century men had reserved the right to trial by battle. Not until 1867 did Parliament abolish that privilege. Nations now had a court but still claimed the right to fight rather than submit their differences to legal settlement. To Davis, as to Bridgman and other internationalists, a league was already in the process of formation. The Hague tribunal, declared Davis in what may have been the first use of the term, had given mankind "the United Nations." Men did not realize it, but they were already citizens of this new body. "And," said Davis, "there is no fact more prophetic than the birth of this union of the twentieth century."[31]

In his first article, Davis did little more than present these conclusions —that a need existed for an international organization already in the process of development. His only constructive suggestion appeared in a call for the signing of arbitral treaties. He devoted much time to study, however, for in a subsequent article in July of 1903 he presented several concrete proposals. He admitted that arbitration alone would not end wars. Only by a more perfect union, in which executive and legislative departments would be added to the infant judicial branch, could nations achieve a warless world. The Hague court was still pitifully weak, with each state retaining full sovereignty and with no power to enforce its decrees. It was, Davis noted, in much the same stage as the United States had been under the Articles of Confederation. Under the latter, however, the congress had been empowered to legislate on some matters, and Davis speculated upon the type of assembly an international organization would need.

He concluded that a structure similar to that of the United States would be ideal. This would include a two-house assembly with representation and voting in the Senate by nations and in the House by population. It would be limited in its authority by the same restrictions upon the federal government that the Constitution of the United States enumerated. In fact, said Davis, "the grant of positive power to the larger organism should be an exact counterpart of the grant of power from the States to the United States."[32]

31. Davis, "The Perpetuation of the Union of Nations," *The Independent*, LV (February 12, 1903), 384–386.
32. Davis, "The Final Outcome of the Declaration of Independence," *ibid.*, (July 2, 1903), pp. 1543–1547.

In the ensuing year, Davis wrote more articles, but he did little more than elaborate upon the points he had already made. In one account, he revealed an uncompromising internationalist spirit. He attacked proposals for a European federation or for an English-speaking arrangement as "too narrow for the times." Conditions demanded a "Universal Union." The belief "that several international unions ought to be formed" had to be destroyed. Such a complex system, Davis warned, might stimulate rather than diminish war.[33]

By the summer of 1904, Davis began to reflect the current agitation for a periodic congress which Bridgman had set in motion. This idea fit perfectly with his own views; hence, he quickly adopted it. In a lengthy article, he reviewed his basic ideas and elaborated further upon his contention that the foundations had been laid, that a world organization could develop as the United States had, and that the United States should serve as a model. Davis then explored in detail the nature and powers of his proposed congress. It should, he suggested, be authorized to regulate coinage, weights, commerce, and navigation. It could legislate concerning the laws of war, including the limitation of armaments, although on the latter point Davis seemed somewhat confused since he also noted that each country would be free to determine its own military needs. Likewise, his provision for the control of commerce seemed to conflict with his insistence that tariff policy remain in the domain of individual states. Davis seemed somewhat vague on whether the union would support its members if attacked, but he implied such an obligation when he warned that the United Nations should not protect governments against internal revolutions.

Among various suggestions, Davis included some of special interest. He proposed that all laws of the congress take effect when ratified by four fifths of the countries representing four fifths of the earth's population. They would automatically be valid after a specified period of time if not vetoed by one fifth of the nations with one fifth of the people of the world. Davis also suggested a unique system of representation where delegates in his House would vote in proportion to population. Each state could cast one ballot regardless of its size; then representation would increase on an ascending scale depending upon numbers of citizens and volume of international trade. Davis provided for regular meetings, although his legislature could convene when needed, and he believed that governments should have the right to withdraw on a three- to five-year notice.[34]

33. Davis, "The Development of the Union," *ibid.*, LVI (May 12, 1904), 1074–1076.

34. Davis, "A World's Congress," *ibid.*, LVII (July 7, 1904), 11–19.

Davis had hoped that his writings would win converts, and he succeeded. Among his followers he soon listed the managing editor of *The Independent*, Hamilton Holt. *The Independent* had shown an interest in world organization for several years, but its comments before to 1903 were probably the work of its editor, William Hayes Ward, and its contributing editor E. P. Powell. Holt, however, soon replaced these men as chief advocate of a league. He became convinced that Davis was right, and from 1903 until his death in 1951 Holt fought unceasingly to create an international system with the United States as a participant. He wrote hundreds of editorials and articles on the subject, delivered thousands of lectures, organized several societies in search of that goal, and eventually merited claim to the title of "America's foremost internationalist."[35]

Editorials in *The Independent* began to reflect Davis's ideas soon after his first contribution to that magazine. Its views, however, soon moved ahead of his. When Davis elaborated upon the powers of his legislature in July of 1904, an editorial noted that Davis had slighted one important topic. A court and congress needed a third branch of government, an executive, if it were to be effective. It admitted that men might not yet be ready for such a far-reaching step, however, and it conceded that for the present the attainment of an assembly would be a significant achievement. A legislature could advise, recommend, appeal "to the reason and conscience of civilized men" and enlist public opinion in support of its actions. It could also delay war by acting as a forum in which words could replace bullets. The editors also solicited the opinion of John Bassett Moore, a noted international lawyer and former counselor of the Department of State, and reproduced Moore's remarks in which he, too, noted that the lack of an executive seemed to be a weakness in much of the planning for a world organization.[36]

The writings and work of Hayne Davis produced another internationalist in addition to Hamilton Holt. This was Representative Richard Bartholdt, a German-American who had come to the United States in 1872 at

35. Holt to Mrs. Charles W. Woodson, March 23, 1942, Holt Papers, Rollins College, Winter Park, Florida; Warren F. Kuehl, "A Bibliography of the Writings of Hamilton Holt," Rollins College *Bulletin*, LIV (September 1959), 1–29; Kuehl, *Hamilton Holt, Journalist, Internationalist, Educator*, pp. 66–69.

36. "The United Nations," *The Independent*, LV (July 16, 1903), 1702; "The Coming Together of Nations," *ibid.*, (July 30, 1903), pp. 1827–1828; "A World Legislature," *ibid.*, LVII (July 7, 1904), 46–47; "A World's Congress," pp. 111–112. It has been possible to identify many unsigned editorials in *The Independent* by referring to office volumes of the magazine in which writings were often initialed. These sets are part of the Holt Papers.

the age of seventeen, entered the journalistic profession, moved west, and became editor of the St. Louis *Tribune*. He first went to Congress in 1893, and thereafter the voters of his St. Louis district returned him to office until he withdrew his candidacy in 1914.

Bartholdt, with his European background, had always revealed an interest in international affairs, and he had supported the Interparliamentary Union since his first contact with that group at its meeting in Christiania, Norway, in 1899. There he became convinced that the participants "were neither dreamers nor cranks, but practical statesmen" in their quest for "the creation and perfection of legal means for the arbitration of disputes which fail of diplomatic settlement."[37]

Bartholdt had sought for some years to elicit interest in the Interparliamentary Union among his fellow congressmen, but not until 1903 did he succeed at least partially in his quest. That year at the meeting of the Union in Vienna, Bartholdt boldly invited the group to convene in the United States in 1904 at the St. Louis Exposition. The delegates responded eagerly, thus placing Bartholdt in an embarrassing position. He had not consulted with either the President or the State Department; he had acted without authorization, yet he had committed his government to the role of host.[38]

About this time, Bartholdt met Hayne Davis for the first time in 1904 at the Lake Mohonk Conference. They immediately united upon a quest that was to be largely responsible for the call for the Second Hague Conference. The first step in that direction had come with the formal organization in Congress of a group of men interested in the Interparliamentary Union. Led by Bartholdt, approximately forty congressmen had assembled early in 1904, elected officers, and invited all present to become members of the Union. Apparently every man did, and within a short time an additional hundred expressed interest in joining.[39] Until that time, only two persons, Bartholdt and Barrows, had been active in the Interparliamentary Union.

The new group in Congress organized a committee of five to prepare a resolution formally inviting the delegates to the United States in 1904 and requesting a special appropriation to defray expenses. Congress responded with a fifty-thousand-dollar allocation. The American group also considered a program of action on the assumption that other countries looked to the

37. Bartholdt, *From Steerage to Congress: Reminiscences and Reflections*, p. 174.
38. Bartholdt, "The Interparliamentary Union . . . ," *Mohonk Report, 1904*, p. 121.
39. Hayne Davis, ed., *Among the World's Peacemakers*, p. 22; Bartholdt, *Steerage to Congress*, pp. 215–216; "An Arbitration Group in Congress," *Advocate of Peace*, LXVI (February 1904), 27–28; Bartholdt, "Interparliamentary Union," p. 120.

United States for leadership. Its members concluded that an official call for a world assembly would be the logical step, and they prepared a resolution requesting the President

to invite the governments of the civilized nations to send representatives to an international conference, to be held at a time and place to be agreed upon by the several governments, and whose purpose it shall be to devise plans looking to the negotiation of arbitration treaties between the United States and the different nations, and also to discuss the advisability of, and, if possible, agree upon, a gradual reduction of armaments.[40]

This proposal, while short of the aspirations of men like Bridgman, Davis, and Holt, at least pointed in the direction they had indicated. The resolution could not have been too drastic or it would have frightened Congress as well as the Interparliamentary Union, which had been conservative in concentrating on arbitration. It was a beginning, however, a fact which the internationalists recognized; hence, they rallied behind it while at the same time looking to the future. As Davis noted in pledging his support to arbitration, governments would have to "go further than that and agree with us to organize a United States of the world." Holt suggested much the same in an editorial preface to Davis's 1904 article on a congress, which appeared while the Interparliamentary Union was in session in St. Louis. Why, he asked, "should not President Roosevelt call a conference of the nations to create an international legislature whose establishment would mark greater progress than the Hague Court?"[41]

Holt was not the only person who saw Roosevelt as the knight to lead them in their quest. At St. Louis, Bartholdt had a similar vision. While reading Frederick Holls's account of the First Hague Conference, he noted the suggestion that future sessions should be held. Hence, Bartholdt drafted a set of resolutions to present to the lawmakers from fifteen nations who came to St. Louis. These urged Roosevelt to call for a second meeting at The Hague and further recommended the assembly of periodic congresses thereafter. Despite some objections to the last idea from some men who saw the proposal as too advanced, the resolution gained approval as presented on September 13.[42]

40. Bartholdt, "Interparliamentary Union," p. 122.

41. Davis, "Remarks . . . ," *Mohonk Report, 1904*, p. 28; Davis, "A World's Congress," p. 11.

42. Bartholdt, "The Calling of the Second Conference of the Hague," *The Independent*, LXIII (July 11, 1907), 66–67; Davis, "The Historic Resolution of St. Louis," *ibid.*, LVII (October 6, 1904), 764–772.

Thus, on September 24, 1904, a delegation from the Interparliamentary Union stopped in Washington at the end of a tour of the United States and called on the President. Albert Gobat, the secretary of the Union, acted as spokesman and argued that arbitration would be greatly advanced by another international assembly. He also observed that "in order to accomplish its duty, this institution must also be made the foundation of a political organization of the world."[43] Roosevelt proved to be somewhat noncommittal in his response. He cautioned the delegates not to expect too much, but he admitted that "very substantial progress" could result from such a meeting if it aided in developing the international responsibilities of states. Hence, Roosevelt promised to do what he could to convene a new conference.[44]

The internationalists hailed these developments. Bartholdt wrote a number of articles and delivered addresses praising the St. Louis meeting, its resolutions, and its promise of the future. He grew so confident in looking ahead that he could see the existing court joined by "an international congress to be followed by an international police, and an agreement between the nations of the world to bow to the supremacy of these institutions." Davis, who had closely allied himself with Bartholdt, likewise publicized the movement. He had served as the press representative of the Interparliamentary Union at St. Louis, and in this job he excelled. His major theme followed the thesis that he had outlined earlier—that the United States was merely fulfilling its destiny to lead and that it was the perfect example of how a broader organization should evolve and function.[45]

The *Advocate of Peace* also viewed the developments with hope. It saw a Second Hague Conference as opening the way to regularly scheduled meetings and believed that that program would become the "one big question" at any assembly. In fact, the entire pacifist contingent soon rallied behind the Interparliamentary Union effort. At the Boston Peace Congress in October 1904, a resolution endorsed the actions taken thus far, com-

43. "To Call Another Peace Conference," *ibid.*, (September 29, 1904), pp. 700–701.

44. *Ibid.*, p. 701.

45. Bartholdt, "The World's Peace Conference," *Harper's Weekly*, XLVIII (October 22, 1904), 1611; Bartholdt, "The Interparliamentary Union and the Cause of International Arbitration," *Advocate of Peace*, LXVII (March 1905), 56–59; Davis, "Historic Resolution," pp. 764–772; Davis, "A Parliament of Nations," *The Outlook*, LXXIX (January 7, 1905), 21–29; Davis, "The President and the Interparliamentary Union," *Harper's Weekly*, XLVIII (October 22, 1904), 1611–1612. Davis, *World's Peacemakers*, pp. 1–86, contains valuable information on the St. Louis meeting and the work of the Interparliamentary Union.

mended Roosevelt for his foresight, and constructively suggested that periodic congresses be the eventual goal. Since this was one of the regular gatherings of international peace workers, it revealed that the idea had come to be universally hailed in such circles.[46]

Hamilton Holt's *Independent* likewise presented an optimistic picture in editorials describing the recent events as part of the inevitable process toward "the creation of a Congress of Nations." Men had responded "to the call of the twentieth century for organized peace and a Parliament of the World." It noted with pleasure that this development had "taken form in the United States" and that henceforth American leadership was assured.[47]

The Independent's observations were essentially correct. A group of highly dedicated converts had appeared who would remain exceptionally active in ensuing years. In Europe, at peace congresses and conferences of lawyers and businessmen, interest and efforts did not compare with those in the United States, and most of the comments by Europeans reflected the American ideal of a periodic congress.[48] From 1905 to 1920, therefore, American citizens assumed the leadership in efforts to organize the world.

46. "The Interparliamentary Conference at St. Louis," *Advocate of Peace*, LXVI (October 1904), 182; "The New Intergovernmental Conference at The Hague," *ibid.*, (December 1904), pp. 227–228; "The Boston Peace Congress," *The Independent*, LVII (October 13, 1904), 876–877.

47. "The Inter-Parliamentary Peace Congress," *The Independent*, LVII (September 15, 1904), 631; "A World's Political Union," *ibid.*, (September 22, 1904), pp. 684–685; "Imperialism and Union of Nations," *ibid.*, (October 6, 1904), pp. 815–816; "Another Hague Conference," *ibid.*, (December 29, 1904), pp. 1516–1517.

48. A few European advocates can be found, but at the turn of the century there seemed to be little real acceptance of either a United States of Europe or a broader type of organization. Lyons, *Internationalism in Europe*, pp. 364–365. The delegates at the Tenth, Eleventh, and Twelfth Universal Peace Congresses in 1901, 1902, and 1903 failed to include resolutions on the subject. The Thirteenth, meeting at Boston in 1904, endorsed the idea, but in 1905 the resolution simply expressed the vague hope that the Hague Conference of 1907 would "adopt measures for the establishment of such federation." *Bulletin Officiel du XIVe Congrès Universel de la paix*, p. 118.

The Road
to the Second
Hague Conference

By 1905, the preliminary steps had been taken toward convening the nations of the world into what subsequently became the Second Hague Conference. Over the signature of Secretary of State John Hay, the United States had issued a circular letter dated October 21, 1904, to the powers present at the first meeting. Hay had acknowledged the role of the Inter-parliamentary Union in reviving the idea, reminded the recipients of the "great work" that had been done, and noted a real need "to complete the postponed work of the first conference." Two months later, Hay again wrote to the various governments. He informed them that in their replies to his first note his suggestions had "been received with general favor." Conditions in the Far East, however, where Russia and Japan were at war, precluded any immediate assembly. The matter, he insisted, should not be forgotten but revived at the earliest possible time. Hay also observed that although the United States had taken the initiative thus far, his government did not wish the responsibility of preparing the program for the new assembly. This could best be done by a formal interchange of ideas through regular diplomatic channels.[1]

That suggestion proved to be a challenge to all persons interested in the proposed meeting, especially the internationalists. With the agenda open, they might do two things. They could determine events if they could in-

1. Scott, *Hague Peace Conferences,* II, 168–174.

fluence the men who would make the decisions, and they would have time to stimulate a public interest on those subjects they wished discussed. Hence, from early in 1905 to June of 1907, they were exceptionally active. However, a great diversity existed in the programs they sought to advance, for by 1905 the internationalists could agree on only one point—the world needed some type of organization. On the subject of the type of league, its scope, its powers, its structure, its location, and even its participants, there was little accord. Arbitrationists, international lawyers, advocates of a periodic congress, federationists, world government advocates, sanctionists, and a variety of plans lying somewhere between these views all sought the same aim by way of different programs. The very diversity of opinions, however, indicates how far and how fully thinking on the subject had progressed.

The largest group interested in the Second Hague Conference was that of the arbitrationists. This was true because nearly everyone could agree to advance this principle. But here, too, views differed. Some men believed that any development should come gradually. They saw the signing of treaties calling for obligatory arbitration as an important step, and they also favored agreements in which governments exempted certain matters. Most of these men displayed little interest in a world organization beyond an occasional congress to gain these ends. The administration of Theodore Roosevelt generally favored such an approach but even so the arbitrationists knew they would have to move cautiously. The Senate would have to approve any agreements, and any radical programs would be doomed to failure.[2]

However, a minority segment of the arbitrationists had learned but little from the Senate's action on the Hay-Roosevelt treaties. Thus, they campaigned for compacts to settle *all* disputes through arbitration or greatly to extend the jurisdiction of the court and hoped that at the ensuing conference nations would adopt such a system.[3]

2. Trueblood, "The Hague Conferences and the Future of Arbitration," *Atlantic Monthly*, XCVII (June 1906), 724–725; "Christian Herald's Great Symposium," *Advocate of Peace*, LXVII (February 1905), 32–33; A. B. Farquhar, "A Business Man's View . . . ," *ibid.*, (April 1905), pp. 87–88; George Gray, "Opening Address . . . ," *Mohonk Report, 1905*, pp. 11–13; "The Next Step for Peace," *The Outlook*, LXXXVI (May 25, 1907), 145.

3. "National Honor!," *The Independent*, LVIII (February 23, 1905), 443–444; "A Victory for Arbitration," *ibid.*, LIX (September 28, 1905), 760; "A Programme for the Hague," *The Outlook*, LXXXI (October 7, 1905), 297–298; Merle Curti, "Bryan and World Peace," *Smith College Studies in History*, XVI (April–July 1931), 143.

International lawyers also showed great interest in the approaching assembly. In terms of number, prestige, and influence, they were in a position to determine government policy to a considerable degree. They primarily favored general arbitration treaties with certain exemptions, but they saw other possible results from a meeting. First, they hoped to revise the structure of the Hague tribunal and establish a genuine court of justice. They found too many weaknesses in the system that originated in 1899. It was not a judicial body, it was not truly permanent, decisions did not have to be based upon a code, it had no authority to determine its own jurisdiction in cases, and it lacked power to enforce its decrees. A new conference might be able to correct some of these shortcomings and create a court of law rather than of arbitration.[4]

The legalists had a second goal. If they could create a real tribunal, it would need statutes upon which to base its decisions. Thus another world assembly might be of value. As Judge Simeon E. Baldwin of the Connecticut supreme court noted, either public or private law had been enhanced by every conference since that of Vienna. Such thinkers sided with those internationalists who favored periodic congresses, since such meetings could advance the structure of international law indirectly and possibly directly if the organization evolved into a legislative body.[5]

The desire to develop a code had been present throughout the nineteenth century, but since the older law societies had not been aggressive in their efforts, new leaders appeared. The members of the Interparliamentary Union often explored the subject and grew in their thinking. Frederick Holls promoted the cause, and Holls and Andrew D. White apparently persuaded Andrew Carnegie to give $250,000 in 1902 to establish "a Library of Inter-

4. Margrave, "The Policy of . . . Adjudication," pp. 271–283; Robinson, *Arbitration,* pp. 98–102; "Justice through Peace," *The Outlook,* LXXXV (April 27, 1907), 919–920; Edwin Maxey, "The Latest Decision at The Hague," *The Arena,* XXXI (June 1904), 584–587; W. L. Scruggs, "Is International Arbitration Practicable?," *World To-Day,* XIII (August 1907), 775–776; "The World's Supreme Court," *The Independent,* LIV (September 11, 1902), 2209; John B. Henderson, "The Hague Tribunal Does Not Go Far Enough," *Mohonk Report, 1904,* pp. 76–78; Charles H. Butler, "How the Hague Court Might Be Made More Effective," *ibid.,* p. 133; N. M. Butler, "Opening Address . . . ," *ibid., 1907,* pp. 16–17; Roderick H. Smith, *Proposed Platform for the American Party,* p. 9.

5. Simeon E. Baldwin, "Equality between Nations and International Conventions as Determining Factors in Shaping Modern International Law," *Advocate of Peace,* LXIX (November 1907), 238; Scott, "The Work of the Second Hague Peace Conference," p. 5; William J. Coombs, "Necessity of the Codification of International Law," *Mohonk Report, 1904,* pp. 149–150.

national Law and Diplomacy for the Permanent Court of Arbitration at the Hague." Finally, at the Lake Mohonk Conferences, a group of legalists formed a study committee in 1905 out of which the American Society of International Law appeared in 1906. Its journal, beginning that year, became an influential organ in advancing the organization's program of peace through law.[6]

Such men placed their faith in the machinery of government and in an ideal of universal justice. They saw nations subscribing to reasonable standards of action and behavior. The legalists had been encouraged by an evolutionary trend which seemed to make their dream inevitable. Developments in arbitration would lead to an organized world based upon law and justice, and any effort which promoted that ideal should be encouraged.[7]

A third group interested in the Hague meeting was that which advocated the assembly of periodic congresses. Both arbitrationists and international lawyers sought such an end, but a large number of men hoped for more than gains in arbitration and law. Such gatherings, they believed, could develop attitudes of peace, promote world co-operation, and advance the goal of federation. Most of these men favored the creation of an advisory congress having no special powers.

The American Peace Society led in endorsing and promoting this program. It found in Hay's note a suggestion that arrangements for the Second Hague Conference be handled through the Bureau of the Administrative Council of the Hague court, and it acclaimed this obscure agency as "the nucleus of a world organization." Its directors formally expressed their pleasure at Hay's letter as "this next great step" and noted in 1906 that the Society should "congratulate itself over the flattering prospect that this long-dreamed-of international assembly, an indispensable condition of the settled and guaranteed peace of the world, is nearing its practical realization."[8] Benjamin Trueblood, both in editorials and in signed articles in the *Advocate of Peace*, sought to convert others. He logically noted the possible gains

6. Carnegie to Holls, August 7, 1902, Holls Papers; "History of the Organization of the American Society of International Law," *Proceedings,* American Society of International Law, 1907, p. 23.

7. Robert Treat Paine, "The Love of Justice as the Motive for Arbitration," *Mohonk Report, 1903,* pp. 122–124; Simeon E. Baldwin, "Reverence for Law," *ibid., 1904,* pp. 71–73; Bartlett Tripp, "Address . . . ," *ibid., 1907,* pp. 47–48.

8. "Mr. Hay's Second Note . . . ," *Advocate of Peace,* LXVII (January 1905), 2; "The Annual Meeting . . . ," *ibid.,* (June 1905), p. 117; "Seventy-Eighth Annual Report . . . ," *ibid.,* LXVIII (June 1906), 134.

from a congress that would meet periodically and conduct its work systematically and continuously rather than have nations rely upon temporary and uncertain gatherings. By 1906, he proclaimed it as "the leading purpose of all the friends of world peace." Furthermore, no one could seriously object to the proposal since it would intrude upon no country or its authority and yet it might do inestimable good. Trueblood insisted early in 1907 that he had not found a serious objection from anyone to the proposition.[9]

At the Lake Mohonk Conference, discussions also turned to the subject of a periodic assembly. There expressions of support became commonplace after 1904. Even Albert K. Smiley departed from the prescribed agenda of arbitration. He passionately declared in 1905 that, although he was in his mid-seventies, he hoped "to live to see a congress of nations, with limited powers, that is, advisory powers at first, establishing international justice, determining the rules by which nations in their intercourse with one another shall be regulated."[10]

The platform of the Mohonk Conference beginning in 1904 carried an endorsement of the idea of an "International Advisory Congress," but apparently some speakers wished a more positive expression of support. Raymond Bridgman, in 1905, introduced a resolution calling for such a statement, but the delegates merely reaffirmed their declaration of the previous year. Another development occurred when Edwin D. Mead proposed a change of name. The words "international organization" should replace those of "international arbitration" in the statement of aims. The delegates took no action on this since most of them still thought it best to concentrate on the older program. The situation, however, soon changed.[11]

At the meeting in 1906, the delegates could no longer resist the current. The idea seemed to be in the clear air of the "lake in the sky." Lyman Abbott, the editor of *The Outlook*, grasped the spirit more clearly than others, and in a dramatic speech he described his "Vision of Peace." Basing his argument upon the evolutionary concept of government, he noted that

9. "How Far Will Arbitration Go?" *ibid.*, (March 1906), p. 51; Trueblood, "Another Year of Arbitration," *Mohonk Report, 1906*, p. 21; Trueblood, "A Periodic Congress of the Nations," *Advocate of Peace*, LXIX (March 1907), 64–66. The American Peace Society also distributed the more popular books and pamphlets on international organization, including Bridgman's *World Organization*, Trueblood's *Federation of the World*, and Lucia Ames Mead's *Patriotism and the New Internationalism*.

10. Smiley, "Remarks," *Mohonk Report, 1905*, p. 169.

11. *Mohonk Report, 1904*, p. 110; *ibid., 1905*, p. 8; Mead, "Remarks," *ibid., 1905*, pp. 138–139.

it was time to strengthen the court created in 1899 and to establish a permanent international body. The Interparliamentary Union, he suggested, should become the official congress of the world "with advisory powers at first, but legislative powers eventually." Beyond that, Abbott could even see some form of executive, but he did not pursue that point. It would come, he predicted, as soon as a legislature could be established. Progress had been so rapid toward this goal that it amazed those who looked back a mere ten years at what men had dreamed then and what had been accomplished.[12]

Abbott's moving oration set the stage for action. Several speakers referred to it, the businessmen's committee endorsed the proposal for a periodic assembly in a separate resolution, and the platform supported the plan to make the Hague Conference "a permanent and recognized advisory Congress of the Nations." This proposition even preceded the one approving a general arbitration treaty.[13]

In the meantime, another current was carrying forward the idea of periodic meetings. This one had been set in motion by Richard Bartholdt, aided by Hayne Davis. Bartholdt had devoted considerable thought to the subject of an international organization since the Interparliamentary Union sessions in St. Louis in 1904. As the leader of the American group in Congress, he directed its discussions at a meeting in Washington early in March of 1905. There the congressmen considered a program for the thirteenth annual session of the Union to be held in Brussels on August 28–31, 1905. The American group agreed to submit three propositions: one, that the Latin American states be invited to participate in the Union; two, that a model arbitration treaty be drafted which would extend the jurisdiction of the Hague tribunal; three, that a periodic congress be established to assemble at stated times, discuss issues, and report to governments.[14]

The last proposal reflected the growing discussions in support of a congress, which had reached groundswell proportions in the United States. Bartholdt, however, realized that the delegates at Brussels would not approve any general resolution without first inquiring into many details on how such a body would operate. Hence, Bartholdt submitted to *The Independent* a draft of twelve proposals on which a league might be based. The magazine published these with an editorial endorsement on May 4 and the

12. Abbott, "A Vision of Peace," *ibid., 1906,* pp. 30–33.
13. *Ibid.,* pp. 37, 100, 112, 120–121, 91, 7–8, 139.
14. "Arbitration Group in Congress," *Advocate of Peace,* LXVII (April 1905), 76–77.

next week printed an article by Bartholdt in which he elaborated upon the points in his plan.[15]

Bartholdt's first three items discussed the structure of a congress. He called for a two-house legislature with a senate in which states would have an equal voice and a lower chamber with membership in proportion to the volume of world commerce. He suggested that delegates serve for terms of eight years. The next three proposals covered procedural matters involving equality for all countries, acceptance of majority rule, and a guaranteed right of withdrawal. The latter provision, Bartholdt noted, might entice states into joining and thus strengthen the union. The next six propositions discussed the jurisdiction and the powers of the congress. It could deliberate only on questions affecting "intercourse between nations," and its acts were to become law if not vetoed by an unnamed number of governments. Members would respect each other's "territorial and political integrity," agree to a policy of reciprocity on tariff matters, and recognize each other as equals in matters of trade. They could arm themselves and retain the privilege of declaring war where no arbitration treaties existed.

In all these points, Bartholdt did not depart drastically from proposals then current in the United States. His plan resembled that of Hayne Davis, who probably played a role in its drafting. Davis had been closely associated with Bartholdt for several months as secretary of the American group, had publicized its work, and was to be present with Bartholdt in Brussels. Bartholdt, however, in ending his program, submitted a rather startling proposition which Davis had not as yet advanced. "The armed forces of all the nations represented to be at the service of the Congress for enforcement of any decree rendered by The Hague Court, according to treaties of arbitration."

This delegation of authority, as Bartholdt explained, would be quite limited in its application and the union would be "very feeble in power." It would, therefore, deprive no country of any sovereignty since all governments could still arm themselves and declare war. Apparently Bartholdt accepted Davis's analogy of trial by battle, since he noted that the right to fight had not stopped in England despite courts and laws, and it would not end between nations. "In due time," however, Bartholdt prophesied, the

15. Bartholdt, "The Parliament of Nations," *The Independent,* LVIII (May 11, 1905), 1039–1042; "The Inter-Parliamentary Union," *ibid.,* (May 4, 1905), 1025–1026. Bartholdt presented his proposals at Brussels. *Address of Hon. Richard Bartholdt,* pp. 1–7.

congress would grow in power and become more "perfect in form and accomplish for nations what a Federal Union like ours accomplished for the constituent states."[16]

Bartholdt sent copies of his *Independent* article to the seventeen other Americans who attended the Brussels meeting so that all could consider his views. While no unanimity existed on the various points, no major differences of opinion appeared, and the three propositions as originally agreed upon were presented when the Union members assembled in Brussels on August 28.[17]

There the proposals for a congress and a model arbitration treaty "absorbed the attention" of several hundred delegates from nineteen nations. At first a skeptical attitude prevailed, for the Europeans apparently feared that a congress would intrude upon their sovereignty. A speech by Bartholdt allayed some of their doubts as they accepted his argument that justice should apply in international matters and that countries, like men, should surrender a degree of their authority in return for the benefits that would be gained. Statements by the Belgian attorney and reformer Henri La Fontaine and an address by Count Albert Apponyi of Hungary further dissipated fears so that on the second day of the conference an entirely different mood prevailed. Apponyi acknowledged the leadership of the United States in the movement for international order, called upon his fellow Europeans to follow the path marked, and moved that two commissions be established to consider the two American proposals. By unanimous vote, the parliamentarians agreed to this action.[18]

Davis and Bartholdt hailed the decision as a great victory for the American program, an opinion generally echoed by other internationalists in the United States. Holt's *Independent* declared it "a substantial success." Samuel Barrows, who as a former representative from New York attended the Brussels assembly, concluded that everyone in the Interparliamentary Union was now ready to accept a world congress.[19] To these advocates, the millennium

16. Martin D. Dubin, "The Development of the Concept of Collective Security in the American Peace Movement, 1899–1917," pp. 52–55.

17. Bartholdt, "The American Proposition for Peace," *The Independent*, LXI (July 5, 1906), 10.

18. *Ibid.*; Bartholdt, "The Introduction of the Peace Movement into Practical Politics," *Mohonk Report, 1906*, pp. 48–49; "The Interparliamentary Conference at Brussels," *Advocate of Peace*, LXVII (October 1905), 192–193; Hayne Davis, "The American Victory at Waterloo," *The Independent*, LIX (October 5, 1905), 777–779; Bartholdt, *Address*, p. 7; Davis, *World's Peacemakers*, pp. 274–276.

19. Davis, *World's Peacemakers*, pp. 113–150; Bartholdt, "Introduction, Peace Movement," pp. 49–50; Davis, "An American Victory," pp. 778–779; "The Council

seemed just ahead. If the Union could formulate a positive program, the official delegates at the Second Hague Conference might well adopt it and thus act favorably upon the proposal for an international organization. In this way, the Interparliamentary Union could become its house of representatives. Even the people, where they knew of the plan, apparently endorsed it. Richmond P. Hobson, a cousin of Hayne Davis and shortly after 1906 a congressman from Alabama, delivered over 200 speeches in 1905 to 200,000 listeners. Although Hobson, a naval hero of the Spanish-American War, might have confused the issue by combining a resolution for a world assembly with that favoring a strengthened navy, he asked his audiences to vote on his proposition. Every time, in 35 states and 246 cities, he found virtually unanimous approval. Indeed, the people might have been willing to go farther than the Interparliamentary Union, for Hobson's resolution implied that administrative machinery and even force might be necessary to maintain peace.[20]

A more cautious analysis of the Brussels meeting, however, might lead to a conclusion quite different from that reached by the internationalists. Rather than a victory, the referral of the proposal for a congress to a committee could be judged a loss. The Union had failed to consider a league by avoiding a vote on the matter. Time would show whether Bartholdt's dream would grow or fade.

The commission, under the chairmanship of Sir Philip Stanhope of England, agreed in principle with Bartholdt's points. Debate centered around the question of a one- or two-house legislature and how delegates were to be named. Its final report appeared on November 19 and contained three recommendations. First, another Hague Conference should be held and thereafter assemble periodically. Second, a special commission should be assigned the task of codifying existing international law, and the congress should then keep it current. Third, a reorganized Interparliamentary Union should become a genuinely representative body associated with the new agency.[21]

---

of Peace at Brussels," *The Independent,* LIX (September 7, 1905), 585–586; Barrows, "International Forces Working Toward a World Congress," *Mohonk Report, 1906,* pp. 52–53; Barrows, "The Bulwarks of Peace," *Advocate of Peace,* LXIX (June 1907), 133.

20. Hobson, "Internationalism and Naval Supremacy," *The Independent,* LX (April 5, 1906), 768–771.

21. "The International Parliament," *The Independent,* LIX (November 16, 1905), 1186; "The Coming Parliament of Nations," *ibid.,* (December 7, 1905), pp. 1360. Davis, on the scene as secretary of the American group, recorded the action in "The World's Peace Makers," *ibid.,* (December 21, 1905), pp. 1436–1438.

This action represented a retreat from the original Bartholdt proposal. It offered no suggestions on how the legislature was to be constituted or what its powers would be. It specifically removed from its jurisdiction any authority to codify law, entrusting that task to another agency. Bartholdt, however, in expressing his elation over the report, optimistically but mistakenly saw only one obstacle left. The Second Hague Conference would have to approve the resolutions, especially if the Interparliamentary Union members supported them. He decided to push forward in the United States by drafting a congressional resolution which directed the President to instruct the American delegates to the Hague Conference to support the plan. Hayne Davis, who had spent four months in Europe carefully steering the American proposition through the commission, likewise viewed the future with optimism.[22]

If the matter had been left to the United States, the proposals might have been adopted at the Interparliamentary Union sessions at London in 1906. A groundswell of enthusiasm appeared in Congress where on April 25 nearly two hundred congressmen affiliated with the Union. Over one hundred of these supposedly practical and realistic men met and agreed to push Bartholdt's suggestions fully at the meeting later that summer.[23]

Around five hundred parliamentarians from nineteen nations appeared in London where the Prime Minister, Sir Henry Campbell-Bannerman, delivered a welcoming address. The presence of such a notable figure, who had referred to a league in 1905, inspired the members with a sense of their growing importance and acceptance. The Americans were especially pleased since the event would give the Union's recommendations additional weight at the Hague Conference. They had caucused prior to the sessions and decided to seek full adoption of the modified Bartholdt resolutions which the Stanhope commission had reported. Democratic Representative John Sharp Williams of Mississippi, at his first meeting of the Union, proposed that the Americans support two additional points. First, he suggested that all debt questions be arbitrated rather than have creditor nations intervene by force to collect their claims, a point the Latin American states had been pushing. Second, Williams noted that it would be wise to pay the judges at The Hague an annual salary and to authorize them to draft an international code. The American group also reached another decision which seemed of little

22. Bartholdt, "The Demand of the Hour," *ibid.,* pp. 1443–1445; Davis, "The World's Peace Makers," p. 1438.

23. "The Interparliamentary Group in Congress," *Advocate of Peace,* LXVIII (May 1906), 98–99; Bartholdt, "Remarks," *Mohonk Report, 1906,* p. 51.

import at the time. It invited William Jennings Bryan to join their delegation. Bryan, in London at the time, seemed to be eligible as a former member of the House of Representatives.[24]

Many comments in London that summer referred to the leadership of the United States in the movement for a world congress, a point which could hardly be disputed. But while the Americans may have been acclaimed, they seemed relatively ineffectual in the face of the more conservative European parliamentarians who proceeded to emasculate Bartholdt's original proposals, ignored his detailed suggestions on the form for an international organization, and modified even more the report of the Stanhope commission. The final resolutions as approved simply noted that it "would be advantageous to give the Hague Conference a more permanent influence in" the organized functions of diplomacy "and that the Powers should agree in establishing periodical meetings of these Conferences." This was far removed from the imaginative propositions of 1905. Furthermore, the Union refused to accept Williams's suggestions to pay judges or to codify international law.[25]

The only startling development at London came when Bryan spoke. He introduced the "cooling-off" idea, which as Secretary of State he later incorporated into treaties. Bryan had carefully studied proposals for the peaceful settlement of controversies and as early as 1905 had spoken in support of referring all disputes to some type of investigation. He suggested at London that where nations refused to submit questions to arbitration they should send them to a separate body. This would bring delay and probably prevent war. Bryan seemed to offer a solution to that knotty problem whereby governments refused to arbitrate questions involving national honor and vital interests. If such matters could be referred to some investigatory body, the moral force of the world could then be applied to compel nations to resolve their difficulties peacefully.[26]

24. Davis, "The Fourteenth Interparliamentary Conference," *The Independent,* LXI (August 16, 1906), 388–389. Dubin, "Collective Security," p. 30, argues that Campbell-Bannerman had been influenced by American ideas, notably those of Carnegie.

25. E. F. Baldwin, "The Parliament of Man, The Federation of the World," *The Outlook,* LXXXIII (August 18, 1906), 889–890.

26. Curti, "Bryan and World Peace," pp. 143–149; "Mr. Bryan's Advice," *The Independent,* LIX (September 21, 1905), 706; Bryan, "The Path to Peace," *ibid.,* LXI (August 30, 1906), 483–486. Bartholdt had included such an idea in his draft of a model arbitration treaty, but it had been eliminated until Bryan called for its acceptance in the preliminary sessions. Davis, "The Fourteenth Interparliamentary Conference," pp. 388–390.

Davis and Bartholdt must have been disappointed with the results of the London meeting, but they never openly admitted a reversal. Perhaps they feared it might harm their cause. They continued to speak of the "victory" at London and to comment on the wise decision to reduce the proposition for a congress to a simple proposal which would arouse little protest. In many respects, they should have been content with partial gains, for the Union did advance the cause of internationalism even though it did not do all the dreamers wanted. It adopted in modified form the arbitration treaty presented by the American group and even strengthened it by adopting the Bryan amendments. Its actions encouraged governments to instruct their delegates at the Second Hague Conference to explore the codification of international law and to discuss disarmament. More important, however, the Americans had gained open debate on a congress. The five hundred parliamentarians present carried to their countries an idea which in a few years people were more ready to accept. Finally, the proposition for an assembly had been referred to the Hague Conference. Bartholdt may have been right when he rationalized that perhaps he could not have expected more.[27]

Other internationalists, however, had no intention of being satisfied with partial gains. With the growing acceptance of the congress idea and the possibility that it might be realized soon, some of them began to explore the "next step." These men, of course, favored arbitration, a court, and an assembly, but they also wished to consider a more perfect arrangement. Generally they tended to favor a world federation, although all of them could not be placed in that neat category. The federation ideal possessed two attractive features; it offered both a means to an end and also a form of government. By adopting a process of union similar to that which the United States had followed, the nations could unite voluntarily into a league. Since this action would be co-operative and evolutionary, it would presumably result in an association without major complications. Federation implied a system similar to that of the United States, where a legislature could pass laws, a court interpret them, and an executive uphold them, while at the same time individual states would be allowed a degree of autonomy.

Raymond Bridgman clearly reflected this trend by 1906. He prepared a lecture that year on "The World Republic," which he used to explore the subject of sovereignty. The inherent right claimed by governments to be the

27. Davis, "Victory for the American Plan," *The Independent,* LXI (August 9, 1906), 309–311; Bartholdt, "The Calling of the Second Conference of the Hague," *ibid.,* LXIII (July 11, 1907), 67; Davis, *World's Peacemakers,* pp. 317–318.

complete masters of all their affairs stood as a major obstacle to the internationalists. Nations would have to delegate some power to a federation if it were to function effectively. Bridgman faced this problem by insisting that sovereignty could be divided. Countries could grant limited authority to a central agency yet retain control of their internal affairs free from the interference of a league. This idea of a divided sovereignty stood at the heart of the federal principle. Bridgman sought to convince men that states, despite talk of absolute rights, were limited in their actions. Men should, therefore, recognize the existence of a "world will" pointing toward union and have their governments relinquish some of their vaunted power.[28]

The idea of federation also appeared in the writings of Hayne Davis. His many references to the United States as a model revealed this view, but Davis contributed more to the movement by converting Hamilton Holt to the cause of world federation. Holt became the most outspoken advocate of this goal. In 1907, he formulated a lecture in which he called for an organization built upon federal principles. As Holt noted, international law still lacked meaning. Where statutes existed within states one could find stability, but nations often used force in their relations with one another. They should seek order and stability by relinquishing part of their sovereignty to a legislature which would draft rules within a prescribed area. Holt claimed that the world stood on the threshold of this important development. The United States had moved in that direction in 1789, and men in the twentieth century were ready to act. Critics argued that this parallel did not apply, since similar economic, political, and social conditions that had existed along the eastern seaboard in the eighteenth century did not exist between nations. Holt, however, insisted that modern communication and transportation made the most distant parts of the earth closer than Charleston and Boston had been then. He argued further that in the United States, with its diversity of people and its vast distinctions, one could find "the world in miniature," yet it functioned smoothly and settled its differences amicably. Since "the germ of the Supreme Court of the World and the International Legislature" already existed in the form of the Hague tribunal and the Interparliamentary Union, men should think of adding "an International Executive." Then a federation would bring peace.[29]

28. Bridgman, "World-Sovereignty Already a Fact," *Advocate of Peace*, LXIX (April 1907), 84–85; Bridgman, "The World's Greatest Era," *Bibliotheca Sacra*, LXIV (October 1907), 717, 719–724.

29. Davis, "The Final Outcome of the Declaration of Independence," best illustrates his position. Holt, "The Federation of the World," typescript copy, Holt Papers.

Holt's *Independent* reflected the ideas of its editor. From 1903 to the end of 1907 it printed eight articles from Hayne Davis and dozens of editorials on international organization. Its boldest act, however, was the publication of "A Constitution of the World" in April of 1907. While relatively brief, the article revealed a federalist ideology and the prevailing concepts of the time.

It called for a periodic congress to meet every five years or on call, and open to all nations. Each government would be entitled to one vote, members would agree to respect "the territorial and political integrity" of other signatories, and there would be equality of commercial opportunity and reciprocal trade accords. There would be "no transfer of political control over territory included in the union without the sanction of the Assembly." Each country would retain the right to maintain its arms and to "use its forces according to its own judgment, save as it may have agreed to resort to arbitration." These same armies would be used to uphold the decisions of the Hague court. There would be a two-house legislature with one house consisting of the executive council of the Interparliamentary Union. Laws passed would take effect after three years if not vetoed by one fourth of the governments represented. The right of withdrawal was guaranteed.[30]

The ideas of Holt, Davis, and *The Independent* had the influential support of a man who at the time enjoyed an outstanding reputation as an international lawyer. This was John Bassett Moore, who had seen long service in the Department of State and been active in arbitration settlements in the 1880s and 1890s. He had compiled a six-volume history of arbitration and had written extensively on the need for an extended legal system. Holt had sought Moore's opinion on the program *The Independent* had been advancing, and Moore had attended a dinner on May 29, 1906, in honor of the American delegates to the Interparliamentary Union meeting in London. Many speakers discussed a parliament but none more forcefully than the usually pragmatic and realistic Moore. He assumed an advanced position, claiming that the pending Hague Conference would contribute substantially to the ideal of a world organization with three well-defined branches of government.[31]

Another proposal for a federation appeared between 1904 and 1907. It came from the eccentric attorney William O. McDowell, who claimed the title of "Peacemaker" in "THE SOCIETY OF THE WHO'S WHO (the intellectual leaders of the world) *bringing into existence* THE UNITED NATIONS OF

30. "A Constitution of the World," *The Independent*, LXII (April 11, 1907), 826.

31. "Peace," *ibid.*, LX (June 7, 1906), 1384–1385; "The Congress of Nations," *Advocate of Peace*, LXVIII (July 1906), 144–145.

THE EARTH." McDowell had been born in New Jersey in 1848, and his title had been conferred upon him in 1891 when a committee of three hundred pacifists met at Independence Hall. He had been influential in founding the Sons and the Daughters of the American Revolution, and he had served as president of the Cuban-American League created in 1898 to aid the Cuban people and to bring the countries of the Western Hemisphere into closer accord. In 1903 he grew interested in the plan for a periodic congress and even designed a flag to fly at The Hague.[32]

By 1905, McDowell believed in a fully developed government. The Interparliamentary Union could serve as its legislature, a judicial body could be modeled after the Supreme Court of the United States, and an executive called the "Peacemaker" could function as president. He would be chosen by the "intellectual leaders of the English speaking world." McDowell included such details as a list of cabinet officers and insisted that the sovereignty of governments would not be eroded. His personality, which reflected egocentric qualities, alienated him from most of the internationalists; hence he worked independently of the existing groups.[33]

Perhaps the most influential American who spoke for a federation of nations, albeit in less detailed terms, was Andrew Carnegie. In 1905, in his Rectorial Address to students in the University of St. Andrews in Scotland, Carnegie suggested that a "League of Peace" be created to allay the dangers of war. He reflected most of the currents at work when he referred to the aims of the Interparliamentary Union, endorsed the idea of periodic congresses, and called for a judicial body similar to that of the American Supreme Court. By 1907, at least 260,000 copies of his speech had been widely distributed in several languages.[34] In the spring of 1907, Carnegie introduced another phrase which later gained widespread acceptance—a League of Nations. While Carnegie still failed to present specific provisions, he added one new element. He suggested "an international police force" similar to the one employed in China during the Boxer uprising in 1900. It would be necessary for any league, he declared, to protect "nations from attack" and "enforce the decisions of properly constituted International Tribunals."

32. McDowell to S. C. Mitchell, April 4, 1924, Mitchell Papers, Southern Historical Collection, Chapel Hill, N.C.; unaddressed letter to the editor, December 9, 1898, McDowell Papers, New York Public Library; *The Peacemaker,* XXII (October 1903), 232; New York *Times,* March 13, 1927.

33. McDowell to Carnegie Institute, June 23, 1905, McDowell Papers; H. C. Phillips to Bartholdt, n.d., Letterbook, September 27, 1904–March 15, 1905, Lake Mohonk Arbitration Conference Papers, SCPC.

34. Carnegie, *A League of Peace: A Rectorial Address . . . 17th October, 1905,* pp. 20–24, 28–31; "Brevities," *Advocate of Peace,* LXIX (April 1907), 82.

While Carnegie preferred that economic pressures be applied first, he agreed that military units should be employed if needed.[35]

Carnegie was not the only federationist of his time who referred to the use of force to maintain peace. Bartholdt's proposal had contained a provision on that subject, and a number of sanctionists had appeared by 1907. Most of them could be classified as federalists since they referred to a three-branch government. The system to them, however, was not as important as the powers conferred. They challenged the contention that moral pressures would deter nations or that states would voluntarily submit disputes to a judicial agency and abide by the decisions. Pacifists claimed that, where controversies had been peacefully resolved, the verdicts had always been honored, and they argued that no military compulsion would be needed. The sanctionists, however, had doubts. They realized that governments had referred only their less important problems to tribunals and that serious controversies would not be easily resolved. Nations involved in a vast arms race preferred to fight for their vital interests and honor rather than rely upon ambiguous principles of justice. Some force, they argued, had to exist to correct this condition.

One advocate of sanctions was a woman, Lucia Ames Mead. She was born in 1856, had established herself as a writer-reformer, and had been active in the Massachusetts Women's Suffrage Association. In 1898, she married Edwin D. Mead and shortly thereafter began to write on the subject which had attracted his interest. She perceived an evolutionary development which would bring a "world legislature." In 1903, she suggested that a police agency would also be needed.

Mrs. Mead injected an argument into discussions on an international organization which later advocates often employed. There were two kinds of force, she noted. One was uncontrolled. It settled controversies by might rather than by justice. The other was the restrained use of police power to compel contestants in a dispute to appear before a court. Nations needed a policing arm just as local governments did. Under a federation, a "World Legislature" could create and control such a force. The latter could also be employed, in turn, to uphold the statutes approved by the congress. Mrs. Mead recognized in 1903 that political machinery had to be developed be-

---

35. Carnegie, "The Next Step—A League of Nations," *The Outlook*, LXXXVI (May 25, 1907), 151–152; Carnegie to Edwin D. Mead, April 6, 1905, George Nasmyth Papers, SCPC; Carnegie, "Introduction," to Davis, *World's Peacemakers*, p. x; Joseph E. Johnson and Bernard Bush, eds., *Perspectives on Peace 1910–1960*, pp. 8–10; Dubin, "Collective Security," pp. 26–30, 53.

fore her ideal could be realized, but she insisted that within one hundred years an international police agency would end anarchical conditions and bring a "reign of law."[36]

In letters to editors, articles, pamphlets, and speeches, Mrs. Mead publicized her views. Her emphasis upon rational and gradual approaches enabled her to gain a sympathetic hearing, and her proposal for force to compel nations to submit their disputes to some international agency for settlement remained alive. It later became the principal plank of the League to Enforce Peace in 1915.[37]

Another federationist who proclaimed the advantages of sanctions appeared by 1907. Walter John Bartnett, an attorney prominent in the American Society of International Law, believed that the states of Europe should "disarm as against one another and retain armies and navies for policing only." Once the benefits of this arrangement became known, other countries, including the United States, would join. The first step would be an agreement whereby governments would "cede to the jurisdiction of the parliament a certain armament . . . for the purpose of executing the decrees of the tribunal; thus enabling all the nations with safety to disarm as against one another, retaining only such armies and navies as they may need for policing purposes." Eventually, executive, judicial, and legislative agencies would evolve.[38]

Even leaders like Davis and Holt added provisions for sanctions to their plans which had originally lacked them. Davis described Bartholdt's recommendations for military action in his Interparliamentary Union proposals as "reasonable." In the United States, where state navies disappeared with the advent of a strong federal authority, so too would national armies give way "to a mere International Police Force" that would effectuate further disarmament and execute "the laws and judgments of the Congress and courts of the United Nations." Holt's *Independent* often published similar views.[39]

36. Lucia Ames Mead, "What Are We to Do?" pp. 142–143; L. A. Mead, "International Police," *The Outlook*, LXXIV (July 18, 1903), 705–706; L. A. Mead, *A Primer of the Peace Movement*, [p. 1].

37. L. A. Mead, "Organize the World," *The Club Worker*, V (March 1904), 96–97; L. A. Mead, "The Future of Arbitration," *The Outlook*, LXXXI (December 30, 1905), 1088–1089; letter to the editor dated September 23, 1904, Springfield (Mass.) *Republican*.

38. Bartnett, "The Federation of the World," *The Arena*, XXXVIII (November 1907), 498–505. He had published his views previously in a pamphlet in 1906.

39. Davis, "Present Prospects for Peace," *The Independent*, LXI (July 5, 1906), 15; Davis, "Disarmament and Union of Nations," *ibid.*, LVIII (June 22, 1905), 1404;

The sanctionists found some acceptance of their ideas in statements of prominent figures, including President Roosevelt. In an address to Congress in December 1904, Roosevelt referred to the need for the United States to exercise "international police power" in maintaining stability in the Western Hemisphere. While he was not thinking of a world body, he did observe in the same speech that little headway could be made in attaining disarmament until some "degree of international control" developed. Nations, he declared, would always have need for some armaments "to serve the purpose of international police." Roosevelt reiterated that point two years later in a letter to Carnegie. Disarmament would be possible only "if there was some system of international police."[40]

At least two eminent legal figures echoed similar views. Justice David J. Brewer of the Supreme Court endorsed Bartholdt's proposition for an army, referred to the Boxer rebellion as an illustration, and argued that some arrangement could surely be found to compel the submission of disputes to arbitration and to uphold the awards. Brewer apparently preferred a form of nonmilitary sanction, but he did not oppose the use of direct arms. John Bassett Moore observed that force to enthrone justice was in 1904 a distant dream, yet he argued that the vision was worth seeking. It should function under an "International Council" and be used to maintain right "under a system of law."[41]

The president of Columbia University, Nicholas Murray Butler, the Boston publisher Edwin Ginn, and Lyman Abbott also spoke in support of sanctions. Butler in 1907 perceived a coming age "which may be described fittingly as internationalism." Countries had grown closer in their relationships, Butler declared, but there would still be times in extreme instances "of disobedience" when "an international police would be needed." Ginn had been presenting a plan for gradual disarmament for years. Governments could reduce their arms, he argued, yet still feel secure if they could be defended "against the aggressions of others." Abbott predicted in 1906 that

<hr />

"Mr. Bryce on Navies," *ibid.,* LIX (September 21, 1905), 700–701; "Our Foreign Entanglements," *ibid.,* LX (February 15, 1906), 405–406; "The Trouble at Algeciras," *ibid.,* (March 8, 1906), pp. 581–582; untitled editorial, *ibid.,* LXIII (August 22, 1907), 470.

40. *Congressional Record,* 58 Cong., 3d sess., 39, pt. 1:19; Roosevelt to Carnegie, August 6, 1906, Morison, *Letters,* V, 345.

41. Brewer, "The Enforcement of Arbitral Awards," *Mohonk Report, 1905,* pp. 37–38; Moore, "The Venezuela Decision from the Point of View of Present International Law," *ibid., 1904,* pp. 64–66.

shortly one armed agency would provide stability "under a common direction and a common control, and no more."[42]

Abbott's connection with *The Outlook* may explain that journal's similar attitude. As early as 1904, it claimed that the armies of the world would someday function as "a great, efficient, scientifically administered international police." Anyone who objected to such a development, it declared, was blind to reality. By 1907, the journal maintained that any court should possess sufficient authority to control recalcitrant nations, and this would mean a police system.[43]

Many less prominent citizens also advocated sanctions. Democratic Representative George W. Taylor of Alabama favored "a navy to maintain peace and to enforce the mandates of an International Court of Arbitration." Another congressman from Pennsylvania, Republican Arthur L. Bates, who had attended the Brussels meeting of the Interparliamentary Union, stood ready to grant the Hague tribunal whatever power it needed to prevent war and uphold its decrees. Philip S. Moxom of Springfield, Massachusetts, a Congregationalist minister, commented in 1904 on the growing acceptance of such ideas. He had raised the subject at a Lake Mohonk session in 1901 and faced a barrage of hostile questions. Moxom had then suggested only a force similar to that used in the Boxer rebellion to maintain order in uncivilized areas and to protect travelers in foreign lands. He had specifically noted it should not be used to uphold the decisions of a court. By 1904, however, he proclaimed such a development to be within "the line of the logical . . . movement and the principle which we represent here," and no one objected.[44]

Attitudes had indeed changed. Even Albert K. Smiley came reluctantly and often momentarily to accept what he had previously shunned. Although a Quaker, Smiley agreed by 1906 that while courts and arbitration should be the most important factor in maintaining peace, "a small army will probably always be required to do police duty and repress mob violence." Another sign of the changing temper appeared at a meeting of Shakers at

42. Butler, "Opening Address . . . ," *Mohonk Report, 1907*, pp. 13–17; Ginn, "Address . . . ," *ibid., 1901*, pp. 20–21; Ginn, "A More Efficient Organization of the Peace Forces of the World," *ibid., 1903*, p. 103; Abbott, "A Vision of Peace," p. 32.

43. "Objections to the Treaties," *The Outlook*, LXXVIII (December 24, 1904), 1007–1008; "Peace and Forcible Disarmament," *ibid.*, LXXXV (April 27, 1907), 909–910.

44. Taylor, "A Regularly Organized International Court Needed," *Mohonk Report, 1905*, p. 50; Bates, "Address . . . ," *ibid., 1906*, p. 76; Moxom, "Address . . . ," *ibid., 1901*, pp. 34–35, 86; Moxom, "The Motives to Which we should Appeal," *ibid., 1904*, p. 69.

Mount Lebanon, New York, on August 31, 1905. These normally pacifist-minded citizens approved a resolution favoring the reduction of armaments to the size of "an international police force."[45]

With pacifists advocating compulsion by arms, it should not be surprising to find military men supporting disarmament as long as some power existed to maintain order. Rear-Admiral Caspar F. Goodrich and Commander Albion V. Wadhams of the Navy and former Civil War officer Horatio C. King apparently perceived the possibility of a gradual reduction of arms and the transfer of certain authority to an international force.[46]

Nevertheless, a large number of traditionalists could not accept the advanced position of some of their contemporaries. They rejected the arguments and insisted that the moral weight of public opinion would suffice. Again and again, they emphasized that in nearly two hundred arbitral cases no nation had ever completely renounced the award.[47]

If the programs of the sanctionists and perhaps even the federalists seemed extreme to some men, there must have been concern over the proposals of a few of the internationalists who wished to create a world organization with even broader powers. Joseph C. Clayton, a New York attorney and editor of the *American Lawyer,* prepared an elaborate draft of a union and published it in his journal in 1907. Any government created should enjoy all the authority needed, said Clayton. He agreed with the evolutionary theory but argued that the world had reached a stage where men should assemble in a convention and draft "a Constitution of the United Nations."

Clayton suggested the creation of a three-branch government headed by an executive called "The Peacemaker." While no evidence connects Clayton and McDowell, this word may reveal some relationship. The new society would enjoy full power in the international realm, but it could not intervene in the internal affairs of states. An emphasis on arbitration reflected the current interest on that subject, and countries could reserve matters of honor, vital interests, and territorial integrity. They could even engage in war to uphold their rights. The main effort would be to have dis-

45. Smiley, "Opening Remarks . . . ," *ibid., 1906,* p. 11; "Resolutions Adopted . . . ," Carnegie Endowment for International Peace Papers, Columbia University, hereafter cited as CEIP Papers.

46. Goodrich, "Address . . . ," *Mohonk Report, 1907,* p. 184; Wadhams, "Address . . . ," *ibid., 1901,* p. 76; King, "Remarks," *ibid., 1907,* p. 133. Aula Gentium, "The Enforcement of International Arbitral Awards," *Law Magazine and Review,* XXXII (February 1907), 157–166, examined in detail the problem of force and arbitration.

47. "A Peace League Among the Nations," *Advocate of Peace,* LXVII, (December 1905), 237–238; *Mohonk Reports: 1901,* pp. 36–38, 86, 87–89, 98; *1902,* pp. 38–39, 40, 93–94, 105; *1903,* p. 33; *1904,* pp. 25, 117; *1907,* pp. 24, 32–33, 37–38.

putes go to a court. If a government resorted to war before utilizing the machinery available, it would be treated as an outlaw and be cut off from the world.

A number of additional proposals made Clayton's plan distinctive. His United Nations would be financed by members, each paying one one-thousandth (one tenth of one percent) of its annual military budget as ascertained by the congress. Armaments would be limited, and no nation could increase its force without approval. Laws would be passed subject to a veto by the chief executive. As first Peacemaker, Clayton suggested that the President assume the title of Theodorus Pacificator Maximus, thus being the first internationalist to nominate Roosevelt for this lofty position.[48]

Other advocates of a more perfect organization included Professor Philip Van Ness Myers of the University of Cincinnati. He incorporated into a history text a chapter on the growing trend of nations to combine. This principle, Myers predicted, would inevitably lead to a European union and eventually to a "World State." The president of the Kansas State Peace Society, George H. Hoss, often referred to a "World-Government" built along federal lines. Its three branches, including an executive agency in the form of a "council," would have the power to uphold "both legislative and court decrees," preferably by nonmilitary means. A similar ambiguous proposal came from Henry M. MacCracken, the Chancellor of New York University. He criticized other plans for a congress. The aim should be "world-government," and he suggested the formation of clubs in colleges and universities to seek the goal already "in men's minds."[49]

MacCracken received verbal support from Wilbur F. Crafts, a Presbyterian clergyman of Washington, D.C., and a founder of the International Reform Bureau. Why not have college students debate the subject of world government and why confine the activities to campuses? Business and church organizations should "study and promote world-government" as a practical goal. Another professor, C. C. Eckhardt of the University of Missouri, used a different term. He saw a "world state" emerging from the evolutionary processes at work.[50]

48. Joseph C. Clayton, *Pax Nobiscum, A Plan for a Tentative Constitution of The United Nations . . .* , pp. 4–16.

49. Myers, *Outlines of Nineteenth Century History,* pp. 116–121; Hoss, "A World-Government—World Peace," *Advocate of Peace,* LXVII (February 1905), 39–41; MacCracken, "The Relations of the Schools and Colleges to the Maintenance of Peace," *Mohonk Report, 1905,* p. 120.

50. Crafts, "College Debates on World Government," *Advocate of Peace,* LXVII (August and September 1905), 182–183; Eckhardt, "The World State," *Popular Science Monthly,* LXIX (August 1906), 147–154.

Between 1905 and 1907, all of these persons had presented their views to influence the discussions of statesmen at the forthcoming Hague Conference. But the people also had to be informed if they were to raise their voice and thus affect the result. Toward this end, the pacifists and internationalists combined in April of 1907 in a dramatic effort to publicize their aims. They organized the National Arbitration and Peace Congress in New York City. The New York Peace Society had co-operated in planning this assembly since it saw it as a means to promote internationalist doctrines. Its constitution reflected the beliefs of its president, Andrew Carnegie, and at least two members of its board of directors, Hayne Davis and Hamilton Holt. It sought the extension of arbitration, the strengthening of the Hague court, and the consideration of measures "for the establishment of a permanent international congress."[51]

The National Arbitration and Peace Congress proved to be an energetic undertaking. It received extensive publicity through a committee headed by Holt, which compiled a scrapbook of 32,977 newspaper clippings that weighed 250 pounds. An exceptional attendance in terms of geographical distribution, numbers, and the prominence of the delegates gave the gathering considerable prestige and testified to the growing acceptance of the peace and arbitration movement in the United States. Carnegie served as president, and among the speakers were Secretary of State Elihu Root, New York Governor Charles Evans Hughes, William Jennings Bryan, and labor leaders Terence V. Powderly and Samuel Gompers. European citizens represented other nations.[52]

At the first sessions of the Congress on a Sunday and Monday, few delegates referred to an international organization. Speakers voiced the traditional pacifist sentiments, endorsed arbitration, and called for the development of the court structure at The Hague. Aside from passing references, only Carnegie, Edwin Ginn, and William Archer, the drama critic of the London *Times*, referred to a "League of Peace" or a federation of Europe.[53]

51. Holt, "The Approaching National Peace and Arbitration Congress," *The Independent,* LXII (March 14, 1907), 614–616; "New York Peace Society," *Advocate of Peace,* LXVIII (March 1906), 65; "The Proposed National Peace Congress," *ibid.,* LXIX (January 1907), 5–6; Frederick Lynch, *Personal Recollections of Andrew Carnegie,* pp. 24–28; Charles H. Levermore, *Samuel Train Dutton,* pp. 81–84; *Minutes,* Annual Meeting, New York Peace Society, May 1, 1907, New York Peace Society Papers, hereafter cited as NYPS, SCPC.

52. "Brevities," *Advocate of Peace,* LXIX (July 1907), 160; Kuehl, *Hamilton Holt,* p. 92; Curti, *Peace or War,* p. 207.

53. *Proceedings,* National Arbitration and Peace Congress, 1907, pp. 21–22, 122–123, 159–160, 52–54, 111, 116–117, 152–153, 88–92.

Such reluctance to speak could not have resulted from the absence of the internationalists. Virtually every one who had advocated a society was present. Their relative silence can be attributed to their desire to discuss only realistic goals. Such a note had been sounded by President Roosevelt in a letter to the Congress and by Secretary of State Root in his address the first day.[54]

Tuesday afternoon, however, the internationalists could no longer be restrained. Edwin Mead suggested that the "Parliament of Man" might be realized at the Hague Conference, and that evening at a session devoted to organized labor and the peace movement an unusual development occurred. The audience voted upon a resolution which a convention of American Federation of Labor delegates at Minneapolis had recently approved. It endorsed in full the Interparliamentary Union's call for arbitration and a congress of nations, and the measure overwhelmingly carried.[55]

Thereafter, the proposal for a periodic congress could not be restrained. The Committee on Resolutions included statements which called upon the United States representatives at the Hague Conference "to urge upon that body the formation of a more permanent and more comprehensive International Union for the regular purpose of insuring the efficient co-operation of the nations in the development and application of international law and the maintenance of the peace of the world." The American delegates should also seek to make the Hague Conferences permanent with regularly scheduled meetings. The resolutions also approved arbitration for all types of disputes except where commissions of inquiry or mediation would suffice. As Bartholdt noted, these statements went beyond the recommendations of the Interparliamentary Union, which would have limited the type of controversy to be submitted to arbitration.[56] By 1907, however, several European nations had signed treaties embodying advanced agreements, and the delegates in New York believed that their action merely reflected that change.

The presence of three outspoken internationalists on the resolutions committee goes far to explain the propositions for a periodic congress. Benjamin Trueblood served as chairman, and John Bassett Moore and Henry MacCracken undoubtedly supported his views. These men, in speaking in support of the resolutions, introduced arguments which soon prompted a barrage of remarks favoring international organization. As Samuel J. Barrows noted in what was obviously a reply to the remarks of Roosevelt and Root, such aims were not unrealistic. They reflected the "practical

54. *Ibid.,* pp. 39, 45, 46, 30–34, 88–89, 296.
55. *Ibid.,* pp. 219, 224–225.
56. *Ibid.,* pp. 297–300.

idealism" which had already carried the world forward at a remarkable pace.[57]

The Congress marked the peak of activity on the part of pacifists and internationalists prior to the Hague Conference, but they had worked in other ways. Circulars, pamphlets, petitions to legislative bodies and civic groups, letters, and articles and speeches reached innumerable Americans. The efforts to indoctrinate began with youngsters in the form of the Young People's International Federation League headed by a New York City teacher and social worker, Mary J. Pierson, and with history books like that of Myers, which enjoyed acclaim as one of the most widely adopted texts of its day. It is little wonder that the internationalists succeeded in later years in winning support for their programs or that in 1907 one observer noted that "almost every speech" at the Mohonk Conference that year "referred to the coming Congress of the World."[58]

The results of their labors appeared in other ways. At least three legislative bodies, those of Massachusetts, Georgia, and Ontario, approved resolutions calling for a regular international congress. Various public organizations followed suit, including six business groups in Colorado Springs. The American Bar Association and the General Assembly of 1907 of the Presbyterian Church, U.S.A., also revealed an interest in the subject.[59]

Thus, before the Hague Conference of 1907, many Americans had been introduced to the idea of a world union and some had become converts. They rejected as obsolete George Washington's warnings against permanent

---

57. *Ibid.*, pp. 310–311, 318–319, 388, 416–417, 299–300. A concurrent resolution approved by the New York legislature on April 11 strengthened the internationalists. It endorsed arbitration treaties and asked the United States to support "a permanent International Congress" meeting regularly "for the purpose of suggesting such changes in the law of nations, and in the method of its administration, as the current of events may make desirable and practicable," *ibid.*, p. 432.

58. The *Advocate of Peace* recorded the extensive work of the internationalists: LXVIII (August 1906), 170–171; LXIX (January 1907), 11; (February 1907), 44–45; (March 1907), 55, 59; (April 1907), 82; (May 1907), 100, (August and September 1907), 185; (November 1907), 234; (December 1907), 255; Pierson, "The Young People's International Federation League," *Proceedings,* Second National Peace Congress, 1909, pp. 389–396; E. D. Mead, "Remarks," *Mohonk Report, 1905,* p. 31; "The Mohonk Conference," *The Independent,* LXII (May 30, 1907), 1277.

59. "Massachusetts Legislature," *Advocate of Peace,* LXIX (April 1907), 80; "Georgia House Resolutions," *ibid.,* LXVIII (August 1906), 171; Elias Rogers, "Remarks . . . ," *Mohonk Report, 1907,* pp. 114–115; James A. Hart, "Remarks . . . ," *ibid.,* p. 107; "International Peace and National Order," *The Outlook,* LXXXIV (September 15, 1906), 98; "The Presbyterian General Assembly," *Advocate of Peace,* LXX (April 1908), 78.

alliances. They talked in all sincerity about a world capital and debated where it should be located. They created a Foundation for the Promotion of Internationalism to discuss the subject and to stimulate action.[60] They also continued their agitation for a federation of English-speaking people, for a United States of Europe, and for a union in the Western Hemisphere.[61]

European proponents of a league continued to acknowledge American leadership.[62] Many of them promoted the idea in their countries, but it had less meaning there than in the United States.[63] Resolutions of endorsement as late as 1906 and 1907 were less prevalent in Europe than in America,

60. Amory W. Bradford, "The Unity of the World," *Advocate of Peace,* LXV (April 1903), 70; "Our Foreign Entanglements," *The Independent,* LX (February 15, 1906), 405–406; "Washington and the World's Peace," *ibid.,* (February 22, 1906), pp. 460–461; "Our Future International Relations," *Harper's Weekly,* LI (August 24, 1907), 1227. The Foundation for the Promotion of Internationalism was proposed by two Dutchmen, Dr. P. H. Eykman and Paul Horrix. Its journal, the *Review of Internationalism,* appeared only briefly in 1907, but many Americans contributed to it. Several societies in the United States co-operated, including the Peace and Arbitration Committee of the International Council of Women (Lucia Mead), Universal Peace Union, Women's International Peace League of America (Mary Frost Evans of Colorado), Department of Peace of the W.C.T.U. (Hannah J. Bailey of Maine), The Society of the "Who's Who" (William O. McDowell). Davis, Bartholdt, and Samuel T. Dutton were especially active. Eykman, "Internationalism and the World's Capitol," *The Independent,* LXI (July 26, 1906), 200–205; Bartholdt, "The Hague as the Seat of a World Government," *Review of Internationalism,* III (August 1907), 242–244; Lucia Mead, "Geneva as World Capital," *ibid.,* pp. 263–266.

61. Robert Stein, "Anglo-Franco-German Alliance," *Advocate of Peace,* LXVII (July 1905), 147–151; "The International Union of the American Republics," *ibid.,* LXVIII (December 1906), 235; "The Third International American Conference," *ibid.,* (February 1906), p. 27; Edwyn Anthony, "Mr. Andrew Carnegie and the Re-Union of the English-Speaking Race," *Westminster Review,* CLXIII (June 1905), 636–642; Beales, *History of Peace,* pp. 252–253.

62. Davis, "World's Peace Makers," pp. 1435, 1437–1438; Davis, "Baron d'Estournelles de Constant," *The Independent,* LX (February 22, 1906), 428; W. T. Stead, "The National Arbitration and Peace Congress in New York," *Review of Reviews,* XXXV (May 1907), 591, 593; Estournelles de Constant, "European Anarchy and American Duty," *The Outlook,* LXXXIII (August 4, 1906), 806–807; "A Peace Missioner," *Advocate of Peace,* LXVIII (August 1906), 180; *Proceedings,* National Arbitration and Peace Congress, 1907, pp. 127, 379–380; Suttner, "How I Wrote 'Lay Down Your Arms,'" *The Independent,* LX (February 1, 1906), 252.

63. Alfred H. Fried, "Internationalism and Patriotism," *Review of Internationalism,* I (April 1907), 33–34; W. T. Stead, "The Century of Internationalism," *ibid.,* pp. 19–28; Suttner, "How I Wrote," p. 252; Davis, "Estournelles de Constant," pp. 426, 428; Kurt R. Grossmann, "Peace Movements in Germany," *South Atlantic Quarterly,* XLIX (July 1950), 292–297; "Brevities," *Advocate of Peace,* LXVII (November 1905), 222; H. S. Jevons, "The Development of an International Parliament," *Contemporary Review,* XCII (September 1907), 313–326; F. W. Hirst, *The Arbiter in Council,* pp. 255–349; Davis, "World's Peace Makers," pp. 1437–1438.

and, even where they appeared, internationalists from the United States contributed significantly in obtaining them.[64] This leadership, however, still had to be tested. Whether all of the endeavors would result in discussion and decision at the Second Hague Conference remained to be seen.

64. The resolution by the Fourteenth Universal Peace Congress in Lucerne in 1905 approved the idea of periodic congresses in vague form. There, of 400 delegates, 50 were from the United States, including Ginn and Trueblood. Their speeches may have influenced the vote, and the platform adopted at Boston the year before also had weight in the considerations. Information on various European conferences can be found in the *Advocate of Peace*, LXVII (October 1905), 200–205; LXVIII (July 1906), 160–161; *ibid.*, (October and November 1906), pp. 220–226; *ibid.*, (December 1906), p. 241.

Optimism
and Education,
1907-1909

Throughout the summer of 1907, the internationalists watched The Hague, where 256 delegates from 44 nations met on June 15 to ponder the future of the world. Men of peace had high hopes that the conference would extend the principles of arbitration through acceptance of a model treaty, and they anticipated a judicial court to replace the existing arbitral tribunal. Other items on the agenda also seemed full of promise. Surely agreements on rules of warfare, on contraband, and on the seizure of private property in wartime would reduce the risk of conflict and promote understanding. Finally, consideration of arbitration and a revised court might lead to the codification of law. Most observers also anticipated discussions on armaments and on additional methods to settle disputes.[1]

The internationalists had other expectations. A conference, they believed, would result in future periodic congresses. That would eventually lead to a permanent body which could at first codify law and later serve as

1. Lyman Abbott, "The Next Step—The Appeal to Reason," *The Outlook,* LXXXVI (May 25, 1907), 152–153; Edward E. Hale, "The Next Step—Justice Between Nations," *ibid.,* pp. 153–154; Jewell H. Aubere, "Richard Bartholdt," *World To-Day,* XII (May 1907), 505–506; Bartholdt, "The Calling of the Second Conference of the Hague," pp. 65–67; Estournelles de Constant, "The Next-Step—International Conciliation," *The Outlook,* LXXXVI (May 25, 1907), 147–151; *Mohonk Report, 1907,* pp. 96, 101.

a parliament to legislate and perhaps uphold the rules with a police force.[2] Certainly the fact that the meeting saw more delegates assembled from more nations than ever before seemed to be a major development in the organization of the world.

Officially, the United States expected far less than most of its interested citizens. Joseph H. Choate, the chairman of the American delegation, quoted Roosevelt to show that the President considered a general treaty of arbitration as the most important goal. He had hopes for other items on the agenda, particularly for a court which would become more permanent and more judicial and enjoy extended jurisdiction. Secretary of State Root realistically assessed the situation, however, when he warned against expecting too much. His instructions of May 31, 1907, underscored that point when he noted that all agreements would have to be by unanimous consent. Controversial questions would have to be referred to future meetings, and no discussions should be carried to a point where they might prompt resentments. Root reviewed all the topics to be considered, but his remarks showed his special interest in the court and arbitration. He, too, hoped that the tribunal could become more judicial and render its judgments according to principles of right and law. He also believed that a model arbitration treaty could be devised, but he warned that its provisions would have to be in accord with what the Senate would accept. Root had two other matters which he seemed to emphasize. For one thing, he wished the Latin American nations to be included under the conventions of 1899; second, he hoped for approval of a resolution which would refer to arbitration controversies arising from the collection of international debts.[3]

After several weeks of discussion, the representatives at The Hague signed a series of treaties on October 18, 1907. These dealt mostly with the rules of warfare, with questions of neutral rights, and with problems of private property rights in wartime. This emphasis led many observers to scoff, since the subject of disarmament had received so little attention. It

2. "Washington and the World's Peace," pp. 460–461; "Bellum Delendum Est," *The Independent,* LXII (June 20, 1907), 1475; Holt, "The Outlook at The Hague," *ibid.,* LXIII (July 25, 1907), 189; "The Coming Hague Conference," *Advocate of Peace,* LXVIII (January 1906), 1–2; "The Workers and Peace," *ibid.,* (December 1906), pp. 239–240; "The First Hague Conference and the Second," *The Outlook,* LXXXVI (May 25, 1907), 158–159; Elbert F. Baldwin, "France and America at The Hague," *ibid.,* (August 31, 1907), pp. 959, 962; *Mohonk Report, 1907,* pp. 52, 96, 101, 121.

3. Roosevelt to Carnegie, April 5, 1907, Morison, *Letters,* V, 638–642; Root, "The American Sentiment of Humanity," *Proceedings,* National Arbitration and Peace Congress, 1907, p. 45; Scott, *Hague Peace Conferences,* II, 181–197.

appeared as if the conference had made substantial headway in humanizing the conditions of war but very little in abolishing it or even in reducing its frequency.[4]

The agreements on arbitration also disappointed many men, including United States officials. The processes remained largely where they had been before. Root had hoped for an accord to "provide for obligatory arbitration as broad in scope as now appears practicable," but all that the world gained was an innocuous resolution endorsing this idea in principle.[5] Debate on the subject had proceeded through various stages. It began with consideration of an agreement under which all disputes of any nature would be submitted for settlement. This commitment proved to be too extreme for most countries, including the United States; hence, discussion proceeded to another possibility. Would nations accept inclusive obligatory arbitration? Under this plan, governments would approve a list of classes of controversies, generally relating to commerce, communication, copyrights, and other nonpolitical matters, and agree to arbitrate differences in those areas. Some thirty items received the serious consideration of a committee in 1907, but the delegates could not agree on a list. This left only the subject of limited or exclusive arbitration, which the United States supported. This proposal called for the submission of disputes unsettled by diplomacy, but it exempted all questions relating to independence, vital interests, and territorial integrity.

After extensive debate in the commission considering the subject, a vote showed more than thirty delegates supporting the proposition and nine opposing. Under the unanimity concept which prevailed, this meant defeat. But the friends of obligatory arbitration rallied. They introduced a compromise resolution which noted that the commission unanimously recognized "the principle of obligatory arbitration." It further declared that in disputes involving "the interpretation and application" of international treaties, obligatory arbitration should be resorted to without qualification. All of the delegates in plenary session later adopted this statement, with three nations, including the United States, abstaining. As Choate said in explaining this stand, approval by the United States would have constituted a retreat from the more advanced position which the commission had favored but not

4. Scott, *Hague Peace Conferences,* II, 362–527; "The United States at the Hague," *Harper's Weekly,* LI (August 17, 1907), 1191; [Rollo Ogden], "Peace by Painful Inches," *The Nation,* LXXXV (August 22, 1907), 156; E. J. Dillon, "The Hague Conference: Aims and Achievements," *Contemporary Review,* XCII (September 1907), 424–426; Curti, *Peace or War,* p. 193.

5. Scott, *Hague Peace Conferences,* II, 189; Margrave, "The Policy of . . . Adjudication," p. 140; Doty, *Durable Peace,* pp. 17–19.

unanimously. The United States, however, did approve unofficially of the principle which all other powers likewise accepted.[6]

The conference also reached indefinite agreement on the subject of a revised court in the form of a more judicial body. Choate had continually kept that subject alive. The delegates favored the creation of such an agency, but they floundered over the method of naming judges. Nearly every nation hoped it might be represented. This would have resulted in a cumbersome and inefficient body, but no one had any suggestion for an acceptable formula. Hence, the delegates, in a special resolution, referred this question to their governments, recommending the establishment of a court as soon as agreement could be reached on the selection of justices.[7]

While most of the internationalists could not have been satisfied with the results of the conference, they sought to convince themselves and others that considerable gains had been made. Hayne Davis and Hamilton Holt had been at The Hague that summer as observers, and they conveyed to readers of *The Independent* their optimistic appraisals. They and others argued that the conventions and statements on the court and arbitration, although not formally accepted, had added substantially to international law. The so-called Porter resolution, which had been approved, further advanced the legal settlement of disputes through the agreement to submit controversies over certain types of debts to arbitration. They found two other aspects of the conference, however, to be of greater significance. First, forty-four nations participated, an advance over the twenty-six of 1899. It proved again that men could come together to discuss common problems. Second, the final resolution, largely the work of the Americans, called for a third meeting. While not setting a date, it seemed to guarantee future action, and it took from the Tsar the power to issue the next call. The world, the internationalists argued, had moved closer to that long-sought American goal of periodic congresses.[8]

Raymond Bridgman and Benjamin Trueblood echoed those sentiments, especially in discussing the last development. The decision on regular con-

6. William I. Hull, "Obligatory Arbitration and the Hague Conferences," *AJIL*, II (October 1908), 731–742; Robinson, *Arbitration*, pp. 36–40, 46–67; Scott, *Hague Peace Conferences*, I, 381, II, 242–243. Article 19 of the draft convention for the court, however, tended to negate even this statement by limiting the jurisdiction of the court to controversies only where parties agreed that the dispute belonged in a category of questions that could be submitted. *Ibid.*, II, 301.

7. Scott, *Hague Peace Conferences*, II, 244–245, 291–309.

8. "The Peace Conference," *The Independent*, LXIII (October 17, 1907), 954–956; Davis, "The Second Peace Conference at The Hague," *ibid.*, (October 31, 1907), pp. 1034–1043; Davis, "The Second Hague Conference," *ibid.*, (November 7, 1907), pp. 1094–1101; *ibid.*, (November 14, 1907), pp. 1143–1150; "The Lock and the Key,"

gresses should be viewed as the "greatest thing" done. It revealed that evolutionary process which would culminate in "a legislative world-assembly." The four-month sessions had laid the foundation for a "future deliberative and federative union." In a burst of enthusiasm, Trueblood predicted that such a body, even with limited powers, could solve "all the problems of international interest" then current.[9] William I. Hull, professor of history at Swarthmore College, viewed the results more calmly, but his vision extended as far. The conferences had created the rudimentary organs for world federation, especially a judicial department. Men could already see the signs. Edwin Mead cautioned that the process would not be rapid, but a federation would come with the United States leading the way.[10]

The legalists likewise interpreted the results as optimistically as possible. James B. Scott, who had served as advisor to the American delegation, described the headway as "a landmark in international development." The plan for a court and its general acceptance meant far more than the fact that it failed to gain approval. "The recognition of the idea," Scott prophesied, "makes the ultimate realization a certainty." The Americans had "forced the idea on the conference," and it stood. David Jayne Hill, one of the delegates, also believed that a court would materialize before too long. The agreements on mediation, good offices, arbitration, and a periodic congress had substantially advanced international law. Hill referred to "a reasonable rate of progress toward the realization of" goals, and he thought that as much had been achieved as anyone could reasonably expect.[11]

Elihu Root, in expressing his government's view, often reiterated Hill's points. In the light of the unanimity rule, the conference had "accomplished a great deal." Root's philosophy also appeared in the President's message to Congress on December 3, 1907, when Roosevelt reported the achievements

---

The Outlook, LXXXVII (October 5, 1907), 240–241; "A United States of the World," Literary Digest, XXXV (September 14, 1907), 361.

9. Bridgman, "The World's Legislature Is Here," *New England Magazine*, XXXVIII (May 1908), 355–361; Trueblood, "The Present Position of the International Peace Movement," *Advocate of Peace*, LXXI (May 1909), 103; Trueblood, "The Successes and Failures of the Second Hague Conference," *ibid.*, LXX (February 1908), 34; "What the Hague Conference Has Accomplished," *ibid.*, LXIX (October 1907), 206–207.

10. Hull, *The Two Hague Conferences and Their Contributions to International Law*, pp. 497–500; Mead, "Peace and Education," *Proceedings*, Second National Peace Congress, 1909, p. 45; Mead, "Some Triumphs . . . ," *Mohonk Report, 1908*, p. 28.

11. Scott, "The Work of the Second Hague Conference," *International Conciliation*, No. 5 (January 1908), p. 27; Scott to William I. Hull, May 27, 1908, Hull Papers, SCPC; Hill, "The Net Result at The Hague," *Review of Reviews*, XXXVI (December 1907), 727–730.

to the nation. He noted that while accomplishments might not have matched expectations, no one could complain.[12]

When all factors are weighed, however, one can only conclude that the internationalists had been overoptimistic. The suggestions of the Interparliamentary Union, which they had spent so much time popularizing, never received serious consideration. All advanced arbitral and court proposals foundered on the rock of unanimity. The powers did not establish a judicial body until the end of the First World War. Even a less ambitious program for a maritime Prize Court, which the conference endorsed as a suitable forward step, never materialized.

The failure at The Hague of the internationalists' proposals may explain why in the ensuing two years most of them operated in more subdued fashion than they had before 1907. Despite their claims of significant advances, they must have been somewhat discouraged. If the results of 1907 had revealed one fact clearly, it was that additional programs of education would be needed before people and governments would accept any venturesome paths toward world organization.

Hence, considerable activity by the leading internationalists soon appeared in the form of educational and organizational efforts. They sought to strengthen existing bodies and programs and to create new ones. The friendship societies which emerged in 1907 and 1908 provide some clue to the frame of mind that stimulated such activity. The Japan Society, formed in May of 1907 and designed to promote better understanding between the United States and Japan, had as its main founder attorney Lindsay Russell. His closest friend, Hamilton Holt, participated in building the Society, in the belief that such organizations would propel mankind toward some form of union.[13] Holt helped establish two similar groups in 1908—the Society for the Advancement of India and the American-Scandinavian Society. In describing the latter's goals, a writer for the *Christian Work* noted that in addition to promoting friendship, encouraging exchange, economic and intellectual, it would bring people "together in closer relationships . . . Its most significant meaning is that it is another step in that federation of the world that is rapidly progressing."[14]

12. Root to Elbert F. Baldwin, September 24, November 1; to Joseph H. Choate, November 12, 1907, Root Papers, Library of Congress; James D. Richardson, comp., *Messages and Papers of the Presidents,* XIV, 7118–7120.

13. New York *Tribune,* May 20, 1907; New York *Journal of Commerce,* May 29, 1907; New York *Town and Country,* December 26, 1908; Kuehl, *Hamilton Holt,* p. 101. Russell had organized the Pilgrim's Society in 1902 and 1903.

14. Springfield (Mass.) *Republican,* March 25, 1908; Kuehl, *Hamilton Holt,* pp. 100–101; *Christian Work,* LXXXVI (December 5, 1908), 220.

Other evidence of similar programs can be found in the creation early in 1907 of an American branch of the Association for International Conciliation. This society had been created by the Baron d'Estournelles de Constant in Europe, and the French senator had campaigned widely for its extension to other lands. Its establishment in the United States paralleled a drive to expand the membership and work of the Interparliamentary Union, and Hayne Davis became the organizing and administrative secretary of the Association for International Conciliation. After the Hague Conference of 1907, the American branch embarked upon an ambitious publication program of pamphlets and leaflets. Nicholas Murray Butler, who often referred to the emergence of an "international mind," became its president.[15]

Another group also enjoyed considerable growth after 1907. The Association of Cosmopolitan Clubs had been founded at the University of Wisconsin in 1903 as a society of foreign and United States students, and the idea spread to other campuses. It became a formally organized movement in 1907, and by 1910 some twenty-four colleges in the United States had chapters. Under the leadership of a former University of Wisconsin student, Louis Lochner, and with the financial support of internationalist Edwin Ginn, these groups sought to develop better understanding between the people of various lands. But, as Lochner noted in 1910, in the clubs "we have the beginning of a world federation scarcely dreamed of by the most sanguine."[16] At least three men who became prominent internationalists, George Nasmyth, George Fulk, and Charles E. Beals, rose through the ranks of the Cosmopolitan Clubs.

A reawakened peace movement also reveals the educational campaign of 1908–1910. The American Peace Society added Beals as a field secretary in 1908, and groups were organized in Buffalo, Cleveland, Seattle, Chicago, Northern and Southern California, Texas, Utah, and Maryland. An Intercollegiate Peace Society became active on campuses. Benjamin Trueblood reported that the circulation of the *Advocate of Peace* reached a record high, and he began a campaign to co-ordinate the work of the many peace agencies. He also continued to preach his brand of internationalism in the form of a congress of nations, and his society promoted the sale of his book as well as those by Bridgman, Davis, and the Meads. The head of the

15. Washington *Star,* March 6; New York *Times,* March 7, 1907; "International Conciliation," *The Independent,* LVIII (June 1, 1905), 1265–1266; Estournelles de Constant, "International Conciliation," *ibid.,* LIX (July 27, 1905), 206–207.

16. Lochner, "The Association of Cosmopolitan Clubs," *Mohonk Report, 1910,* p. 186; Lochner, "Work of the Association of Cosmopolitan Clubs," *Advocate of Peace,* LXXII (April 1910), 88–89.

Pacific Coast operation, Robert C. Root, as well as Beals, frequently spoke on the theme of world federation.[17]

By far the most active of the younger peace associations, especially in advancing the idea of international organization, was the New York Peace Society. After its formation in 1906, it led in planning the first National Arbitration and Peace Congress, and it grew rapidly. Carnegie served as its president, but he was not the only internationalist among its leaders. In addition to Hayne Davis and Holt, John Bassett Moore, Lindsay Russell, Frederick Lynch, and Professor Samuel Train Dutton of Columbia served on its board of directors. They were already committed to the goal of a world organization by 1908 and were later to promote that cause. In 1908 the Society hired William H. Short, a young minister from Minnesota, as its secretary. He, too, became a convert. Thus the internationalists virtually assumed the helm of the New York group. The platform adopted in February 1910 resolved that "the Hague Conferences become automatic, periodic and self-governing, that the International Court of Arbitral Justice be constituted, and that a Universal Obligatory Arbitration Treaty be framed, to the end that a 'Federation of the World' be realized."[18] These words reflected sincere convictions. The New York Peace Society shortly thereafter helped create a World-Federation League which became a subsidiary of the Society, and in 1914 its members led in forming the League to Enforce Peace.

The New York Peace Society became the most ambitious agency spreading the gospel of internationalism within these years. Such experienced journalists as Holt, Lynch, and Davis obtained widespread publicity for its programs and broad distribution of its literature. It organized an active mailing file of over twelve thousand prominent citizens and maintained an impressive speaker's bureau.[19]

The internationalists, especially Edwin Mead, also sought to acquaint people with their ideals by informing them about the schemes of early

17. "News from the Field," *Advocate of Peace,* LXX (July 1908), 158; "Editorial Notes," *ibid.,* LXXI (June 1909), 124–125; "Buffalo Meeting . . . ," *ibid.*; "News from the Field," *ibid.,* LXX (November 1908), 236; "The New Chicago Peace Society," *ibid.,* LXXII (February 1910), 30–31; Beals, "International Fraternity," *ibid.,* LXXI (March 1909), 57–59; George Fulk, "The Intercollegiate Peace Association," *Proceedings,* Second National Peace Congress, 1909, pp. 371–373; [Holt], "The Next Step in the Peace Movement," *The Independent,* LXVIII (April 7, 1910), 771–773.

18. Boston *Transcript,* May 2, 1907; Curti, *Peace or War,* p. 200; *Minutes,* Executive Committee, February 25, 1910, NYPS Papers.

19. William H. Short, "Peace Society of the City of New York," *Advocate of Peace,* LXXII (January 1910), 19.

planners. The Great Design and Penn's proposals merited the most attention, but the views of St. Pierre, Bentham, Kant, Ladd, Burritt, and Lorimer received the attention of writers and speakers.[20]

Educational programs operated in other ways. Fannie Fern Andrews, a social reformer and former teacher, organized the American School Peace League in 1908 in Boston. As secretary, she directed the agency, which enjoyed financial support from Edwin Ginn. The Peace League formed branches in nearly every state, prepared and mailed quantities of literature to teachers, sponsored essay contests, and introduced peace day (May 18) into the nation's schools. The National Education Association and the United States Commission of Education eventually became its allies.[21]

Mrs. Andrews passionately believed that teachers had an obligation to convey to children the ideal of peace and inform them that the United States should play a role in the evolving structure of international life. The American School Peace League, therefore, sought to teach students that the peace movement was not passive and negative but active and constructive. By intelligent planning, men and women could advance programs of arbitration, courts, and law, which would bring justice, organization, and good will. She declared in 1908 that "eventually the international congresses will culminate in a world legislature, where the representatives from every government will legislate for the common welfare." Judicial and executive departments would "complete the rounding out of a world republic."[22]

Reflecting her beliefs, the League became an effective agency in introducing the ideas of the internationalists to the nation's youth. She sponsored essay contests on the Hague Conferences and on "The United States, the Exemplar of an Organized World." She sought to have civics courses add "instruction in International Government" and to have educational asso-

20. Mead, "An Early Scheme to Organize the World," *ibid.*, LXX (January 1908), 18–19; Trueblood, "The Present Position of the International Peace Movement," *Proceedings,* Second National Peace Congress, 1909, p. 92; F. W. Hirst, "The Logic of International Co-operation," *International Conciliation,* No. 14 (January 1909), pp. 3–6; "News from the Field," *Advocate of Peace,* LXX (January 1908), 10–11; Frederick D. Hicks, "The Equality of States and the Hague Conferences," *AJIL,* II (July 1908), 551–554; J. B. Scott, review of Bridgman, *World Organization,* and Trueblood, *Federation of the World, ibid.,* pp. 725–727.

21. *Christian Science Monitor,* December 3, 1910; F.F. Andrews, "The American School Peace League," *Advocate of Peace,* LXXI (November 1909), 237–238; Curti, *Peace or War,* pp. 202–203, 210–211; E. D. Mead, "The World Peace Foundation: Its Present Activities," *World Peace Foundation Pamphlets,* II (July 1912), 28–29.

22. F.F. Andrews, "The Relation of Teachers to the Peace Movement," *Education,* XXVIII (January 1908), 279–289; Andrews, "The American School Peace League," *Proceedings,* Second National Peace Congress, 1909, pp. 46–50.

ciations awaken to the "cooperative process, leading to world unity." At the annual meeting of the League in Denver in July of 1909 the main theme was "The Practical Program for World Organization." It included such topics for discussion as "A regular World Congress, at first advisory, but with powers gradually increasing," and "An international police."[23]

Another more powerful educational agency appeared in New York as a result of the efforts of the internationalists there when they persuaded Carnegie to create the Carnegie Endowment for International Peace in 1910. Carnegie had long been interested in such a project. They had submitted various plans to him, but he had rejected them. Late in 1908, however, Holt, Dutton, Mead, Albert K. Smiley, and Lynch drafted a proposal which they presented to Carnegie through Nicholas Murray Butler. It called for the creation of an endowed institute to seek the advancement of arbitration and good will. Carnegie remained unmoved, but revised suggestions and continual pressures from these men finally resulted in a decision to establish a ten-million-dollar endowment.[24]

Carnegie's creation, however, proved to be cautious in its programs and a disappointment to the internationalists. Not one of the most active of them received appointment to the board of trustees. Apparently Carnegie followed the advice of Root, who became the Endowment's first president, in determining the list. Hence, the more conservative legalists directed the new association and its work.[25]

A second endowment, the World Peace Foundation, appeared in 1910 as a result of Ginn's generosity. He had been supporting an "International School of Peace," and the new body carried that name until early in 1911. Ginn had frequently advocated a world league, and he considered calling his new agency the "International Foundation for the Promotion of International Organization and International Peace." He named to his board of

23. *Program, American School Peace League,* Fannie Fern Andrews Papers, Radcliffe College; *American School Peace League, 1909,* pp. 8–12; *The Independent,* LXVII (September 9, 1909), 615.

24. Butler to Carnegie, January 8; Carnegie to Butler, January 11; Dutton to Carnegie, February 18, 1909, Carnegie Papers; Butler to Holt, December 7, 18, 1908, January 12, February 5, 12, 1909; Holt to Butler, December 31, 1908, February 11, 1909, Butler Papers, Columbia University. Levermore, *Samuel Train Dutton,* pp. 92–96, 110, and Kuehl, *Hamilton Holt,* pp. 98–100, have accounts of the Endowment's founding.

25. Curti, *Peace or War,* p. 205; "Reminiscences of Sir Norman Angell," Oral History Research Office, Columbia University, hereafter cited as OHRO; Ginn to D. S. Jordan, February 10, 1911, David Starr Jordan Papers, Stanford University; New York *Tribune,* December 25; New York *Evening Post,* December 17, 1910; Kuehl, *Hamilton Holt,* pp. 99–100.

directors three men, Holt, Edwin Mead, and James A. Macdonald of the Toronto *Globe*, who had long been committed to that ideal. In addition, he appointed Mead secretary, which made him executive officer. The Foundation, said Ginn, would educate people about war and their duties to maintain peace. In this respect, despite Ginn's advocacy of an international police force and a judicial and executive system, the Foundation remained moderate in supporting such programs until the outbreak of the World War.[26]

One other educational body emerged shortly after the Hague Conference. Hayne Davis "conceived and organized" what became the Peace and Arbitration League in 1908. It began at a meeting October 11–17 at Greensboro, under the auspices of the North Carolina Peace Society. President Roosevelt had seen the preliminary proposal for the League, endorsed it, and agreed to serve as honorary president. It called for state congresses to call attention to the conventions of the Second Hague Conference, to direct thought toward a third meeting at The Hague, to develop arbitration, and to remain fully prepared while this structure evolved.[27]

The Peace and Arbitration League summarized these aims with the statement that "The Practical Program for Peace is Adequate Armament and Effective Arbitration." A second internationalist active in the society, Richmond P. Hobson, seemed to emphasize naval strength over pacific machinery, and this stand aroused considerable outcry. It appeared to many men that the preparedness advocates had taken refuge behind a false banner to promote their cause. The *Advocate of Peace* labeled it "the Davis-Hobson insane policy." Holt, in *The Independent*, expressed shock at his friend's action. He called it a "suspicious program" designed to trick the nation, a charge which brought to an end his fruitful labors with the man who had converted him. Davis appealed to Holt. He wished "to dissipate the cloud of misconception" between them, but efforts to heal the breach failed.[28]

26. Ginn, "The World Peace Foundation," *World Peace Foundation Pamphlets,* I (April 1911), 1–6, 8–9, 12; Dubin, "Collective Security," p. 22; "Mr. Carnegie's Greatest Gift," *The Independent,* LXIX (December 15, 1910), 1341.

27. Davis to Holt, undated letter [October 1908], Holt Papers; Roosevelt to Davis, May 30, 1908 (copy), Davis Papers; New York *Tribune,* May 30, 1908; "Is it a Peace Society?," *Advocate of Peace,* LXX (April 1908), 77–78; Davis, "The North Carolina Peace and Arbitration Congress," *The Independent,* LXV (October 8, 1908), 827–832.

28. "The American Peace and Arbitration League," undated typed outline of program and work [1909], Davis Papers. "A Bizarre Peace Congress," *Advocate of Peace,* LXX (November 1908), 230–231; [Holt], "A Suspicious Program," *The Independent,* LXV (October 8, 1908), 853–854; Davis to Holt, November 30, 1908, Holt Papers.

Holt may have been oversuspicious, for Davis undoubtedly believed in his program, as did Congressman John Sharp Williams and Senator James B. McCreary, who had been active in the Interparliamentary Union. The latter became president of the new society, which boasted an impressive roster of supporters. Davis may have endorsed preparedness, but he had not abandoned his faith in justice. He had included such proposals as "Mutual guarantees by the nations to respect each other's territory and sovereignty, and to arbitrate all other questions." The Peace and Arbitration League continued for several years, campaigning more for battleships than for arbitration, and Davis's name declined in prominence in its councils.[29] He virtually retired from the arena, writing only a few articles on international organization until the struggle over ratification of the Treaty of Versailles in 1919 and 1920. Then he again joined his old cohort Holt.

Virtually all of these educational activities by the pacifists and internationalists centered upon one basic theme. The arbitral structure recommended at The Hague had to be attained. This could be done by four developments. First, nations should sign bilateral agreements to arbitrate disputes. Second, the judicial court should replace the tribunal recommended in 1899. Third, the model arbitration treaty should be circulated and approved by the nations. Fourth, the Prize Court should be established. To the internationalists these were essential foundations which had to be laid before they could move ahead.

In the United States, they centered their efforts upon the first two aims. They believed it strategically sound to commit their government first to limited arbitral agreements with friendly powers rather than to seek approval of any universal obligation. In view of the fate of previous treaties and the failure of all ambitious proposals at The Hague, an oblique approach seemed best. The plan for a court did not require great effort since it had already been officially endorsed. It would only be necessary to keep the idea alive.

One theme emerged in discussions over the correct course of action. Reason should prevail. Governments should submit their disputes to arbitral processes just as on the domestic level men settled their differences without conflict. This idealistic belief, which totally ignored the inadequate

29. "And on Earth, Peace, Good-Will Toward Men," *Army and Navy Life,* XIII (December 1908), 512–514; Davis to Diego Mendoza, June 28, 29, 1910, Davis Papers; Dubin, "Collective Security," pp. 45–49. Lucia Ames Mead described many of the new societies in *Educational Organizations Promoting International Friendship,* pp. 3–14.

machinery and the insurmountable obstacle of sovereignty, seemed logical in those years before 1914 when world wars seemed so far away. They used the rational argument, however, to persuade politicians and statesmen that some step should be taken to advance the machinery of arbitration.[30]

The internationalists did not delay long before beginning their campaign of persuasion. It started in November of 1907, when Holt suggested to members of the New York Peace Society that they exert pressure upon officials to negotiate treaties of arbitration. Carnegie broached that subject to Roosevelt and Root shortly thereafter. A few weeks later Carnegie again reminded the President of the task ahead when he expressed his pleasure at provisions for arbitration in the recently concluded Central American Peace Conference treaty and offered to erect a Pan-American building in Washington.[31]

Just before Christmas, on Holt's initiative, the New York Peace Society appointed a three-man committee to urge action on arbitral agreements. Whether such pressures influenced Roosevelt is not clear, but early in 1908 Root negotiated the first of a series of accords which eventually included twenty-four countries. As Root told Carnegie, it was time to get "the arbitration business on its legs again." It apparently had been embarrassing to Root to see his government lag behind when he had spoken so forcefully in favor of arbitration.[32]

The new agreements were said to be compulsory, but they contained no obligatory features. They were limited in scope to problems of a legal nature or to those arising from any misunderstanding over treaty provisions. They excluded questions of national honor, vital interest, and independence. Moreover, they called for the Senate's approval of the *compromis* or agreement on what to arbitrate in each instance where the government wished to act. That had been the proviso added by the Senate to the Hay accords of 1904 which Roosevelt had then refused to accept. How Root persuaded Roosevelt to change his mind cannot be determined, but he apparently convinced the President that these agreements achieved every-

---

30. The application of logic appears clearly in the resolutions of the arbitration and peace congress of 1907. *Proceedings,* National Arbitration and Peace Congress, 1907, pp. 296–297.

31. *Minutes,* Executive Committee, November 6, 1907, NYPS Papers; "A Compulsory Arbitration Treaty with Japan," *The Independent,* LXIII (November 14, 1907), 1179–1180; Carnegie to Roosevelt, December 15, 1907, Root Papers.

32. *Minutes,* Board of Directors, December 21, 1907, NYPS Papers; Root to Carnegie, February 25, 1908, Root Papers; J. B. Scott, "Elihu Root," *The Independent,* LXVI (February 4, 1909), 230.

thing that could be expected at that moment. When he transmitted the documents to Roosevelt, Root reminded him that gradual steps might bring nations to a higher level of practicing "their peaceful professions." The Hague Conferences had advanced the world to this stage; now carefully drafted arbitral treaties seemed necessary. Root had always maintained that peace suffered if a country agreed to certain provisions which it might not honor during a crisis.[33] This philosophy had been described by the nineteenth-century authority on international law James Lorimer as the "reciprocating will." Agreements, said Lorimer, were meaningless unless the signatories were ready to accept and honor what they signed.[34] Root's treaties fully echoed those sentiments.

While many men regretted the limited scope of the new accords, most persons accepted them as the best attainable. Any advance was better than none. Later treaties could contain more ambitious proposals. Hence, Root received the acclaim of pacifists and internationalists for his efforts. Such accolades reached their climax in February of 1909 at a mammoth banquet in his honor sponsored by the New York Peace Society. More than five hundred guests paid tribute to him and in so doing revealed the public support behind his arbitral policy.[35]

They also honored Root, however, for keeping alive another aim of the internationalists, the establishment of a court of justice. He had done this, in part, by helping create the Central American Court of International Justice in 1907. He had also aided by continually endorsing the plan approved at the Hague Conference. In fact, in the spring of 1908 James B. Scott reported Root's hope that the permanent court would be established by the time of the third Hague assembly, which most men thought would be scheduled for 1915.[36]

Root's successor as Secretary of State continued the quest for a court. In April 1909, Philander C. Knox indicated that his department was exploring the proper channels by which the goal could be attained. Such action prompted further agitation from pacifists and internationalists. On June 28, Bartholdt introduced a concurrent resolution calling for a study

33. "The Senate and The Hague," *The Independent,* LXIV (March 19, 1908), 650; Richard W. Leopold, *Elihu Root and the Conservative Tradition,* pp. 58–59.

34. Philip Marshall Brown, *International Realities,* p. 41.

35. "The Arbitration Treaties," *The Independent,* LXIV (February 27, 1908), 478; "The Limits of Anglo-American Arbitration," *Living Age,* CCLVII (April 4, 1908), 53–55; New York *Times,* February 27, 1909; "The Optimist," *Christian Work,* LXXXVI (March 13, 1909), 347.

36. Scott, "Remarks," *Mohonk Report, 1908,* pp. 23–26; Holt, "How the Press May be Made a Greater Influence for Peace," *ibid.,* p. 157.

of the methods nations might follow in appointing judges and for the creation of a commission to explore the problem. Two valuable years had elapsed. Steps had to be taken to make the court a reality by 1915.[37]

Nothing developed from these efforts or from those on behalf of a maritime Prize Court. The London Naval Conference of 1908–1909 included in its final agreements provisions for such a body, but the failure of Great Britain to ratify the Declaration of London ended that dream.

Thus, despite modest gains, the efforts to supplement or consolidate the work of the Second Hague Conference did not proceed well in the years from 1907 to 1910. The goal of arbitration advanced in limited fashion in the form of the restricted treaties, the two courts came no closer to attainment, and efforts to formulate or codify law gained little support. Such men as Scott could speak in 1909 of "the triumph of the new diplomacy which seeks the settlement of international controversies by the appeal to reason, and which recognizes that permanent peace can only be based upon the principles of justice," but those noble words echoed against the barriers which the internationalists knew existed.[38]

These obstacles may have been a moderating influence; for the ideas of a periodic congress, of a union of English-speaking people, of a United States of Europe, and of a Pan-American federation found fewer advocates than in the years prior to 1907. At the Lake Mohonk sessions in 1908, at an Arbitration and Peace Congress in Philadelphia that same year, and at the Second National Peace Congress at Chicago in 1909, speakers referred to these proposals less than at meetings shortly before. The Mohonk platform especially reflected the change. Resolutions in 1906 and 1907 clearly endorsed a periodic congress. In 1908 the statements were so vague as to be meaningless.[39]

While the internationalists may have become more subdued, they did not abandon their quest. As idealists, they had no recourse other than to promote their ideals. Bridgman continued to emphasize the inevitability of the evolutionary process toward regular assemblies. A third Hague Conference could place the capstone on the developing peace structure. More

37. Knox to William I. Hull, April 17, 1909, Hull Papers; J. B. Scott, "America and the New Diplomacy," *International Conciliation,* No. 16 (March 1909), pp. 9–10; "A Supreme Court of the World," *The Outlook,* XCII (June 5, 1909), 313–315; "Mr. Bartholdt's Resolution in Congress," *Advocate of Peace,* LXXI (July 1909), 149; *Congressional Record,* 61 Cong., 1st sess., 44, pt. 4:3912.

38. Scott, "America and the New Diplomacy," p. 10.

39. "The Pennsylvania Arbitration and Peace Conference," *AJIL,* II (July 1908), 611–615; "Platform of the Pennsylvania Arbitration and Peace Congress," *Advocate of Peace,* LXX (July 1908), 161–162; *Mohonk Report, 1908,* pp. 7–8.

conservative thinkers like Scott agreed. The meetings at The Hague had made headway in preparing for a court, a legislature, and an executive.[40] A third gathering in 1915 might achieve agreement on regular congresses "thus raising the international and occasional conference to the dignity of an established institution." This in turn might bring "an international assembly capable of legislating ad referendum for the nations because composed of representatives of the nations." Scott, however, did not perceive such a body in the same light as did many internationalists. He thought more in terms of a diplomatic union in which governments would cooperate; he did not believe that a political federation would or could be attained.[41]

Nicholas Murray Butler also accepted the inevitability thesis. He saw "the political organization of the world" proceeding apace while men talked about it. While Butler continued to discuss the "federation of the world's legislatures," he, like Scott, believed in a limited body consultative in nature. He agreed with Root that "the public opinion of the world is the true international executive" and that no formal agency would be needed to enforce peace. Slowly, as the "high ethical and political ideals of civilized man assert themselves," he declared, nations would achieve a political organization. Americans should "lead in this undertaking" or "contribute powerfully toward it."[42]

This belief reflected the spirit of constructive internationalism which Bartholdt proclaimed in these years. In a resolution jointly sponsored by Senator McCreary, he called for the creation of a commission to study plans for international and judicial co-operation. Such a body would enable the United States to have a fully prepared agenda whenever the governments of the world might again choose to meet. All former presidents would automatically serve on it. The proposal, however, died in committee.[43]

While such men concentrated on the evolving Hague structure, a few Americans preached about a more advanced type of union. Carnegie re-

40. Bridgman, "The World's Legislature Is Here," *New England Magazine,* XXXVIII (May 1908), 355–361; Scott, "Recommendation for a Third Peace Conference," *AJIL,* II (October 1908), 821–822; Scott, "Some Subjects Likely to be Discussed at the Third Hague Peace Conference," *Proceedings,* Second National Peace Congress, 1909, pp. 240–241.

41. Scott, "Remarks," *Mohonk Report, 1908,* p. 23; Scott to Holt, September 21, 1909, Holt Papers.

42. Butler, "Opening Address . . . ," *Mohonk Report, 1909,* pp. 19–21; Root, "The Sanction of International Law," *AJIL,* II (July 1908), 452–455.

43. "Work for Our Ex-Presidents," *The Independent,* LXIV (February 13, 1908), 379–380; "Ex-Presidents as Peacemakers," *Advocate of Peace,* LXX (February 1908), 27–28; *Congressional Record,* 60 Cong., 1st sess., 42, pt. 1:843, 899.

mained the leader in proposing a league of peace, since he stimulated further consideration of the topic. In April of 1909, Carnegie presented his views to the New York Peace Society. Men had a duty "to urge in season and out of season the precious truth that lasting peace is only to be attained by an international league of peace, prepared, if necessary, to enforce peace among erring nations, as we enforce obedience to law among erring men; this league finally to be perfected by an international supreme court." The Society thus adopted a resolution "That in the League of Peace, suggested by the Prime Minister of Great Britain to the last Peace Conference in London, this Society sees the true and most feasible solution to the problem."[44]

Shortly thereafter, in sending his regrets at not being able to attend the Second National Peace Congress in Chicago, Carnegie observed that "a League of Peaceful Nations" would soon be attempted. His letter resulted in a resolution "that the nations of the world by joint agreement, by a league of peace among themselves," should bring an end to war.[45] This action prompted further comment, especially at the Lake Mohonk Conference and in the press.[46]

Carnegie's statements often contained a reference to force although he never elaborated upon the subject. Other sanctionists also remained ambiguous in their remarks. Richard Watson Gilder, the editor of *Century Magazine*, observed that an "armed peace" to prevent wars did not seem unreasonable. Neither was a "Supreme Court whose decrees would be enforced by the navies of the world." Even the *Advocate of Peace* in something of an aberration from its usual reluctance to approve of force agreed that when "such a world-league of peace is once formed,—and the day of its formation we do not believe to be very remote,—it will then be very easy for this great league, by a small international police or otherwise, to prevent any two members of the league from breaking the peace." Since the *Advocate of Peace* editorial insisted that all civilized nations be members, its suggestion would have virtually eliminated wars.[47]

44. Carnegie, "The Wrong Path," *Advocate of Peace,* LXXI (May 1909), 105; Short, "Peace Society of the City of New York," *ibid.,* (June 1909), p. 144. The reference is to Campbell-Bannerman.

45. *Proceedings,* Second National Peace Congress, 1909, pp. 487, 345.

46. S. T. Dutton, "The Need of More Effective Organization in the Peace Movement," *Mohonk Report, 1909,* pp. 27–28; William I. Buchanan, "Some Essentials of International Arbitration," *ibid.,* p. 127; "Mr. Carnegie and the Limitation of Armaments," *Spectator,* CIII (July 10, 1909), 52–53.

47. Gilder, "The Passing of War," *Mohonk Report, 1909,* p. 183; "A League of Peaceful Nations," *Advocate of Peace,* LXXI (May 1909), 98.

Spokesmen for nonpacific organizations had no qualms about endorsing force. The *Scientific American* noted that disarmament could not succeed without a court backed by an international army. The National Grange adopted a report from its Committee on International Peace in 1909 which called for effective action to achieve a "united world" under "a great world's court to settle international differences; an international police force to give effect to the decrees of this court; and the end of the burdens of armies and navies."[48]

Other advocates of sanctions presented their ideas. One novel proposal came from Theodore S. Woolsey, an authority on international law and a professor at Yale. Why not begin by keeping the peace at home in the Western Hemisphere, Woolsey asked? A concert of nations could maintain stability, promote trade, and protect the area against external threats. Such a coalition, Woolsey noted, had already begun. The Pan-American Conferences, the agreements between the Central American republics which had created a bureau and court, and the growing interest of the Latin American countries in arbitration pointed to some form of union and "an American police power in the hands of all the stable, responsible and orderly states of this hemisphere."[49]

Of the sanctionists, Mrs. Mead and Edwin Ginn remained the most consistent. Their main theme, presented in numerous articles and speeches, emphasized that power could not be ignored as a reality of international life. Therefore, it should be channeled to work for peace, not against it. Mrs. Mead favored a police agency and also suggested the use of non-intercourse against recalcitrant nations. Ginn proposed a disarmament system by which nations would contribute five to ten percent of their arms "to form an *International Guard* or *Police Force*." Governments would then no longer need to retain vast armies and navies, and they would then be ready to disarm.[50]

Another advocate of sanctions, Cyrus Street, presented his views

48. "To Keep the Peace," *Scientific American,* C (May 29, 1909), 402; "The Grange and Peace," *World Peace Foundation Pamphlets,* I (1913), 4, 8–9.

49. Woolsey, "An American Concert of the Powers," *Scribner's Magazine,* XLV (March 1909), 365–368.

50. L. A. Mead, "Armaments and Peace Forces Not Analogous," *Mohonk Report, 1908,* p. 172; L. A. Mead, "Some Common Fallacies," *Proceedings,* Second National Peace Congress, 1909, pp. 256–257; L. A. Mead, "The Next Step in the Organization of the World," *Christian Work,* LXXXV (November 28, 1908), 701–702; Ginn, "An International School of Peace," *Advocate of Peace,* LXXI (November 1909), 236; Dubin, "Collective Security," pp. 17–22.

publicly in September of 1908 in Council Bluffs, Iowa, and in November he published for the first time a small magazine entitled *The United Nations*. He first thought about an international organization around 1863 when he moved from Iowa to California, but he had done little to publicize his views. Street operated a real estate firm in San Francisco and served as the secretary and land officer of the Immigration Association of California.[51]

While the world was moving closer to the vision he had seen years before, Street still saw obstacles. Nations, however, should create an organization

vested with legislative, judicial and executive functions, with power to make, judge and execute laws; and to provide for the final disposal of all their armies and navies, and for any army and navy under the sole command of the UNITED NATIONS to *enforce* peace and prevent war *ever* occurring again.[52]

Street, like the other sanctionists, said little about operational details.

Of all the internationalists of the era, whether advocating a federation or a league of peace backed by an army, Hamilton Holt continued to be the most active. He showed no attachment to any single program. He co-operated with the evolutionists in seeking arbitration treaties, a court of justice, and periodic congresses. He advanced the federation idea by lecturing on the subject several hundred times between 1907 and 1910. He believed in the educational process and carried his messages to all areas of the nation. Finally, he endorsed a fully organized political structure with executive, judicial, and legislative functions. If sanctions were needed, he was for them.[53]

Another internationalist, William O. McDowell, was one of the few sanctionists to present his ideas in detail. He apparently converted the editor of the *Journal of American History*, Francis Trevelyan Miller, for the magazine dedicated one entire issue "to the United Nations of the World." Miller also printed McDowell's "First Draft of a Constitution for the United Nations of the World" and described it as "the germ which may

51. *Builders of a Great City, San Francisco's Representative Men*, II, 327–328; Street to Holt, July 14, 1910, Holt Papers.
52. *The United Nations*, I (November 1908), 1–4. I am indebted to Mr. John Murray of Los Angeles, who spent several years exploring Street's career. The only extant copies of his journal are in the Holt Papers, in the Los Angeles Public Library, and at the Bancroft Library at Berkeley. These bear various places of publication—Berkeley, Council Bluffs, and Aurora, Illinois.
53. Kuehl, *Hamilton Holt*, pp. 73–74, 90–93; "The International Parliament," *The Independent*, LXIII (September 26, 1907), 765–767; Holt, "A Great Work on Peace," *ibid.*, LXVII (September 9, 1909), 598–600.

be nurtured into one of the greatest documents in the annals of mankind." He hoped it might stimulate discussion and action, and a year later he indicated that the response had been "aggressive and healthful."[54]

McDowell paid great attention to details, but his constitution reflected his earlier ideas. He called for a three-branch government with power to act for the peace and welfare of mankind. The executive, or "Peacemaker," would be aided by five associates. One was to be a woman and the others would represent racial groups. He listed a cabinet of thirty-one officers, including secretaries for womanhood, childhood, the arts, religion, knowledge, original research, and peace. In discussing his judicial system, McDowell easily bridged the chasm over naming judges which had divided the Hague Conference. His "Peacemaker" would have all appointive authority subject to confirmation by the "United Parliaments."

There would be a limit on his government's powers since it would have no right to intrude in the internal affairs of states. It could, however, maintain a police force, outlaw and regulate the manufacturing of armaments, and abolish all national armies and navies. A "peace budget" would be levied against members on the basis of one tenth of one percent of their military allocations. Half of this amount would go to the United Nations and half to the contributing governments to be used for peaceful purposes. A fee upon interstate mail would also provide income. Details on a flag, an amending process, and on rules of procedure reveal the amount of thought McDowell devoted to his scheme.[55]

One other internationalist who appeared in the period under consideration merits study because of the radical nature of his proposals. Oscar T. Crosby published a plan in 1909 under the title, "The Constitution of the United States of the World." Crosby lived in Virginia where he enjoyed a reputation as an engineer, explorer, author, and businessman; and during the next decade he was to play an active role in efforts to achieve an organization.

Crosby perceived a trend toward brotherhood and unity despite emotions and national loyalties. Men should "give substance to the dream" by

54. [Miller], "Can the Nations of the World be United Under a Constitution? . . . ," *Journal of American History*, II (third quarter 1908), 533–534; [Miller], "America's Appeal for United Nations," *ibid.*, (fourth quarter 1908), p. 535; Miller, editorial preface, "America—Guardian of World Peace," *ibid.*, (first quarter 1909), p. 39.

55. McDowell, "First Draft of a Constitution for the United Nations of the World," *ibid.*, II (fourth quarter 1908), 537–542.

supporting a constitutional amendment to allow the creation of a confederation of states. In a draft resolution, Crosby presented the details for such
a body. It was much simpler than McDowell's, for Crosby called for an
international court as the operating center of his government. It could
determine its own procedures, set its budget, and use "violence by the armed
forces" available to it. It would hear cases between members and nonmembers, present its decisions, execute its decrees "by arms" if necessary,
aid members in suppressing rebellions, and "repel any attack, or . . . repress preparations therefore, by any state against any member-state." Despite Crosby's limited structure of government, he presented one of the
most radical proposals of his day. The court could conscript an army,
demand the abolition of armaments and fortifications, and then prevent the
rebuilding of any military units other than those needed for a nation's internal order or to maintain its colonial possessions.[56]

Another plan for an international force appeared in May 1909 from a
retired naval officer, Arthur H. Dutton. The answer to war and the clue to
disarmament lay in the creation of "an international army; a composite,
compact, thoroughly trained, well-equipped and mobile force." Each nation should contribute to it on the basis of its population until five hundred
thousand men were under arms. A naval force should also be formed, with
ten thousand men, a contingent of cruisers and gunboats, and a transport
fleet to move the army. Both of these units would be under the control of an
"International Court of Arbitration" and would be used "to compel obedience to its decrees," to uphold disarmament agreements, and to suppress
revolts. Dutton also considered minor problems of languages, finances, command, and an arms-inspection system.[57]

What impact these educational efforts, plans, and writings of the internationalists had upon the American mind in the months following the
Hague Conference of 1907 cannot be determined, but they kept alive more
ambitious ideas at a time when the primary emphasis tended to be on
arbitration and a slowly evolving Hague structure. Whether cautious or
advanced in their proposals, they persisted in their dream. Bartholdt felt
its presence when he observed that the American people liked the idea of
a world organization based upon law. It had been part of their experience.
Such remarks along with discussions of plans prompted one editorial writer

56. Crosby, *The Constitution of the United States of the World,* pp. 1–12.
57. Dutton, "National Disarmament and An International Army," *World To-Day,*
XVI (May 1909), 489–493.

to conclude in 1909 that the topics of "the federation of nations, and international parliaments and tribunals, are no longer debated with scholastic nicety as mere intellectual exercises; they are escaping from the academic into the practical sphere, and are being taken seriously by men of affairs."[58]

58. Richard Bartholdt, "Popularizing and Organizing the Peace Movement," *Proceedings,* Second National Peace Congress, 1909, p. 331; "The Peace Congress," *The Dial,* XLVI (May 16, 1909), 315. Many writers expressed the concept of a growing cosmopolitan spirit without emphasizing the need for a politically organized world. Paul Reinsch, "Interdependence *vs.* Independence of Nations," *Proceedings,* Second National Peace Congress, 1909, pp. 116–119; William I. Hull, "The Advance Registered by the Two Hague Conferences," *ibid.,* pp. 205–207; "An Age of Internationalism," *Review of Reviews,* XXXVI (November 1907), 528–529; Victor Duras, *Universal Peace,* pp. 7–8.

Aggressive
Revival

After nearly three years of sporadic and uncertain effort following the Second Hague Conference, the internationalists embarked upon two crusades in 1910 and 1911. First, they sought congressional approval of a resolution for a commission to explore the possibility of a world federation. Second, they joined in the struggle to advance arbitration through a series of treaties which they hoped might result in their eventual goal of union. In these undertakings, they achieved a notable first by organizing for the first time. Thus they no longer preached their message in totally disorganized fashion.

The background of their activities can be found in their efforts to interest Theodore Roosevelt in an international organization. He occupied a position of exceptional prominence in the world of his day. Moreover, he possessed an ability to dramatize or popularize issues. Even more important, as president he had revealed considerable interest in the maintenance of peace as his actions in referring disputes to the Hague court, his cautious endorsement of limited arbitration treaties, his efforts to settle the touchy Moroccan question in 1905, and his offer of good offices in 1905 in the Russo-Japanese War revealed.

Roosevelt, however, proved to be an immense challenge to the internationalists. Carnegie had often told him about the need for a league and asked Roosevelt to contact the German Kaiser about erasing dangers of war.

Roosevelt at times expressed his displeasure at Carnegie's irrational enthusiasm, but he did not ignore the latter's ideas, as his references to an international police force disclose.[1]

Holt's *Independent* also sought to convince Roosevelt that destiny summoned him to be a peacemaker. And it was in *The Independent* in 1909 that Henry Granger, a New York mining engineer, called upon Roosevelt to become the first "World President" under a league. An international conference, said Granger, could draft a constitution, form an armed force, and, with Roosevelt as leader, attain peace and prosperity. As Granger noted, Roosevelt's prestige, popularity, and abilities would make him the one man acceptable to everyone.[2]

The Independent hastened to endorse Granger's proposition, and in the New York Peace Society the internationalist-minded members pondered what they could do to promote this scheme. They began by reprinting two thousand copies of Granger's article and *The Independent's* editorial and circulating these at the Chicago Peace Congress and the Mohonk Conference in 1909. Later that summer, at Carnegie's urging, the Society distributed three thousand additional copies, and as a result of these activities a group of dedicated adherents decided to organize.[3]

The men who assembled had an intense interest in international organization. Several of them—Holt, Walter John Bartnett, William H. Short, and Oscar T. Crosby—had already devoted their energies to that cause. They were joined by John Temple Graves, the editor of the New York *American*, F. Milton Willis, a poet, and Judge George M. Nelson. They organized the World-Federation League and elected Holt president. Shortly thereafter, they persuaded Bartholdt to accept a title as honorary vice-president.[4]

1. Carnegie to Roosevelt, August 27, 1906, February 14, 1907, May 12, November 15, 1908, Roosevelt Papers, Library of Congress; Burton J. Hendrick, *The Life of Andrew Carnegie,* II, 305–307, 324–325; Dubin, "Collective Security," pp. 30–33; Roosevelt to Carnegie, August 6, 1906; to Arthur Spring Rice, July 1, 1907, in Morison, *Letters,* V, 345, 699.

2. "Mr. Roosevelt: Past and to Come," *The Independent,* LVII (November 17, 1904), 1162–1163; "Theodore Roosevelt, Peacemaker," *ibid.,* LIX (September 7, 1905), 584; "Washington and the World's Peace," *ibid.,* LXI (February 22, 1906), 460–461; "Theodore Roosevelt's Great Opportunity," *ibid.,* LXII (January 10, 1907), 103–104; Granger, "Roosevelt—A Suggestion," *ibid.,* LXVI (April 22, 1909), 853–854.

3. "The Task of Mr. Roosevelt," *ibid.,* (April 29, 1909), p. 927; *Minutes,* Executive Committee, April 30, 1909, NYPS Papers; Holt, "Practical Next Steps for Peace," *Mohonk Report, 1909,* pp. 122–123; Short, "Peace Society of the City of New York," *Advocate of Peace,* LXXI (July 1909), 167–168.

4. Kuehl, *Hamilton Holt,* p. 78; "A Commission on World-Federation," *Christian Work,* LXXXIX (July 23, 1910), 107.

This league sought, not to change existing nations or to intrude upon their domestic concerns, but "only to lessen the occasions of war" and to hasten "the day of establishment of *some* form of central government empowered to keep the peace." This vague statement appealed to all internationalists since it left the type of structure undefined. But the members of the World-Federation League had organized as an action body and not as a study group. Hence, they drafted a joint resolution to send to Congress. Its introductory sections noted the growing ties of communication and understanding and the need to "give public expression to a form of articles of International Federation" for transmittal to other countries. It then called for the presidential appointment of a commission of five men instructed to act in three ways.

FIRST: To urge upon the attention of other Governments the fact that relief from the heavy burden of military expenditures and from the disasters of war can best be obtained by the establishment of an International Federation.

SECONDLY: To report to Congress, as soon as practicable, a draft of articles of a Federation limited to the maintenance of peace, through the establishment of a Court having power to determine by decree all controversies between nations and to enforce execution of its decrees by the arms of the Federation . . . and controlled solely by it.

THIRDLY: To consider and report upon any other means to diminish the expenses of Government for military purposes and to lessen the probabilities of war.

In an explanatory statement, the League suggested that the world body and its authority could be obtained through the further development of the Hague Conferences and court. With grants of power, those agencies could perform legislative and judicial functions and thus be able "to settle *all* controversies between nations." It would even have at its disposal "an armed force to execute" the decrees of the judges. It suggested the names of Roosevelt, Carnegie, Root, Joseph H. Choate, and Bartholdt, as possible commissioners.[5]

An intensive propaganda campaign late in 1909 and early in 1910 sought to prepare the way for congressional action. Both *The Independent* and Graves's New York *American* promoted the scheme; and since the latter journal was part of the Hearst chain, other newspapers in that network supported it. Bartnett wrote articles for the New York *Tribune* and the New York *Evening Post*; and on January 16, the New York *Times* published an interview with Representative James A. Tawney, Republican of Minnesota, in which he called for a "world-wide federation" to insure peace. Finally, on

5. *World-Federation League*, undated leaflet, Holt Papers.

April 5, Bartholdt introduced the resolution which called for "the appointment of a commission to draft articles of international federation, and for other purposes."[6]

This proposal went to the House Committee on Foreign Affairs, and while it awaited action an event of importance occurred when Theodore Roosevelt, on May 5, addressed the Nobel Peace Committee and discussed a league. Roosevelt had not been able to deliver such a speech in 1906 when he had received the award, for he had then been occupied with his presidential duties. In 1909, however, he had embarked upon a hunting expedition in Africa and then planned a tour of Europe. He had accepted several speaking engagements but had refused an invitation from the Nobel Committee. Carnegie had learned that members of the Committee felt offended and that Roosevelt's attitude might prejudice them in the future against American nominees.[7]

To prevent such an unfortunate situation, Carnegie cabled Roosevelt, and the latter agreed to speak. Hoping he could also influence what Roosevelt might say, Carnegie enlisted Holt's aid. Carnegie sent Roosevelt an editorial from *The Independent,* and Roosevelt apparently used it as an outline for his address. Holt suggested that Roosevelt act vigorously by advocating a court of justice similar to that of the Supreme Court of the United States. He should also call for arbitration treaties which guaranteed the "territorial integrity and sovereignty" of the signatories and which agreed to arbitrate all questions except those involving national honor. Holt ended his editorial with the usual plea of the internationalists. Roosevelt should call attention to the fact that a "United Nations" could be achieved by developing "the Hague Court into a real international court, the recurring Hague Conferences into an international legislature, and then adding an international executive, should one be deemed necessary."[8]

Holt's words reflected the sincere desire of the World-Federation League men to have Roosevelt head the commission they hoped to see formed. They

6. [William Hayes Ward], "Work for Roosevelt," *The Independent,* LXVIII (February 3, 1910), 278–279. Many of the articles and editorials appear in a 128-page booklet, *The Peace Movement: The Federation of the World,* printed by the World-Federation League, pp. 44–49, 68–70, 89–98, 104–106, 119–121; *Congressional Record,* 61 Cong., 2d sess., 45, pt. 4:4310.

7. Herbert H. D. Pence to Carnegie, February 8, 1909, Roosevelt Papers. The above and following account of Roosevelt's Christiania address are based upon Ruhl Bartlett, *The League to Enforce Peace,* pp. 26–27, and Kuehl, *Hamilton Holt,* pp. 75–77.

8. [Holt], "Mr. Roosevelt at Christiania," *The Independent,* LXVIII (February 17, 1910), 376–377.

recognized the former president as a powerful figure, but even he could not have performed all the tasks they set for him. Holt alone at one time suggested he serve as a delegate to the Pan-American Conference in 1910, attend the third Hague Conference, "visit the chancelleries of the principal nations," prepare to lead the peace movement, and "bring the nations under a federal law made, executed, adjudicated and sanctioned by the peoples of the world."[9]

The World-Federation League men received momentary encouragement, however, when they read Roosevelt's speech before the French Academy at the Sorbonne on April 23. He admitted there that a statesman had a duty to find "some other agency for force in the settlement of international disputes." Shortly thereafter Roosevelt wrote Carnegie that what he would say to the Nobel Committee would "represent very nearly all that is efficient and useful that I can accomplish."[10] At Christiania, Norway, he suggested the adoption of arbitration treaties covering all subjects except national honor. He presented Holt's arguments for strengthening the international tribunal along lines similar to those of the Supreme Court, and he referred to the United States Constitution as a model for "a species of world federation for international peace and justice." He closed his address with an appeal and a proposal. Governments should seek disarmament, and the "great Powers" should "form a League of Peace, not only to keep the peace among themselves, but to prevent, by force if necessary, its being broken by others." He noted the lack of any genuine executive or sanctions to uphold the decisions of the court and called attention to the need for individual governments to maintain their own defenses "until the establishment of some form of international police power, competent and willing to prevent violence as between nations." A combination of the larger countries could perform this task, Roosevelt declared, and the statesman who would act to create "such a combination would have earned his place in history for all time and his title to the gratitude of all mankind."[11]

The members of the World-Federation League hailed these words. Roosevelt, said Holt, had endorsed all that *The Independent* had ever advocated. The world was ready for federation now that it had a man of Roosevelt's caliber ready to act. Crosby also praised the address. With "Roosevelt's explosive and near-belligerent leadership," the accomplishments of the

---

9. [Holt], "Work for a Nobel Prize Winner," *ibid.*, (February 24, 1910), pp. 429–430.

10. Roosevelt, "Duties of the Citizen," *ibid.*, (April 28, 1910), pp. 900–901; Roosevelt to Carnegie, April 22, 1910, Morison, *Letters*, VII, 75.

11. "International Peace," *Works of Theodore Roosevelt*, XVI, 305–319.

proposed commission would be startling if he would assume its leadership.[12]

The general response to Roosevelt's suggestions also seemed favorable. *Christian Work*, the New York *Tribune*, the St. Louis *Star*, *The Nation*, and *The Chautauquan* found nothing irrational in his words. Even *The Outlook*, which generally held that moral force would be sufficient to uphold the decisions of international courts, agreed "absolutely and without qualification with the principles" in the speech. Three or four major powers in a new holy alliance could prevent wars. Only the *Advocate of Peace* sounded a pessimistic note. Such a league could hardly materialize, it declared. Developments would more likely be in accord with past achievements and along "purely pacific lines."[13]

The time of Roosevelt's speech proved to be especially convenient for the World-Federation League, since two days later, on May 7, 1910, the House Foreign Affairs Committee held a hearing on Bartholdt's resolution. Under the friendly chairmanship of David J. Foster of Vermont, the leaders of the League had a chance to testify. Crosby sought to convince the congressmen that there was nothing visionary in the proposal to create a world federation. The idea was old; it was time to act. The plan would obligate no one since the commission would only study and make recommendations. Any detailed project for a union would be submitted to governments for analysis and amendment. In this way, an acceptable and workable constitution could be created. Representative John N. Garner of Texas wanted to know the cost and time involved in the study, to which Crosby replied that such matters could be left to others.

When Representative J. Sloat Fassett of New York suggested cutting out the sections on federation, Crosby argued that the main aim was "to place finally before the world" this idea and to commit the United States to that goal. Fassett observed in friendly fashion that this provision actually determined what the verdict should be before the jury was chosen and noted that the commission should be free to reach its own conclusions. He sug-

12. [Holt], "The Federation of the World," *ibid.*, pp. 1043–1044; Crosby to the editor, New York *Times*, May 14, 1910.

13. "Ex-President Roosevelt and International Peace," *Christian Work*, LXXXVIII (May 21, 1910), 679–680; "Mr. Roosevelt's Recipe for International Peace," *Literary Digest*, XL (May 14, 1910), 961–962; St. Louis *Star*, May 5, 1910; *The Nation*, XC (May 12, 1910), 471–472; "Mr. Roosevelt's Peace Plans . . . ," *The Chautauquan*, LIX (July 1910), 175–177; "A Holy Alliance," *The Outlook*, XCV (May 7, 1910), 12–13; "Ex-President Roosevelt's Nobel Peace Prize Address," *Advocate of Peace*, LXXII (June 1910), 122.

gested that it be authorized to investigate and report upon any means to diminish war.

Crosby sought to stand firm on the point of federation, but he committed a strategic error. In trying to convince the congressmen that the idea of federation was essential, he argued that regardless of the commission's instructions it would undoubtedly recommend that course of action. Republican Representative Edwin Denby of Michigan noted that since Crosby seemed so certain of the outcome he could not object to Fassett's suggestion. Further questions revealed another obstacle when Denby inquired about the powers of the commission and what its relation would be to the secretary of state. Congress did not wish to usurp any of the authority delegated to that department. Crosby left the stand shaken and admitting a willingness to accept the half-loaf of an uninstructed commission.[14]

Holt followed Crosby as a witness. He insisted that a world federation offered mankind the best hope for peace, that events had moved far toward that goal, and that Congress now had a momentous opportunity. He opposed any change in the resolution and cited Roosevelt's address of two days before to indicate the popularity of the proposition. A commission would, he noted, enable the United States to have a fully planned agenda for the anticipated third Hague Conference. He sought to dismiss any concern over its powers by noting that the commissioners would be authorized only to inquire, to discuss, and to report. He again referred to Roosevelt's closing words to indicate that the former president would be compelled to serve as chairman and that this would insure success. He ended with a positive assertion that peace would come only through a federation

entered into by agreement, in which there will be some sort of an international legislature to make the laws, courts to interpret them, and international police to enforce them. That is the only practical way to obtain peace and disarmament. We must organize the world.[15]

Other witnesses included Professor Ernst Richard of Columbia University, who introduced a supporting statement from the two-million-member German-American Alliance, and Charles T. Root, the publisher of *Iron Age*. Richard noted that trends toward world federation, while Root emphasized how valuable it would be to support a definite and constructive peace

14. House Committee on Foreign Affairs, *Hearing on International Federation for the Maintenance of Peace,* 61 Cong., 2d sess., May 7, 1910, pp. 1–11.
15. *Ibid.,* pp. 11–15.

program. Judge Nelson, Urbain J. Ledoux representing Ginn's International School of Peace, and Philadelphia businessman William S. Harvey also testified. Several times the congressmen returned to the subject of the commission's authority and the wisdom of committing it in advance to what it should report. The hearing ended with an appeal by Crosby that "the word 'federation' in any general wreck which may befall the clauses as drawn shall be saved."[16]

The World-Federation League advocates now realized that Bartholdt's resolution had to overcome the obstacles of both tradition and practical politics. Therefore, they sought to strengthen its chances in every possible way. For one thing, they continued to negotiate personally with the members of the House Foreign Affairs Committee. They also knew that Roosevelt's Christiania address was the weightiest argument on their side, and Holt persuaded Representative Foster to introduce into the *Congressional Record* his *Independent* editorial of May 12, 1910. Edwin Mead aided by obtaining a resolution of endorsement in the platform of the New England Arbitration and Peace Congress which met at Hartford, Connecticut, from May 8–11. Finally, President Taft felt the pressure from the federationists. They apparently arranged for him to meet with the members of the House Foreign Affairs Committee, and there Taft announced that he favored the resolution and hoped to appoint Roosevelt chairman.[17]

On June 4, the House Committee presented its report in the form of H.J. Resolution 223 offered by William S. Bennet of New York. It authorized the appointment of a commission of five men

to consider the expediency of utilizing existing international agencies for the purpose of limiting the armaments of the nations of the world by international agreement, and of constituting the combined navies of the world in an international force for the preservation of universal peace, and to consider and report upon any other means to diminish the expenditures of government for military purposes and to lessen the probabilities of war.[18]

This proposal eliminated all reference to world federation; hence, it reflected only in small measure the desires of the men who had sponsored

16. *Ibid.*, pp. 15–27.

17. New York *Tribune*, May 8, 1910; Holt to Crosby, May 5, 14, 1910, Crosby Papers, Library of Congress; David J. Foster to Holt, May 14, 1910, Holt Papers; *Congressional Record*, 61 Cong., 2d sess., 45, pt. 6:6315; *Report*, Proceedings, New England Arbitration and Peace Congress, 1910, p. 113; Short, "The New York Peace Society," *Advocate of Peace*, LXXII (June 1910), 148; New York *Times*, June 3, 1910.

18. *Congressional Record*, 61 Cong., 2d sess., 45, pt. 7:7432, pt. 8:8545.

Bartholdt's resolution. They saw in the last phrase, however, some chance that their hopes might be realized. They liked the clause on disarmament, too, since that had been one of their underlying aims, and Bennet had introduced another resolution on March 10 which had called for an international conference to discuss the limitation of arms. They also supported the suggestion to combine the navies into a police force. Granger had proposed such in his article, and World-Federation League publications had endorsed the idea. Representative Bennet had reflected such publicity in a resolution he introduced on March 30 calling for such action.[19] All these suggestions had now been incorporated into one bill.

The World-Federation League supporters and other internationalists, through articles, editorials, and pamphlets, sought to convince congressmen and the American people that the Bennet measure would lead to a world federation. They felt assured of House passage, but to insure favorable action in the Senate, the New York Peace Society sent nearly five thousand letters to prominent persons and periodicals requesting them to use their influence in support of the proposal.[20]

The House on June 20, operating under the rule of unanimous consent, approved Bennet's resolution with only an added proviso that the commission should report within two years and that its expenditures should not exceed ten thousand dollars. This seemed a small sum compared to the appropriations for armaments, but the congressmen had been assured that any expense would be met from unnamed sources outside the government. On June 24, with the Senate acting as a committee of the whole, Henry Cabot Lodge introduced the measure and it passed without debate.[21] This action reflected in part the growing spirit of internationalism, but it revealed even more a growing concern over armaments. Bartholdt's resolution and the proposals of the World-Federation League gained much of their prominence

19. *Congressional Record*, 61 Cong., 2d sess., 45, pt. 4:4025. The combined resolutions had originally been H. Res. 553, H. Con. Res. 36 and 45, H.J. Res. 187. They became H.J. Res. 223. A special report, "Universal Peace," included extracts from Roosevelt's Nobel Address, a dialogue between Bennet and Fassett from the *Congressional Record*, and an article by Holt, "The Federation of the World." House *Report* No. 1440.

20. Holt, "The Federation of the World," *The Survey*, XXIV (June 11, 1910), 432–434, appeared in many newspapers as a syndicated item. Short, "Work of the New York Peace Society for June," *Advocate of Peace*, LXXII (July and August 1910), 177. A copy of Short's letter dated June 21 is in the Fannie Fern Andrews Papers. The World-Federation League sent out 4,971 reprints of Holt's *Survey* article, including 3,989 to magazines and newspapers. Short to Crosby, June 29, 1910, NYPS Papers.

21. *Congressional Record*, 61 Cong., 2d sess., 45, pt. 8:8542, 8545–8547, 8713, 8874.

because they appeared at the same time as an administration proposal for substantial increases for naval construction. Many congressmen reflected the concern of their constituents when they accepted even impractical suggestions which might block the trend toward greater and greater armaments.

Almost immediately the internationalists began a campaign to persuade Roosevelt to head the commission and to get Taft to name the other four members. Virtually all of Roosevelt's statements pointed to an acceptance, and commentators agreed that he would be an excellent choice and that the commission's task was a realistic one. Roosevelt, however, seemed to be in demand, for other men also had tasks for him. Democratic Representative Joseph T. Robinson of Arkansas introduced a resolution which asked Congress to appropriate half a million dollars and invite parliamentarians everywhere to an assembly in the United States. Robinson set no time for the meeting, but speculation immediately began that Roosevelt should serve as its presiding officer with title as "president" of the world's parliaments. With such activity, it is understandable that the *Christian Work* predicted that "internationalism is to be the great achievement of this century."[22]

But such optimism soon faded when Roosevelt refused to assume the hero role thrust upon him. Taft discussed the subject of the commission with Roosevelt, found him interested and willing to offer suggestions, but he would not serve. The President then explored the possibility of naming Carnegie, William Jennings Bryan, J. P. Morgan, and the New York banker James Speyer, but Taft considered the chairmanship as the most important position and refused to act until he had filled it.[23]

Holt obtained interviews with both Roosevelt and Taft in the hope that he could break the impasse, but he made no headway. Roosevelt insisted it would be futile to continue to advance his name. He pledged Holt to secrecy on the reasons for his refusal, but he apparently pleaded a lack of time and stated his belief that the venture was hopeless. His recent talks with the heads of European countries, especially the Kaiser, had convinced him that nothing could be gained.[24]

22. Bennet to Holt (telegram), June 24, 1910, Holt Papers; New York *Times*, June 30, 1910; "The Commission for World Peace," *Advocate of Peace*, LXXII (July and August 1910), 153; "America's Official Peace Commission," *The Chautauquan*, LX (September 1910), 5–6; New York *Times*, July 3, 1910; "A Commission on World-Federation," p. 107.

23. Taft to Bartholdt, July 3; to Philander Knox, July 7; to Carnegie, June 30; to William Barnes, June 30, 1910, Taft Papers, Library of Congress.

24. Kuehl, *Hamilton Holt*, pp. 84–85; Roosevelt to Holt, July 15, Roosevelt Papers; Holt to Short, July 15, NYPS Papers; Roosevelt to Sir George Trevelyan, October 1, 1911, Morison, *Letters*, VII, 377–379, 398.

Graves, Bartnett, and Holt, however, did not abandon hope. Their editorials and articles tried to rally popular support behind the commission, and in a lengthy essay in the *North American Review* Holt explored fully the subject of a world federation. He traced the historical progress toward greater co-operation, noted the growing acceptance of the idea of an international organization, and concluded that the peace commission could take the next step by recommending a plan of action. It could succeed in its aim of combining the navies into an effective force only after a league existed which could compel nations to settle their disputes by judicial process. A federation, therefore, would be the only practical recommendation the commission could make.[25]

Holt took advantage of the opportunity to do some rethinking about his own and other men's proposals for an effective association. He reviewed Bartholdt's ideas of 1905 which the Interparliamentary Union had considered, Carnegie's rectorial address of 1905, a suggestion of José Batlle y Ordóñez of Uruguay at the Second Hague Conference, and Roosevelt's ideas expressed in his Christiania speech. He found several points in common, especially their emphasis upon justice, a court system, sanctions, and their agreement on the need for a league. He perceived danger, however, in any organization which sought to prevent war by utilizing force too much. "Constitutional safeguards" needed to be incorporated into any plan to prevent oppressive action. Three propositions, he declared, might serve as the basis of a league built upon principles of right.

1. Each nation in the League to respect the sovereignty and territorial integrity of the others.
2. The armies and navies of the members of the League to be at its service to enforce the decrees of the International Tribunal in all questions that the members of the League previously agree to refer to arbitration.
3. The armies and navies of the League to sustain any member of the League in a dispute with an outside nation which refuses to arbitrate.[26]

The federationists did not confine themselves to writing. They gained an endorsement of the commission at the Universal Peace Congress in Sweden

25. [Graves], "Peace and the American Peace Commission," New York *American*, August 17, 1910; Bartnett, "Recent Progress in the Peace Movement," Boston *Herald*, September 23, 1910; [Holt], "An American Peace Commission," *The Independent*, LXVIII (June 30, 1910), 1455–1456; [Holt], "The Problems Before the Peace Commission," *ibid.*, LXIX (July 14, 1910), 93–95; Holt, "The United States Peace Commission," *North American Review*, CXCII (September 1910), 301–316. The World-Federation League distributed these and other articles in two booklets, *The Federation of the World* and *The American Peace Commission*.
26. Holt, "The United States Peace Commission," pp. 311–315.

that summer which represented the views of six hundred delegates. Bartholdt drafted a resolution for the Interparliamentary Union meeting which called for a plan of federation with judicial, legislative, and executive powers and which further requested co-operative action on the part of other governments in naming commissions similar to that of the United States. In this way, the world would be prepared for the third Hague Conference. The internationalists also continued to badger Taft about appointments, and they grew increasingly strident as the weeks passed. Taft and members of the State Department, however, cautioned patience. They apparently hoped that the commission could achieve its results without Roosevelt if they could find the proper persons.[27]

The plan, however, soon hit a major snag in the persons of Nicholas Murray Butler and Elihu Root. They met in mid-August at The Hague, discussed the idea, and concluded "that there was serious danger in it for the prestige & influence of the country." They felt uncertain as to what the commissioners would do, feared that their tasks were ambiguous, and worried that as representatives of the United States they might make their government appear ridiculous. The two men informed Taft of their views and suggested that he first sound out official attitudes before he made any appointments.[28]

Holt learned of this opposition in a conversation with Root and shortly thereafter tried to convince Butler that he and Root did not understand the purpose or function of the proposed body. It would not commit or embarrass the government because it would be entirely advisory. Butler, however, did not agree. He argued that European conditions were in a state of delicate balance which could be upset by inquiring Americans. Also, currents were already moving in a desirable direction. Butler informed Taft that he had taken a careful measure of European leaders and views and discovered that the time was inopportune for the proposed commission to act.[29]

Secretary of State Knox heeded the advice of Root and Butler. He wrote ten governments, and the exchange of letters, which took time, prompted concern among the World-Federation League men. They thus continued their efforts to arouse public opinion and to exert pressure upon administra-

27. "Growth of the World Peace Idea," *Review of Reviews*, XLII (September 1910), 285; "More Peace Commissions," *The Independent*, LXIX (September 1, 1910), 499–500; Holt to Taft, July 26; World-Federation League to Taft, (copy), July 11, 1910, Holt Papers; Holt to Short, August 5, 1910, NYPS Papers; Huntington Wilson (Acting Secretary of State) to Crosby, August 4, 1910, Crosby Papers.

28. Root to Taft, August 20, 1910, Taft Papers.

29. Holt to Butler, October 31; Butler to Holt, November 3, 1910, Butler Papers; Butler to Taft, November 5, 1910, Taft Papers.

tive leaders, especially Root and Knox. Early in 1911 Crosby invited thirty-five senators and congressmen to dinner to discuss the commission. At the Third National Arbitration and Peace Congress at Baltimore in May 1911, the subject arose a number of times in speeches, and the delegates eventually approved a resolution calling upon Taft to act in appointing the five men.[30]

A less concerted drive appeared in the attempt to persuade foreign governments to create similar commissions. As Secretary of the New York Peace Society, Short had spent much of the summer of 1910 in Europe discussing the idea, and in the spring of 1911 the World-Federation League considered sending representatives abroad to stimulate official interest. The League also kept in touch with Senator Henri La Fontaine of Belgium, the head of the Permanent International Peace Bureau in Berne, Switzerland, and that agency sought to influence favorable European replies to the official inquiries from the United States. Other European pacifists, notably the Baroness von Suttner and W. T. Stead, followed all action regarding the Bennet measure, with Stead and other writers virtually demanding action in England. Perhaps these voices stimulated a response, for in March the House of Commons approved a resolution, 276 to 56, in favor of an international naval force.[31]

All these efforts failed, however. The peace commission died, for Taft followed the advice of Butler and Root and never appointed the five men. An unsigned State Department memorandum in summarizing the replies from the powers stated that, despite expressions of interest, governments had "considerable hesitation" about participating. Under the circumstances, it seemed unwise to proceed. The last official action came in June of 1912 when Bartholdt obtained congressional approval of a bill extending the life of the proposed commission another two years.[32]

30. Taft to Holt, December 23, 1910, Taft Papers; *Minutes*, Executive Committee, NYPS, November 2, 1910, NYPS Papers; "A Great Opportunity Neglected," *Advocate of Peace*, LXXII (November 1910), 229–230; "The Commission on Armaments," *ibid.*, (December 1910), p. 257; D. S. Jordan to Butler, December 24, 1910, CEIP Papers; [Gustav Stickley], "Peace: By the Editor," *Craftsman*, XIX (December 1910), 225–229; "Brevities," *Advocate of Peace*, LXXIII (April 1911), 79; Eugene A. Noble (ed.), *Proceedings*, Third American Peace Congress, p. 387.

31. New York *Sun*, April 27, 1911; Suttner, *Memoirs*, I, vi–vii; Stead, "England's Lost Leadership of Peace," *Contemporary Review*, XCIX (February 1911), 222–230; "The Peace Policy of President Taft," *Living Age*, CCLXVIII (February 11, 1911), 372; "A Review of the World," *Current Literature*, L (May 1911), 466. There is evidence that other European governments considered the subject. A. Shadwell, "Is Peace Possible?" *Nineteenth Century*, LXXXIV (July 1918), 20.

32. Taft to Fiorello H. LaGuardia, January 15, 1919; Unsigned State Department Memorandum dated June 2, 1911, Taft Papers; "Brief Peace Notes," *Advocate of Peace*, LXXIV (July 1912), 161.

While the world may not have been ready for the ambitious project contemplated by the Bennet resolution, a case can be made for the other side. In the first place, the replies the State Department received could have been interpreted in more optimistic fashion. None of the ten powers flatly refused to co-operate; three expressed a willingness to discuss the matter; two wished to be kept informed; three doubted that practical results could be attained; one called the resolution "too vague"; and one did not fully respond. Second, no query reached the lesser nations of Europe or Latin America, where friendly attitudes prevailed. Indeed, a number of governments felt offended that they had not been consulted, for they wished to co-operate.[33] Finally, one wonders what the results would have been if Knox had interpreted the replies in a fashion similar to that of Secretary of State Hay when he proclaimed the assent of nations to his first "Open Door" notes. Had Taft announced a favorable response and named an American commission, other countries would have been forced to follow suit. The subsequent discussions would not have led to disarmament, an international navy, or a world federation, but they might have prompted consideration of these subjects in official circles. Statesmen might then have been better prepared to explore them in 1918–1919 and arrive at a more intelligent arrangement than the one which emerged at Paris at that time.

The conservative views of Root and Butler also merit examination, although Root did not influence the outcome as much as Butler. Root served on the Senate Foreign Relations Committee which reported the measure favorably, and he voiced no opposition during the formal vote. He could have blocked, or at least altered, the proposal in committee. Butler's advice, therefore, carried more weight when he warned Taft not to proceed. He did not recall his role too accurately in later years when in 1938 he described the Bennet resolution as remarkable in its vision. He remembered discussing the commission with European statesmen, but he incorrectly observed that Taft had asked him to undertake that task because "ordinary diplomatic channels" could not be used.[34]

It seems, therefore, that Butler and the State Department assumed much of the function which the commission would have performed had it been appointed. Their queries were little different from those the commis-

33. Belva A. Lockwood to Taft, February 25, 1911, Taft Papers; to Root, March 24, 1911, CEIP Papers; Department of State Archives, file 500a 166 1/2 contains replies which reveal a favorable response. National Archives, Washington, D.C.

34. Butler, "The United States Must Lead," *Vital Speeches of the Day*, IV (August 1, 1938), 623–624; Butler, "Wait and See," *ibid.*, V (November 15, 1938), 85–86.

sioners would have asked. The conclusions, however, might have been quite different. The commissioners would have reflected a broader internationalist view than that of Butler and Root.

The efforts related to the Bennet resolution were not the only ones of the world-organization advocates in 1910 and 1911. They also sought arbitration treaties broader in scope than those approved under Roosevelt and Root. An increasing number of persons questioned the traditional arrangement that exempted questions of vital interests and national honor, since only the country involved could determine what subjects were vital or the degree to which honor or independence was threatened.[35] Moreover, nations could use these exclusions to avoid bringing certain disputes before the world for settlement. The North Carolina Arbitration and Peace League and even Theodore Roosevelt observed that every effort should be made "to secure agreements with all the governments to respect each other's territory and sovereignty and to arbitrate all other questions."[36]

While most internationalists favored broader accords, they supported any type of agreement. They realized that every treaty moved the world toward a more complete state of co-operation and a greater degree of justice and respect for law. Since these last two principles were vital to any workable organization, it was important to encourage them. Also, a future league could be built upon a web of agreements involving many governments. It was part of that evolutionary process at work. Hamilton Holt expressed it succinctly when he stated that first Congress should approve an arbitration treaty with Great Britain, "second, the League of Peace; third, the Federation of the World."[37]

Two events late in 1909 and early in 1910 stimulated the renewed interest in arbitration. First, Secretary Knox suggested on October 18 that the proposed Prize Court, which had been discussed since the last Hague Conference, be imbued with powers that would make it the genuine judicial body endorsed in 1907. Then, on March 22, 1910, President Taft, in an address before the American Peace and Arbitration League in New York

35. Scrapbooks of clippings for 1909 and 1910 compiled by H. C. Phillips, the secretary of the Lake Mohonk Conferences, reveal the changing attitudes, Mohonk Papers. "Broader Arbitration Treaties," *The Independent*, LXVI (May 13, 1909), 1036–1037.

36. "President Roosevelt and the Navy," *The Independent*, LXV (July 30, 1908), 275–276; Roosevelt to Hayne Davis, May 30, 1908, cited in *Congressional Record*, 61 Cong., 2d sess., 45, pt. 9:330–338.

37. "New England Peace Congress," *Advocate of Peace*, LXXII (June 1910), 123; *Mohonk Report, 1910*, p. 156; Holt, "Universal Peace," *Cosmopolitan Magazine*, LI (August 1911), 291.

City, shocked his listeners by suggesting that all disputes, without exception, be settled by arbitration.[38]

Arbitrationists and internationalists acclaimed his leadership, became bolder in their advocacy of unlimited treaties, and began to urge action in the form of an agreement with some friendly government.[39] Taft responded by negotiating two trial treaties with Great Britain and France. According to the provisions, all justiciable disputes were to be arbitrated and all other questions were to be referred to a six-man joint high commission of inquiry. The latter would decide whether the case was judicial in nature and hence subject to arbitration or whether it should be settled in some other way. Five members of the commission had to agree before they could present their decision.

Taft realized that the Senate could be an obstacle, so he had consulted with senators in drafting the treaty in the hope that a form could be found which would be acceptable. Chances for approval thus seemed better than any previous time. Editorials and committees of influential citizens voiced their support, and the sessions of the Third National Arbitration and Peace Congress in May of 1911 proved to be a focal point of popular agitation. In mid-June, some twenty peace and arbitration societies united in a joint endorsement of the treaties.[40]

But by August 3, when the governments formally signed the documents, voices of opposition had been heard. The most influential critic proved to be the unpredictable Roosevelt. He expressed his opinion even before he knew the exact provisions, noting that it would be absurd to agree to arbitrate all questions when the American people would never settle certain matters in this way. If the nation were attacked or if honor or independence

38. "Secretary Knox and International Unity," *AJIL*, IV (January 1910), 180–184; "Reception and Banquet," American Peace and Arbitration League *Bulletin*, No. 18.

39. Short, "The New York Peace Society," *Advocate of Peace*, LXXII (May 1910), 114; William J. Bryan, "The Forces That Make for Peace," *Mohonk Report, 1910*, pp. 172–173; "National Honor," *The Independent*, LXVIII (March 31, 1910), 715; Carnegie, "Peace *versus* War: The President's Solution," *Century Magazine*, LXXX (June 1910), 309–310; Carnegie to Taft, December 10, 1910, Taft Papers; *Report*, Proceedings, New England Arbitration and Peace Congress, pp. 113–114.

40. J. A. Baker, "The English House of Commons for Arbitration with America," *Mohonk Report, 1911*, pp. 125–126; Smiley, "Some Events of the Past Year," *ibid.*, pp. 19–20; "An Unlimited Arbitration Treaty with Great Britain," *Advocate of Peace*, LXXIII (February 1911), 25–26; "Unlimited Arbitration with England," *Literary Digest*, XLII (March 25, 1911), 557–559; "Muffling the War-Drum," *ibid.*, (April 1, 1911), pp. 612–613; New York *Times*, March 31, 1911; Edwin D. Mead to N. M. Butler, April 6, 1911, CEIP Papers; Noble, *Proceedings*, p. 386; Springfield (Mass.) *Republican*, June 22, 1911; John P. Campbell, "Taft, Roosevelt, and the Arbitration Treaties of 1911," *Journal of American History*, LIII (September 1966), 280–281.

seemed threatened, it would be better to fight than negotiate. Alfred Thayer Mahan, the second outspoken opponent, concurred. The renowned naval expert observed that until the world had a fully developed system of law, men could not entrust everything to arbitration. Furthermore, certain subjects like the Monroe Doctrine were not generally recognized by other countries, and this policy must be safeguarded. Like Roosevelt, Mahan argued that some wars could be justified. The third opponent, Henry Cabot Lodge, did not voice his views publicly. He agreed "absolutely with" Roosevelt, but as a member of the Senate Foreign Relations Committee he believed that opposition would be futile. As of June he could see no result save approval in the form in which the treaties had been negotiated.[41]

But the Senate again proved to be an insurmountable barrier. The treaties had fully considered that body's previous objections, especially its demand for a voice in the *compromis* or special agreement to submit each dispute for settlement. The advice and consent of the Senate had to be given before each question could be referred to some body. The Committee on Foreign Relations, however, soon nullified the intent and concept of the accords. First, it destroyed their all-inclusive nature by adding an amendment listing exceptions. These included immigration, state indebtedness, and the Monroe Doctrine. It then repudiated the most significant advance, the provision for a joint high commission to determine the justiciability of disputes. Only the Senate could consider and determine "whether the matters in difference are arbitrable."[42]

The Committee's report appeared on August 15, too late for action at that session of Congress. During the period of adjournment, the supporters of the treaties wasted no time in arousing opposition against the amendments. The battle continued throughout the fall and winter, with Taft standing firm against changes and joining in the public appeals. Popular opinion, thus aroused, appeared in the form of mass meetings, resolutions, memorials, petitions, and letters and telegrams which came "pouring in upon the Senate."[43]

The critics naturally condemned the Senate's jealous regard for its prerogatives, but the issues went deeper than that. Two differences of opinion

---

41. Roosevelt, "The Arbitration Treaty with Great Britain," *The Outlook*, XCVIII (May 20, 1911), 97–98; Roosevelt, "A Proper Case for Arbitration," *ibid.*, XCIX (October 14, 1911), 365–366; Mahan, "Diplomacy and Arbitration (II)," *North American Review*, CXCIV (July 1911), 124–125; Lodge to Roosevelt, June 3, 1911, Roosevelt Papers.

42. Senate *Report*, Committee on Foreign Relations, 62 Cong., 1st sess., Doc. 98, pp. 3–8, 37–40, 19.

43. Taft conducted a twenty-four-state speaking tour late in 1911 in which he dis-

emerged in the debates. One of these involved the decision to arbitrate all types of justiciable disputes. Taft and his supporters claimed that certain subjects which the opponents wished to exclude could not be arbitrated anyway. The Monroe Doctrine, state debts, and immigration did not fall into a category which made them international. They were domestic matters which could not be invoked under the agreement. Senator Root agreed in part with this reasoning, but he saw no harm in adding a reservation that the Senate construed this to be the case. Precedent, argued Root, supported such a course, and it might in the future prevent misunderstandings and avoid dangerous difficulties.[44] The Senate Committee's insistence upon an amendment to exclude these subjects, as well as Root's proposal, really destroyed the spirit of the accords and the one important advance—that of including all justiciable questions in the realm of arbitration. Yet even as revised, the treaties represented a significant gain. The Senate did not insist upon the inclusion of the terms "national honor" or "independence."

The second point of conflict hinged upon the proposed joint high commission to determine the justiciability of a dispute. The Committee on Foreign Relations destroyed this provision by insisting that the Senate have the determining voice on that subject. The idea of the joint commission was an advance of marked significance. Taft viewed it as such. In the same way that his successor considered Article X the heart of the Covenant, Taft believed this proposal to be "the centre and the point of the whole plan."[45] It sought to elevate arbitration to a more judicial level; it suggested a reasonable solution to the old problem of deciding whether a question fell within the principles of law and equity. As Root and others indicated, this matter had long been established in domestic law by giving the courts authority to decide upon their jurisdiction and whether cases fell within the scope of the law. Professor William I. Hull noted that the joint commission would

---

cussed the treaties. He also wrote articles—"The Pending Arbitration Treaties," *Century Magazine*, LXXXIII (January 1912), 459–466, and "The Dawn of World Peace"—in the *International Conciliation* series. The Carnegie Endowment for International Peace organized a citizens' committee to urge ratification. Its efforts are recorded in a letterbook, "Arbitration Treaties, 1911–1912," in the CEIP Papers. "The Peace Treaties and the People," *The Independent*, LXXII (January 18, 1912), 156–157; "The Arbitration Treaties," *Advocate of Peace*, LXXIV (February 1912), 29; "The People Want Peace Assured," *ibid.*, (March 1912), p. 53; "The Arbitration Treaties," *ibid.*, LXXIII (September 1911), 193–194.

44. Senate *Report*, Doc. 98, pp. 9–10; J. B. Scott to George Turner, November 6, 1911, CEIP Papers.

45. Taft, "World-Peace and the General Arbitration Treaties," *World's Work*, XXIII (December 1911), 146.

play the role of a grand jury to investigate and indict and thus determine the type of hearing to be held.[46]

The Senate's concern over the joint high commission is difficult to fathom. In the first place, the interest of the United States seemed protected by the fact that it would name three of the six members. Even then the United States could control the outcome since all decisions had to be approved by at least five of them. Any two Americans could block action. Taft appeared ready to accept an amendment to allow the Senate a voice in confirming the commissioners, but this assurance did not allay senatorial fears. In the second place, if the commission decided that a dispute was arbitrable, the Senate could still have refused to submit the case for decision. The matter would first go to the President, who would draft the special agreement or *compromis*, which in turn would require the approval of the Senate. The commission's reports under this arrangement could only be described as advisory, since the Senate would have the final voice. Its power to advise and consent would not have been affected if the proposal had been allowed to stand. Taft may have expressed an accurate observation when he noted that the men who objected to the treaties may really have been opposed to the principle of arbitration.[47]

All of the arguments of the arbitrationists seemed of little weight when the Senate voted on March 5, 1912. It approved a reservation excluding certain types of disputes and by amendment eliminated the joint high commission. The vote on that point stood 42 to 40. The Senate then approved the treaties 76 to 3.

An analysis of the outcome reveals some striking parallels with the Senate's action in 1919 and 1920 over joining the League of Nations. In 1911, Lodge's position on the Foreign Relations Committee allowed him to play a key role. Then, as in 1919, he claimed to be for the issue in principle but in favor of some modification. His actions and efforts did much to determine the outcome. Edwin Mead dramatically characterized Lodge's work by quoting the Old Testament. "He said, art thou in health my brother? And he took him by the beard to kiss him and smote him under the fifth rib and shed out his bowels."[48]

46. Root, "The Importance of Judicial Settlement," *Proceedings*, International Conference, Judicial Settlement of International Disputes, 1911, pp. 11–14; Root to Marburg, February 2, 1910, Theodore Marburg Papers, Library of Congress; Hull, "The International Grand Jury," *The Independent*, LXXII (January 4, 1912), 12–14.

47. Taft, "World-Peace," pp. 148–149.

48. "Senator Lodge's Criticism of the Treaties," *Current Literature*, LII (April 1912), 376; Holt, *Treaties Defeated*, pp. 233–234; Mead, "Aftermath of the Treaties," Boston *Herald*, March 19, 1912.

Taft, too, found himself in a role comparable to the one he played some years later. He hesitated to accept any changes, even Root's interpretation of the treaty, because he feared that any sign of concession would weaken his side and strengthen the Senate in its demands. Taft sat in the same judgment seat in 1919 when he had to decide whether to accept reservations. He also occupied the chair which Woodrow Wilson owned during the later fight, and Taft felt in 1911 some of the abuse and criticism that fell upon Woodrow Wilson in 1919. Like Wilson, he also faced the dilemma of what response he could expect from the other signatories regarding an amended treaty, for Taft had been informed by the British ambassador, Lord Bryce, that both the British and French governments did not favor the changes.[49]

Politics also entered the picture as in 1919 and 1920, only in something of a reverse pattern. The Democrats, with the exception of three men, voted against the joint high commission. Democratic Senator Gilbert M. Hitchcock of Nebraska opposed the modest provisions of the Taft treaties in 1912 but in 1919 stood stalwartly in support of the more advanced Covenant. Interestingly, Governor Woodrow Wilson of New Jersey approved of the treaties in their original form. Perhaps the one political difference was that Taft could not count on his own party in 1912. By that time the insurgency movement had already begun, and it partially explains the pattern of voting.

Finally, the constitutional question of the Senate's power, the delegation of authority, and the belief that the interests of the nation should be safeguarded loomed as large in 1912 as in 1919. In both instances, the Senate acted to maintain its authority and to protect the nation from what it deemed an unwise move. Bartholdt watched the action from the House with a feeling of helplessness and expressed the frustration of the internationalists. "We cannot enter into international agreements and at the same time maintain intact in every respect what is called sovereign power or senatorial prerogative." It was necessary, he declared, to sacrifice a degree of "sovereignty in order to meet the obligations imposed by agreements with the family of nations."[50] The Senate, nevertheless, succeeded in its aim in 1912 as it did in 1919; hence, in their revised form the Taft treaties barely went beyond those of Root. They agreed to arbitrate disputes which could be arbitrated but only after the Senate decided upon the proper course of action.

Taft had to decide what to do about the amended treaties, and he faced

49. Memorandum by Taft, October 17, 1911, CEIP Papers; Taft to W. J. Bryan, January 16, 1912; to Carnegie, December 29, 1911, Taft Papers.
50. Bartholdt, "Let the Arbitration Treaties be Ratified Unchanged," *Advocate of Peace*, LXXIII (September 1911), 201.

considerable pressure to obtain the acceptance of the signatories to the Senate's changes. Eventually, he withdrew them. They fell too far short of his goal of developing "an arbitral court whose jurisdiction should be increased ultimately to include all possible disputes of an international character." Taft remained relatively silent over the fate of the treaties, but he was probably as dismayed at the outcome as the other supporters of arbitration. They struck back at the Senate by castigating the men they viewed responsible. Edwin Mead reflected their sentiments in a letter to Nicholas Murray Butler in which he described his feelings "at the present wretched and outrageous performance."[51]

Although the Taft treaties died, the enthusiasm for arbitration continued, as did discussions on the parallel subjects of a court and international law. Taft's efforts had actually stimulated the concept of justice which lay at the base of both these ideals. Disputes had to be settled fairly and according to set standards. This meant action through courts and the acceptance of rules impartially and judicially administered.

This concept of justice revealed itself in various ways. It had become "more important than peace," declared *The Outlook*. Root reflected this philosophy when he observed in 1909 that "peace can never be except as it is founded upon justice," and Nicholas Murray Butler called justice "the one real and continuing ground of security for both men and nations."[52]

Adherents to this principle, however, realized that the same obstacles existed for a court as for treaties of arbitration. Therefore they resorted to the familiar tactics of education and the old evolutionary hypothesis in the hope that changing attitudes would bring an international judicial system. Discussions at The Hague in 1907 as well as the creation of a Central American Court of Justice that year had seemed to confirm the wisdom of their methods. The latter agency had had considerable impact in encouraging the legalists, for as a working model it stimulated suggestions for a broader body. Philander Knox reflected such desires when in October of 1909 he suggested the creation of a Prize Court "with the jurisdiction and functions of a court of arbitral justice." Knox expressed views which paralleled those of the internationalists as he argued his case. The trend of the

51. Henry A. Atkinson, *Theodore Marburg: The Man and His Work*, p. 118; Lord Bryce to Taft, March 27, 1912, Taft Papers; Trueblood to Butler, March 11, 1912, CEIP Papers; Carnegie to Taft, April 2, 1912; Taft to J. B. Scott, December 17, 1912, Taft Papers; Mead to Butler, March 8, 1912, CEIP Papers.
52. "Peace, Strength, and Justice," *The Outlook*, CIV (May 17, 1913), 94; "Address by the Honorable Elihu Root," *International Conciliation*, No. 18, (May 1909), p. 4; Butler, "Opening Address . . . ," *Mohonk Report, 1910*, p. 16.

world was toward "unity, at the same time preserving national organization." Each country, he declared, "is likely to see itself forced to yield something of its initiative, not to any one nation, but to the community of nations in payment for its share in the 'advance of richness of existence.' "[53]

In his suggestions for a Prize Court, Knox was actually trying to solve the sovereignty issue which had led all governments to demand representation on the bench of the body proposed at the Hague Conference. The Prize Court would presumably be dominated by the major powers since they were the maritime carriers; hence, they would select the judges. This seemed to be a partial solution, but it still fell short of the ideal. Hayne Davis and Holt considered conditions and suggested the creation of nine circuit courts, each possessing jurisdiction in an area determined by geographic and other interests. This system would enable every country to appoint its own judges. The nine chief justices of the circuits would then sit as a supreme tribunal to which matters would be brought on appeal. Cases involving governments in two different circuits could be heard by a panel made up of judges from the two.[54]

Knox, Taft, and spokesmen in the State Department led by solicitor J. B. Scott worked at the problem and thus raised the hopes of many persons. Scott announced at the Lake Mohonk Conference in May of 1910 that official response to a circular note indicated that the court might soon be attained.[55] His words stimulated additional interest in judicial processes that year, the centennial of the birth of Elihu Burritt, and two new organizations appeared. Theodore Marburg, a wealthy Baltimore publicist, led in forming the American Society for Judicial Settlement of International Disputes. The second body emerged within the Carnegie Endowment for International Peace as a Division of International Law with Scott as its director was formed. In seeking to determine what international law was or should be, the Division embarked upon a number of historical studies which it published.[56]

The legalistic approach to peace, however, remained essentially con-

53. Knox, "International Unity," *International Conciliation*, No. 28 (March 1910), pp. 10, 4–5.

54. "The Judicial Arbitration Court," *The Independent*, LXVIII (April 28, 1910), 935–937; Davis, "The Foundations of International Justice," *ibid.*, (March 10, 1910), pp. 504–513; Holt, "The World Court," *ibid.*, (May 19, 1910), pp. 1093–1095.

55. Scott, "Progress Toward an International Court of Arbitral Justice," *Mohonk Report, 1910*, pp. 73–74; Trueblood, "The Eighty-Second Annual Report . . . ," *Advocate of Peace*, LXXII (May 1910), 107.

56. Scott, "Elihu Burritt," *ibid.*, (June 1910), pp. 131–134; Butler, "Opening Address . . . ," *Mohonk Report, 1911*, p. 24; Scott to J. B. Moore, June 13, 1911, CEIP Papers.

servative in its programs. Not many persons accepted the reasoning of the more imaginative world-organization advocates that a league should be created and empowered to legislate and to uphold the decisions of a court. Most of them, like Professors of International Law George Grafton Wilson of Harvard and Paul S. Reinsch of Wisconsin, saw the need but could not agree to such. Some men like W. O. Hart, a New Orleans attorney, Peter W. Meldrim, a former president of the Georgia Bar Association, and Dean Henry Wade Rogers of the Yale Law School did advocate a union of nations, but they were exceptions.[57] A considerable difference of opinion existed which seemed to create an unbridgable gap between the two groups and their ideologies. The more radical internationalists could not appreciate the gradualist approach of most of the lawyers who thought that a court should first be established and that a body of laws could then develop from decisions and other forms of precedent.

The growing activity on behalf of a court, plus discussions on the Bennet resolution and the Taft treaties did, however, stimulate a wider interest in an international organization than ever before. References to a league of some type appeared with ever greater frequency between 1910 and 1912. In many instances, however, these statements merely reflected an acceptance of the idea with no sign of intensive thought.[58] Older proposals continued to be publicized, especially those of the American Peace Society for periodic congresses or for a federation based upon a co-operative arrangement. Cyrus Street also continued to advance his ambitious plan

57. Wilson, "Bases of International Legislation," *Mohonk Report, 1912,* pp. 116–120; Reinsch, "The Relation of Legality to International Arbitration," *ibid., 1911,* pp. 108–112; Hart, "Universal Peace Impossible Without an International Code," Noble, *Proceedings,* p. 112; Meldrim, "Why a Real International Court is Needed," *Mohonk Report, 1912,* pp. 91–94; Rogers, "The Present Problem . . . ," *Report,* Proceedings, New England Arbitration and Peace Congress, pp. 28, 33, 35, 37.

58. Smiley, "Opening Remarks . . . ," *Mohonk Report, 1910,* p. 12; William Sparling, "Canadian Churches and Peace," *ibid., 1911,* p. 164; "Business and Internationalism," Mohonk Business Men's *Bulletin,* No. 9; George L. Clark, "By War or Law?" *Advocate of Peace,* LXXIII (March 1911), 64; "Brevities," *ibid.,* (October 1911), p. 222; [O. G. Villard], "Progress Towards Peace," *The Nation,* XCII (January 5, 1911), 4; "The Unification of Nations . . . ," *Biblical World,* XXXVII (June 1911), 355–358; James A. Tawney, "The Cost of Armed Peace . . . ," *Yearbook,* NYPS, 1911–1912, p. 40; Theodore Marburg, "A Modified Monroe Doctrine," *South Atlantic Quarterly,* X (July 1911), 228–230; Henry Wallace, "Educate the Poor—And Stop War," *World's Work,* XX (June 1910), 13088–13089; Eunice B. Peter, "Democracy and the Cure for War," and Katherine Warren, "International Peace," in *International Peace, Winning Essays,* pp. 14–15, 19; Helen Anderson, "International Peace," *ibid.,* pp. 19–21; *Report,* Proceedings, New England Arbitration and Peace Congress, pp. 28, 37, 44, 52, 72, 83–89, 102, 119.

throughout the Middle West. He organized an International Association of the Friends of Peace which attracted a number of prominent citizens. He endorsed the Bennet resolution but would have preferred a call for "a COMPLETE international government." Street claimed that by 1911 he had personally presented his program to more than ten thousand people and that through publications and the daily press he had reached millions. He had "almost universally found the people in favor of the plans advocated by me and the newspapers ever ready to make them known."[59]

While Street's claims may appear exaggerated, some evidence indicates that people did respond to suggestions for an international organization. Residents of Weyamvega, Wisconsin, did. During a baccalaureate service for the high school graduating class on June 4, 1910, the audience approved a resolution supporting obligatory arbitration treaties, a court of justice, regular congresses, and "a solemn compact of peace" to make war impossible. All the ministers, high school teachers, and members of the graduating class signed this statement.[60]

The Middle West reflected the activities of other propagandists who campaigned throughout the area. Charles Beals, who had assumed the secretaryship of the Chicago Peace Society, delivered many addresses on a union, and Professor Hubert M. Skinner of Lincoln-Jefferson University offered an extension lecture on "the Federation of the World." Both of these men noted the growing trend toward co-operation and predicted that before too long the details which would unite nations would be completed. Representative Bartholdt also carried the message of the internationalists through the Mississippi Valley through his work in Congress and the Inter-parliamentary Union.[61]

Most of these spokesmen did not concern themselves with details, but a few of the plans between 1910 and 1912 did explore in varying depth programs of action or did discuss the provisions on which a league should be based. One of these reflected the continuing interest of William O. McDowell to establish his United Nations. Representative Robinson re-

59. "The Anglo-American Arbitration Treaty," *Advocate of Peace*, LXXIII (June 1911), 122; Trueblood, "The Breaking Down of National Boundaries," *ibid.*, (November 1911), pp. 255–257; *The United Nations*, III (August 1911), 1–5; "A Declaration of Independence by Citizens of the World," and "The New Peace Movement," typed proposals sent with Street to Holt, July 9, 1910, Holt Papers; Street to Carnegie, January 30, 1911, CEIP Papers.

60. "Brevities," *Advocate of Peace*, LXXIII (October 1911), 221.

61. Beals, "The Chicago Peace Society . . . ," *ibid.*, (April 1911), p. 87; Skinner, *The Federation of the World*, p. 3–11.

introduced his resolution on December 15, 1910, to invite all members of "the parliaments and national legislative bodies of the world" and all the judges of any international courts to the United States for a congress. The measure also requested six hundred thousand dollars to cover costs and for "peace propaganda," and McDowell explained to the House Committee on Foreign Affairs on January 19, 1911, that the funds would be well spent. The legislators and judges would consider important international questions, seek to achieve justice by formulating proposals for a court, and thus approve a recommendation of the Hague Conference. The appropriation, McDowell explained, would simply attain a goal suggested by Bartholdt in 1909 that all nations contribute one tenth of one percent of their military budgets for peace purposes. Robinson conceded, in supporting McDowell's testimony, that the proposal could be described as visionary. Parliaments, however, constituted the one place where power did exist and where it might be possible to get some constructive action. Some twenty-five thousand lawmakers would be involved.[62]

In New York City, McDowell's suggestion prompted the formation of a committee to support the resolution and to seek New York as the site for the conference in 1913. McDowell reported in October of 1911 that he had pledges for a six-hundred-thousand-dollar hospitality fund and two million dollars for the construction of an assembly hall. He also united with Bartholdt in a campaign to persuade congressmen to join the Interparliamentary Union in the hope that this action would aid in achieving the goal. He obtained the signatures of 372 of the 482 senators and representatives in Congress in the hope that this achievement would set an example for other nations. If the Interparliamentary Union could enroll a large percentage of the men in every legislature, its meetings would truly represent all lands. These ambitious plans failed, but the efforts did not die. On July 9, 1912, Democratic Representative William Sulzer of New York introduced H.J. Resolution 335 which again called for an assembly of parliamentarians and invited them to meet in the District of Columbia in the fall of 1915. Congress failed to act upon this proposal also.[63]

62. H.J. Res. 250, 61 Cong., 3d sess., December 15, 1910; House Committee on Foreign Affairs, *Hearing on Joint Assembly and Meeting of the Parliaments and National Legislative Bodies of the World in the United States*, 61 Cong., 3d sess., January 19, 1911, pp. 1–2, 4–5; New York *Times*, July 3, 6, 1910, contains information on the origin of the idea.

63. *Hearing, Joint Assembly*, pp. 5–6; McDowell to all congressmen (copies), [October 1911]; McDowell to Butler, October 10, 1911; to Root, October 9, 1911, CEIP Papers; McDowell to J. P. Morgan, December 23, 1912, McDowell Papers; *The Peace Movement*, I (September 1912), 294.

Another plan of considerable detail appeared around 1911. Robert W. Mason of Lewiston, Maine, published it in a pocket-sized pamphlet entitled *A Constitution for World-Wide Federation*. Mason suggested the creation of a symbolic figure comparable to "Uncle Sam." He would be "Uncle Nat" and represent the "United Nations of the World." Mason prepared a constitution modeled after that of the United States which called for a three-branch government with no authority over the internal matters of countries.

Mason endowed his legislature with impressive powers. It could tax, borrow, regulate international commerce, and establish a "Tariff Bureau" to keep rates reasonable. It could issue its own currency, control international mail, and make all laws that were necessary and proper for its operation and for the maintenance of peace. The chief executive could veto bills, but the parliament could repass them by a two-thirds vote.

The world president enjoyed other authority. He served for a term of eight years, acted as commander-in-chief of a "Peaceguard," and possessed the right "to secure peace throughout the United Nations." Mason suggested a novel way of choosing this man. Each government could nominate two men, but only one could be a citizen of that country. This slate of names would then be referred to the parliament, which would select the executive. No one nation could have one of its citizens serve more than once every thirty-two years.

Mason's proposals for a judiciary revealed little knowledge of the legalistic problems or processes in international relations. He merely called for a supreme court and whatever lesser bodies would be needed. He did, however, include other proposals of interest. He listed a set of guarantees similar to those of the "Bill of Rights." He also provided that all legislation of the United Nations be subject to the veto of the chief executive of any member state. If a man did not exercise that right, he automatically assumed the responsibility of administering the law within his domain. As Mason observed, this proposal would force the international government to be responsible to its members. It would have to act wisely or lose support and become ineffective. Mason did not stop to consider what the consequences of his nullification proposal would have been had it been incorporated in the Constitution of the United States. His plan, nevertheless, received widespread distribution and prompted comment in several lands.[64]

A third detailed suggestion appeared in *The Independent* in 1911 as part of a series planned by Holt as a set of "Federationist" papers. He had

64. Mason, *A Constitution for World-Wide Federation*, pp. 1–24.

reasoned that, as proponents of the Constitution had written in its support in 1787 and 1788, so now men should present the case for an international federation. The author, who signed his contribution "Justus," speculated upon what kind of structure should be created. He called for a congress in which all countries would be equal at first and decide matters by unanimous consent. Eventually, as conditions changed, a fairer method of representation and voting should be devised. His court proposals contained suggestions for an appellate system identical to that devised by Holt and Davis. Its judgments would be based upon a set of standards which included "mutual guarantees to respect national territory and sovereignty," pledges to accept the decisions of the court where they fell within its defined jurisdiction, and promises to submit disputes to arbitration. To develop the concept of justice, members should also agree to "compel obedience to decisions" and supply armed forces for that purpose.

The United States, Justus argued, could sign such an agreement as readily as it supported the Monroe Doctrine, for it would be upholding right. Such action would not be an entangling alliance but "an effective compact for widening the area of law duly declared and adjudicated, in accordance with principles for which this nation has risked everything in the past and of which it is still the chief exponent." The force employed would never be used arbitrarily, said Justus, and he included another provision to insure fairness in this respect. Each nation could decide in every instance whether it would participate in a program of military action where two members engaged in a quarrel over territory.[65] This proviso provided a loophole for the United States and its constitutional clause on the warmaking power, but it also exposed a weakness. Could any league count upon a force when needed if the contributing countries held such discretionary rights?

Mason's plan for a "Peaceguard" and the provisions for a similar agency in the proposals of Justus and the Bennet resolution reflected a growing advocacy of sanctions which disturbed many internationalists. Was some military arm needed, or would the moral weight of law and right be sufficient in any world organization to maintain peace? A debate of no small proportions emerged over this question because the planners had reached a crossroads. Should they include provisions for force and if so to what degree? Should they renounce force and trust that nations, like men, would respect their commitments and obligations?

Evidence of this conflict appeared in the World-Federation League

65. Justus, "The Federationist, (II) Possibilities of the United States Peace Commission," *The Independent*, LXX (April 20, 1911), 829–835.

where Crosby, who became president in 1910, favored a court with an army at its disposal to uphold decisions and maintain peace. Crosby did not agree with the federationists who called for a government modeled after that of the United States. Legislative and executive functions, he argued, could all be performed by a court. This court could appoint any officers that it needed to execute whatever the judges directed, and its decisions would establish precedents which would eventually have the same weight as if passed by a legislature. Such men as Holt and Short refused to accept such a narrow program or one which conferred extensive authority on any single agency of an international organization. They knew how reluctant nations were to submit certain types of disputes to a tribunal, especially those involving territory, and they wondered how governments could confer such sweeping authority upon judges when they could not reach agreement at The Hague in 1907 on the simple formula of appointing justices to a court with far less authority or jurisdiction. They feared that Crosby's league would become tyrannical and even provoke war. To Crosby, such arguments failed to consider the reality of international life. The judicial path seemed to be the only one that nations had been willing to accept. They would not create legislatures or executives; hence the court should be empowered to act in the absence of these agencies. It would be fairer because it would base its decisions upon legal and judicial grounds.[66]

Crosby believed that the New York Peace Society, which had incorporated the World-Federation League as a department in April of 1910, had grown lazy in championing the programs of the League. It reflected the more conservative approach of its members who shied away from advanced ideas. The best the World-Federation League officials could do was suggest a compromise in which they urged the creation of a court and a "co-related military power adequate for the enforcement of the decrees of the Court," but they left the question of sanctions in an ambiguous state.[67]

In his discussions with Crosby, Holt reflected the dilemma on sanctions in the minds of the internationalists. He had been an early advocate of force, although he had never formulated specific rules for its application. Then, at the Third National Peace Congress in Baltimore in May of 1911, he completely repudiated this principle. As president and presiding officer, he had

66. Crosby to Short, November 23, 1910; to Holt, December 1, 1910; draft of proposed program with Holt's annotations [November 1910]; Crosby to Short, January 31, 1911, NYPS Papers.

67. Crosby to Short, January 31, 1911, January 3, 1912, NYPS Papers.

prepared an address in which he called for a league of peace supported by an army. Theodore Marburg, the chief organizer of the meeting, warned Holt that such views would alienate many pacifists in attendance. It would be wiser to suggest an association built upon voluntary action and omit references to sanctions. "Social ostracism," Marburg believed, would be a more effective tool. Only on the rarest of occasions, and then only to uphold the decrees of the court, should force be employed.[68]

Holt apparently agreed, for in his speech he reverted to his theme that war had to give way to law, that nations had to act toward each other as men did in their daily relationships, and that "the political organization of the world, therefore, is the task of the twentieth century." Governments could continue along the evolutionary path as in the past or accelerate matters by creating a league of peace. Such a union, Holt cautioned, should not "attempt to use force for any purpose whatsoever." It would be unnecessary and "beget suspicion."

Five provisions for a union, Holt claimed, would make it effective even though it lacked a police power: (1) Countries should agree to arbitrate all disputes. (2) A court should decide upon controversies. (3) Nations should meet periodically to determine rules which would serve as laws unless vetoed by a member within a given time. (4) Armaments were to remained untouched by any league. (5) Any government could withdraw at will. The ratification of the Taft treaties, Holt declared, would point the way to such a union. These would bind states together until they could agree upon some universal accord.[69]

The resolutions at Baltimore reflected this conservative approach. They endorsed the arbitration treaties, called for a strengthened court and the creation of the peace commission authorized by the Bennet resolution, and urged the United States to negotiate with other countries

looking to the formation of a league of peace planned simply to settle by amicable means all questions of whatever nature which may arise between the contracting powers, with no idea of the employment of force to impose the will of the league on any of its members nor to force any outside power to join the league, nor to force any outside power to arbitrate a dispute, nor to enforce the decisions of an international tribunal of any character, nor to use force in any other way.[70]

68. Kuehl, *Hamilton Holt*, pp. 93–94; Marburg, *League of Nations: A Chapter in the History of the Movement*, I, 38; Marburg, "The Significance of the International Court . . . ," *Mohonk Report, 1910*, pp. 87–88.
69. Holt, "A League of Peace," Noble, *Proceedings*, pp. 5–12.
70. *Ibid.*, pp. 385–391.

This rejection of sanctions appeared in the expressions of other men. Albert K. Smiley argued that public opinion would be far more effective than armaments. J. B. Scott agreed to the point that he denied a need for an economic boycott against lawbreakers. A common pacifist view appeared in the *Advocate of Peace* when it endorsed the Bennet resolution but dismissed the idea for a combined navy as only incidental to the larger goal of advancing peace. Even Raymond Bridgman observed that nations supporting a reign of law should place honor and public opinion above that of a police force. The latter would be unnecessary, and other writers seemed to agree.[71]

Unlike Holt, however, many internationalists could not abandon sanctions. Lucia Ames Mead and Edwin Ginn refused to modify their earlier proposals, and other persons suggested that any league would need some form of compulsion to be effective.[72] In most instances, however, they failed to elaborate upon this point. A few programs deserve examination, nevertheless, because of the spokesman or ideas involved. Former Representative Charles A. Towne observed late in 1911 that the progress toward an organized world had been so rapid that in ten to fifteen years men would see a tribunal which would hear all controversies, initiate investigations of questionable acts, and "be clothed with all the physical power necessary for enforcing its mandates and compelling obedience to its decrees."[73]

The Republican Club of New York City also favored a police agency

71. Smiley, "Remarks . . . ," *Mohonk Report, 1910*, p. 200; Scott, "Some Needs of the Peace Movement," *ibid., 1911*, pp. 39–41; Scott to D. S. Jordan, May 2, 1911, CEIP Papers; Bridgman, *First Book of World Law*, pp. 284, 301; "International Peace," *The Outlook*, XCV (June 18, 1910), 334–335; "International Police or International Public Opinion," *ibid.*, XCVIII (August 12, 1911), 847.

72. Lucia Mead, "Internationalism and Patriotism," *Journal of Education*, LXXI (February 3, 1910), 127, (April 7, 1910), 375; Ginn, letter to editor dated April 13, *The Nation*, XCII (April 20, 1911), 396; Ginn, "The World Peace Foundation," *The Independent*, LXX (February 9, 1911), 297–298; Charles W. Eliot, "The Fears Which Cause the Increasing Armaments," *Mohonk Report, 1910*, pp. 99–100; Butler, "Opening Address . . . ," *ibid.*, p. 23; William Dudley Foulke, "Arbitration the Shortest Road to International Justice," *ibid., 1911*, pp. 100–101; Marcus M. Marks, "The Practical View of the Peace Question," *Advocate of Peace*, LXXIII (May 1911), 107; E. Morris Fergusson, "Arbitration and Force," *The Outlook*, XCVIII (June 3, 1911), 269–270; Paul U. Kellogg, "Of Peace and Good Will," *American Magazine*, LXXI (April 1911), 745; James S. Barcus, *First President of the World: A Prophecy*, p. 12; Thomas W. Kincaid, "Should There Be An International Navy?," U.S. Naval Institute *Proceedings*, XXXVII (1911), 91–93; A. L. Bancroft, "An Enforced Peace of the World," holograph copy, CEIP Papers.

73. Towne, "Universal Peace Movement," Senate Doc. 289, 62 Cong., 2d sess., pp. 9–10.

to uphold decisions of a court even if this meant war. Only in this way would men ever attain legislative and executive bodies in an organization. Charles W. Eliot, the retired president of Harvard, noted in 1910 that any force should be overwhelming in its application. The combined fleets of the world, he thought, could effectively uphold the decisions of a court and protect private property on the high seas in wartime.[74] Eliot became quite vocal in presenting this solution and in the next few years may have convinced many people of the correctness of his position.

Another proposal came from Caspar Goodrich, who expanded upon his earlier ideas and concluded that the earth would have seen more peace if Great Britain and the United States had united to avert war in the nineteenth century. They could still do this, Goodrich argued, by supporting any nation which submitted a dispute to the Hague court and by moving against the other party which refused to do so. "A visible and overwhelming police to compel acceptance of its judgments even against a party *in absentia*" should also be part of the plan. Goodrich feared in 1911 that agreement on such a principle was many years away; yet the League to Enforce Peace after 1915 endorsed the compulsory submission of controversies to pacific settlement.[75]

The subject of sanctions had thus gained considerable currency by 1910 and 1911. Plans, however, usually referred to military force rather than economic pressure, and it should be noted that before 1914 the latter idea had few adherents. Carnegie had hinted at it, Justice Brewer had mentioned it, and Mrs. Mead had explored the subject; but they did not elaborate upon it. One of the most novel proposals appeared in 1911 when several men suggested an International Society to Control the Finances of the World in the Interest of Peace. They hoped to create a neutral bank or some agency which would accumulate a vast reservoir of funds which could then be applied to keep nations peaceful. Yet they remained vague in discussing its application.[76]

Butler's "international mind" had thus developed in many ways by 1912. Even governments had shown an inclination to explore the subject of a league. In the United States the actions and statements by such officials as Taft and Knox seemed to confirm Frederick Lynch's observation that in the

74. Republican Club, *Universal Peace*, pp. 11, 14–15; Eliot, "Fears Which Cause the Increasing Armaments," pp. 99–100.

75. Goodrich, "Wanted—An International Police," *Living Age*, CCLXX (August 26, 1911), 544–549.

76. C. E. Creecy to J. B. Scott, May 18, 1911; W. P. Dewey to Carnegie, April 27, 1911; plan by J. M. Ross, CEIP Papers.

twentieth century men would see the unification of the world and that the internationalists who led in that movement would go down in history.[77] The events of the next two years, however, did not suggest a promising future for his prophecy. The activities of 1910 and 1911 were not followed by equally impressive efforts.

77. Howard H. Bridgman, "Our Country the World," *New England Magazine*, XXXXV (November 1911), 326; Knox, *The Spirit and Purpose of American Diplomacy*, pp. 55–56; Lynch, "The Leaders of the New Peace Movement in America," *The Independent*, LXIX (September 22, 1910), 629–638.

Years of Decline, 1913-1914

By the summer of 1912, the peace movement in the United States had reached a peak of activity and popularity. Likewise, the judicial concept for the settlement of disputes had been growing. For the internationalists, however, the situation did not look promising. Most of the leaders seemed to be discouraged, and their efforts in the months before the outbreak of war in the summer of 1914 were more restrained and less widespread than at almost any period since 1900.

One of the reasons for this decline can be found in the very activities of the peace workers. Their cause had become respectable. At the Third National Peace Congress in 1911, a president of the United States addressed such a body for the first time, and there, too, one could find an impressive roster of the names of leading citizens. To strengthen their voice, most of the peace groups had federated in 1912, and the American Peace Society had moved its headquarters to Washington in order to be near the center of political activity.[1] Operating under subventions from the Carnegie Endowment for International Peace, the reorganized agency increased mem-

---

1. Curti, *Peace or War*, pp. 199–200; Kuehl, *Hamilton Holt*, p. 93. The declining interest in an international organization can be seen most clearly in the records of the Fourth American Peace Congress at St. Louis in 1913. Only a few speakers referred to a league, and the subject did not appear in the resolutions. *Book of the Fourth American Peace Congress.*

156 Seeking World Order

bership rolls, organized new branches, and circulated vast amounts of literature.[2]

While the pacifists continued to campaign against armaments, to portray the horrors of armed conflict, and to counteract war scares, they turned increasingly to positive programs of action. They supported the renewal of the Root treaties in order to advance arbitration, they explored the feasibility of an international court of justice, they endorsed the efforts of Secretary of State Bryan to conclude conciliation pacts in 1913 and 1914, and they enthusiastically laid plans for a gigantic celebration in 1915 to commemorate one hundred years of peace with Great Britain.

The internationalists did not hesitate to co-operate with the pacifists in pursuing these constructive goals. This was especially true of arbitration, where everyone applauded the successful effort in 1913 and 1914 to renew several of the general treaties Root had concluded in 1908 and 1909. The task was not easy, for the United States in its official actions had seemed partially to repudiate arbitration by refusing to submit three outstanding controversies to arbitral settlement. One of these involved the interpretation of a treaty, the Hay-Pauncefote accord of 1901, when a dispute arose during the Taft administration over the collection of tolls in the Panama Canal. The United States insisted upon its own interpretation, which claimed exemption for some of its vessels, while Britain maintained that the ships of all nations should be charged equal rates. Under the terms of the arbitral agreement in effect with Great Britain, this was a matter which should have been referred to the tribunal at The Hague. The United States, however, assumed an obstinate position from which it eventually retreated.

The second issue concerned a dispute with Mexico during the Wilson administration, which eventually included armed intervention at Vera Cruz. While no arbitral agreement existed between the two governments, the controversy was one that might have been referred to the Hague court. In the third instance, the United States would not tolerate any hearing over why Colombia lost Panama in 1903. The refusal of the United States to act in these instances seriously weakened the principle of arbitration. Theodore Roosevelt observed that even the most innocuous agreements appeared to be little more than scraps of paper which the nation would not honor if its

2. "The Annual Meeting and Reorganization of the American Peace Society," *Advocate of Peace*, LXXIV (June 1912), 129–130; "Report of the Activities . . . American Peace Society . . . 1912–1913," CEIP Papers; A. D. Call, "The Recent Developments of the Organized Peace Movement . . . ," *Mohonk Report, 1914*, pp. 34–37.

interests seemed threatened. The events supported his oft-stated warning that "foolish and sweeping" provisions in treaties which would not be honored would do more harm than good to the cause of peace. Even Holt's *Independent* admitted that the American people seemed inclined "to agree to arbitrate anything and be unwilling to arbitrate any specific thing."[3]

The foremost authority on arbitration, John Bassett Moore, agreed with this conclusion. In looking back in 1914, Moore noted that progress had been painfully slow if not retarded. First, the United States had insisted upon exempting certain types of disputes. Then, after 1909, the Senate had blocked efforts at further advance. Before the Root treaties, Moore observed, differences had often been submitted for settlement by executive agreement. The amendments to those accords, however, required the drafting of special treaties and effectively nullified one channel of action. He warned men not to boast about gains when the world seemed to have slipped backward.[4]

The proponents of arbitration did not like to admit even a degree of failure, but some of the legalists among them capitalized upon the situation to advance their ideal of courts, laws, and justice. Nations, they declared, would submit controversies more freely to judicial hearing if clear-cut rules existed. These men spoke with conviction and often between 1912 and 1914, most notably at the National Conferences of the American Society for Judicial Settlement of International Disputes in Washington in 1912 and 1913.[5] Despite widespread discussions, however, no new ideas appeared.

The desires of the pacifists and internationalists did, however, culminate in an abortive movement of interest. This was the crusade for a third Hague

3. Roosevelt, "The Foreign Policy of the United States," *The Outlook*, CVII (August 22, 1914), 1011–1015; letter to editor, "Arbitration and Panama," *ibid.*, CIII (January 18, 1913), 111–112; "Arbitration, General and Specific," *The Independent*, LXXVII (February 9, 1914), 186.

4. Moore, "International Arbitration—A Survey of the Present Condition," *Mohonk Report, 1914*, pp. 14–17.

5. "Clearing of the International Situation," *Advocate of Peace*, LXXVI (March 1914), 50; [Holt], "A Great Peace Victory," *The Independent*, LXXVII (March 2, 1914), 291; Helm Bruce, "Remarks . . . ," *Mohonk Report, 1913*, p. 112; Lyman Abbott, "Arbitration as a Means for the Promotion of International Justice," *ibid.*, pp. 13–15, 17; George G. Wilson, "The Promotion of Internationality Through Arbitration and Judicial Processes," *ibid., 1914*, pp. 155–157; John M. Clark, "Some Lessons from the Work of the Supreme Court . . . ," *ibid.*, pp. 157–158; Henry B. F. MacFarland, "The International Court of Arbitral Justice," *ibid.*, pp. 108, 110–111; Samuel Graham Jr. to Carnegie, January 1, 1913, CEIP Papers; *Proceedings*, Third and Fourth National Conference[s] American Society for Judicial Settlement of International Disputes, 1913, 1914.

Conference. A span of eight years had elapsed between the first two meetings, and it seemed logical to assume that another assembly should be scheduled for 1915. It would provide an opportunity to create a more judicial agency and to reach accord on a code of law.[6]

The internationalists had been demanding for years that governments act to plan the agenda for such a gathering. The problem, however, proved to be one of protocol. Who would issue the call? The leaders of the Carnegie Endowment for International Peace—Butler, Root, and Scott—all perceived the project as one of great potentiality, as did Richard Bartholdt in Congress; and their efforts may have been important in persuading President Taft on June 10, 1912, to appoint a National Advisory Committee to consider the matter.[7]

The State Department did not act, however, even though a number of European governments named official commissions to explore the subject. This depressing situation worried the internationalists in the United States, who saw the third Hague Conference as one more step toward their ideal of a periodic congress of nations. If no one moved to issue a call, their dream would be shattered.[8]

This concern prompted considerable agitation late in 1913 and early in 1914 to stimulate action in Washington. Rumors had begun to circulate that the response of most countries to such an assembly had been so unfavorable as to threaten the venture. The United States would have to move boldly as in 1905; hence, on January 19, Bartholdt introduced a resolution requesting the secretary of state to act upon the convention of 1907 in which the nations had agreed to a third session. Stimulated by such demands, the Wilson administration announced in February that it had consulted with the government of the Netherlands to determine the latter's willingness to serve as host and that it had dispatched a circular letter on the subject.[9]

6. Edward A. Harriman, "The Work of the Hague Conferences—Past and Future," *Mohonk Report, 1914,* p. 94; "The Third Hague Conference," *The Outlook,* CVI (February 21, 1914), 383; *Mohonk Report, 1913,* p. 9.

7. "Preparation for the Third Hague Conference," *Advocate of Peace,* LXX (February 1908), 25–26; "Mr. Bartholdt's Resolution in Congress," *ibid.,* LXXI (July 1909), 149; Wilbur F. Gordy, "Education and the Petition to the Third Hague Conference," *National Education Association Journal . . . 1909,* pp. 89–91; J. B. Scott, "The Third Hague Conference," *Mohonk Report, 1912,* pp. 123, 126–127.

8. N. M. Butler to J. B. Scott, June 27; Scott to Butler, July 3, 1912, CEIP Papers; "The Third Hague Conference," *Advocate of Peace,* LXXV (November 1913), 224.

9. [Holt], "Call the Third Hague Conference Without Delay," *The Independent,* LXXVI (December 4, 1913), 429–431; N. M. Butler to H. C. Phillips, December 11; to Root, December 27, 1913, CEIP Papers; Henri La Fontaine to D. S. Jordan, Decem-

A national committee of prominent citizens organized to urge Wilson to call for a meeting openly, but such efforts failed to elicit any official response. By June the international situation seemed so hopeless that *The Independent* despairingly noted that no assembly could be held until at least 1916 or 1917.[10] It has often been assumed that the clash of arms in 1914 doomed the third Hague Conference, but it had little chance of being called on schedule if a war had not come. The armaments race and the aura of suspicion permeating the diplomacy of the time would have undermined the venture. The mood and attitude of nations by 1914 was far different from what it had been in 1899 or even 1907.

This situation must have been evident to the internationalists, for it was not the only sign that the atmosphere which had fostered their dreams had changed. The Bryan cooling-off agreements of 1913 and 1914 offered further proof of the changes in thinking. Bryan had revived the idea which David Dudley Field had advocated and which had appeared in the provisions of the Hague conventions of 1899 and 1907. Bryan had discussed it in 1905 and 1906, and it had originally been in Bartholdt's proposals for the Interparliamentary Union in 1905 and 1906. Governments which could not solve their disputes through the channels of diplomacy or arbitration should agree to submit their differences to a special commission for investigation. No signatory had to accept the report, but each would be obligated to resort to some machinery for peace. In this respect, the Bryan treaties represented a gain because under Part II of the Hague Conventions of 1899 and even as revised in 1907 the response of governments was entirely voluntary. The Bryan accords also contained a second principle in the form of the "cooling-off" idea. The belief that any delay might avert war had been expressed many times before 1913, and that concept had been implicit in the Taft treaties.[11] But Bryan inserted a proviso under which the

---

ber 26, 1913, Jordan Papers; David S. Patterson, "The Travail of the American Peace Movement, 1887–1914," pp. 331–336; *Congressional Record,* 63 Cong., 2d sess., 51, pt. 2:1956; *ibid.,* 1st sess., pt. 2:1179; *Papers Relating to the Foreign Relations of the United States, 1914,* pp. 4–5, 10–11.

10. "Clearing of the International Situation," *Advocate of Peace,* LXXVI (March 1914), 49; "From All Parts," *The Peace Movement,* III (March 15, 1914), 125–126; "Things International," *The Independent,* LXXVIII (June 22, 1914), 533.

11. Dubin, "Collective Security," pp. 57–59; Curti, *Peace or War,* p. 225; [Holt], "Mr. Bryan's Peace Triumph," *The Independent,* LXXIX (August 24, 1914), 261–262; F. Holls, "Abstract of Address," *Mohonk Report, 1900,* p. 13; Scott F. Hershey, "Address . . . ," *ibid.,* p. 52; "The Model Arbitration Treaty," *The Independent,* LVI (January 7, 1904), 47; Root, "Nobel Peace Prize Address," Robert Bacon and J. B. Scott, eds., *Addresses on International Subjects by Elihu Root,* pp. 158–174.

signatories promised not to resort to arms for at least a year while the inquiry was in progress.

The Bryan agreements, however, proved to be a setback for the internationalists in at least two ways. First, they contained no reference to arbitration. When Bryan first assumed office, he had expressed a desire to negotiate arbitral pacts similar to those drafted by Taft. But the documents he formulated provided only "for investigation and report to an International Commission" of "all disputes" which could not be resolved in other ways. Arbitration had been eliminated, and it would have been weakened more had not Bryan renewed the Root treaties. Second, another clause in the Bryan compacts reserved to the signatories "the right to act independently" after the commission submitted its report.[12] Thus the legal and moral principles which the internationalists had been working to advance received a setback. In method and procedure, the treaties fell short of the judicial goal envisaged for over a decade. They thus provided additional evidence that the United States and other nations were still unwilling to be bound by any agreements which might limit their action. They were ready to examine disputes but not to accept decisions.

Of course, few men openly admitted any loss of ground. In fact, press response to Bryan's proposals had been generally favorable from the beginning. Even such internationalists as Holt hailed the pacts when the Senate approved them. Some defenders of arbitration, however, notably Taft, continued to speak on its behalf. As late as 1914, he still sought to defend the provisions of his treaties and to refute the Senate's claim to power, but his arguments carried little weight.[13] Arbitration, for all effective purposes, made no new headway in the two years prior to July 1914.

Paradoxically, as this means of resolving difficulties deteriorated and as nations moved closer to war, discussions of justice and law increased. This development occurred largely because of the organized efforts of certain groups, notably the Carnegie Endowment for International Peace. It conducted campaigns directly through an elaborate program of publications and indirectly through subventions to various organizations devoted to the judicial settlement of controversies. The aims of these agencies remained

12. "Secretary Bryan's Peace Plan," *Advocate of Peace*, LXXV (May 1913), 97; William M. Malloy, comp., *Treaties . . . and Agreements Between the United States . . . and Other Powers, 1910–1923*, III, 2666–2667.

13. "A Pacifist in Charge of Our Foreign Relations," *Literary Digest*, XLVI (May 31, 1913), 1207–1209; "Mr. Bryan's Peace Triumph," pp. 261–262; W. H. Taft, *The United States and Peace*, pp. 100–130.

essentially what they had always been—the creation of a genuine court and the development of law.

The actions of the Endowment may also explain why the internationalists succeeded less in their cause after 1912. The leaders of the Endowment moved cautiously and believed "that we should be very conservative." In fact, J. B. Scott, who became secretary as well as director of the Division of International Law, continually expressed doubts about proposals for "an international police, for a league of peace, for neutralization, or for the political federation of the world." These programs seemed to be "opposed to the current of history" and the development of the United States. The use of courts, arbitration, and law seemed natural and more logical. The major suggestion for an organization which Scott supported was the one calling for periodic congresses. He saw in this proposal the possible development of a code. Basically, Scott believed in a loose "juridical union within the larger union of the society of nations." Root agreed with such reasoning. Governments would not as yet accept any extreme proposals for world federation or an effective league.[14]

A number of other agencies worked in similar ways to advance the principles of justice. The American Association for International Conciliation, the American Peace Society, the American Society of International Law, and the Society for the Judicial Settlement of International Disputes all sought a law-oriented system. The very prominence of these bodies between 1912 and 1914 reflects further the declining position of the more advanced internationalists.

All of the established groups, however, did not endorse such limited aims. The World Peace Foundation advocated some imaginative proposals, largely because of Ginn, the two Meads, and Holt. They lectured extensively under the auspices of the Foundation, delivering addresses, "The United States and the United World" and the "Federation of the World." The Foundation's main work, however, consisted of educational programs in the schools, colleges, and civic groups. It supported the American School Peace League and continued to print Ginn's International Library. It thus made Bridgman's *World Organization* available as well as Carnegie's *A League of Peace*, Edwin Mead's *Organize the World*, and Mrs. Mead's *Patriotism and the New Internationalism*. The Foundation also presented Kant's plan for a league

14. Scott to L. Renault, June 15, 1911, CEIP Papers; Scott, "The Constructive Peace Movement," *World To-Day*, XXI (February 1912), 1789–1792; Scott, "The Third Hague Conference," *Mohonk Report, 1912*, pp. 127–128.

and Sully's *The Great Design of Henry IV*, and it began publication in 1911 of a pamphlet series which in the next three years presented several items which discussed an international organization.[15]

While this endowed agency promoted a world union, moneys were not readily available for campaigning; hence, additional funds were needed. Some of the advocates turned to the federal government for support and received a response which seems remarkable. They did obtain modest appropriations. Congress usually approved funds for the Interparliamentary Union after it made such a grant for the first time in 1910. Bartholdt had requested five thousand dollars but happily settled for half that amount. He sought fifty thousand dollars in 1912 to underwrite a meeting in the United States, and in 1914 the House acted on his request.[16] The war, however, nullified any chance for such an assembly.

Bartholdt also co-operated indirectly with McDowell in the latter's effort to persuade Congress to pay the cost of a meeting of all the world's parliamentarians in New York in 1915. A building had to be constructed and vast plans made. McDowell obtained official support in New York for his venture, and his American Peace League conducted a crusade which gained endorsements from 390 societies, clubs, and organizations. McDowell also approached Secretary of State Bryan and President Wilson, but they refused to act. Resolutions to obtain appropriations from Congress failed.[17]

15. Mead, "The World Peace Foundation . . . ," *World Peace Foundation Pamphlets,* II (July 1912), 18–20; Ginn, *The International Library,* pp. 1–8; Peter Filene, "The World Peace Foundation . . . ," *New England Quarterly,* XXXVI (December 1963), 480–483, 489–490. Pamphlets discussing an international organization included "Sir Edward Grey on Union for World Peace," I (April 1911), Edwin Mead, "Heroes of Peace," II (January 1912), and J. A. Macdonald, "William T. Stead and his Peace Message," II (July 1912).

16. Bartholdt, "Government Support for the International Headquarters of the Interparliamentary Union," *Advocate of Peace,* LXXII (March 1910), 61–63; "Brevities," *ibid.,* (May 1910), p. 101; [Holt], "A Congressional Appropriation for Peace," *The Independent,* LXVIII (May 5, 1910), 999–1000; "Interparliamentary Conference," *Advocate of Peace,* LXXIV (February 1912), 31; "Brief Peace Notes," *ibid.,* LXXV (April 1913), 78; "War and Peace Measures Before Congress," *ibid.,* LXXVI (February 1914), 44; "Brief Peace Notes," *ibid.,* (July 1914), p. 155.

17. McDowell to Andrew D. White, Joseph H. Choate, and William H. Short, February 3, 1913; to Bartholdt, August 28, 1913, SCPC Papers; McDowell to Wilson, February 4, 1913, Wilson Papers, Library of Congress. McDowell to Joseph Tumulty, August 30, 1913, Department of State Archives, 500D/17, National Archives. Several resolutions sought government support for such an assembly in addition to those cited in Chapter Seven. H.J. Res. 335, *Congressional Record,* 62 Cong., 2d sess., 48, pt. 9:8810; H.J. Res. 359 and 361, *ibid.,* pt. 11:11762, 11861; H.J. Res. 153, *ibid.,* 63 Cong. 2d sess., 51, pt. 1:32; H.J. Res. 85, *ibid.,* 62 Cong., 1st sess., 47, pt. 1:881.

Actually, McDowell and Bartholdt labored less vigorously than they had in earlier years. McDowell confined his interest to this one project, and Bartholdt rarely spoke as openly as before. His most notable attempt to keep internationalist proposals alive came at the conference of the Interparliamentary Union in Geneva in 1912. There he introduced and defended a resolution urging governments to insert into arbitration treaties a provision to guarantee the territorial integrity and the sovereignty of nations in their internal matters. This suggestion met bitter opposition from the European delegates, who wanted no such pledge. They argued, in what was later to become a standard point, that such a clause would lead to injustice and perpetuate inequities.[18]

Most of the other leading internationalists likewise campaigned with less enthusiasm than before or disappeared from the battleground. Davis wrote not a single article between 1912 and 1914; Carnegie remained relatively silent, still appealing occasionally to Roosevelt to take up the mantle of leadership. He did establish another foundation in 1914, the Church Peace Union, but at that time it did not seem related to the movement for an international organization. Holt delivered his lecture on "The Federation of the World" dozens of times but utilized *The Independent* only infrequently in discussing that subject. He seemed to be discouraged by the various setbacks. The World-Federation League faded away, its supporters unable to sustain sufficient interest to keep it alive. Occasionally there were suggestions that the peace commission authorized by the Bennet resolution be appointed, but such proposals disappeared as rapidly as they appeared. Edwin Ginn died early in 1914, still proclaiming the advantages of a police force, and Benjamin Trueblood suffered a nervous breakdown on June 7, 1913, which left him incapacitated until his death in October of 1916.[19]

Only Raymond Bridgman produced an item of significance. He elaborated upon an idea which the United Nations later developed. A world body, Bridgman argued, should give proper consideration to the needs and uncertainties of the underdeveloped areas of the earth. Revolutions and other

18. "The Interparliamentary Conference at Geneva," *Advocate of Peace*, LXXIV (November 1912), 234.

19. Carnegie, "Peace by Arbitration," *The Independent*, LXXVII (February 16, 1914), 229; "The Outcome of the Peace Treaties," *ibid.*, LXXII (March 21, 1912), 633; "The Need of the Peace Commission," *ibid.*, LXXIII (August 1, 1912), 276–278; D. S. Jordan, "Foreclosing the Mortgage on War," *World's Work*, XXIV (June 1912), 208; E. D. Mead, "The American Peace Party and Its Present Aims and Duties," *World Peace Foundation Pamphlets*, III (April 1913), 6; Ginn, "Organizing the Peace Work," *ibid.*, (July 1913), pp. 4–5.

forms of internal dislocation in those lands could jeopardize the lives and property of men everywhere. Since nations would rarely assume individual responsibility to act, Bridgman suggested

the creation of a new organ of the executive department of the world government, which shall serve as a bureau of national assistance to all peoples that are not capable of maintaining stable government, and for the relief of citizens who are so oppressed by their governments that they will rebel unless relief is secured.[20]

The problem of administering this agency, Bridgman admitted, would be difficult to solve, but he believed the larger powers should have more voice since they would assume much of the responsibility. The military force could be requisitioned from their armies. It would be welcomed where it went because it would arouse less suspicion than contingents from individual countries. Where people did resist, the bureau would administer the government, "always acting under the laws of the country."[21]

Bridgman pursued his ideal of an organized world in other ways. In 1911 he produced another book of essays, *The First Book of World Law*, in which he continued to emphasize the evolutionary trend toward political unity. In keeping with this philosophy and his old methods, Bridgman also worked between 1910 and 1913 to gain approval of a petition in the Massachusetts legislature. Republican Representative Samuel W. McCall of that state then introduced it into Congress as H.J. Res. 100. As revised, it called for the President "to instruct the delegates of the United States to the next Hague Conference and to the next Pan American Conference to" incorporate into future treaties a clause that they would respect each other's territory and not expand their lands by conquest. Bridgman believed that such agreements would bind governments together and make unity much easier.[22]

The declining activity of most of the internationalists did not prevent the appearance of some new advocates who before 1912 had devoted only limited attention to the subject. Theodore Marburg had been active in pacifist and judicial circles and may have been attracted to broader programs as a result of his work in organizing the Third National Peace Con-

20. Bridgman, "A Bureau of National Assistance," *Bibliotheca Sacra,* LXX (October 1913), 545–551.
21. *Ibid.,* pp. 551–561.
22. *Congressional Record,* 62 Cong., 1st sess., 47, pt. 2:1260; House Committee on Foreign Affairs, *Report on Increase of Territory by Conquest,* 62 Cong., 2d sess., May 15, 1912, pp. 1, 4–8.

gress. There he came into contact with Holt, and a lifetime friendship began. Marburg presented his views in an article in *The Independent* in which he proposed that enlightened states unite to oversee the "backward lands" and to guarantee justice, morality, and liberty in such communities. Marburg did not believe that the major powers would allow a federation to be formed which would regulate their internal affairs or resolve their individual external troubles. But he did think governments might agree on some form of co-operative action for international problems.[23]

The second new spokesman came from Buffalo, New York, where he first developed his views in October 1911 after reading Ladd's *Essay on a Congress of Nations*. Roderick Smith, a broker, drafted a plan for a league, which he revised after discussions with friends in Buffalo. In February of 1913, he printed it in the form of a pocket-sized pamphlet of thirty pages. Smith suggested that the United States invite the powers of the world to unite "in establishing a Court of Nations and a Congress of Nations" at The Hague and to "provide for an International Army and Navy for the purpose of securing, protecting and guarding the rights of nations."[24]

Despite his advocacy of force, Smith emphasized a judicial process in his plan. Governments should agree to submit disputes to a tribunal which would decide issues on the basis of "justice and right" and upon laws approved by the assembly. The judges would have limited authority, having no jurisdiction over domestic affairs, the Monroe Doctrine, or "the European System." Decisions would be subject to review by the members, and parties in a case could appeal to the congress for a new trial or for changes in laws to correct inequities.

Smith's congress would be in charge of the court and the armed force, and he delegated other duties to it. It would regulate coinage, mails, weights and measures, copyrights, piracy, disarmament, discovery, and other matters involving general relations of nations. For an agency with this much authority, Smith said little about its membership. He avoided that subject save for a remark that it should be representative and be based on some process of apportionment. The congress could convene the force against any government which refused to utilize the machinery for the pacific settlement of dis-

23. Marburg, "The Backward Nation," *The Independent*, LXXII (June 20, 1912), 1365–1370.

24. Roderick H. Smith, *One of the Assets of the American Money Enterprise*, pp. 1–30. Smith quoted St. Pierre, Kant, and Franklin. Of contemporary internationalists, he apparently knew only Ginn and Holt. His early views can be found with a letter to Root, January 12, 1911, CEIP Papers.

putes, but the force could not be employed "to enforce the decrees of the Court of Nations." Only a limited application of power would be needed. In this respect, Smith's idea paralleled very closely those of the men who in 1915 organized the League to Enforce Peace.

In advocating force, Smith did not stand alone, since the idea of a combination of a few powers into a league to prevent war remained alive. In most instances, however, the proponents of such a course provided no details on how it should work.[25] Yet a few of them did elaborate. The proposal for a Western Hemisphere union to maintain peace in the Americas appealed to some men, and on April 23, 1913, Representative James L. Slayden of Texas introduced H.J. Res. 72. It called for an agreement between the "Governments of America" to provide "for the mutual guaranty of their sovereignty and territorial integrity." William I. Hull, possibly inspired by this action as well as by his country's willingness to settle the Mexican quarrel by mediation, responded with a "Solution of the Monroe Doctrine Problem." The United States should not be required to police the New World alone. "The tools of the new internationalism" should be applied so that the Hague structure could assume a greater responsibility in settling disputes judicially and in upholding decisions.[26] As a Quaker, Hull preferred pacific means to accomplish the latter, but as a last resort he accepted the possibility that arms in the form of "a genuine police force" might be needed. As a historian, Hull observed that Americans had once been urged "to think *continentally*," but now they should "think *internationally*."[27]

Two other outspoken advocates of military sanctions were clergymen. Dean Charles R. Brown of the Yale Divinity School and the Moderator of the Congregational Church declared that the world needed more than conferences, courts, and other devices if it were to eliminate war. The "new internationalism" might require "a great international police force exerting

---

25. David Davies, *The Problem of the Twentieth Century*, p. 107; George M. Stratton, "The Double Standard in Regard to Fighting," *International Conciliation*, No. 59 (October 1912), p. 12; J. W. Hamilton to Carnegie, February 26, 1913, (copy) SCPC; "A Practical Universal Peace Plan," *The Peace Forum*, II (November 1913), 19.

26. *Congressional Record*, 63 Cong., 1st sess., 50, pt. 1:357; Hull, "The Hague Solution of the Monroe Doctrine Problem," *Mohonk Report, 1914*, pp. 135–143; Hull, "The Abolition of Trial by Battle," *Editorial Review*, IV (April 1911), 345–346.

27. Hull, "International Interpretation of United States History," *History Teacher's Magazine*, V (May 1914), 135–139; Hull, "International Police, but Not National Armaments," Swarthmore College *Bulletin*, VII (September 1909), 24.

military pressure." The Unitarian minister William C. Gannett of Rochester, New York, believed that the force should also be used to uphold rules on which the nations had agreed, and it should serve with public opinion as "an International Protectorate . . . against national crimes."[28]

Robert Stein, a geologist from Washington, D.C., asked men to form another type of protectorate. The world had seen an evolving pattern of peace, and the time had come for the four major powers—Great Britain, France, Germany, and the United States—to unite and form a "Trust of Civilization." This agency would use arms to keep the peace, but Stein supplied no details on this point. John Bates Clark, with Sir George Paish of the London *Statist*, talked in terms of a "Standing Committee of the Powers" to protect the interests of mankind. It would be a league of ministers, "not a parliament of man," and it should begin modestly by having the Third Hague Conference create a permanent secretariat. This action would not bring "a world state," but it would be "a long step toward it."[29]

A more imaginative proposal came from Democratic Senator Thomas P. Gore of Oklahoma. He thought that nations should create "an international peace guarantee fund." Countries spent billions of dollars a year on armaments. They should reduce the amount to five hundred million and contribute an equal sum to a peace fund. The money would be invested in government bonds and in the stock of the major industries of the world. The contributors would then establish an international force to see that quarrels were adjudicated and that any wronged state received a monetary indemnity.[30]

Gore was not the only person who hoped to see arms reduced and a strong association organized. The World Peace Foundation became involved in 1914 in supporting a proposal which called for the major powers to reduce their armaments and then "jointly and severally agree to go to the aid" of the others "with the forces at their disposal in the event of any one of them being attacked on account of a reduction of armament." A number of congressional resolutions in 1913 and 1914 also played upon the theme that

28. Brown, "The Church and the New International Order," *Mohonk Report, 1914*, pp. 207–209; Gannett, "International Good-Will as a Substitute for Armies and Navies," *World Peace Foundation Pamphlets*, II (January 1912), 11–12.

29. Stein, *An International Police to Guarantee the World's Peace*, pp. 6–12, 20–21; Clark and Paish, "A Proposed Standing Committee of the Powers," *Mohonk Report, 1914*, pp. 121–124.

30. Gore, "The Foreign Policy of the United States," *Annals*, American Academy of Political and Social Science, LIV (July 1914), 280–281.

the third Hague Conference or some other agency should be handed the problem of reducing arms.[31] Many internationalists, however, could still not accept sanctions in any form.[32]

The year 1912 saw one other development in the history of the movement for a world organization. Two Americans helped lay a philosophical foundation beneath the various developing ideas. Frank Boas, professor of anthropology at Columbia, noted that in his field of study scholars observed a continual trend toward ever-enlarging units of society. Boas could see no reason to think that nations represented "the largest attainable social units" or that they would remain permanent. Sociologist Franklin H. Giddings, also of Columbia, presented an even more profound analysis. He quoted Herbert Spencer's observation that the smaller units of society tended to grow and then claimed that war seemed to be pushing men toward a "social integration." The greater the threat, the more effort responsible leaders exerted to achieve some equilibrium. Such progress came slowly, irregularly, and often by chance, Giddings claimed. It explained the development of the imperial system and the balance of power concept. The only hope lay in a continuing development of reason and law rather than of might, for few people wanted to see any one nation or coalition dominate the world.[33]

Giddings thus revealed philosophical and political concepts which underlay the crusade for an international organization, something most of the advocates did not discuss. The modern movement had emerged with the rise of democracy and self-government. Its very foundations rested upon ideals of co-operation, reason, and justice. Authoritarian concepts stood as an insurmountable obstacle, as Roosevelt had discovered when he sought to persuade the Kaiser to discuss a league of peace and as the war was soon to prove. Many internationalists had often quoted Kant's observation on

31. Denys P. Myers, "A Plan for Reduction of Armaments," *Mohonk Report, 1914*, p. 117; *Congressional Record*, 63 Cong., 1st sess., 50, pt. 3:2419 (S. Res. 136); *ibid.*, 2d sess., 51, pt. 1:32 (H.J. Res. 153); pt. 6:5074 (H. Res. 381); *ibid.*, 1st sess., pt. 15:14889 (H.J. Res. 341); *House Report* No. 416, 63 Cong., 2d sess.

32. F. H. Boardman to D. S. Jordan, June 12; Atherton Brownell to Jordan, November 16, 28, 1913, Jordan Papers; Alfred Hayes, "The Federation of the World," *South Atlantic Quarterly*, XII (October 1913), 369–373; R. M. MacIver, "War and Civilization," *International Journal of Ethics*, XXII (January 1912), 135–138, 142–145; Samuel J. Elder, "Judicial Determination in International Awards," *New England Magazine*, XLVII (May 1912), 140; Samuel T. Dutton, "The Federation of Peace," *The Independent*, LXXIV (January 23, 1913), 183–184; J. W. Van Kirk, *Worldism*, pp. 9–12.

33. Boas, "An Anthropologist's View of War," *International Conciliation*, No. 52 (March 1912), pp. 9, 13; Giddings, "The Relation of Social Theory to Public Policy," *ibid.*, No. 58 (September 1912), pp. 5–6, 8–10, 12–13.

the need for self-government, but no one expressed its significance more clearly than Giddings. The importance of democracy in achieving an organized world may go far to explain why the United States had become a leader in the movement and why the internationalists had concentrated upon educational campaigns, petitions, and congressional resolutions.

The Americans, of course, continued to enjoy the support of European advocates, for discussions had continued there between 1907 and 1914. There, too, proposals varied. Naturally a school existed which called for a European federation. One of the most vocal spokesmen was the German-born Englishman Sir Max Waechter. He led in founding a European Unity League and often labored with the Italian prince Orazio di Cassano-Zunica. The Russian sociologist Jacques Novicow died in 1912, but he had kept his book, *La fédération en Europe*, current by describing the tendencies toward unity in the form of arbitration treaties, congresses, plans for a court, and the Interparliamentary Union. Among less vocal spokesmen for a European association were the French journalist Francis de Pressensé, Winston Churchill, Lord Courtney of Penwith, and Sir Henry Campbell-Bannerman.[34]

Several other men who endorsed a European union also called for a wider federation. W. T. Stead, probably the foremost European internationalist until his death on the *Titanic* in 1912, presented his views often and with passionate determination. On the Continent, Walther Schücking, Alfred H. Fried, and Hans Wehberg of Germany, Váler Smialovzky of Hungary, E. Duplessix of France, and Albert Gobat of Switzerland all saw the vision clearly.[35]

Stead and Duplessix as well as Havelock Ellis endorsed the use of sanctions. Professor M. C. van Vollenhoven of Leyden and Professor Georg

34. Waechter, "The Federation of Europe; Is It Possible?," *Contemporary Review*, CII (November 1912), 621–630; Salvatore Cortesi, "The Federation of Europe," *The Independent*, LXVII (July 15, 1909), 121–123; Cassano, "European Federation," *Advocate of Peace*, LXXI (November 1909), 229–232; Cassano to J. B. Scott, September 4, 1913, CEIP Papers; Francis W. Fox, "The Federation of Europe," *Advocate of Peace*, LXXI (December 1909), 255–256; "Brief Peace Notes," *ibid.*, LXXVI (April 1914), 79; *Official Report*, Seventeenth Universal Congress of Peace, p. 65.

35. James A. Macdonald, "William T. Stead and His Peace Message," pp. 12–13; Stead, "To the Picked Half Million," *World Peace Foundation Pamphlets*, III (September 1913), 3–16; "Pan-European Bureau," *Advocate of Peace*, LXXI (December 1909), 248–249; "News and Notes," *American Political Science Review*, III (November 1909), 610–611; V. and T. Smialovzky, *Through Darkest Imperialism . . .* , p. 64; Gobat, "The International Parliament," *The Independent*, LV (May 14, 1903), 1148–1150; *Official Report*, Seventeenth Universal Congress of Peace, 410–442; "The World's Peace Confederacy," *The Peace Forum*, I (April 1913), 13; H. Ellis, "The War against War," *Atlantic Monthly*, CVII (June 1911), 751–761.

Grosch of Germany expressed their views clearly. Other advocates endorsed the concept in ambiguous fashion. At the Universal Peace Congress at London in 1908, the delegates accepted four principles on which to build a "Society of Nations." These included a legislative body, a court, an executive, and a reduction in arms to the size of a police force. By 1913, however, van Vollenhoven found it difficult to have the subject included on the agenda for the Twentieth Universal Peace Congress at The Hague.[36] In Europe, as in the United States, the topic attracted less attention than earlier.

The European advocates continually acknowledged that leadership in the movement belonged to the United States. They realized that the American form of government provided men with a convenient model to be copied and that the people most familiar with it should undertake the task of creating a world union. Moreover, many European governments, especially those on the Continent, lacked the democratic environment needed, and they did not encourage discussion on the subject even in ambiguous terms. This meant that the crusade had to develop in the New World.[37]

And there, despite the more limited efforts in 1913 and 1914, the dream of an international organization remained alive. It had been planted so firmly that the First World War did not destroy it but rather saw it grow. Scholars have tended, in seeking the origin of the League of Nations, to look no farther back in history than to the year 1914, but no revolution took place that summer or in the ensuing four years, especially in the United States. Americans were fully aware of the concepts when men began to talk about a league after the war began. The favorable public reaction which appeared in response to appeals for a postwar association can be traced in large measure to the work of the internationalists between 1900 and 1914. Even more significantly, however, the plans which proved to be the most popular from 1915 to 1919 were those which built upon the ideas and thinking of the prewar era. Nicholas Murray Butler expressed that point clearly in a

36. Ellis, "War against War," p. 761; "Progress in International Law," *The Outlook*, LXXXVIII (March 14, 1908), 609; "Sounding the Slogan of Peace Anew at the Hague," *Advocate of Peace*, LXXV (October 1913), 233–234; "Twentieth International Peace Congress," *ibid.*, pp. 197–198, 203; Grosch, "International Police Force," *The Peace Movement*, III (June 15, 1914), pp. 248–252; van Vollenhoven, "The Enforcement of Sanctions in International Law by Means of an International Police System," *ibid.*, II (June 15, 1913), 265–272; *ibid.*, (July 15, 1913), pp. 305–308; *ibid.*, (September 15, 1913), pp. 345–346; Beales, *History of Peace*, p. 274.

37. Waechter, "The Federation of Europe," pp. 624–625; Henri La Fontaine to J. B. Scott, January 20, 1913, CEIP Papers; Smialovzky, *Imperialism*, p. 64; Stead, "Internationalism as an Ideal for the Youth of America," *The Chautauquan*, LIV (May 1909), 335–337.

speech in 1917 when he asked his audience if they realized "the world owes to us very much of the progress which had already been made toward international organization when this war broke out?"[38]

While no one proposal had gained widespread acceptance by 1914, certain principles had emerged as part of internationalist thought in the United States. First, Americans had accepted the argument that an evolutionary process seemed at work, that any future society should build upon precedents and practices previously established. Second, they had come to believe in a democratic league modeled after their own nation—a federal union, a voluntary association in which men as well as countries would have some voice. The third belief followed naturally. Any agency should be built upon legal and judicial foundations. No other idea had appeared with greater frequency or consistency in the plans and discussions prior to 1914. The internationalists may have varied in their emphasis but not in their faith in these principles. Hamilton Holt summarized this philosophy in an oft-quoted phrase: "Peace is the outcome of justice, justice of law, law of world organization."[39] In these concepts, too, one finds that emphasis upon reason which continually appeared in American projects. Fourth, Americans had as yet to decide what to do about sanctions. They did agree that any military force should function under a system of law and justice, but they could not agree on how this police agency should operate, when it should be applied, or how it should be composed.

One might have thought that a war would have altered American thinking on these points. The clash of arms certainly disrupted the evolutionary developments of the previous fifteen years; it challenged democratic concepts everywhere; it defied all belief in law and justice; and it seemed to indicate a need for a supranational body with exceptional powers if the world was to avert such a catastrophe in the future. American internationalists, however, did not abandon any of these four principles. It should not be surprising that their ideas did not markedly change. They had spent years in developing them, and once they recovered from the shock of the war they set to work anew to create organizations and educate people for the task ahead.

38. *A World in Ferment*, p. 192.
39. "The Temple of Peace," *The Independent*, LXXV (September 4, 1913), 533; Kuehl, *Hamilton Holt*, pp. 63, 120.

Reawakened
Interest

The outbreak of war in the summer of 1914 found most Americans psychologically unprepared to cope with the event. This was especially true of pacifists and internationalists. They had labored for years to prevent such an occurrence, and the insignificance of their efforts left them impressed with their helplessness. At least one hundred thirty peace groups existed in the world in 1914; sixty-three of these were in the United States. The American Peace Society had enlarged its branches from seven in 1909 to thirty-one, and its paid membership had increased substantially. It claimed to be "the largest peace society in the world."[1] Yet it could do nothing to check warfare, and neither could the million-dollar foundations created by Ginn and Carnegie. The years of effort, the application of money, and the efforts to reorganize and consolidate pacifists into an efficient cooperative body had been meaningless.

What then could men do? The enormity of that question and its impact can be seen in the paucity of plans or comments about an international organization throughout July and August. Men had reached an impasse; they did not know where to turn. That they did not immediately suggest programs for a league of nations can be easily explained. First, virtually all

1. Beales, *History of Peace*, pp. 277–280; Curti, *Peace or War*, p. 201; A. D. Call, "The Recent Development of the . . . Peace Movement . . . ," *Mohonk Report, 1914*, p. 35.

thought and action in regard to world co-operation immediately before 1914 had been channeled along the lines of arbitral, legal, and judicial agreements. The war had proven how ineffective such machinery could be in time of crisis. Second, governments had insisted that participation in any international agency be completely voluntary. They thus nullified any chance of establishing an effective association since they would not support it. This condition did not change; indeed, the war stimulated a nationalistic spirit which accented even more the independence of states. Third, the prewar peace structure had been built upon treaty agreements, and any future league would have to rest on the same foundation. The war, however, had shattered the assumption that treaties had meaning. They had become "scraps of paper." The obligation of countries to honor their commitments had become meaningless. How then could any effective international body be established upon a voluntary basis?

The best evidence of the helpless situation appeared in the frustrating dilemma of what could be done about a third Hague Conference. The National Citizens' Committee, formed in the spring of 1914, continued to function, and as late as December of that year interested persons met to discuss the situation. Edwin Mead, in commenting upon this gathering, expressed what was already a dying thought when he noted that "in the regularizing and immense strengthening of the Hague Conferences and their conventions lies our hope." The dream of a third session at The Hague soon faded away.[2]

A few men did prepare suggestions for a league in August and September, but only after those months did plans appear with frequency. One of the first men to express his ideas was Charles W. Eliot. In a letter to President Wilson on August 6, he proposed that the members of the British Empire, the United States, France, Italy, Japan, and Russia unite in an "offensive and defensive alliance to rebuke" the Central Powers. A blockade, enforced co-operatively by these governments along with agreement on their part to renounce territorial ambitions, completed Eliot's scheme. Force, he noted, was essential to protect "civilization against a savagery" and to insure peace in Europe. Wilson apparently considered this idea but renounced it because, as he wrote Eliot, public opinion would not support it.[3]

2. "Peace Paragraphs," *The Independent,* LXXVIII (April 6, 1914), 57; *Yearbook,* NYPS, 1914, p. 12; E. D. Mead, "Annual Report," *World Peace Foundation Pamphlets,* IV (December 1914), 21; "Reminding us of the Hague Conference," *Advocate of Peace,* LXXVII (July 1915), 161.

3. Eliot to Wilson, August 6, 1914; Wilson to Eliot, August 14, 19, 1914 (copies), Edward M. House Papers, Yale University.

Eliot did not confine his efforts to the President. He also presented his views to officials of the Carnegie Endowment for International Peace. His suggestions, however, proved to be too controversial for Eliot's fellow trustees. Thus, he turned to the public forum by writing to the editor of the New York *Times*. That paper observed in an editorial that Eliot's desire to check war, "enforce order, justice, and peace," and promote free trade was no longer a dream. In fact, it marked the culmination of a generation of intelligent thought and planning. The principles upon which the United States had been built could be extended throughout the world.[4]

Eliot had proposed an international tribunal, the abolition of standing armies, and the creation of an armed force which would act against violators of treaty commitments. He had suggested the use of a police power as early as 1907 to maintain peace; in 1910 he called for an international navy to protect private property and trade in time of war. Countries that participated, he observed, might also agree to some limitation on armaments. In 1913, he again suggested "concerted action" to uphold rights and justice.[5]

Eliot, however, never elaborated upon his views. He presented only the skeleton of an idea. In a long interview with Edward Marshall in the New York *Times* and in an exchange of letters with New York banker Jacob H. Schiff, Eliot referred to a league only rarely and then in the broadest terms. In fact, Eliot, in discussing the subject, acknowledged that no one could see how a federation could be attained.[6]

Shortly after the war began, a Yale mathematician, Irving Fisher, prepared an article for the New York *Times*. He noted the possibility that countries would support "an international agreement backed up by military force—a league of peace such as Mr. Carnegie once proposed, but provided with some form of international police." The laws by which nations lived, said Fisher, needed effective sanctions. He therefore suggested that the Hague tribunal be moved to a safe area, that the governments establish a "league of nations," and that they create "a small international police force to enforce, if necessary the decrees of the court of arbitration." States would agree to submit their disputes to the judges and also "sanction the use of the international police to enforce the decrees of that court against any re-

4. Eliot to S. N. D. North, August 5, 1914; to J. B. Scott, September 7, 1914; Scott to Eliot, September 30, 1914, CEIP Papers; New York *Times*, December 28, 1914.

5. Eliot, "Address . . . ," *Mohonk Report, 1907*, pp. 91–92, 137–138; Eliot, "The Fears Which Cause the Increasing Armaments," *ibid., 1910*, pp. 97–102; Eliot, *The Road Toward Peace*, pp. 10–56.

6. Eliot, *Road Toward Peace*, pp. 127, 129–150; "The Eliot-Schiff Letters," *Current History*, I (January 9, 1915), 465–472.

fractory member of the league." Fisher acknowledged that his body would be "a rudimentary super-government," but it would also be an insurance company. It would be cheaper to pay the premium than to support vast armament programs or fight wars. To safeguard the members from any arbitrary action by the league, Fisher suggested that its authority be limited to peace-keeping except where nations agreed to extend its powers.[7]

Fisher was a newcomer to the scene, as was the young economist Roger Babson. Shortly after the war began, he observed that the world needed some type of international organization. The Hague court should be supplemented with a "legislative branch." Delegates would represent countries, but their voting power would be in ratio to their "fighting strength." He also envisaged some type of executive in the form of a commission elected by the congress. His government would "inaugurate and enforce the international policies agreed upon." This would be done by a call upon the members to supply "united navies and armies" when needed. Babson's league would be democratic in structure and operation, have no authority over the internal affairs of nations, and be restricted entirely to interstate matters which might lead to war. Babson also gave it some control over trade, communication, tariffs, and immigration. Indeed, he believed that any political structure would emerge from a "commercial federation." Like Eliot, he would also have granted it authority to neutralize sea lanes in time of conflict. Babson believed that the United States had reached a stage where it might fight to uphold such policies.[8]

Another proposal drafted late in the summer of 1914 came from Lars P. Nelson of Denver, Colorado. He prepared a congressional resolution which called for the creation of a popularly elected "International Senate" to function as "a permanent World Government." It would control armaments, act as a legislature, and serve as a supreme court from which there could be no appeal. It would guarantee the territorial integrity of members, but its coercive power would be confined to public opinion and economic sanctions. Aside from this limited concept of force, Nelson's plan came closer to being a call for a supranational agency than any other at the time. He criticized internationalists like Holt, who called for a limited organization. No country should have the right to veto legislation or be allowed to withdraw. A league had to "have absolute authority to be effective."[9]

7. New York *Times*, August 16, 1914; Bartlett, *League to Enforce Peace,* p. 29.
8. Babson, *The Future of World Peace*, pp. 69–77, 80, 93–97, 106–108.
9. Nelson to Trueblood, November 28, 1914, Trueblood Papers; Nelson to D. S. Jordan, November 10, 1914, Jordan Papers. Nelson claimed that he published an early draft of his plan in 1907.

Edgar D. Brinkerhoff, an accountant of Fall River, Massachusetts, also published one of the earliest complete schemes after the outbreak of war. It appeared on October 31 in a pamphlet on the "Constitution of the United Nations Of The Earth." Its details and length suggest that it had been written before July. He called for a world government, using the Constitution of the United States as a model. The congress could tax, regulate commerce, coin money, and maintain an army and navy. The union would protect members from external threats and on request come to their aid to suppress internal violence. A section on limitations of powers allowed countries control of their internal affairs, but only in a nominal way. Brinkerhoff's autocratic inclinations appeared in a provision that the constitution would take effect when accepted by eighteen nations, including the major powers, and that all others would then be required to join within ten years.[10]

A few other newcomers to the internationalists' ranks also summarized their ideas quite early. C. E. Grunsky, the president of the American Engineering Corporation in San Francisco, prepared in October a "Constitution of the United World" in which he called for a coalition to settle disputes, limit arms, uphold decrees of a court by force, and possess a vast number of economic and political powers. It would operate under a president, a cabinet, a legislature, and a court. Attorney and author Alfred O. Crozier drafted a scheme in August and mailed it to President Wilson. He too called for a "government of governments" with authority to enforce decrees and impose the will of the organization upon its members. Members had jurisdiction over their domestic affairs, but the "Nation of Nations" could control waterways, military bases and property, and even private business dealings. It could collect damages from aggressors, tax, and expel a state for nonpayment. Crozier paid but scant attention to judicial concepts.[11]

Another early and unusual proposal came from John van der Willen of Greeley, Colorado. He suggested the establishment of six regional unions as the basis for a universal league. Each group would send one man to serve on a central body which would act for the union and direct the international army. Elijah W. Sells of New York thought that a more complete government would be needed, and he introduced one idea of merit. States should contribute one third of their average budgets for the previous five years to the union and at the same time reduce their armaments by half. The organi-

10. Brinkerhoff, *Constitution for the United Nations Of The Earth,* pp. 5, 7–20.
11. Grunsky, *The Next Step,* pp. 12–14, 17–20; Crozier, *Nation of Nations: The Way to Permanent Peace,* pp. 6, 29–71.

zation would expend fifty percent of this income and invest the remainder in interest-bearing bonds. After twenty-five years, it would have an estimated guaranteed annual income of $450,000,000. Sells, a public accountant, provided detailed figures on costs and expenditures, the size of the forces needed, and the number of representatives from each nation.[12]

After September, more and more persons expressed interest in a league. They voiced opinions, however, rather than plans, and when they supplied details these reflected proposals already circulating.[13] Some of them were persons of prominence, including William Dean Howells and Louis Brandeis. The latter had reservations about many of the schemes being advanced, but he presented one idea which most planners had ignored. Some provision should be made for "the longing for self-expression" of governments great and small. No international organization should obliterate nations or restrict them unduly.[14]

The older spokesmen for world union were not to be outdone by these newcomers. They too explored the situation in the light of the war. Oscar Crosby led in publishing a forty-four-page pamphlet in August. He had written most of it while in Japan in the summer of 1914. He discussed the causes of the war, emphasized the need for an effective judicial body, and reverted to his idea of an armed tribunal. It should have power to support its decrees, to intervene where needed to stabilize governments or dependencies, and to protect members against attack. If nations would create a *"central force"* to uphold the court, countries might then disarm with safety. To achieve his goal, he had Senator John F. Shafroth of Colorado introduce a resolution which asked for an "International Court of Decree and Enforcement." Shafroth included numerous details on its organization,

12. John van der Willen to J. B. Scott, August 24, 1914, CEIP Papers; Sells, *A Plan for International Peace,* p. 5–20.

13. S. L. Fridenberg, *An Appeal for International Union,* pp. 5–6, 19–27; Carroll L. Riker, "International Police of the Seas," *Congressional News and Bulletin,* I (June 15, 1916), 12–15; Harry Hunt, "Now for a United States of the World." Detroit *Tribune,* October 18, 1914; H. L. Adamson to editor, *The Forum,* LII (November 1914), 779–780; Benjamin R. Andrews, "Education for Internationalism," *Teachers College Record,* XVI (January 1915), 69–70; Frank Crane, *War and World Government,* pp. 21–24, 34–36, 60–63, 80, 89–90, 99, 189–190, 196, 206, 211–214, 218–220, 227–230. Crane published a syndicated newspaper column which reached millions of readers. *Ibid.,* p. 7. Indicative of interest was the summary by George W. Nasmyth, "Ten Constructive Peace Programs," *The Survey,* XXXIII (March 6, 1915), 618–619.

14. [Howells], "Editor's Easy Chair," *Harper's Magazine,* CXXIX (November 1914), 960–961; Brandeis, "An Essential of Lasting Peace," *Harper's Weekly,* LX (March 13, 1915), p. 259.

its powers, and its operation, all of which reflected Crosby's scheme.[15] Crosby did not stop here, however, for early in 1915 he organized an Armed International Tribunal Association.

A second thinker to express his views did so privately in letters to President Wilson. William O. McDowell first wrote on July 30 with an appeal for a special session of Congress to enact the Sulzer-Robinson and Bartholdt measures which called for the convening of an international parliament. In a subsequent letter he called Wilson's attention to his constitution for a United Nations which had appeared in the *Journal of American History* in 1908.[16]

A third prewar advocate presented his ideas on September 23 in an article in *The Outlook*. Theodore Roosevelt discussed the war, its impact, and the future. If nations were to prevent comparable conflicts, he concluded, they would have to place force behind their treaty commitments. A judicially oriented league with "collective armed power" behind the decrees of the judges would be a sound move.[17]

Subsequently, Roosevelt wrote a series of articles for the New York *Times* and one for *The Independent* in which he spelled out his position. First, the major countries should unite in a "World League of the Peace of Righteousness." Second, they should reconstitute an "amplified Hague Court" and appoint men who would not represent nations but justice. Roosevelt provided no answer, however, to the insurmountable problem statesmen had faced on this subject since 1907. Third, states should agree on a list of national rights. These would include such matters as immigration, territorial integrity, and domestic questions. Then, "all should guarantee each of their number in the possession of these rights." This was certainly a sweeping obligation which only a few men had dared to propose. Finally, they should submit all other matters to the tribunal, accept the decisions, and "unite with their military forces to enforce the decree of the court as against any recalcitrant member." While he noted that disarmament might eventually be achieved under such an arrangement, Roosevelt did not elaborate upon that point.[18]

Internationalists, the New York *Times* observed in an editorial, had

15. Crosby, *The Constitution of an International Court of Decree and Enforcement*, pp. 35–41; Crosby to Short, January 4, 1915, NYPS Papers; *Congressional Record*, 63 Cong., 3d sess., 15, pt. 3:2941–2942.

16. McDowell to Wilson, July 31, 1914, May 12, 1915, McDowell Papers.

17. Roosevelt, "The World War: Its Tragedies and Its Lessons," *The Outlook*, CVIII (September 23, 1914), 169, 173, 175–178.

18. New York *Times*, October 4, 11, 18, November 1, 1914.

been proposing the same things for years. Why Roosevelt spoke as he did, however, remains a puzzle. He had been silent on a union since 1910, his correspondence in July and August reflects no profound interest in the matter, and he soon refused to co-operate with other internationalists in seeking a program of action. Lord James Bryce sent him some proposals for a league in the winter of 1914–1915, and Roosevelt initially commended them since he saw in them a program nearly identical to his. Yet by March of 1915, he wrote Bryce that he had but little interest in formulating details on the subject. Perhaps his utterances revealed less of a commitment to international organization than a desire to find some issue with which to embarrass President Wilson.[19]

In his *Independent* article, which appeared on January 4, 1915, Roosevelt elaborated upon three additional points which reveal that possibility and further disclose his ideas. For one thing, he left no doubt that he considered the membership of the United States essential to any association, and he castigated the Wilson administration for not honoring its obligations under the Hague treaties. Roosevelt incorrectly charged that the German attack upon Belgium violated principles of right and justice which the signatories should have upheld. They should respond in such instances with "their whole strength . . . against any nation which refuses to carry out the agreement, or which, if it has not made the agreement, nevertheless violates the principles which the agreement enforces." Governments could still make much progress "along the lines of the Hague Conventions." Second, Roosevelt suggested two categories of membership. "Contracting powers" would be responsible for maintaining the peace. They would appoint judges and be the voting members. Lesser states could join, enjoy the benefits, and co-operate, but they would have no rights until they gained sufficient statue to assume a share of the responsibility. Roosevelt's third point involved the controversial subject of the status quo. The rules under which the tribunal would act, he stated, would have to begin by stabilizing world conditions at some particular point in time.[20]

Two other prewar internationalists also voiced their views in the winter of 1914–1915. Both Raymond Bridgman and Richard Bartholdt resorted to their earlier methods of working through resolutions. Bridgman drafted

19. *Ibid.*, October 18, 1914; William C. Olson, "Theodore Roosevelt's Conception of an International League," *World Affairs Quarterly*, XXIX (January 1959), 340–341, 344–345, 350–351; William B. Howland to Roosevelt, December 17, 1914, Roosevelt Papers.

20. Roosevelt, "Utopia or Hell," *The Independent*, LXXXI (January 4, 1915), 14–16.

a petition which the Massachusetts legislature considered on January 21. It called for the Congress of the United States to invite all other governments to unite in "a World State" with legislative, executive, and judicial departments. It declared that this organization would not be hindered by national sovereignty. In February, both houses of the Massachusetts assembly approved the measure. Bartholdt's resolution reflected Crosby's views, for it called for an "international court of decree and enforcement for the adjustment of disputes" between governments. It would have a police force at its disposal, and all nations were to relinquish their naval vessels. The armies would be reduced to one soldier per thousand inhabitants. This plan went to the House Committee on Foreign Affairs, which never issued a report.[21]

Bartholdt was not the only representative to introduce into Congress a measure on a league. Republican William M. Calder of New York presented H.J. Res. 432 to the House on February 27, 1915, in which he called for a committee to plan for a combined navy from the neutral states to patrol sea lanes. Representative Charles F. Curry of California submitted H.J. Res. 396, which requested the president to call a world conference to achieve disarmament and to create "an international legislature, an international court, an international army and navy police, and for other purposes." Two less ambitious men, Democratic Representatives Walter L. Hensley of Missouri and Robert H. Gittens of New York, asked for a peace congress at the end of the war at which the powers would presumably discuss some form of co-operation.[22]

Bartholdt and Bridgman soon withdrew from the battle, although their reasons for doing so remain unclear. Neither became attached to the organizations formed in 1915 nor acted vigorously upon established convictions. Andrew Carnegie followed the same pathway, for his age and health soon forced him to retire from virtually all outside activities. He did, however, express his views in an article in *The Independent* on October 19 and in an interview published in the New York *Times* on November 26, 1914. He still called for a league "of powerful peace nations, resolved to preserve the peace themselves and also, if absolutely necessary, to enforce it upon others." This could be done, said Carnegie, by insisting that disputes be settled at the Hague Conferences or before some tribunal. Decisions would

21. Massachusetts *House Journal* (1915), pp. 151, 283, 448, 473–474; Massachusetts *Senate Journal* (1915), pp. 189, 266, 289, 305, 324, 361, 371; New York *Times,* January 20, 1915; *Congressional Record*, 63 Cong., 3d sess., 52, pt. 2:1917.

22. *Congressional Record*, 63 Cong., 3d sess., 52, pt. 5:4888; *ibid.*, pt. 1:899; *ibid.*, pt. 2:1484; *ibid.*, pt. 3:2365; New York *Times*, February 28, 1915.

be rendered by majority vote and "be binding upon the powers." Thus he still believed in military sanctions to uphold the peace, but he had not developed his ideas.[23]

Other prewar internationalists did not greatly alter their views as a result of the struggle in Europe. Neither Lucia Mead nor Fanny Fern Andrews expressed an immediate opinion on an organization, but they soon became supporters of the League to Enforce Peace.[24] Nicholas Murray Butler insisted that the goal of union might still be achieved through education and understanding. A European federation seemed inevitable, said Butler, as he admitted that the old machinery had failed. "New and constructive methods" had to be found, but he refused to join in efforts to find them. When the leaders of the League to Enforce Peace sought to enroll him in their ranks, he claimed that his position with the Carnegie Endowment for International Peace did not enable him to lend his name to any other peace group. This was a false excuse, because he later allowed the World's Court League to use his name.[25]

None of these individual planners possessed sufficient interest or influence to rally men behind them. Only those advocates who had been most fully organized in the prewar years seemed capable of that task. Most of them had joined the New York Peace Society where they had influenced that body's campaign for the Bennet resolution, and it absorbed the World-Federation League. Of its internationalists, no one was more important than Hamilton Holt, and it was under Holt's leadership that the League to Enforce Peace appeared in 1915.[26]

The chain of events began with a series of lectures to the New York Peace Society by former president Taft in 1913. Holt had persuaded Taft to assume this task, had obtained permission to print them in *The Independent*, and had agreed to help Taft arrange them for book publication. It had been Holt, therefore, who had suggested to Taft that he include the subject of

23. Carnegie, "A League of Peace—Not 'Preparation for War,' " *The Independent*, LXXX (October 19, 1914), 89–90; New York *Times*, November 26, 1914.

24. L. A. Mead, "America's Danger and Opportunity," *The Survey*, XXXV (October 23, 1915), 90–92; L. A. Mead, "The Woman's Peace Party," *Advocate of Peace*, LXXVII (February 1915), 35–36; *Addresses Given at . . . The Woman's Peace Party*, pp. 5, 6, 8, 14.

25. New York *Times*, October 18, 1914; Butler, "The Work of Reconstruction," *Advocate of Peace*, LXXVI (November 1914), 235; Butler, *The Changed Outlook*, pp. 8–9; Butler to George H. Perris, February 9, 1915; Short to Butler, May 3, 1915; Butler to Short, May 6, 1915, CEIP Papers.

26. Bartlett, *League to Enforce Peace*, pp. vii, 27; Kuehl, *Hamilton Holt*, pp. 125–126.

world federation in one of his addresses. Taft accepted this advice and Holt supplied much of the data for this lecture. Taft expressed no unique opinions, but his words committed him to an ideal, gave him prominence in the movement, and influenced his later decision to assume the presidency of the League to Enforce Peace.[27]

Holt forged the next link in the chain with a plan printed in *The Independent* on September 28, 1914. He had drafted his proposal after considerable thought and discussion, especially with William Short. At least eleven days before his editorial appeared, he had summarized it in a speech in Boston, so his ideas represented no hasty rush into print. In fact, the essential points reflected ideas long current; but the war, he noted, had forced mankind to reconsider the possibility of a league. Now there could be no doubt about its need or of the fact that the United States should participate. The time had come to issue a "Declaration of Interdependence."

Developments in international law and the establishment of the Hague tribunal, Holt argued, offered hope for a future "parliament of man." Governments should create a "court with jurisdiction over all questions," and there should be "conferences with power to legislate on all affairs of common concern, and an executive power of some form to carry out the decrees of both." Such a league would be "a first step toward world federation" which would "not offer insuperable difficulties."[28] The chief problem was that of sanctions. Force, Holt observed, could be used for aggression, for defense, and for protection. Mankind should limit its application to the last by creating an international army and navy. As nations contributed arms to this agency, they could disarm and rely upon the league. They would then support it with fervor.[29]

Holt listed five principles upon which such a union could be built. These included his proposal on disarmament, a pledge by which members would "mutually agree to respect the territory and sovereignty of each other," a provision to settle by arbitration "all questions" which could not be resolved by diplomacy, an assembly to meet periodically to "make all rules to become law unless vetoed by a nation within a stated period," and a clause providing for withdrawal and for expulsion.

27. Kuehl, *Hamilton Holt*, p. 127; Taft, *U.S. and Peace*, pp. vii, 133–182.

28. Kuehl, *Hamilton Holt*, pp. 119–121; William H. Short, "How the League of Nations Came to Be," mimeographed copy of speech, 1926, Short Papers, Rollins College; Holt, "The Way to Disarm: A Practical Proposal," *The Independent*, LXXIX (September 28, 1914), 427–429.

29. Holt, "Way to Disarm," pp. 428–429.

In expounding upon these principles, Holt added other points. He believed that only two matters—land and independence—were vital to countries. If these could be guaranteed by a pledge to respect them, most wars would cease, and all other problems could be arbitrated. He added the provision for a veto to prevent coercion by the league against any one power. The right of withdrawal further insured justice, and the clause on expulsion had been included for two reasons. Members could eliminate any state which indefinitely blocked action, and governments which violated their pledge to respect the territory and independence of nations could be punished in this way.[30]

In terms of length, detail, constructive thought, and—except for Roosevelt—influence, Holt's editorial equaled or surpassed all contemporary suggestions. It circulated widely in *The Independent*, appeared in a condensed version in newspapers, reached thousands in reprint form, and was republished as a pamphlet by both the Church Peace Union and the American Association for International Conciliation. Holt possessed a flare for publicity, and he solicited the opinions of dozens of notable persons, presented their views on his plan in *The Independent*, and thus kept interest alive.[31]

Nor did he rest with his original scheme. Within two weeks, Holt prepared another editorial to rectify an apparent weakness in the first. He had not, he noted, elaborated sufficiently on how his police force would function or what authority it should possess. It should defend members and uphold "international law and order." It would compel the submission of disputes to a court, aid members against outside powers which ignored the pacific machinery, and "enthrone law and suppress arbitrary action." This emphasis upon justice reflected Holt's concern that the union never act in arbitrary fashion or "become a League of Oppression." The United States should be willing to support such a noble venture, Holt argued. If the Constitution imposed a barrier, it should be amended. All obstacles had "to give way."[32]

Response to Holt's proposal was generally favorable. Many persons and newspapers acknowledged that the time had come to abandon traditional policies and assume new obligations. A few commentators added suggestions of their own, including one for an economic boycott and another for a tax upon nations equal to their armaments budget, which would be used to

30. *Ibid.*

31. Kuehl, *Hamilton Holt*, pp. 122–123.

32. [Holt], "The Enforcement of Peace," *The Independent,* LXXX (October 12, 1914), 43–44.

maintain the police force. Some writers feared that the scheme was too visionary and that it would be impossible to get governments to agree or to honor their commitments. Only a few editors, notably those of the *Army and Navy Journal* and the Chicago *Tribune*, raised major objections.[33]

Holt's plan, however, had a lasting impact, not because of the publicity and commentary it aroused, but because it stimulated a small group of internationalists to action. The first development appeared in the New York Peace Society where they formed a Plan of Action Committee which met throughout October, November, and December of 1914. The second step came with a suggestion by Theodore Marburg that a series of dinners be held at which the participants would analyze Holt's editorial to see if they could improve upon it. From these gatherings, agreements emerged which led to the League to Enforce Peace. The founding of that organization has been recounted in detail in other studies; hence, it is important here only to explore the ideas expressed in the various meetings and to analyze the final program in terms of earlier and later proposals.[34]

The first discussions in the New York Peace Society were dominated by Holt and Short, who knew exactly what they wanted. Even so, Holt found it difficult to steer the subject away from plans for a conference to stop the war and to keep the topic confined to a union of nations to enforce peace. However, the discussants finally emerged with a plan which went beyond Holt's editorial. It suggested an exceptional program of sanctions. The treaty creating the organization "not only might arrange the boundaries of the States and their colonies but might guarantee the territories so established against attack either from within or from without the League." Any nation threatened "would have a right to call on all remaining members of the League to assist in defending it." This provision for mutual defense would enable governments to reduce armaments and still feel secure; it would also prevent the police force from becoming too large or independent. The plan further suggested the renewal of the Hague Conferences, the establishment of "a complete International Court of Justice," the signing of a treaty providing for the submission of all disputes to arbitration or to the court, and the convening of periodic meetings of the powers to promote "measures

33. "The League of Peace, Comment and Criticism on the Plan . . . ," *ibid.*, (October 26, 1914), pp. 125–126; "The League of Peace: Further Comment . . . ," *ibid.*, (November 16, 1914), p. 252; *Army and Navy Journal*, LII (October 3, 1914), 137; Chicago *Tribune*, October 13, 1914.

34. Contemporary accounts appear in Short, "How the League of Nations Came to Be," and in Marburg, *League of Nations: A Chapter . . .* , I, 43–68. This study relies largely upon Bartlett, *League to Enforce Peace*.

of common interest" and to remove "in their incipient stage causes of contention."[35]

The New York Peace Society approved the report of this committee, but Holt and Short doubted whether the Society possessed the dynamic leadership for an aggressive campaign. Therefore, Holt acted on Marburg's advice that they invite a number of scholars to dinner to discuss Holt's editorial. After these men arrived at some definite conclusions, they could solicit the opinions of statesmen and individuals who had practical experience in such matters. Marburg admitted that he had been wrong in his advice to Holt in 1911. He now agreed that force had to be an essential ingredient in any union.[36]

Hence, at four meetings at the Century Club in New York City on January 25 and 31, March 30, and April 9, 1915, a group of prominent citizens debated the best course to follow. Most of those attending the first three dinners sympathized with the stated goal of a league. What they had to agree upon were the terms or conditions under which it would operate.

Discussions at the first session touched upon a number of topics. Should the organization be formed through diplomacy or by conference? How extensive should its powers be? What role should force play? While they could not answer all these questions, the participants did agree on several points. They opposed my association with extensive authority; it should be "a Confederation of Governments rather than a Federation." It should insist that all controversies between members "be settled amicably." This formula would keep peace within the league; but there had to be some protection against aggression from outsiders. Hence, they accepted, with four dissenting votes, a resolution that the league guarantee "members against the invasion or impairment of its territory or sovereignty by an outside nation." Finally, they agreed that membership be open as fully as possible and that the United States should lead in seeking such an organization.[37]

---

35. Short, "How the League of Nations Came to Be"; Bartlett, *League to Enforce Peace*, pp. 30–33; Plan of Action and Executive Committees to Members and the Constituency (printed brochure), January 6, 1915, NYPS Papers.

36. Kuehl, *Hamilton Holt*, pp. 125–126.

37. *Minutes*, January 25, 1915, League to Enforce Peace Papers, Harvard University, hereafter cited as LEP Papers; John H. Latané, ed., *Development of the League of Nations Idea: Documents and Correspondence of Theodore Marburg*, II, 703–706, contains a summary by Marburg. Participants with the number of meetings attended were: FOUR—Holt, Short, John Bates Clark, Harold J. Howland, William B. Howland; THREE—Marburg, Franklin H. Giddings, Frederick Lynch, William I. Hull, Irving Fisher, George H. Kirchwey, John Hays Hammond; TWO—Westel W. Willoughby, James A. Stewart, George A. Plimpton; ONE—Theodore S. Woolsey, James

At the second dinner, discussion began anew, with no one committed to the resolutions already adopted. Hence, the participants reconsidered their previous motions and redrafted them. They accepted a statement that disputes between members be settled amicably and that an offending power face the "united forces of the League" if it did not co-operate. This more precise and limited clause gained the unanimous support of the discussants. They then adopted a resolution introduced by Irving Fisher which obligated them to the principle "that the use of military force by the League be sanctioned." They next agreed that controversies should be submitted to existing tribunals or to "a true international court of justice" and that the union would begin to operate whenever the governments adhering to it "represent a sufficient preponderance of military power to enable it to enforce its decision."[38]

The third session did not take place until March 30. Two significant developments marked this meeting. For one thing, Holt sought unsuccessfully to obtain approval for a legislative assembly even though he expressed a readiness to accept the Hague Conferences as such. Second, the participants adopted certain changes in response to the Bryce-Dickinson "Proposals for the Avoidance of War," which had been received in the United States on February 24. Lord Bryce and Sir Willoughby Dickinson had organized a discussion group in England which had formulated a set of principles on which a union might be based. Their ideas, especially the provisions on how differences should be resolved, impressed the men at the Century Club. The members of an association, according to the "Proposals," would agree not to resort to war until they had selected one of three agencies to which to refer a dispute. They could take justiciable questions to an arbitral tribunal or a court of justice, and all other matters would go to a Council of Conciliation which could also determine whether a controversy was justiciable or not. The five-point program adopted by the Holt-Marburg body on March 30 combined the best ideas from both groups.

1. The function of the League of Peace shall be to guarantee that no dispute to which a member of the League is a party shall be settled by other than amicable means, the guarantee to be maintained when necessary by the use against the offending nation of the united forces of the nations of the League.

L. Tryon, Frank Crane, George C. Holt, Frederick N. Judson, Everett P. Wheeler. At the fourth session, a number of new persons appeared—Albert Shaw, Leo S. Rowe, Henry S. Pritchett, A. Lawrence Lowell, Darwin P. Kingsley, Andrew D. Humphrey, William C. Dennis, J. Reuben Clark, Jr., James M. Beck, and William Howard Taft.
   38. Latané, *Development*, II, 706–709; *Minutes*, January 31, 1915, LEP Papers.

2. Disputes not settled by diplomacy to which a member of the League may be a party shall be referred for settlement to existing institutions, such as the International Committee of Inquiry, the Permanent Court of Arbitration, good offices, mediation, or to other institutions to be established for that purpose. The early creation of an International Court of Justice is held to be especially important.

3. The League ought to be formed as soon as practicable but not until the nations adhering to its constitution shall represent a sufficient preponderance of power to enable it to maintain the guarantees of the League.

4. Initiative for the formation of a League of Peace ought to be taken by the United States immediately without waiting for the ending of the present war.

5. The nations of the League shall provide an assembly to meet periodically to discuss affairs of common concern.[39]

The Bryce "Proposals" reflected a much more judicial concept toward the settlement of disputes than did this American program. The Englishmen also revealed a better grasp of the historical evolution toward a world organization. They embodied ideas which had been circulating for years, especially in the United States. Lord Bryce must have been familiar with American internationalist thought. He had attended the sessions of the Interparliamentary Union in 1906 where he surely heard of Bartholdt's plan and Bryan's proposal. He had served as ambassador in America during the discussions over the Bennet resolution and the Taft arbitration treaties, had participated in the Peace Congress in Baltimore in 1911, had contributed articles to Holt's *Independent*, and had welcomed the Bryan "cooling-off" pacts. It is not surprising, therefore, that the "Proposals" contained ideas which had appeared in the Taft and Bryan agreements. Both had distinguished between justiciable and nonjusticiable disputes and provided for councils of conciliation.

The Englishmen did contribute something new, however, for they sought to define the word "justiciable." Controversies fell into that category if they raised any questions involving the "interpretation of a treaty as to any question of international law, as to the existence of any fact which, if established, would constitute a breach of any international obligation, or as to the nature and extent of the reparation to be made for any such breach." The League to Enforce Peace had avoided this touchy subject, but the Bryce-Dickinson definition proved to be so sound that its basic formula appeared later in Article XIII of the Covenant and subsequently in the statutes creating the

---

39. *Minutes*, March 20, 1915, LEP Papers; Latané, *Development*, II, 709–713. The Bryce "Proposals" in typescript can be found in the CEIP Papers and the Holt Papers.

Permanent Court of International Justice and the International Court of Justice.[40]

The "Proposals" also explored the idea of conciliation more fully than ever before. They suggested that the Council be a permanent agency. The Taft treaties had included a provision for such a body, but it was to be created by governments whenever needed. The Bryan accords provided for established commissions but not for a universal one as did the Bryce plan. It would be of considerable size, since each "Great Power" could name three members to it. The Council of Conciliation became the heart of the structure because of its functions. It could decide nonjusticiable questions, invite nations to submit controversies to it, and publish its findings and recommendations. It could also suggest a course of action on matters not referred to it whenever peace was threatened, and it could propose a program of disarmament.

The Bryce propositions thus relied upon existing machinery but called for significant improvements. Governments were to promise not to resort to war until they had exhausted every channel created. Then, after a year to eighteen months, a country could embark upon hostilities if it so wished. If it did so then, the signatories would consult regarding a course of action. If it chose to fight before it honored its treaty commitments, the other signers would automatically refuse to support it and go to the aid of the state attacked, taking "diplomatic, economic or forcible" action.

The word league did not appear in the "Proposals." No such aim was implied, for the clause on sanctions specifically noted that any decision would be made not by the Council but by the "Powers acting in concert." It is difficult to see how the proposal for an automatic response can be reconciled with this point. The internationalists in the United States realized this when they retained in their propositions of March 30 their opinion that a league with an assembly should be formed. These clauses took their program far beyond the Bryce plan. And they recognized the difference when they insisted upon retaining a clear program of guaranteed sanctions to be applied by the organization.

The influence of the Bryce "Proposals" continued at the fourth meeting of the Holt-Marburg group on April 9. Several of the participants of the

---

40. Dubin, "Collective Security," p. 128; Dickinson, "The Way Out," *War & Peace*, I (September 1914), 345–346. The arbitration treaties of 1911 and Taft had defined justiciable disputes in brief fashion as controversies which could be settled by the "application of the principles of law or equity." Taft, "The Dawn of World Peace," *International Conciliation*, Special Bulletin, November 1911, pp. 7, 11.

earlier dinners attended to explain their work to the practical statesmen who appeared. They included such international lawyers as William C. Dennis and J. Reuben Clark, Jr., and such attorneys as James M. Beck, a former United States Assistant Attorney General. The most notable figures, however, were Darwin P. Kingsley, president of the New York Life Insurance Company, A. Lawrence Lowell, president of Harvard, and Taft. Taft's presence represented a singular victory. Members of the New York Peace Society had tried to persuade him to accept the leadership of a committee they were organizing, but Taft had turned them down. Holt and Short, however, had reasoned with Taft and had finally broken his resistance.[41]

All of the diners had received copies of the previous discussions, the resolutions, the Bryce "Proposals," and projects by Holt, Fisher, and Marburg. Holt informed them that there were two ideas—a court and a league—implicit in the American plan. One implied the other, for the machinery to settle disputes could not stand alone. Taft disagreed with this view, which had been embodied in the resolutions. They were too ambitious. They required the United States to enter "a defensive alliance with European nations which would bind us to take part in an European war if such should arise." He favored a judicial system with conferences to formulate laws. The league could come later. Once countries signed treaties agreeing to submit their quarrels to an organization they would in time then consider how decisions should be enforced.[42]

The sanctionists must have been discouraged at Taft's words, but another newcomer, Lowell, arose to defend their propositions. He replied that international law meant nothing if not enforced. The United States might not be prepared, he admitted, to uphold arbitral awards, but it might be ready to compel the submission of disputes "to a proper tribunal." This would be especially true of nonjusticiable questions, said Lowell, for they would be more likely to result in war. In any case, the application of force "should be automatic instead of subject to the decision of a meeting of the powers."[43]

While other moderate voices that day called for delay and for less ambitious action, the sanctionists won. The acceptance of some of Taft's suggestions, however, reveals the spirit of compromise. He proposed that nations agree to send justiciable disputes to a court and that for other issues they

41. Kuehl, *Hamilton Holt*, p. 127; Charles S. Macfarland, *Pioneers for Peace Through Religion*, p. 235; Taft to George W. Kirchwey, February 5, 1915, Taft Papers.
42. *Minutes*, April 9, 1915, LEP Papers; Short to Taft, April 6, 1915, Taft Papers.
43. Bartlett, *League to Enforce Peace*, p. 36.

sign treaties similar to the Bryan pacts for a cooling-off period of a year. Then, if nations violated these pledges they would face "the joint force of all the members of the League."

The final agreements appeared as four resolutions.

1. That it is the opinion of those present that it is desirable for the United States to form a League of all the great nations in which all justiciable questions between them would be submitted to a judicial tribunal.

2. That members of the League shall jointly use their military force to prevent any one of their number from going to war or committing acts of hostility against any member before the question at issue has been submitted to the tribunal.

3. That nations shall be compelled to submit non-justiciable questions to a Council of Conciliation before going to war, under the same penalty as provided above.

4. That conferences between the parties to this agreement shall be held from time to time to formulate and to codify rules of international law which, unless some nation shall signify its dissent within a stated period, shall thereafter govern in the decision of the aforementioned tribunal.[44]

The first and third provision borrowed heavily from the Bryce "Proposals," but since the men who formulated those had been impressed by the Taft and Bryan treaties, even these points could be traced to Americans. The major distinction from the English plan continued, however, with American insistence upon a real league and, as Lowell had argued, automatic sanctions. Also, the last resolution revealed a further distinction. Holt had finally won his point that in some way international laws should be formulated as well as codified.[45]

Taft later expressed surprise at the degree of agreement and at the "snap" of the final proposals, but he did not abandon the venture. He reviewed the resolutions, edited them, and supported them publicly. Hence, in ensuing weeks, through speeches, articles, and editorials, the "founding fathers" of the new movement presented their program to the people. Behind the scenes, they also circulated their ideas to win waverers to the cause and to inform statesmen of their actions. Marburg kept in touch with the Bryce group and also sent President Wilson and the State Department detailed information on every meeting. At the Lake Mohonk Conference in May 1915, these advocates virtually dominated the discussions. The platform endorsed the major provisions, but the delegates there rejected the one on

44. *Ibid.*, pp. 36–37.

45. I am indebted to Professor Martin Dubin of Northern Illinois University for allowing me to read a manuscript, "A Prelude to the Covenant," in which he examines the impact of the Bryan treaties upon Bryce and other Englishmen.

force. A few men, like Eliot, had argued that the clauses should be stronger, but most of the speakers thought otherwise.[46] Surely a vast campaign would be needed to persuade the American people on that point.

The league men, therefore, kept building. They formed a national committee and called for an organizing meeting on Bunker Hill Day, July 17, in Independence Hall. While a more auspicious date might have been picked, Taft's schedule determined the time. Holt had suggested the Philadelphia setting for a movement which would present to the world a declaration of interdependence, but this idea was not original with him.[47]

At Philadelphia some three hundred delegates discussed the original declaration and adopted it with only a few changes. For one thing, the phrase, "subject to the limitation of treaties," was added to the clause on justiciable disputes to clarify that point. It would, as Marburg explained, allow states to negotiate treaties in which they could exempt specific questions from obligatory action. This also revealed an awareness of the Senate's objection to all-encompassing arbitration accords.

A second, more important, revision came in the provision on sanctions. The delegates agreed that in addition to military force economic pressures might also be applied. Several men had proposed such a change before the meeting, and their view prevailed. Thus, the plan read that "The signatory powers shall jointly use forthwith both their economic and military forces against any one of their number that goes to war, or commits acts of hostility against another of the signatories before any question arising shall be submitted as provided in the foregoing." The sanctionists won an even greater victory in naming the society. It was to be the League to Enforce Peace.[48]

Since considerable misunderstanding developed at the time and later over this word "enforce," it should be noted that it involved a carefully limited application of power. The association did not guarantee the territory or independence of members, and its rules applied exclusively to them. The platform said nothing about disarmament or a police force; it avoided the

46. Taft to Mabel T. Boardman, April 12, 1915, Taft Papers; [Holt], "The League of Peace at Mohonk," *The Independent*, LXXXII (May 31, 1915), 340; Latané, *Development*, I, 23–45; Marburg to Taft, May 23, 1915, Taft Papers; *Mohonk Report, 1915*, pp. 9–10; Eliot, "Hopes for the Future," *ibid.*, pp. 156–160.

47. *Minutes*, April 9, 1915; Holt to Lowell, May 25, 1915, Holt Papers.

48. Bartlett, *League to Enforce Peace*, pp. 39–41; Charles R. Ashbee, *The American League to Enforce Peace*, pp. 21–22; Short to Holt, June 3, 1915 (copy), Taft Papers; Marburg to Bryce, July 16, 1915, in Latané, *Development*, I, 48. Speeches and discussions at this meeting were published as *League to Enforce Peace, American Branch*.

subject of who could join or whether the union would be an indissoluble one; and it did not provide for any response where wars broke out after governments had followed the rules and first submitted the dispute for settlement. It concentrated entirely upon compelling nations to bring their differences to the machinery of a league. Lowell clearly expressed the reasoning involved. Any concerted action by countries after the outbreak of fighting would be futile. An international organization to be effective had to prevent war, not end it once it began. The leaders of the League to Enforce Peace reiterated those points over and over again. As Marburg wrote, it "was fundamentally a league to compel inquiry before nations are allowed to fight." Taft expressed it another way by noting that "the whole League shall use its entire power to require any member of the League that wishes to fight any other member of the League, to submit the issue upon which that member desires to go to war to a machinery for its peaceful settlement before it goes to war."[49]

The entire program reflected the assumed success of the arbitral system and developments in creating commissions of inquiry in the prewar years. They had presumably proven that wars would not come when governments allowed their differences to be discussed and took time to have tempers cool. All disputes should be resolved in this way, and since nations had not been willing in every instance to utilize the pacific machinery available voluntarily, they had to be compelled to do so. This idea had been evolving for years. The League to Enforce Peace planners simply built upon what had gone before. First, they restated the type of system to be erected; then they provided alternatives for governments so that states could raise no objections about rigid formulas or requirements; third, they abandoned the voluntaristic philosophy for a compulsory feature. While the latter represented a notable step, it reflected a discussion which had been current for years. They devised a moderate program which seemed reasonable. Finally, they accepted the suggestion that international laws should be formulated and codified. Despite much advocacy here, nations had made but little headway in adopting such a principle; hence it was the most radical feature of the platform.

The society formed at Independence Hall was not the only one founded in the winter and spring of 1914–1915. At least a dozen groups appeared which included some plan for an international organization. One of these represented the leading social workers of the nation led by Paul Kellogg,

---

49. Lowell to C. R. Ashbee, June 1, 1915, Lowell Papers, Harvard University; Marburg, *League of Nations*, I, 73; *League to Enforce Peace* (undated leaflet), Holt Papers; Marburg to Bryce, November 29, 1916, Latané, *Development*, I, 212–213.

Lillian Wald, and Jane Addams. They invited prominent citizens to a discussion at the Henry Street Settlement as early as September 29. At least two of the men present, Holt and Professor George W. Kirchwey of Columbia, later participated in the League to Enforce Peace discussions. The boldest suggestion called for a Pan-American congress to have the countries of the Western Hemisphere "act in concert" in placing the subject of arms limitation before the Hague Conference.[50]

They continued their conversations, however, and in March *The Survey* printed their statement. It revealed a paramount concern over the causes of war and other world problems, but one paragraph dealt with a league. Treaty-making should be elevated to a position where it could "lay the foundations for that world organization which" should establish permanent peace. In a special editorial accompanying the statement and in articles, *The Survey* committed itself to a program of a federation with an "international police" to protect commerce, and with a duty to maintain trade on the high seas and the access to all waterways.[51]

A more forceful group which enjoyed the support of Jane Addams and Holt also appeared. It began with the Emergency Federation of Peace Forces, headed by Louis Lochner. He had become secretary of the Chicago Peace Society, and he started his work after the Socialist-pacifist Rosika Schwimmer delivered a speech in Chicago in November of 1914. The formation of the Emergency Federation on December 19 revealed that the Middle West, too, felt the impact of war and wondered what could be done. A mass meeting on January 17 resulted in a call for an assembly in Chicago on February 27–28, at which time the delegates changed the name to the National Peace Federation.[52]

At those sessions at which Jane Addams presided, many speakers, including Holt, explored a course of action. The final platform urged an immediate conference of neutral countries to act as a mediation body to which the belligerents could submit their cases. It then recommended a set of principles for the postwar world. These included "(a) An international court for

50. Lillian Wald to William I. Hull, September 24, 1914, Hull Papers; Jane Addams, *Peace and Bread in Time of War*, pp. 2–3; *Minutes*, September 29, 1914, Emily G. Balch Papers, SCPC.

51. "Towards the Peace That Shall Last," *The Survey*, XXXIII (March 6, 1915), part II; "Federation of Governments, A Possible Solution to Peace," *ibid.*, (March 6, 1915), 631–632; Mercedes M. Randall, *Improper Bostonian: Emily Greene Balch*, p. 136.

52. "The Emergency Federation of Peace Forces," *Advocate of Peace*, LXXVII (February 1915), 42–43; "The Significance of the Chicago Conference," *ibid.*, (April 1915), pp. 78–79; Lochner to Butler, January 11, 1915, CEIP Papers.

the settlement of all disputes between nations; (b) An international congress, with legislative and administrative powers . . . (c) An international police force; . . . (d) non-intercourse, as the sanction and enforcement of international obligations." A call for disarmament, the neutralization of trade routes in wartime, and other current aims of the extension of democracy and the popular control of foreign policy completed the plan. As permanently organized, it named Holt president, Miss Addams vice president, and Lochner secretary.[53]

Jane Addams did not confine her activities to the two organizations described. She also led the women of the world in a peace crusade, beginning in the United States with a rally in January 1915 in Washington, D.C., at the annual meeting of the National Federation of Women's Clubs. The platform reflected pacifist goals, but it contained provisions endorsing a "Concert of Nations," the substitution of "Law for War," and an international police force.[54]

Miss Addams later led a delegation of women to The Hague where in April they introduced their program. This included clauses supporting "A Concert or League of Nations open to all States," education "on the principles of world organization," a reconstructed Hague system with a judicial court, and regular conferences to "formulate rules of international law to govern in the decisions of the world court." The resolutions adopted at The Hague embodied these ideals with ones for a Council of Conciliation and Investigation, for mediation, and for a greater role for women in important affairs.[55]

Although she supported such plans, Miss Addams refused to embrace the program of the League to Enforce Peace when it emerged. "Its liberal concessions as to the use of warfare" did not seem to be what the world needed at the time. Miss Addams maintained this conservative outlook until 1919 when she spoke for the League of Nations under the auspicies of the League to Enforce Peace. Her stand then was much more compatible with

53. Kuehl, *Hamilton Holt*, p. 108; "Tentative Program," Holt Papers; Randolph S. Bourne, comp., *Towards An Enduring Peace: A Symposium of Peace Proposals and Programs, 1914–1916*, pp. 264–266.

54. *Ibid.*, pp. 268–269; "Women for Peace," *The Independent*, LXXXI (January 25, 1915), 120.

55. James W. Linn, *Jane Addams: A Biography*, pp. 301–305; Mary Chamberlain, "The Women at the Hague," *The Survey*, XXXIV, (June 5, 1915), 219–222; "Tentative Program for discussion . . . ," typed carbon, F. F. Andrews Papers; "Resolutions Adopted by the International Congress of Women," *The Survey*, XXXIV (June 5, 1915), 218.

her response at Chicago in 1915 and with her approval of the Bennet resolution's call for a naval police force in 1910.[56]

Other societies which emerged in the winter of 1914–1915 reveal efforts on the state level. In Kansas, Andrew M. Brodie, a Presbyterian minister, and Governor Arthur Capper formed the International Peace and Equity League. It called for disarmament, a world court, and force to uphold the decrees of the latter. In Massachusetts, activities centered in the churches and the Massachusetts Peace Society. A program prepared by the Bay State's Federation of Churches on February 5 and sent to 2,500 ministers included provisions for international action "in groups, under a representative form of government, which should include a legislature, judiciary, and an executive." The latter would act as a police agency "to preserve order, prevent war, and protect life and trade." A less ambitious call, over the signature of the Rev. William W. Iliffe of Brookline, included a call for a greater reliance upon law, a court, and "some means of compulsion." Iliffe organized the Christian Peace League, which listed Holt's name as a vice president along with Mrs. J. Malcolm Forbes of Boston who in future years became a loyal supporter of the League of Nations.[57]

In the Massachusetts Peace Society, Professor Jay William Hudson, the director of the education department, delivered several addresses on a union with force at its command. In Boston, at the World Postal League, a movement to achieve a federation through the unification of the communications systems of the earth and the creation of an international postal structure was started. And in Boston a number of women began a mail campaign through their clubs. A statement solicited signatures to a "protest against war" and for a "call on my Government to work with all governments toward world-wide disarmament and an international court of justice, properly policed, because I believe that this alone can secure that absolute necessity of civilization—world-wide peace."[58]

In New York, the center of internationalist activity, several groups emerged. One of these reflected the ideas of Charles H. Ingersoll, the president of the watch company bearing his name. He organized the United States

56. Addams, *Peace and Bread*, pp. 195, 197; Addams to Holt, July 13, 1910, Holt Papers.

57. Brodie to CEIP, May 10, 1915, CEIP Papers; "Brief Peace Notes," *Advocate of Peace*, LXXVII (March 1915), 59; "Brief Peace Notes," *ibid.*, (April 1915), p. 84; *The Christian Peace League*, leaflet, SCPC.

58. "Among the Peace Organizations," *Advocate of Peace*, LXXVII (January 1915), 6; *ibid.*, (March 1915), pp. 55–56; "Brief Peace Notes," *ibid.*, LXXVI (November 1914), 230.

of Europe Association. It sought disarmament, an end to the war, and a European federation. Ingersoll presented no details other than to indicate that the United States should help in its formation.[59]

New York City also became the headquarters for what in time proved to be the only organization outside of the League to Enforce Peace to have any real or lasting influence—the World's Court League. It developed from the International Peace Forum, a prewar body created by businessman John Wesley Hill and by John Hays Hammond, a mining engineer and former president of the American Society for Judicial Settlement of International Disputes. One of its leaders, John Temple Graves, had been active in the World-Federation League.

The International Peace Forum had long advocated a legal system under a court of justice and, like other Americans, its leaders asked what had gone wrong in 1914. They decided to re-examine their program at a meeting in New York City in December 1914. The speakers proclaimed the need for a judicial body, and the final resolution requested Congress to call a conference after the war to achieve disarmament and to establish "a Court of Arbitral Justice" and "an International Police Force able to enforce the decrees of the court." Hammond, however, could not endorse the last point. He considered an armed peace little better than war in terms of economic costs. Hill, too, argued against the proposition. When he first read the platform of the League to Enforce Peace, he wrote Taft to protest. Taft held an honorary presidency in the International Peace Forum, and Hill could not understand how anyone could support a program based upon compulsion.[60]

Hammond and Hill decided that additional discussions might advance their ideal of a judicially organized world; hence, they called a World Court Congress at Cleveland for May 12–14, 1915. There, Hammond presided and speakers included former Secretary of State Knox, J. B. Scott, and several men who had attended the League to Enforce Peace dinners, including Taft and Marburg.

The resolutions revealed a reaction against some of the propositions then being advanced. These legally oriented men limited their program to a court

59. *The United States of Europe*, leaflet dated August 21, 1914, with form letter signed by Ingersoll announcing organization meeting, Holt Papers.

60. Each issue of *The Peace Forum* printed its platform on the table of contents page. "A World Tribunal with Teeth," *The Peace Forum*, III (February 1915), 16–17; Hammond, "Address," *ibid.*, pp. 6, 8; "A Business Man on Armed Peace," *ibid.*, p. 22; Hill to Taft, June 2, 1915, Taft Papers.

of justice and the codification of law. This was the only program nations might be willing to accept and one which the United States could legitimately espouse. The delegates explored but could not agree on other matters, including the election of judges, the jurisdiction of the court, and the powers to be conferred. Hence, they provided for a standing committee of one hundred under the chairmanship of Hammond, and from this body the World's Court League emerged.[61]

Two groups in New York also proved to be active, especially the New York Peace Society, which continued its discussions after the creation of the League to Enforce Peace. The Niagara Peace Society in February and March called for a world congress at Niagara where a league of nations built on the Hague structure could be formed. It would settle disputes judicially, have force at its disposal, and disarm along lines suggested by Holt.[62]

Established national associations also contributed to the discussions on international organization. The American Peace Society stood midway between the cautious and the venturesome proposals being formulated. It believed that the court advocates at Cleveland had placed the cart before the horse. A "Congress of Nations" had to precede and perfect a judicial system. But the American Peace Society doubted whether such a body should be established along the lines suggested by the League to Enforce Peace. It rested its case upon the old evolutionary concept that periodic conferences could achieve what was necessary. While it agreed that in some instances the use of a police power might be needed, such force should be applied only in isolated emergencies.[63]

The Socialists in the United States also accepted the ideal of a union of governments. It had long been a Socialist aim to unite working men everywhere, but by the spring of 1915 Socialist leaders were discussing an "Inter-

61. "To Infuse Personal Morality into Nations," *Literary Digest*, L (June 12, 1915), 1405–1406; New York *Sun*, June 13, 1915; "World Court Congress," *Advocate of Peace*, LXXVII (May 1915), 108–109; "Brief Peace Notes," *ibid.*, (June 1915), p. 135; Jeremiah W. Jenks, "An International Court of Justice," *Review of Reviews*, LI (June 1915), 735. Abstracts of addresses and resolutions are in *The Peace Forum*, III (June 1915), 5–32.

62. Buffalo *Express*, February 14, 1915; "Among the Peace Organizations," *Advocate of Peace*, LXXVII (March 1915), 56–57.

63. "The Cleveland World Court Congress," *Advocate of Peace*, LXXVII (June 1915), 130–131; "A League of Peace," *ibid.*, (May 1915), pp. 105–106; "War on Its Last Legs," *ibid.*, (April 1915), p. 77. The director of the New England Department of the Society, James L. Tryon, delivered a number of speeches on "International Federation and Police" early in 1915. "Field Department Notes," *ibid.*, (February 1915), p. 34.

national Federation." The party eventually called for a *"United States of the World"* with a court system, a congress, an executive, and an "International police force."[64]

Since the World Peace Foundation had always favored an association of nations, it supported the emerging movement vigorously. In October 1914, it published a pamphlet containing Victor Hugo's famous address on a United States of Europe, and on July 12, 1915, it voted to support the program of the League to Enforce Peace. Ginn had died and Mead suffered a nervous breakdown in 1915, but the other internationalists on the board of directors kept the Foundation committed.[65]

Of the various groups interested in peace, only the Carnegie Endowment seemed to be hostile to the goal of a diplomatically oriented league of nations. Its conservative directors wished to avoid controversial subjects; a "wait and see" policy might be best. Yet the Endowment did not publicly oppose any of the new schemes. In fact, by subsidizing certain societies, it indirectly paid the fees of internationalist speakers, and its support of the New York Peace Society enabled that body to work as it did in helping to organize and support the League to Enforce Peace.[66]

By the summer of 1915, the plans of men and the labors of new and established groups certainly had spread the idea of a league throughout the land. A receptive press aided them in that task. *The Independent* and *The Outlook* led, followed by *The Nation*. The *Christian Work*, headed by Frederick Lynch, had been a leader for years, and Lynch participated in the League to Enforce Peace discussions. Charles Fremont Taylor of *Equity*, a Philadelphia-based reform magazine, argued that a world government should be created under a constitution which would subordinate national sovereignty to a supreme authority. Harrison Gray Otis of the Los Angeles *Times* also called for an organization with extensive power. He published in May of 1915 a revision of a plan which he claimed to have conceived in 1912. It included provisions for an executive, a flag, an international bank and currency, and a grant of power to his world government in the form of a police force to "preserve, maintain, defend and guarantee the terri-

64. "American Socialists and Peace," *ibid.*, p. 29; Bourne, *Enduring Peace*, pp. 271–272.

65. Hugo, "The United States of Europe," *World Peace Foundation Pamphlets*, **IV** (October 1914); "World Peace Foundation Work in 1914," *ibid.*, (December 1914), pp. 26–27, 35, 39; "Annual Report, 1915," *ibid.*, **V** (December 1915), 13–14, 16.

66. George A. Finch to S. L. Fridenberg, November 23; Scott to J. G. Schmidlapp, February 2, 1915, CEIP Papers.

torial integrity, the national autonomy, and independent sovereignty, and the peace of every member."[67]

Thus the foundations of a new movement had been laid by the middle of 1915. "We have societies galore advocating a parliament of man," J. B. Scott observed as early as February, "and an equally large number of organizations and people advocating a supreme court of the world, all of them making innumerable suggestions and proposals at different times."[68] Scott might have added that most of these plans and planners showed little imagination and that their thinking resulted in markedly similar ideas. Virtually every proposition had been developed in the prewar discussions of the internationalists. The significance of the movement in 1914 and 1915 and thereafter lay, therefore, not in originality but in the exploration that occurred. It was a time of searching to discover which propositions seemed practical and which ones nations might be willing to accept.

67. Frederick Lynch, *The Last War*, pp. 70–71; [R. Ogden], "World-Citizenship," *The Nation*, C (January 14, 1915), 42–43; Taylor, "World Government vs. World War," *Equity*, XVII (November 1915), 264; Taylor to Endowment, March 24, 1915, CEIP Papers; Otis to editor, Los Angeles *Times*, May 23; Otis, "Plan to End War," *ibid.*, May 24–26, 31, 1915. Evidence that Otis drafted his plan prior to 1914 can be found in Taft to Root, June 19, 1913, CEIP Papers.

68. Scott to J. G. Schmidlapp, February 2, 1915.

Divergent
Views

With the establishment of the League to Enforce Peace in June of 1915, American internationalists could look to the future. They had nearly two years in which to formulate their ideas before their nation declared war in April of 1917, but, unfortunately for their cause, they looked in different directions. The League to Enforce Peace dominated in planning, in leadership, in educational and propaganda efforts, and in influence, but it still represented only a part of the movement in the United States for some type of organization. Other views existed in almost as many numbers as there were persons to espouse them, but they can be grouped in four categories—"generalists," judicialists, constructive advocates of a league, and spokesmen for a supranational government.

The generalists proclaimed an ideal but never committed themselves to any specific program. They probably reflected the thinking of most citizens who found the idea of an international organization attractive. Such persons reiterated a common theme that mankind needed some agency to prevent war and that men should embark upon the venture. Many of them cavalierly called for the abandonment of isolationism and challenged their nation to assume its duties in the world.[1]

1. Faries, *Rise of Internationalism*, pp. 168–174; Amos S. Hershey, "Some Problems of Defense," *Annals*, American Academy of Political and Social Science, LXI (September 1915), 266–268; John H. MacCracken, "The Basis of a Durable Peace,"

Generalists often tied the idea of a society of nations to other goals which they considered more important. This was true of antipreparedness spokesmen, those who wished to uphold the freedom of the seas, the advocates of mediation to end the war, groups concerned with immigration policy, and liberals who hoped to spread democratic, social, and economic reforms throughout the world. In every instance, they endorsed a league largely because it would help them gain their aims.

The opponents of preparedness, for instance, believed that the formation of an association of nations would result in disarmament; hence, they argued that their government should not expend vast sums for its armed forces since these would eventually be reduced. Often, however, these persons had their arguments turned against them. The preparedness spokesmen noted that since no league existed the nation would still have to rely upon its own resources. Furthermore, they claimed that in the future, peace and justice would have to be maintained by military sanctions; hence, the United States should remain prepared.[2]

Generalists primarily concerned with the freedom of the seas endorsed an international organization because they hoped it would solve many of the problems arising from the war—the blockade, search and seizure, and the use of the submarine. A league could solicit pledges from its members to honor the principle of the freedom of the seas and even neutralize trade routes and place them under its guarantee.[3]

The advocates of mediation became quite vocal between 1914 and 1917, and several societies appeared. The National Peace Federation, the American Neutral Conference Committee, the Women's Peace Party, and

---

ibid., LXVI (July 1916), 35, 42–43; Max Heller, "A Precedent for Humanity," *Advocate of Peace*, LXXIX (March 1917), 85–86; Mary E. Wooley, "Women and the World Crisis," *ibid.*, (April 1917), pp. 118–119; W. H. P. Faunce, "Holding to the Dream," *ibid.*, LXXVII (August 1915), 193; [Rollo Ogden], "The New Europe," *The Nation*, CIII (November 23, 1916), 480; Josiah Royce, "The Hope of the Great Community," *Yale Review*, V (January 1916), 269–291; Darwin Kingsley, *The United English Nations*, pp. 12–13; Nehemiah Boynton, "The American Spirit in Internationalism," *Mohonk Report, 1916*, pp. 224–226; Elizabeth Knopf, "World Unity," *The Peace Forum*, II (July 1914), 14; H. A. Overstreet, "The Next Step in International Control," *Four Lights*, VI (April 7, 1917), 3.

2. "National Security and International Peace," *The Outlook*, CX (June 23, 1915), 409–411; Elizabeth Tilton, "Pacifists Fight!" *The Survey*, XXXV (February 26, 1916), 636–637; "An Animal of Extinction," *ibid.*, XXXVI (May 6, 1916), 165; Hudson Maxim, *Defenseless America*, pp. 31–33, 37, 53.

3. "A Counsel of Wisdom," *The Independent*, LXXXV (January 31, 1916), 145–146; John Cadwalader, Jr., "The Best Way to Enforce Peace," *Current History*, IV (June 1916), 466.

the Neutral Conference for Continuous Mediation sought mediation as their primary goal and a world organization as a lesser aim. Their reason for uniting the two ideas is not apparent, since in nearly every instance the proposed league was not to be created until the war ended. Thus it could not have served as the mediating agency. Most of the supporters of this program, however, apparently believed that such an association would be useful in future conflicts.

Julia Grace Wales of the University of Wisconsin, Jane Addams, and Louis Lochner acted as the leading proponents of this idea, although they had help from one established internationalist, Hamilton Holt. Miss Wales drafted a plan in August of 1914 for a conference of neutral nations which gained the endorsement of the assembly of women pacifists in January and of Lochner's National Peace Federation.[4] These groups, with others, then sought unsuccessfully to persuade the Wilson administration to call a meeting of nonbelligerents. Their crusade began early in 1915 when Senator Robert M. La Follette of Wisconsin introduced a resolution calling for the appointment of a commission to explore the possibility. La Follette reflected both the agitation in his home state and the interest of his wife, who was active in the Women's Peace Party. The fourth provision of the La Follette resolution referred to the creation "of an international tribunal where any nation may be heard on any issue involving rights vital to its peace and the development of its national life, a tribunal whose decrees shall be enforced by the enlightened judgment of the world." The neutral governments which would unite to end the war could also act as a federation to establish rules for the neutralization of major trade routes and provide for their preservation in wartime.[5] None of the mediation groups succeeded in their task, but through their spirited efforts they helped spread the idea of an international organization.

The generalists who concerned themselves with immigration policies in calling for a society of nations were primarily interested in attitudes and laws affecting Orientals in the United States. They believed that a world organization with a court and commissions of conciliation might see that national groups were treated with fairness and allay war scares similar to those which had disturbed relations between Japan and the United States.[6]

4. Addams, *Peace and Bread*, p. 9; Linn, *Jane Addams*, pp. 298–299; Curti, *Peace or War*, p. 242; Kuehl, *Hamilton Holt*, pp. 108–109.

5. Kuehl, *Hamilton Holt*, pp. 109–110; "A Conference of Neutral Nations," *Advocate of Peace*, LXXVII (March 1915), 53–54; C. D. Eastman, "The Minimum Program of Enduring World Peace," *The Peace Forum*, III (May 1915), 29–33; *Congressional Record*, 63 Cong., 3d sess., 52, pt. 4:3230.

6. *A Petition to the President and Congress . . .* , printed leaflet, SCPC.

The editors of the *New Republic*, with their desire for democratic, social, and economic reforms, believed that some type of league should be formed to better the conditions of mankind everywhere. Yet they were generalists because they rarely offered concrete suggestions about how the league should be created or how it should function. They noted that a regional organization would not suffice, that ideals of democracy should prevail, that principles of law should be respected and upheld, and that warlike tendencies should be eliminated. By the time the United States entered the war in 1917, the editors seem to have endorsed the program of the League to Enforce Peace, but the *New Republic* still remained uncommitted on what it really desired.[7]

The second category of internationalists, the judicialists, existed in considerable number after 1914. They were the heirs of the arbitrationists and older evolutionary theorists who believed that the future should be built upon the past. They continued to refer to a developing Hague system, to call for a genuine judicial court, and to insist that periodic congresses, rather than a permanent league, would provide the world with a sufficient organization to maintain peace. While ten years earlier their program had seemed revolutionary and somewhat startling, by 1915 it seemed conservative and even unrealistic.

The judicialists thus faced a major problem in presenting their case to the American people, because it appeared by the summer of 1914 that philosophy based upon the Hague system had been rejected. Arbitration had been dealt a blow because of the refusal of governments to utilize it except for insignificant matters; then in embarking upon war nations completely ignored the machinery available at The Hague. It seemed impossible to believe that nations would voluntarily agree to settle their major differences peacefully. A few persons continued to proclaim the advantages of arbitration or to ask what had happened, but the world knew.[8]

7. "The End of American Isolation," *New Republic*, I (November 7, 1914), 9–10; "Timid Neutrality," *ibid.*, (November 14, 1914), pp. 7–8; "Lowes Dickinson's Plan," *ibid.*, (January 2, 1915), pp. 6–7; "The Deeper Preparedness," *ibid.*, III (July 3, 1915), 218–229; Walter Lippmann, "Sinews of Peace," *ibid.*, V (November 20, 1915), part II, 7–8; John Dewey, "Force, Violence and Law," *ibid.*, (January 22, 1916), pp. 295–296; "Mr. Wilson's Great Utterance," *ibid.*, VII (June 3, 1916), 102–104; "Editorial Notes," *ibid.*, VIII (September 2, 1916), 102; "International Security," *ibid.*, IX (November 11, 1916), 36–37; "Moving Toward Peace," *ibid.*, (November 25, 1916), p. 83; "The Background of American Hesitation," *ibid.*, X (March 31, 1917), 247–248.

8. "The Lake Mohonk Conference," *The Outlook*, CX (June 2, 1915), 241; Henry Olerich to Albert Shaw, March 23, 1917, Shaw Papers, New York Public Library; Marburg, "World Court and League of Peace," *Judicial Settlement of International Disputes*, No. 20 (February 1915), p. 3.

It is remarkable that international law did not suffer the same catastrophic dismissal, but it did not, and this proved to be the salvation of the judicialists. They argued that international law had not been given a chance. Arbitration had been tried and failed. It had collapsed, men now said, because governments had mistrusted a machine that had no fixed standards to guide it. Some of the legalists even argued that if a genuine judicial body had existed and if its decisions had been based upon a formulated set of rules, nations might have taken their disputes there in 1914.[9]

A court of justice could be established, the statutes on which it would rely could be determined, and in periodic conferences nations could serve as a legislature to draft new rules. Most of the legalists believed that no permanent organization other than a court had to exist. A revived and strengthened prewar peace structure would suffice.

The judicialists, with their emphasis upon a court and periodic assemblies, did not propose much more than William Ladd had suggested seventy-five years before. Since the American Peace Society had long endorsed this formula, it became one of the major supporters of the judicial approach. It noted, as Ladd had done, the distinction between the two ideas of a congress and a court.[10] "The problems involved in a League of Peace, a World State, Concert of Powers, and the like, would naturally come under the former, while the various views relating to an international judiciary, an international police, and the like, will find expression in the latter."[11]

The commitment of the Society to the spirit of internationalism cannot be denied. In the summer of 1915, it even considered changing the name of the *Advocate of Peace* to "The American INTERNATIONALIST, a journal of international organization." Yet the society remained conservative in what it endorsed. It claimed as late as October of 1915 that it viewed all proposals with an open mind, but it had already chosen its path. It endorsed neither "wild nor impossible schemes," and it argued that any plan "must take the form of an International Legislature and an International Judiciary."[12]

---

9. William I. Hull, "Six Sanctions of the International Court," *Judicial Settlement of International Disputes*, No. 25 (May 1916), pp. 3–6; W. R. Vance, "The Vision of a World Court," *ibid.*, No. 28 (February 1917), pp. 6–7, 12–13.

10. "Annual Report of the Executive Director," *Advocate of Peace*, LXXVII (June 1915), 143–144; "Our Program," *ibid.*, (August 1915), pp. 186–187.

11. "Fifth International Peace Conference," *ibid.*, (June 1915), p. 132.

12. Arthur D. Call to Butler, July 23, 1915, CEIP Papers; "Our Basis of Consistency," *Advocate of Peace*, LXXVII (October 1915), 211–212; "Our Program," *ibid.*, (August 1915), pp. 186–187.

Furthermore, the Society in August of 1915 issued an indirect challenge to the League to Enforce Peace in an editorial attacking force. The old pacifist reliance upon public opinion still endured. Moreover, plans for a league overlooked "the necessity for first establishing an International Legislature and an International Court, out of which such an international police must develop if it develops at all."[13]

Confronted by a new and popular organization moving in another direction, the American Peace Society faced a dilemma. Its proponents saw the widespread endorsement of the League to Enforce Peace but insisted that only their plan of a congress and court could be universally accepted. Yet the more radical proposals attracted such enthusiastic support that those members who endorsed the League to Enforce Peace or presented suggestions which went beyond those of the parent organization must have embarrassed the Society.[14]

This lack of a united front may explain why the American Peace Society revised its constitution in 1916. The new constitution created regional divisions closely affiliated with the national body and abolished the semi-autonomous state branches. That year, the Society also gained a new president, George W. Kirchwey, who seemed an unusual choice, since he had participated in three of the discussions which preceded the creation of the League to Enforce Peace. But Kirchwey had grown unhappy when the League drafted and approved its final platform. He had not voted for the plank on force at the Philadelphia meeting in June of 1915, and he subsequently voiced opposition to that program.[15]

The American Peace Society, however, continued to co-operate with the internationalists. A conference of delegates from several pacifist and pro-league groups was organized, meeting October 26–27, 1916, to seek a program on which all could unite. The seventy-three persons who attended could not agree, and a continuation committee assumed the task of drafting a questionnaire and compiling the results. The tabulation showed widespread agreement and disagreement and some inconsistency. On questions

13. "Ten Objections to an International Police," *Advocate of Peace*, LXXVII (August 1915), 188.

14. "What Should Peace Societies Do?" *ibid.*, (December 1915), pp. 258–259; "Among the Peace Organizations," *ibid.*, (July 1915), p. 164; *ibid.*, (December 1915), pp. 278–279; James L. Tryon to Jordan, June 12, 1915, Jordan Papers.

15. "Facts About Our Organization," *Advocate of Peace*, LXXVIII (November 1916), 290; "The Philadelphia Program," *ibid.*, LXXVII (July 1915), 157–158; Kirchwey, "How America May Contribute . . . ," *Annals*, American Academy of Political and Social Science, LXI (September 1915), 231–234; Kirchwey, "The Inconsistency of Trying to Enforce Peace," *Mohonk Report, 1916*, pp. 131–136.

relating to a world organization, eighty percent approved of additional conferences at The Hague "to formulate and codify law to govern international relations." A similar percentage favored the creation of a league in which the signatories would agree to submit disputes to courts and councils of conciliation, but less than fifty percent would accept military sanctions to compel such submission.[16] Such differing views revealed the depth of the cleavage in the ranks of the pacifists and internationalists.

The American Peace Society probably anticipated the results of the survey, for it had already committed itself to a platform which it thereafter presented as its belief. It accepted a ten-point statement which the American Institute of International Law had formulated and adopted at a meeting in Havana on January 22, 1917. The "Recommendations of Havana" fully reflected the cautious judicial approach. They called for the assembly of a third Hague Conference, for agreements on periodic meetings thereafter, and for an interim committee to procure and register all declarations and conventions and to call these to the attention of the world "in order to insure their observance." For nonjusticiable disputes, nations were to resort to arbitration, good offices, mediation, and "an international council of conciliation." Justiciable matters would "be decided by a court of justice" except where governments wished to rely upon arbitration.[17]

In adopting the "Recommendations of Havana," the American Peace Society indirectly revealed the degree to which it had fallen under the domination of the Carnegie Endowment for International Peace, which had been instrumental in promoting that declaration. The Society relied heavily upon subsidies from the Endowment, but in fairness it should be noted that it also agreed with the policies of the Endowment.[18]

The Carnegie organization's James Brown Scott had formulated the Havana principles, had publicized them, had presented them at the meeting in Cuba, and had moved their adoption. Scott thus revealed his continuing faith in a "judicial union." Nations should be invited, not summoned, to

16. "The Conference of Peace Workers," *Advocate of Peace*, LXXVIII (December 1916), 320–321; "Brief Peace Notes," *ibid.*, p. 340; "The Conference of Peace Workers," *ibid.*, LXXIX (April 1917), 115–116; "Where Peace-Workers Stand," *ibid.*, pp. 101–103; New York *Times*, February 20, 1917; New York *Sun*, February 21, 1917.

17. "American Peace Society's Program," *Advocate of Peace*, LXXIX (February 1917), 43; "The Havana Meeting of the American Institute of International Law," *ibid.*, (March 1917), pp. 77–78; "Second Meeting of the American Institute of International Law," *ibid.*, p. 71. "A Governed World" appeared in each issue of its journal in 1917 and 1918 as its declaration.

18. Kirchwey, "Statement of the President to the Directors," *ibid.*, (June 1917), pp. 168–173; A. D. Call to Robert C. Root, March 12, 1917 (copy), CEIP Papers.

court, Scott argued, for "this very loose union of states which we call the society of nations" could not stand the strain of compulsion. Plans which took the world much beyond the stage to which it had advanced would be doomed to failure.[19]

Scott believed that the machinery already existed to perform whatever functions would be needed. The Hague Conferences represented gains which should not be lightly cast aside. In his private correspondence, Scott revealed views which placed him in irreconcilable opposition to the League to Enforce Peace program. Such groups threatened "the success of the really great and constructive things which were well under way before they took them in hand." Furthermore, governments would never accept the advanced proposals of the League to Enforce Peace. If they did, "the inevitable result would be the subordination of justice to force, instead of the subordination of force to justice, for which we are working in our quiet, modest, and unobtrusive way."[20]

Another judicialist in the Carnegie Endowment, Nicholas Murray Butler, agreed with Scott, but he looked at the world with a broader perspective. He believed that basic principles underlay international law and organization, that mankind had to be educated regarding these, and that until men accepted them there could be no hope. He too found much in the League to Enforce Peace which he could not approve. Despite many invitations, he refused to join, and late in 1916 he attacked it under the cloak of anonymity.[21]

In a series of letters to the New York *Times*, writing under the pseudonym of Cosmos, Butler admitted that a "new international order" would be required. It would be "sanctioned and protected by international law and supported by an international guarantee so definite and so powerful that it cannot and will not be lightly attacked or shaken in the future by any Power." These words seemed to indicate an acceptance of military force, but Butler's subsequent statements revealed otherwise. Any structure should be built upon the idea of public right and upon the spirit of the international mind. The Hague Conferences had moved the world in this direction, and

19. Scott, "The Organization of International Justice," *Advocate of Peace*, LXXIX (January 1917), 10–22; Scott, "The Form of the Agreement and the Cooperation Necessary . . . ," *Mohonk Report, 1916*, pp. 18–19.

20. Scott, *Mohonk Report, 1916*, p. 16; Scott to William I. Hull, February 11, 1916, Hull Papers.

21. Butler to Secretary, American Association for International Conciliation, in "Among the Peace Organizations," *Advocate of Peace*, LXXVII (November 1915), 255; Butler to Talcott Williams, January 23; to J. B. Scott, January 27, 1917; to Samuel T. Dutton, January 29, 1917; to Marburg, August 10, 1915, CEIP Papers.

a third meeting should be held. There nations could seek those principles upon which they could agree. They should make no promises they would not keep, Butler warned, for such would actually harm the movement for world order. He believed that the war would allow countries to go much farther than before 1914, and he suggested that the qualifications of national honor and vital interests be removed from agreements.[22]

Since some union would be formed, Butler proposed that it be built upon a court of justice, commissions of inquiry, periodic congresses, and declarations setting forth the "fundamental rights and duties of nations." The United States would co-operate in any league if it did not depart unduly from traditional paths, violate accepted standards or policies, or require the abandonment of its responsibilities in the Western Hemisphere. The nation should move cautiously and then stand firmly behind the principles it accepted.[23]

Scott arranged for the Endowment to publish the Cosmos articles in book form, supervised their translation into several languages, and helped obtain an exceptional distribution for the volume.[24] Hence, the views expressed by Butler became, for practical purposes, the program of the Carnegie Endowment for International Peace.

The judicial approach to world order received further impetus from 1915 to 1917 from the World's Court League. Its modest and evolutionary philosophy as presented in its magazine appealed to many men and women. The Women's Peace Party, many lodges of the Royal Order of the Moose, and the National Federation of Women's Clubs adopted its platform. The New York Peace Society agreed to co-operate, the World Peace Foundation lent it money, the Carnegie Endowment for International Peace subsidized it, and Butler and Scott granted it the use of their names.[25]

The World's Court League organized branches in several states, sponsored an assembly in New York City in 1916, and attracted a number of prewar internationalists who refused to affiliate with the League to Enforce Peace. These included Simeon E. Baldwin, James B. McCreary, and William I. Hull. At the conference of the American Society for the Judicial Settlement of International Disputes in December 1916, the court formula gained

22. Cosmos [Nicholas Murray Butler], *The Basis of Durable Peace*, pp. 63, 66, 69–95.

23. *Ibid.*, pp. 97–102, 85, 106–111.

24. Scott to Adolph S. Ochs, December 28, 1916, CEIP Papers.

25. Samuel T. Dutton to Jordan, December 13, 1916, Jordan Papers; "Many Organizations Endorse World Court Movement," *World Court*, III (June–July 1917), 320.

additional support when many speakers acclaimed it as the only one which would ever work.[26]

The League to Enforce Peace understandably looked with concern upon these developments. Officials of the larger body, however, could not attack the smaller since the judicial element lay at the core of their own proposals. Moreover, many of them had co-operated in forming the World's Court League. Soon it became embarrassing to have the names of its leaders attached to both groups: an uninformed person might conclude that the two societies had identical aims. Hence, late in 1916, the League to Enforce Peace requested its major supporters to withdraw from all similar organizations.[27]

This action precipitated a movement to unite the two. The World's Court League officials entered into discussions in an optimistic frame of mind. Since their platform included the "irreducible minimum" for an international structure on which all men could agree, they hoped to win acceptance of their views. They may have planned to ensure victory by obtaining Elihu Root's consent to serve as their president, but he pleaded reasons of health in declining their invitation. Several conferences did little save reveal an uncompromising position on both sides. The best the representatives could do by April 1917 was agree not to attack or oppose each other, to continue discussions about a possible joint publication, and to explore further the plan to merge.[28] Thus, as late as 1917, two major organizations of internationalists existed. They could reach accord on a common goal but not on the means to attain it.

The failure of these men to unite should have taught them a lesson, one they still had not learned when the nation had to consider the Treaty of Versailles in 1919. How could they expect the Senate to agree on a league when its supporters could not? For a time during merger discussions, it appeared as if the Society for the Judicial Settlement of Disputes would co-operate with any new body. This would have brought Root, Butler, and Scott in as participants, and the Carnegie Endowment might then have

26. Addresses can be found in *Proceedings*, Sixth National Conference, 1916.

27. Short to Taft, November 27, 1916; Taft to Samuel T. Dutton, December 5, 1916, Taft Papers; *Minutes*, Executive Committee, December 16, 1916, LEP Papers; "The World's Court League," *World Court*, II (December 1916), 261–262.

28. S. T. Dutton to Executive Committee, Carnegie Endowment, January 26, 1917; to Butler, January 19, 26, 1917; to J. B. Scott, February 10, 1917, CEIP Papers. F. C. Bray to William I. Hull, January 17, 1917, Hull Papers; *Minutes* of Conferences, January 30, February 17, March 20, 1917; undated "Tentative Statement" on possible points of agreement and *Minutes*, Executive Committee, April 1917, World's Court League folder, SCPC.

placed its resources behind the operation. But a suggestion that the groups combine on a broad platform and leave details to the future did not gain support.[29] If the internationalists could not agree on such an ambiguous program, would they ever be able to unite in endorsing a particular constitution or covenant?

Further evidence of the diversity of views can be found in the judicially oriented advocates who remained independent in their thinking and only rarely affiliated with established societies. William I. Hull had participated in some of the dinners at the Century Club, but as a pacifist he could not fully accept the sanctions of the League to Enforce Peace. He turned from that organization and most of the others, giving the World's Court League only nominal support, because he suspected them of endangering "the constructive peace programme of the Hague Conferences, including preeminently the Court of Arbitral Justice." They not only distracted people from these ends, but they also sought "to substitute for a genuine international court and genuine national sanctions, an ex parte tribunal and armed alliances."[30]

Hull lectured extensively and wrote numerous articles between 1915 and 1917 on the historical evolution toward international organization and on current proposals. He considered none of them as realistic as the one based on the Hague Conferences. Future developments should come gradually through meetings and discussions rather than be imposed through some plan. Hull hoped that public opinion and economic pressures would allow a league to govern effectively, but he conceded that a police force might be acceptable if it could operate in a legitimate fashion.[31]

John Bassett Moore stood aloof from the formal agencies and other men in discussing a judicially organized world. The League to Enforce Peace continually sought to enlist him in its ranks because of his reputation as the leading authority on arbitration, but Moore shied away. He had been involved in planning the League but decided its program was too elastic, undefined, and impractical. He worried about how force would be applied and kept asking for a definition of aggression. Nevertheless, he contributed to

29. "Tentative Statement," Dutton to Lowell, April 10, 1917 (copy); Dutton to Butler, April 10, 1917, CEIP Papers.

30. Hull to Scott, January 26, 1916; to Esther E. Baldwin, January 26, 1916, Hull Papers.

31. Hull, "Three Plans for a Durable Peace," *Annals*, American Academy of Political and Social Science, LXVI (July 1916), 12–15; Hull, "International Organisation," *Bookman*, XLV (April 1917), 138–141; Hull, "Why the Apparently Helpless Supreme Court Succeeds," *World Court*, II (January 1917), 338–353; Hull, *Preparedness: The American Versus the Military Programme*, pp. 258–259, 265.

the movement through articles and speeches. To Moore, no association could succeed unless men wanted it to work. Those advocates who called for force behind a court did not realize this. They based their case upon a false assumption that arbitration had failed. It had not, but nations and people had. Men had to consider how governments could be persuaded "to accept not the results but the process of arbitration," and this involved sentiment, feelings, and "the aspirations of humanity." Thus in arbitration, conciliation, and international conferences to formulate law, nations could best find their way.[32]

The third person who believed in the judicial and evolutionary approach, Elihu Root, enjoyed prestige as a respected statesman, and internationalists of every ilk sought his support. Root lent his name to certain organizations, but he usually expressed personal views rather than those of any society. He was a gradualist in his thinking, as his instructions to the American delegates to the Second Hague Conference revealed when he told them to think of "the foundations which may be laid for further results in future conferences." Root also told them to seek a judicial court and agreements for periodic meetings automatically convened.[33] He followed, therefore, the Ladd tradition of internationalism.

As early as August of 1914, Root observed that some organization would emerge as a result of the conflict. As a member of the Senate Foreign Relations Committee, however, he refused to allow his views to be published. Yet privately he agreed with Charles Francis Adams that there was an irresistible movement "towards Tennyson's 'Parliament of man, and Federation of the world,' with a Hague Tribunal and International Police in reserve." There would have to be a court. That in turn implied law, which meant agreement on the rules to be followed and on sanctions for enforcement. But this would be an exceptionally difficult program to formulate, Root believed, and it should be considered by experts and not by amateurs or pacifists.[34]

32. Richard Megargee, "The Diplomacy of John Bassett Moore: Realism in American Foreign Policy," pp. 286–297; Moore to Lowell, July 3, 1915, Lowell Papers; Moore, "The Peace Problem," *Columbia University Quarterly*, XVIII (June 1916), 210–225; Moore, "International Cooperation," *International Conciliation*, No. 100 (March 1916), 8–9, 11–14.

33. Scott, *Hague Peace Conferences*, II, 184.

34. Memorandum of Interview with William H. Short, August 6, 1914, enclosed with letter of Holt to Root, August 7, 1914; Root to Holt, August 8, 1914; Adams to Root, February 6; Root to Adams, February 11, 1915, Root Papers. Martin D. Dubin, "Elihu Root and the Advocacy of a League of Nations, 1914–1917," *Western Political Quarterly*, XIX (September 1966), 439–455, contains a detailed account of Root's views.

Yet Root did not contribute substantially to the plans emerging. He claimed to be too tired. He did respond to a request by Lowell to state his opinion on the League to Enforce Peace platform, however. In his reply, Root both praised and questioned its aims. The society could serve a useful purpose by educating people, and he endorsed the proposition that justiciable matters be referred to a genuine court. He did not believe, however, that any commission should be empowered to determine the justiciability of a question. Each nation should reserve that right for itself and should be free to utilize any part of the machinery for peace. This was "the essence of independence," Root declared, and in expressing this opinion he stood exactly where he had been in the debate over the Taft accords of 1911–1912. The Monroe Doctrine and immigration controversies would never be submitted to a court. The United States would break its treaties before it would do so; hence, any agreements committing it to such a course would in the long run harm rather than advance justice.

The use of sanctions also worried Root. It would mean the abandonment of the policy of isolation and entangle the nation "in the international politics of Europe." He concluded, however, that there would have to be "some kind of sanction for the enforcement of the judgment of the court," but such a program would have to be carefully devised.[35] The automatic use of arms as in the League to Enforce Peace proposal could result in injustice. If armies were to march against a nation which refused to submit its disputes to pacific settlement, the United States might end up fighting "the wrong country" and aiding "the real aggressor." No one could assume under the League to Enforce Peace plan that the guilty party would always be the one who would not co-operate in resolving differences peacefully. Furthermore, a nation in the right which refrained from war and followed the machinery might be swallowed by an aggressor while it waited for a league to act.[36]

Root did not alter his views. As late as February 1917, he still believed that some organization would develop, doubted that the United States would join a league, and thought that it was dangerous to formulate concrete provisions on its structure or duties. All efforts to educate the people to their responsibilities merited support as long as they did not insist upon "a final and authoritative program."[37] Thus, Root endorsed the internationalists' efforts in only a qualified way.

35. Lowell to Root, July 28; Root to Lowell, August 9, 1915, Lowell Papers.
36. Root to Holt, December 3, 1915, Holt Papers; Root to Lowell, January 14, 1916, Lowell Papers; Leopold, *Elihu Root*, pp. 129–130.
37. Short, "Memorandum of a Conference . . . ," February 26, 1917, Taft Papers.

The concepts of law which these men reflected had great appeal, and many books and articles which endorsed the judicial approach to peace appeared between 1915 and 1917. These revealed a basic difference in thought between those writers who believed in erecting permanent machinery, preferably in the form of a league with some authority, and those who believed in the court-and-congress approach of the judicialists. It would not be possible, the latter argued, to enforce laws until men and governments were ready to recognize and honor them. Until that day, no machinery would work regardless of how elaborate it might be.[38]

These disparate views paralleled the ideological differences which had existed for years between pacifists and internationalists. The former had argued that the world would never see peace until men in their hearts wished to end wars. The internationalists assumed that some system could be devised which, despite men's nature, could be made to work. Their philosophy had grown popular, especially after the war began, because it seemed that an effective union might have averted the conflict. They now found it disconcerting to hear many legalists still say that the moral spirit behind the laws or any association would still be the determining factor.

But the advocates of a league believed that such assumptions had to be ignored. Mankind could not wait for the millennium. The spokesmen for a league did not disagree with the legalistic emphasis of the judicialists; they simply wanted to go farther. They recognized that nations had to move beyond the dream of a revised prewar peace structure, that the old voluntaristic philosophy had been unrealistic, and that some element of compulsion would be needed to make governments respect their commitments and international law.

The supporters of a league were in accord on certain points. They wanted no supranational body or federation which might possess authority over its members. Their ideas paralleled those of Americans who after 1776 wished a loose confederation which would serve as the agent of the states. They also made a distinction between a league and an alliance. The first would be formally organized and function as a unit; it would not be a coalition of governments acting only after consultation. Here agreement ended, however. Some men emphasized the judicial ideal in the agency to be created, as did

38. Jessie S. Reeves, "The Justiciability of International Disputes," American Political Science *Review*, X (February 1916), 70–79; "Peace and International Law," *The Outlook*, CXI (December 29, 1915), 1011–1012; Samuel P. Orth, "Law and Force in International Affairs," *International Journal of Ethics*, XXVI (April 1916), 339–346; "Justice and Peace," *Advocate of Peace*, LXVII (January 1905), 4–5; Carlton J. H. Hayes, "The Peace of Nations," *Columbia University Quarterly*, XIX (March 1917), 179–182.

the League to Enforce Peace. Others thought in terms of a legislative body. An even greater divergency of views appeared over the subject of sanctions. Some people believed that the weight of public opinion would suffice; others suggested economic pressures; yet others called for military force. They also disagreed upon how or when any of these three should be applied. The League to Enforce Peace limited the use of force to compel nations to take their disputes to the machinery created, but other planners thought it should be utilized to uphold the decisions of the court, and some believed it should be exerted even more vigorously to maintain peace and uphold the political independence and territorial integrity of members.

Most advocates of a league compromised their differences sufficiently to support the League to Enforce Peace. It thus became the most active and influential internationalist society in the world. It became the leading spokesman for the league idea because it had a program which seemed reasonable and realistic, because it had dedicated and intelligent leaders, and because it operated in an efficient, intelligent, and skillful manner. Moreover, it raised an impressive amount of money, and its sound financial condition enabled it to conduct vast information campaigns. This work usually took precedence over all other activities. It sought to present its program to the American people, but even more it wished to create a public opinion favorable to the general ideal of a league. By early 1917, it had distributed over one million copies of its literature. The Speakers' Bureau, in March of 1917, formulated plans to reach over five million listeners that summer.[39]

Behind this dynamic crusade lay one belief: the nation had to be organized to influence the decision of the Senate. All would be in vain unless two thirds of the senators favored a postwar union. Hence, the League to Enforce Peace sought to persuade state legislatures to adopt resolutions favoring an international organization and to gain from political parties an endorsement of that ideal. It succeeded in the Democratic platform of 1916, but its efforts in regard to the Republicans proved to be less satisfying. The Republican standard-bearer, Charles Evans Hughes, favored an association based on an expanded judicial structure, conferences, co-operation, and guarantees to maintain order, but the platform remained vague. It reflected the judicial outlook of such Republicans as Root and Butler when it expressed a belief "in the pacific settlement of international disputes" and

39. Bartlett, *League to Enforce Peace*, pp. 61–65; *Minutes*, Executive Committee, May 25, 1916, Lowell Papers; *The League Bulletin*, No. 9, September 1916; Taft to Miss Delia Torry, December 3, 1916, Taft Papers; "Report of Publicity Committee," November 18, 1916; "Report of Speaker's Bureau," March 17, 1917, Lowell Papers.

referred to "the establishment of a world court for that purpose." The League to Enforce Peace did achieve a major aim in 1916, however, for no prominent figure in either party publicly dissented from the international statements of platforms or candidates.[40]

The success of the League to Enforce Peace can be explained in other ways. It organized branches in nearly every state and won to its standard several existing pacifist groups. The New York Peace Society initially served as its central office with William Short as secretary of both organizations until November of 1916. Through the efforts of Holt, the Church Peace Union also joined the crusade. In giving two million dollars to establish it, Carnegie had hoped to disseminate the gospel of peace within organized churches of all denominations and to gain their co-operation in the struggle against war. The Church Peace Union soon went beyond these goals to reflect the league ideal of its donor, since it had in its ranks many internationalists, especially its secretary, Frederick Lynch, and Holt. It had reprinted the latter's editorial on the "Way to Disarm," and it allocated money to secure the services of clergymen to preach sermons on the League to Enforce Peace program.[41] The World Peace Foundation continued to appropriate funds for the propaganda campaign, the Massachusetts Peace Society became a virtual branch, and under Fannie Fern Andrews the American School Peace League distributed literature to the teachers of the nation. Elsewhere, the Intercollegiate Peace Association, the International Polity Clubs, and the Pennsylvania Arbitration and Peace Society endorsed the main points of the League's platform.[42]

The League succeeded, too, because it won to its ranks national leaders

40. Marburg to Taft, December 2, 1915, Taft Papers; Marburg to Aristide Briand, January 16, 1917, in Latané, *Development*, I, 248; Short to Taft, December 11, 1916; to Taft, January 17, 1917, Taft Papers; *Minutes*, Committee on Management, February 16, 1916, Lowell Papers; *Minutes*, Executive Committee, October 11, 1916, April 21, 1917, LEP Papers; Jack E. Kendrick, "The League of Nations and the Republican Senate," pp. 11–14.

41. Bartlett, *League to Enforce Peace*, pp. 62–64; *Minutes*, Directors and Advisory Council, October 20, 1915, NYPS Papers; Short to Jessie M. Short, January 22, 1917, Short Papers; Lynch, *Personal Recollections*, pp. 155–163; Macfarland, *Pioneers for Peace*, pp. 21–23, 30–31, 36, 54–55; *Minutes*, Executive Committee, May 4, 1916, Church Peace Union Papers, New York City; *Minutes*, Executive Committee, League to Enforce Peace, January 20, 1916, Lowell Papers.

42. "Annual Report, 1915," *World Peace Foundation Pamphlets*, V (December 1915), 13, 16–17; Charles H. Levermore to Jordan, February 14, 1916, Jordan Papers; F. F. Andrews to Marburg, July 21, 1915, Andrews Papers; Intercollegiate Peace Association leaflet, October 25, 1915; *Minutes*, Board of Directors, Pennsylvania Arbitration and Peace Society, June 19, 1916, SCPC.

in every area of endeavor. It also sought political balance in its prominent representatives. Since Taft, Lowell, Marburg, and Holt gave it a predominately Republican cast, it tried to lure in Democrats. It did not, however, succeed fully. William Jennings Bryan remained aloof and eventually challenged some of the League's propositions. Moreover, the Wilson administration leaders refused to associate with it. Even a few Republicans—Roosevelt, Lodge, Root, and Butler—would not join.[43]

A Committee on Information also enlisted prominent journalists in the cause. A select list of 763 newspapers which reached 91 percent of the nation's readers received press material, and by December of 1916 some 129 had committed themselves editorially to the League's program while only 38 had written against it.[44] Moreover, through Holt's *Independent* and Herbert Houston's *World's Work*, the society had two national magazines which virtually served as semiofficial organs.

Because of such organized efforts, many Americans accepted the formula of the League to Enforce Peace. Taft reported "great interest" wherever he spoke. A poll of nearly six hundred chambers of commerce and trade organizations in forty states showed virtually unanimous agreement in support of an association built upon judicial principles. The same returns indicated endorsement by substantial margins of economic and military sanctions to compel the submission of disputes to agencies for peaceful settlement. The businessmen's group at the Lake Mohonk Conference in 1916, representing thirty-five organizations, also endorsed the League's aims. Labor union members also approved the ideal through their delegates, and Samuel Gompers and the A. F. of L. became dedicated converts.[45]

Despite its successes, however, the League to Enforce Peace had its problems. Because of the attitudes of peace and judicial advocates, the society failed to gain the universal acceptance it desired. Indeed, it often felt compelled to refute some of the criticisms and objections of its opponents. Furthermore, it faced dissension within its ranks. Some supporters abandoned it when their interpretations of its planks were ignored, occasional conflicts erupted over procedures, and men continually raised questions regarding its work.[46]

43. Bartlett, *League to Enforce Peace*, pp. 43, 55–56, 70–72, 82.

44. *Ibid.*, p. 64; *The League Bulletin*, No. 14, December 21, 1916.

45. Taft to Lowell, April 3, 1917, Lowell Papers; *Minutes*, Executive Committee, September 17, 1915, LEP Papers; "An International Supreme Court and Business Sentiment," *The Outlook*, CXII (January 12, 1916), 53; "Declaration . . . ," *Mohonk Report, 1916*, p. 215; Philip Taft, *The A.F. of L. in the Time of Gompers*, p. 343.

46. Lowell, "The League to Enforce Peace," *North American Review*, CCV (Jan-

Among these differences, one prompted more debate than any other. Was the League to Enforce Peace wrong in its policy of sanctions? Not only organized peace and judicial spokesmen answered yes; other individuals also did.[47] William Jennings Bryan declared that the American people would never allow a world body to reach a decision for war which would commit the United States. It would violate the Constitution, entangle the nation, allow European powers to apply force in the Western Hemisphere, and, most important of all, abandon those principles for the pacific settlement of controversies which the world had been developing for years.[48]

Other men challenged the League to Enforce Peace for other reasons. They approved in general but thought it did not go far enough. Some of these persons never spelled out their views; others believed that an international organization should use force to do more than compel nations to submit their disputes for settlement. Some of them emphasized economic sanctions and insisted that commercial and financial pressures be applied to isolate all lawbreakers and aggressors. Still other men argued that the decisions of the court should be upheld.[49] The New York attorney Everett P. Wheeler, who headed the Committee of International Law and Arbitration of the New York Bar Association, voiced this alternative as much as anyone, and his group endorsed such a policy. The League to Enforce Peace had no effective

uary 1917), 25–30; Marburg, "Remarks," *Mohonk Report, 1916,* pp. 139–142; Marburg, "The League to Enforce Peace—A Reply to Critics," *Annals,* American Academy of Political and Social Science, LXVI (July 1916), 50–59; Andrew B. Humphrey to Taft, December 29, 1915, Taft Papers; *Minutes,* Executive Committee, June 29, 1915, December 16, 1916, LEP Papers.

47: Simeon E. Baldwin, "International Outlawry As An Alternative for Force," *World Court,* II (December 1916), 290–293; [Samuel Danziger], "Force a Dangerous Agent," *The Public,* XIX (August 4, 1916), 722; A. H. Snow, "Cooperation versus Compulsion in the Organization of the Society of Nations," *Mohonk Report, 1916,* pp. 100–108; "Feasibility of the President's Peace-Program," *Literary Digest,* LIV (February 3, 1917), 231–232.

48. Bryan, "Four Objections to Proposals of the League to Enforce Peace," *World Court,* II (December 1916), 288–290; Taft and Bryan, "The Proposal for a League to Enforce Peace," *International Conciliation,* No. 106 (September 1916), pp. 21–25; *Mohonk Report, 1916,* pp. 100–136.

49. George B. Adams, "America's Obligation and Opportunity," *Yale Review,* V (April 1916), 481; Ralph Barton Perry, "What Is Worth Fighting For?," *Atlantic Monthly,* CXVI (December 1915), 827–831; "The Path to Peace," *The Outlook,* CXIII (May 31, 1916), 243–245; "Will the United States Fight to Preserve the Peace of the World?," *Current Opinion,* LXII (February 1917), 84; Lucia Mead, "The Sanction of Non-Intercourse," *Mohonk Report, 1915,* pp. 46–47; Theodore S. Woolsey, "War and Disarmament," *ibid.,* pp. 72–73; "An International Supreme Court and Business Sentiment," pp. 53–54; Lindley M. Garrison, "The Problem of National Defense," *Mohonk Report, 1915,* p. 81.

answer to any of these men other than to maintain that countries would not as yet go that far. They might be willing to move modestly in that direction, as the platform advocated, but it would be unrealistic and perhaps fatal to attempt more.[50]

Another difficulty of the League to Enforce Peace lay in its deceptively simple program. It contained principles so basic that many persons could subscribe to them, a quality which attracted members. But other people wanted specific details. They asked about the Monroe Doctrine, the obligations of membership, the degree of sovereignty which would be lost, and what domestic questions would be determined by an international organization. The leaders of the League resisted such queries. They wished "to advocate the principle, not to draft a treaty."[51]

To meet criticisms, they often sought to explain their platform in speeches, articles, and interpretive clauses. They referred to early plans and planners, to historical precedents in the form of courts, councils of conciliation, and international conferences, and to the evolutionary tendencies at work. They also pursued another tack by challenging alternative suggestions. Their plan would entail no drastic departure, they argued, from traditional paths.[52] Eventually the League had to consider a more detailed program, but it had only begun an informal study when the war came in 1917.

The League to Enforce Peace did not enjoy a monopoly as the only pro-league society in the United States prior to April of 1917. Other citizens pondered the subject and formed groups. The Central Organization for a Durable Peace became the most active of these, and it attracted the attention of several of the most spirited internationalists in the nation. The Central

50. Everett P. Wheeler, "A World Court and International Police," *Judicial Settlement of International Disputes*, No. 26 (August 1916), pp. 11, 14–15; J. W. Hamilton to Jordan, October 4, 1915, Jordan Papers; Lowell to Robert S. Hall, June 19, 1915, Lowell Papers.

51. "Will the United States Fight to Preserve the Peace of the World?," p. 83; "Brief Peace Notes," *Advocate of Peace*, LXXIX (February 1917), 57; Short to Jordan, August 11, 1915, Jordan Papers; Lowell, "Introduction," Robert Goldsmith, *A League to Enforce Peace*, p. xi.

52. "Historical Light on the League to Enforce Peace," *World Peace Foundation Pamphlets*, VI (December 1916), 6–25; Lowell, "A League to Enforce Peace," *Atlantic Monthly*, CXVI (September 1915), 392–400; Oscar Straus, "Rebuilding the Foundations of International Peace," *Current History*, IV (August 1916), 905–911; Marburg, "World Court and League of Peace," *Annals*, American Academy of Political and Social Science, LXI (September 1915), 276–283.

Organization had emerged from a conference of thirty peace-workers at The Hague early in April of 1915. The delegates had gathered from several lands; hence, the Central Organization became the only world-wide society seeking peace through a league. They approached the problem by formulating a statement of principles on which they would invite discussion and study.[53]

This "Minimum Program" reflected many current pacifist desires with its provisions for the abolition of secret treaties, popular control of foreign policy, reduction of armaments, freedom of the seas, and guarantees of religious freedom and equality. It suggested an international association based upon Hague Conferences "at regular intervals" and permanently organized. Governments should then agree to submit all their disputes to a court of arbitration or of justice or to a "Council of Investigation and Conciliation." It then inserted a clause on sanctions. "The States shall bind themselves to take concerted action, diplomatic, economic or military" against countries which resorted to war before utilizing the machinery of peace. This phrase had been presented by G. Lowes Dickinson, one of the British delegates, who thus inserted the thinking of the Bryce "Proposals."[54]

Only one American, Fannie Fern Andrews, participated in the conference at The Hague. On her return, she sought to implement in the United States the plan of the Central Organization, which called for study groups in each nation. She extended invitations to many of her friends and attracted such internationalists as Holt and Lynch, judicialists like Dutton, Hull, and former president of Adelphi College Charles H. Levermore, and such peace leaders as Kirchwey, Lochner, Jordan, and Jane Addams. At their first meeting, on September 28, 1915, they elected Holt chairman, Lynch secretary, and Mrs. Andrews international corresponding secretary.[55]

In subsequent months, the American branch sought financial support, conducted educational campaigns, and formulated studies on the "Minimum Program." Members wrote essays, ten of which the Central Organization published. They explored such diverse topics as annexation, plebiscites, nationalities, the Hague Conferences, freedom of the seas, limitation of armaments, and force. None of these, however, contained original ideas of

53. Doty, *Durable Peace*, pp. 32–43.

54. *Ibid.*, pp. 60, 64, 70, 130–133; *Central Organisation for a Durable Peace*, leaflet, April 1915, Holt Papers; E. M. Forster, *Goldsworthy Lowes Dickinson*, pp. 165–166.

55. F. F. Andrews to Jordan, June 16, 1915, Jordan Papers; *Minutes*, September 28, 1915, Holt Papers.

importance. The articles on sanctions by Holt, Taft, and Houston did little more than comment upon the program of the League to Enforce Peace.[56]

Despite the enthusiasm of the American members, the Central Organization aroused little interest in the United States, mainly because it competed with the more popular League to Enforce Peace. It attracted only a few persons not already in that society. The dilemma of its leaders can be seen in Jordan, who had not been an internationalist prior to 1914. He had joined the League to Enforce Peace despite his concern over sanctions, but he found the Central Organization more acceptable because it tempered its military proposals with pacifist principles. Jordan, however, reflected a middle-ground position which few other persons found inviting. His unsuccessful efforts to raise a modest sum to cover the cost of publishing the studies of the Central Organization reveals that fact. Furthermore, while a few prominent members of the League to Enforce Peace supported the new society, other leaders, like Marburg and Short, attacked the Central Organization plan because of its pacifist aims.[57] Hence, the American branch never became an important operation.

Other advocates of a league of nations expressed their views without affiliating wholeheartedly with any of the established societies. Many lesser-known individuals resorted to the mails in circulating plans, a condition which prompted Jordan to complain that he knew of at least one hundred schemes, many of which had been sent to him for his comments.[58] The idea had become popular.

A few proposals gained a respectable degree of publicity. Late in December of 1916 an assembly of clergymen and laymen in New York City drafted a statement on lasting peace. Bearing the signatures of eight hundred churchmen, their message listed as a first principle "the establishment of a League of Nations."[59]

56. New York *Times*, May 17, 1916; F. F. Andrews, "A World Plan for Durable Peace," *The Independent*, LXXXVI (June 12, 1916), 446–447. Fifty-nine of the studies appeared in four volumes, B. de Jong van Beek en Donk, ed., *Recueil de Rapports*.

57. Jordan, *Days of a Man*, II, 665; Jordan to Mrs. Jordan, June 21, 1915; to Darwin Kingsley, August 18, 1915; to B. de Jong van Beek en Donk, January 19, 1916; to W. J. Bryan, May 11, 1916; Mrs. Andrews to Jordan, February 10, December 19, 1916; Henry Haskell to Jordan, December 27, 1916, Jordan Papers; Marburg to Jong van Beek en Donk, May 6, 1916, in Latané, *Development*, I, 108–111.

58. Jordan to George A. Williams, August 18, 1915; to Samuel W. Packard, December 18, 1915, Jordan Papers.

59. *The Peace Negotiations of the Nations: Suggestions for Adequate Guarantees for Lasting Peace*, p. 1.

The ideal also gained a hearing when Senator Henry Cabot Lodge spoke in its favor. While Lodge never joined the League to Enforce Peace and later had reservations about an international organization, he believed in a co-operative approach to the world's problems. In 1915, he expressed the need for some form of agreement which carried countries farther than they had been willing to go before the war. He insisted, however, upon one qualification. Any treaty had to be practical so that governments would respect it. They should find some way to maintain order, and they could do this by being "so united as to be able to say to any single country, you must not go to war, and they can only say that effectively when the country desiring war knows that the force which the united nations place behind peace is irresistible." Men had to pursue this Utopian step without "thought of personal or political profit or with any idea of self-interest or self-glorification."[60]

Lodge resisted all efforts to lure him into the League to Enforce Peace. He apparently placed its provisions for arbitration and conciliation in the category of "impractical," especially if this meant submitting to a tribunal such questions as immigration. He further argued that it would be impolitic of him to join since he served on the Senate Foreign Relations Committee. Yet Lodge did appear at the annual meeting of the League to Enforce Peace in Washington where on May 27, 1916, he spoke again in favor of an international organization. He had not altered his views. The old voluntarist philosophy could be carried no further. Force had to be placed behind the desires of governments. He believed that despite obstacles and difficulties his country should abandon the narrow interpretation of Washington's warning about alliances. It should "join with the other civilized nations of the world if a method could be found to diminish war and encourage peace."[61]

Late in the winter of that year, however, Lodge had second thoughts. Indeed, by January of 1917, the officers of the League to Enforce Peace viewed him with suspicion. He had cooled toward that organization when he thought it had become enmeshed in efforts to end the war through mediation, an unthinkable act in light of Lodge's belief that German autocracy had to be destroyed. That same conviction led him to question discussions about a union until Germany was defeated. He expressed his new concerns in a

60. John A. Garraty, *Henry Cabot Lodge: A Biography*, pp. 343–344; Lodge, "Force and Peace," *Annals,* American Academy of Political and Social Science, LX (July 1915), 204, 210–12; Lodge, *War Addresses, 1915–1917*, pp. 32–43.

61. Lodge to W. S. Bigelow, April 5, 1916, Lodge Papers, Massachusetts Historical Society; Lodge to Lowell, May 1, 1916, Lowell Papers; League to Enforce Peace, *Enforced Peace,* pp.164–167.

speech in the Senate in which he acknowledged his changed opinion. Careful consideration had led him to see difficulties and to become aware that mere "verbal adherence to a general principle" would not be enough. "Everything . . . depends upon the details," he observed, and these should be determined only by a "most solemn and binding" treaty.[62] Thus Lodge, while not fully abandoning the ideal of a league, had certainly qualified what had once been an endorsement.

Other advocates of a league had no such qualms, especially those who wished to create an effective organization. Some favored a defensive league in the form of an alliance, a goal which ran counter to the prevailing belief of most internationalists that any society should be open, democratic, and just. Benjamin Ives Gilman of the Boston Museum of Fine Arts saw one arrangement in the form of a treaty between the United States and France in which each government announced its desire to act on behalf of peace either singly or jointly. Other nations would then be invited to subscribe to this formula. Charles Eliot, however, remained the most outspoken advocate of a militarily oriented league. Eliot never worried about consistency. At various times, he proposed a European union, an association of Allied governments, and even a "League of Pacific Powers."[63]

Eliot did not stand alone in advocating a regional league, for other men also perceived that an international organization could be built upon smaller units. Henry W. Ballentine, the Dean of the Law School at the University of Illinois, observed that "a series of supernational governments and a sea government, each charged with some portion of the world's problems" could "evolve into a world state." The same idea appeared in one of Walter Lippmann's early books. In a critical analysis of the League to Enforce Peace, he suggested that nations begin with "a series of local world governments." John Bates Clark also argued that the existing alliances in Europe provided a degree of security which should not be abandoned at the end of the war. Any new arrangement would have to recognize these "defensive

62. Lodge to Lowell, December 22, 28, 1916, January 30, 1917, Lowell Papers; Lowell to Taft, January 23, 1917; Taft to Mrs. Taft, January 27, 1917; Lodge to Taft, January 23, 1917, Taft Papers; Lodge, *War Addresses*, pp. 264–279.

63. Gilman to Lowell, January 24, 1916, Lowell Papers; Eliot to the editor, New York *Times*, July 18, 1915; Eliot, "Inferences from Eleven Months of the European Conflict," *Current History*, II (August 1915), 856–858; Eliot, "How Can America Best Contribute Toward Constructive and Durable Peace?," *Annals*, American Academy of Political and Social Science, LXI (September 1915), 243–244; Eliot, "Criticisms of the Peace Societies," *Advocate of Peace*, LXXVII (November 1915), 238–239; "Dr. Eliot's Recent Views," *ibid.*, (August 1915), p. 190; Eliot to Butler, July 8, 1916, CEIP Papers.

unions" and possibly build upon them by adding machinery to settle disputes peacefully.[64]

Historian George L. Beer kept alive the dream of an English-Speaking Union, and he gained an important convert in Darwin Kingsley. The most prophetic discussion of a regionally oriented world society, however, came from a professor of law at Columbia. Ellery C. Stowell looked at nations realistically. The process of unity, he declared, had already forced governments into alliances along geographical and political lines, and this trend would continue. The weaker states would be forced to associate with the stronger until eventually there might be two major "competing political groups." They would be loosely formed, vie with each other for the support of minor countries, and negotiate to seek compromises on their major differences. If one of them overcame the other, a new "macrocosm" consisting of dissident governments would appear. The hope of the future, said Stowell, lay in the development of a spirit of "internationalism" which would bind the world together politically and economically.[65]

The most popular discussion of a geographically limited organization of states centered upon the proposal for a Western Hemisphere union. Woolsey's suggestion of 1910 had gained converts. Hayne Davis in 1910 had presented a plan for an American court of justice with guarantees by members to respect each other's territories, and Holt had called for a congress to go with this body. Theodore Roosevelt noted on October 24, 1913, in Rio de Janeiro, that the American republics had similar interests and that more than anywhere else it might be possible "to work out some scheme of common international conduct which shall guarantee to every nation freedom from molestation by others." In July 1914, Holt revived the idea in an editorial in which he suggested a regional agreement to arbitrate all disputes and to have governments meet periodically to formulate laws for the Western Hemisphere. Countries, he suggested, should be free to join or withdraw at will and also be allowed to maintain their armies.[66]

64. Ballentine, "Shall the United States Join a League to Enforce Peace?," *Advocate of Peace*, LXXIX (February 1917), 55; Lippmann, *The Stakes of Diplomacy*, pp. 140–145; Clark to Short, [1917], LEP Papers; Clark, "Existing Alliances and a League of Peace," *Mohonk Report, 1915*, pp. 57–61.

65. Beer, "America's Part Among Nations," *New Republic*, V (November 20, 1915), 62–64; Kingsley, *The United English Nations*, pp. 11–22; Stowell, "Plans for World Organization," *Columbia University Quarterly*, XVIII (June 1916), 226–240.

66. Davis, "The Foundations of International Justice," *The Independent*, LXVIII (March 10, 1910), 508–513; [Holt], "An International Judiciary," *ibid.*, pp. 536–538; Roosevelt, "American Internationalism," *The Outlook*, CV (November 1, 1913), 474; Holt, "Basis for a League of Peace," pp. 83–84.

Not long after, Carnegie, a careful reader of *The Independent*, wrote Wilson to observe that a "Union of Peace" could be built around the ambassadors of the American republics. They might be able "to deal with such questions as may arise between countries." Wilson, he advised, could make a contribution by keeping in mind the need for an association of nations. Late in 1914 and early in 1915, several other persons picked up the theme. It would indeed be possible, wrote Philip Marshall Brown, a professor of international law and diplomacy at Princeton, to create "a genuine American legislative assembly" which could unite the nations on a foundation of law.[67]

The suggestion for a Pan-American league called forth one of the first public expressions of interest in such a union from President Wilson. On January 6, 1916, he proposed a formal pact in which the states of the Western Hemisphere could combine in a pledge to guarantee each other's territory and political independence. Wilson had shown some awareness of the movement for an international organization as early as 1887 in an article in the *Political Science Quarterly*, but the topic held no great appeal for him. In the ensuing twenty-five years he mentioned it only a few times.[68] His casual remarks reveal him as one of those many generalists of the prewar era who believed in a federation without devoting much thought to it.

Wilson, however, had been influenced by the currents about him. He had joined the American Peace Society in 1908, delivered addresses at pacifist meetings, and must have been introduced to the Ladd-Trueblood concept of a congress of nations and a world court. He knew of the evolutionary trends at The Hague and recognized the importance of arbitration when he endorsed the Taft treaties in 1911.[69] Once in the White House, Wilson heard the clamor of the internationalists, for they forced their views upon him. McDowell, Holt, Crosby, Carnegie, and others wrote him, often sub-

---

67. Carnegie to Wilson, [n.d., marked received September 26, 1914], Wilson Papers; "Information Desk," *The Peace Forum*, III (June 1915), 40; "A Pan-American League of Peace," *Advocate of Peace*, LXXVII (June 1915), 132–133; "The Americans Against the World," *World Court*, I (October 1915), 110–111; "Pan-Americanism," *New Republic*, I (December 19, 1914), 9–10; Frank Allaben, "The World's Need of International Government," *Journal of American History*, X (third quarter 1916), 435–436; Brown, "Pan American Unity," *Mohonk Report, 1915*, pp. 36–44.

68. Harley Notter, *The Origins of the Foreign Policy of Woodrow Wilson*, pp. 43–44, 114, 142; Arthur S. Link, *Wilson The Diplomatist: A Look at his Major Foreign Policies*, p. 94; Ray Stannard Baker, *Woodrow Wilson and World Settlement*, I, 326.

69. *Advocate of Peace*, LXX (November 1908), 232; "The Fourth American Peace Congress," *ibid.*, LXXV (March 1913), 49–50; Notter, *Foreign Policy*, pp. 128–129, 238.

mitted proposals, and Marburg kept him posted on developments within the League to Enforce Peace and on discussions abroad.

Wilson's mind absorbed some of these ideas, as his Pan-American proposal reveals. Representative James L. Slayden had pushed that proposition in Congress in the form of resolutions, and Bryan wrote Wilson to solicit his support. Slayden's statement calling "for the mutual guaranty of . . . sovereignty and territorial integrity," was strikingly like that subsequently voiced by Wilson. In the fall of 1914 when Carnegie raised the subject, the President thanked him for a suggestion which might "later bear fruit." Late in November 1914 and throughout ensuing months, Colonel Edward M. House, Wilson's close advisor, discussed the topic intermittently with the President, and at a meeting on December 16, 1915, Wilson digressed on the points which he presented at the Pan-American Scientific Congress on January 6, 1916.[70]

Wilson's thoughts on a broader league followed the same ambiguous path. His brother-in-law, Dr. Stockton Axson, reported in 1924 a conversation in the fall of 1914 in which Wilson declared that "there must be an association of the nations, all bound together for the protection of the integrity of each, so that any one nation breaking from this bond will bring upon herself war; that is to say, punishment, automatically." Throughout 1915, as internationalist activities increased, Wilson became familiar enough with the league idea that he considered the possibility of combining it with an effort at mediation in October and November. This might bring the war to an end and at the same time establish conditions to stabilize Europe. He did not as yet, however, suggest that the United States join such a body.[71]

Even as late as February 1, 1916, Wilson had not publicly advanced that point. In Des Moines, in a speech, he noted the absence of an effective court, expressed the hope that such an agency might materialize as a result of the war, and added that there might also be "some sort of joint guarantee of peace on the part of the great nations of the world." On May 8, he hinted at the possibility of American membership in a talk with delegates from the American Union Against Militarism. Peace would have to be upheld by

70. Notter, *Foreign Policy*, pp. 273–274; Baker, *Wilson: Life and Letters*, VI, 83; Charles Seymour, *The Intimate Papers of Colonel House*, I, 207–234. John Chalmers Vinson, *Referendum for Isolation: Defeat of Article Ten of the League of Nations Covenant*, contains a summary of scholarly efforts to trace the origins of Wilson's ideas on a league, pp. 24–34.

71. New York *Times*, February 4, 1924; Baker, *Wilson: Life and Letters*, VI, 124–126, 131.

force, he declared, and the United States could not escape this responsibility. Then, in the ensuing two weeks, Wilson pondered the problem in depth and formulated his ideas.[72]

He had reason to proceed cautiously, because he had agreed to address the League to Enforce Peace delegates in Washington at their first annual meeting. The President observed to House that his message might well "be the most important I shall ever be called upon to make." The leaders of the League to Enforce Peace had sought for weeks to enlist Wilson in their ranks, for they had carefully followed his remarks. He had at first refused their invitation to speak, pleading a lack of time, but Taft and Short turned to House who persuaded Wilson to reconsider. Hence, on May 27, the President in his speech committed the United States to a league of nations.[73]

The President made several points. He spoke of the right of self-determination, of a world free from aggresssion, of the need to respect the territorial and political integrity of nations, of the necessity to prevent future conflicts, and of an association of nations in which the United States would be a member. Wilson, however, offered no concrete suggestions on any of these matters. He referred only to basic principles, for he believed it to be unwise as yet to elaborate upon details.[74]

Wilson's words cheered the internationalists. Holt compared Wilson's message with that of President James Monroe in 1823. It was "a declaration of interdependence." Most of the members of the League to Enforce Peace also acclaimed the speech as an endorsement of their program even though Wilson had carefully indicated he did not mean it to be such. Many observers, including editors, also agreed on the significance of the President's remarks. He had committed the nation to join an international organization. In this respect, they judged correctly. No other current head of a government had as yet publicly espoused the idea of a league of nations.[75]

72. Ray Stannard Baker and William E. Dodd, eds., *Public Papers of Woodrow Wilson: The New Democracy*, II, 70–82; "Three Presidents on the League to Enforce Peace," *The Independent*, LXXXVI (May 22, 1916), 264; Baker, *Wilson: Life and Letters*, VI, 203–205, 212, 216–222.

73. Baker, *Wilson:Life and Letters*, VI, 216; Bartlett, *League to Enforce Peace*, pp. 53–56; Short to Taft, April 12, 1916; Wilson to Taft, April 14, 1916; Short to Taft, May 9, 1916, Taft Papers; Taft to Wilson, May 9, 1916; Wilson to Taft, May 18, 1916, Wilson Papers; *Enforced Peace*, pp. 159–164.

74. *Enforced Peace,* pp. 160–164; Arthur S. Link, *Wilson: Campaigns for Progressivism and Peace, 1916–1917*, pp. 23–26.

75. Holt to Wilson, May 29, 1916, Wilson Papers; [Holt], "A Declaration of Interdependence," *The Independent*, LXXXVI (June 5, 1916), 357; "A Bill of Rights for the World," *The Survey*, XXXVI (June 10, 1916), 281–282; "America's Part in

Henceforth, that goal became "the central pillar of Wilson's peace programme." It appeared a number of times throughout the fall of 1916 as Wilson campaigned for re-election, most notably at Omaha on October 5, where he left no doubt that the United States would be a participant. The President, however, continued to qualify his statements. When he spoke to the Senate in January of 1917, he pointedly noted that membership would be predicated upon a just peace acceptable to the United States. Even if the United States remained a neutral it would have to "join the other civilized nations of the world in guaranteeing the permanence of peace upon" terms of right and justice, and he employed the analogy of many internationalists in proposing that governments "adopt the doctrine of President Monroe as the doctrine of the world." When Wilson delivered his war message to Congress in April, he left no doubt that a league had become a part of his peace program. There had to be "a partnership of democratic nations."[76]

While Wilson generally supported and encouraged the idea of a league, his remarks about protecting and guaranteeing territorial integrity must have appealed to persons in the fourth category of internationalists—those who favored the creation of a supranational government with executive, legislative, and judicial powers and with national sovereignty subordinated to the larger unit. While this proposal drew less attention than the others, a sizable number of Americans flirted with it. The Friends' National Peace Conference in 1915 approved a resolution to establish a court, a "legislative body," and a "world government." In New York, Charles L. Clist founded the World-State League to educate people to the necessity of entrusting affairs to "a world-congress, court, executive and police force." The World Peace Association distributed literature from the rural village of Jenkins, Minnesota, which urged men "to strengthen the United Nations, and to make of it a truly democratic WORLD GOVERNMENT." Other men referred to "a world state," a "supreme authority," and an agency to which countries could transfer "powers essentially sovereign."[77]

World Democracy," *World's Work*, XXXII (July 1916), 254–256; "President Wilson's Peace-Plan," *Literary Digest*, LII (June 10, 1916), 1683–1685; Bartlett, *League to Enforce Peace*, p. 51.

76. Baker, *Wilson: Life and Letters*, VI, 416; Baker and Dodd, *Public Papers*, II, 348, 408.

77. "Friends' National Peace Conference," *Advocate of Peace*, LXXVII (October 1915), 229; postcard of World Peace Association, Holt Papers; George E. Roberts, "The Economic Motive as a Factor in War," *Mohonk Report, 1916*, p. 212; William D. Parkinson, "The Spread of Federalization," *Unpopular Review*, VI (July–September, 1916), 15; E. A. Hayes to Jordan, January 29, 1916, Jordan Papers.

When such persons elaborated upon details, they revealed a stereotyped uniformity in their thinking. They referred to a three-branch government modeled after that of the United States. It would decide and uphold law, police the earth, and regulate or abolish armaments.[78] Raymond Bridgman's peition to the Massachusetts legislature reflected this as did a proposal from John Bigelow, a retired army officer. He dismissed most of the current proposals for a league and concluded that only a world citizenship would do. By popular plebiscite, people could surrender their national rights to "The United Republics, or the United Nations of the World."[79]

Two similarly inclined advocates labored industriously to advance their cause. George H. Shibley, an attorney in Washington, D.C., organized a group of professional men into a League for World Peace. It planned to publish a *World State* quarterly and conduct research. Shibley hoped the war could be ended, that a European union could be formed, and that the United States might then join to form a "World State or Federation of the World." He attacked the proposals of the League to Enforce Peace as unsound. They allowed nations to exist as independent powers, thus inviting continued anarchy. They unrealistically emphasized arbitral, judicial, and legal methods. Shibley maintained that the League's "assertion that some questions are non-justiciable is directly opposed to the attainment of real International Government and Permanent Peace and Ultimate Disarmament." An agency responsive to the people should formulate rules of conduct, and nations which then violated them should face court action and punishment.[80]

Oscar Crosby also challenged the League to Enforce Peace. He continued to advocate an Armed International Tribunal with a court functioning as an executive agency. Its decisions should be upheld. If an organization only compelled the submission of disputes to a tribunal, it still left governments with a legal license to kill under certain conditions. Furthermore, the League to Enforce Peace platform incorrectly presumed that nations would always behave like gentlemen and agree on what constituted warlike action. The world needed an effective machine.[81]

78. Henry Olerich to Scott, October 18, 1915; L. Lincoln Wirt to Henry Haskell, July 7, 1915, CEIP Papers; C. F. Bertholf to Lowell, July 28, 1915, Lowell Papers; Newman Moon to Jordan, April 13, 1917; J. W. Miller to Jordan (two undated letters [February–March 1916]), Jordan Papers.

79. Bigelow, *World Peace*, pp. 205, 215–217, 223.

80. Shibley, *The Allies Pledged to a United States of Europe*, pp. 9–14, 22–23; Shibley to Jordan, November 21, 1915, Jordan Papers.

81. Crosby to Short, February 3, 14, 1915, NYPS Papers; Crosby to G. Lowes

Crosby continued to work through congressional resolutions. He apparently collaborated with Representative Walter L. Hensley in drafting a proposal which Hensley attached as a rider to a naval appropriations bill. It requested the President to call a conference where delegates could explore the creation of some agency to which governments could submit disputes and seek disarmament. It authorized the President to appoint a commission of nine citizens to represent the United States and provided for an appropriation of two hundred thousand dollars. If the assembly could be held before the naval moneys were spent, the construction of the ships should stop. The preparedness spokesmen accepted this resolution since it gave them votes which they needed; hence, on August 26, 1916, the measure passed with only one man speaking against it.[82]

Crosby did not stop here. He again joined Senator Shafroth, who on May 18, 1916, introduced S.J. Res. 131. It proposed a constitutional amendment "authorizing the creation, with other nations, of an international peace-enforcing tribunal or tribunals for the determination of all international disputes." It further asked the President to negotiate treaties to establish this structure and to supply the funds to maintain whatever administrative and military establishment might be needed.[83]

These resolutions on an international organization were not the only ones considered by Congress between 1915 and April of 1917. Robinson in the Senate and Republican Martin B. Madden of Illinois in the House presented S.J. Res. 213 and H.J. Res. 66 calling for a meeting of all the parliamentarians of the world, thus showing that McDowell had not abandoned his quest. Democratic Representative Charles B. Smith of New York sought approval of H.J. Res. 359 to solicit from governments a statement which would "lay the foundations for the establishment of a court of nations, a congress of nations, and international army and navy, and for other purposes." H.J. Res. 362, submitted by Henry T. Helgesen of North Dakota, called for a committee to plan "for an international police of the seas," and David J. Lewis of Maryland in H.J. Res. 373 asked that other countries be

---

Dickinson, February 26, 1916, Lowell Papers; Crosby, *The Armed International Tribunal Association*, pp. 2–6; Crosby, "An Armed International Tribunal . . . ," *Annals*, American Academy of Political and Social Science, LXVI (July 1916), 32–34.

82. Baker, *Wilson: Life and Letters*, VI, 214n; Crosby to Baker, July 13, August 3, 1928, Crosby Papers.

83. Crosby to House, June 10, 1918, House Papers. Crosby wrote several letters which Shafroth had printed as government documents. S. Doc. 987, 63 Cong., 3d sess.; S. Docs. 245, 378, 535, 64 Cong., 1st sess.; *Congressional Record*, 63 Cong., 3d sess., 52, pt. 3:2941; *ibid.*, 64 Cong., 1st sess., 53, pt. 1:375; *ibid.*, pt. 8:8228.

invited to "a conference to discuss a government for the international community." Lewis had been concerned that Congress approve a statement showing that it shared Wilson's aspirations "for some sort of joint guaranty of peace." His bill did not indicate this, however, because the President thought such a move might invite criticism of the idea.[84]

The American people by April of 1917 had thus been exposed to a wealth of plans and arguments on behalf of some type of world organization. Resolutions in Congress, statements by the President, and extensive propaganda efforts by organized and unorganized advocates had scattered the idea widely. As one commentator observed, "Never before has there been such a campaign for internationalism, never before have there been such potent arguments in its favor." Fannie Fern Andrews classified these as essentially patriotic, democratic, and humane, because Americans were being awakened to their "obligation to serve the world."[85] Through her School Peace League and the National Education Association, she did as much as anyone to spread such sentiments. A statement of principles by the latter society called for an end to nationalism and for a new loyalty to "international patriotism."[86]

It is clear that such efforts had an effect upon American thinking, but it is exceedingly doubtful whether the man-in-the-street by 1917 knew just what kind of an organization he should support. Even the proponents could not agree on that point. One can, however, arrive at certain conclusions about the stage of the crusade as the United States entered the war. First, a belief had become commonplace that some type of society should be created. A difference of opinion did exist over whether it should be formed immediately or not until the end of the war, but even here most planners seemed ready to be opportunistic and act at the best time. Second, the internationalists seemed in agreement that a league should be open to all nations. A few of them thought only major countries should be included and

84. *Congressional Record*, 64 Cong., 2d sess., 54, pt. 4:3254; *ibid.*, 65 Cong., 1st sess., 55, pt. 1:439; *ibid.*, 65 Cong., 1st sess., 55, pt. 1:991; *ibid.*, 64 Cong., 2d sess., 54, pt. 2:2023; *ibid.*, pt. 3:2216, pt. 4:3534; *ibid.*, pt. 1:635–636, 668; *Minutes*, Executive Committee of League to Enforce Peace, May 12, 1916, Lowell Papers; Baker, *Wilson: Life and Letters*, VI, 416.

85. Carl C. Eckhardt, "What We Have to Build On," *The Survey*, XXXVI (August 5, 1916), 484; F. F. Andrews, "The Education of the World for a Permanent Peace," *National Education Association Journal . . . 1915*, pp. 246–251; Andrews, "The New Citizenship," *ibid.*, pp. 702–705; Andrews, "What the Public Schools Can Do . . . ," *ibid., 1916*, pp. 93–96.

86. "Declaration of Principles," *School and Society*, II (September 11, 1915), 361–367.

some men would have excluded the Central Powers, but reason seemed to dictate a broad base for membership.

A third accord existed on the subject of the powers and structure of a union. Only a very few advocates called for a world government. Even the older ideal of a federation had been pushed aside because it implied a broader grant of authority than most thinkers wished to see. Hence, the word "league" became popular. It expressed what was wanted—an association based upon certain agreements with authority to act only on specified matters and in stated ways. Furthermore, a pragmatic attitude prevailed which led the vast majority of proponents to exclude pacifist ideals and wartime issues from the jurisdiction of any society. Thus, disarmament, neutral rights, trade questions, immigration, and the democratic formulation of foreign policy appeared in the schemes of only a few men and groups.

Fourth, the judicial concept dominated in virtually all plans. It had become an essential ingredient in the philosophy of nearly all internationalists because they believed that the gains of the previous decade should not be lightly abandoned. A few of them still referred to arbitration, but most of them had moved to other legal methods to settle disputes which were more logical and realistic.

Fifth, the exponents of union had not as yet resolved their differences over sanctions. They debated two issues. One involved the question whether a league should apply any force at all. Most advocates by 1917 had decided that it should, but a sizable minority continued to argue otherwise. The other concerned the degree to which sanctions should be used. After considerable discussion on this point, a majority of internationalists agreed that force should be applied only in limited and legal fashion. One can find expressions to the contrary from individuals, including Wilson, who suggested some form of compulsion to impose or to maintain peace in an arbitrary fashion by force of arms, but there is little evidence to indicate popular support for this idea. The nation, however, was still to have several months in which to explore this subject and the other questions relating to a league. Perhaps a better consensus would be reached by the time the statesmen assembled around the peace table.

An Idea
Grows

The entry of the United States into the war in 1917 virtually guaranteed the world of a future international organization. Wilson's expressions on that point left no doubt about the future. Furthermore, American involvement meant that any structure would be a democratic one, built, presumably, by the victorious Allies rather than by the autocratic Central Powers. Hamilton Holt quickly reminded men of Kant's dictum that peace would come not only when nations could be politically organized but also when the people ruled.[1]

Wilson's pledges and his open support of a league encouraged internationalists in other lands to express themselves. They had been exploring the subject with varying degrees of intensity since 1914. In the Netherlands, where the Central Organization for a Durable Peace operated, and in Belgium, a number of individuals engaged in speculative planning.[2] Henri La Fontaine, who had won the Nobel peace prize in 1913, had taken refuge in London, whence he often spoke for a democratic and judicially oriented league. The United States should lead, he declared. After 1917, he advocated a law-making society with court and administrative machinery to make

1. [Holt], "Pure Reason," *The Independent*, XC (April 14, 1917), 99.
2. Nico Van Suchtelen, *The Only Solution—A European Federation*; J. Kuiper, *De geheele wereld één Republiek*; J. D. Reimen, Jr., *The Solution of the International Crisis*; A. J. Barnouw, "Caliban Regenerated," *The Nation*, CIII (September 7, 1916), 217–218.

war illegal, require the submission of disputes to peace-making bodies, and guarantee the territory and independence of all nations. In Holland, a European Federation Committee appeared late in 1914 to propagandize for a union in which the United States and other countries would eventually participate, and individual writers often echoed that theme.[3]

In other European neutral states, similar speculation had been possible. Dr. O. Jersild of Denmark proposed a European armed force to maintain peace. Christian Lange, the Norwegian secretary-general of the Interparliamentary Union, suggested that members of that body conduct a survey on the problems of an international organization. August Schvan, a native of Sweden living in England, proclaimed the advantages of "a world citizenship" and a small police force, and Christen C. Collin of Norway revived Kant in calling for "a League of Right" supported by armed force. As in the United States, few of the European pacifist societies altered their programs to embrace any extensive brand of internationalism.[4]

In the belligerent countries, especially on the continent, talk about peace in any form seemed treasonable; hence, groups or individuals interested in an association of nations remained silent or worked clandestinely. By 1914, however, the idea had been infused into German and Austrian thought and it could not be stifled. A *Bund Neues Vaterland* furtively advocated a union in general terms.[5] Even the German government gave a temporary stamp of approval to the ideal when Chancellor Bethmann-Hollweg declared on November 9, 1916, that Germany would be willing to join a league. At least one American, Charles Macfarland, the executive secretary of the Federal Council of Churches, claimed responsibility for that statement, but it proved

3. La Fontaine, "America's Opportunity," *The Survey*, XXXVI (August 5, 1916), 473–474; La Fontaine, "On What Principles is the Society of States to be Founded?," *Annals*, American Academy of Political and Social Science, LXXII (July 1917), 89–92; G. Heymans, "To the Citizens of the Belligerent States," *Towards an International Understanding*, No. 10, pp. 15–16.

4. O. Jersild, "Thoughts on Peace and Peace Guarantees," *Recueil de Rapports*, IV, 197–212; C. Lange, *The Conditions of A Lasting Peace*, pp. 3, 9, 13; Beales, *History of Peace*, p. 300; Schvan, "Six Essentials to Permanent Peace," *Annals*, American Academy of Political and Social Science, LX (July 1915), 226–229; Collin, *The War Against War*, pp. 76–77, 160–161; Doty, *Durable Peace*, pp. 24–26; "A Manifesto by Members of the International Peace Bureau," *Advocate of Peace*, LXXVI (December 1914), 250–252; Jong van Beek en Donk, "The Movement in Neutral Countries," *The Project of a League of Nations*, No. 15 (August 1917), pp. 21–25.

5. Doty, *Durable Peace*, pp. 24–26; Beales, *History of Peace*, pp. 295–296; G. Grosch, "Die Friedensorganisation der Staaten," *Internationale Organisation*, No. 9/10 pp. 39–52, 65–72; Graf Ottokar Czernin, "International Arbitration: An Austrian View," *Living Age*, CCXCIX (November 23, 1918), 480–484.

to be meaningless. Bethmann-Hollweg fell from power in June 1917. Finally, near the end of the war, another Chancellor, Prince Maximilian of Baden, endorsed German membership, and the *Reichstag* voted its approval. By then, a German League of Nations Society had appeared.[6]

Although French internationalists faced opposition, they, too, explored the subject. The *La Paix par le Droit* society in 1915 formulated a "minimum program" based upon the Hague structure which called for the obligatory arbitration of all disputes. This theme received the endorsement of the *Ligue des Droits de l'Homme* a few months later.[7] Most of the French statements, however, revealed little awareness of the detailed schemes emerging elsewhere.

After the United States entered the war, Frenchmen intensified their discussions. The government, according to rumors, desired a society which could guarantee peace through economic and military pressures and even uphold the decrees of a court after nations had been forced to submit their disputes to that body. M. J. de Sillac, who had attended the Hague Conference in 1899, visited the United States late in 1916 where he examined current proposals, and by 1918 as Minister of Foreign Affairs he encouraged the formation of an official study group which relied heavily upon the ideas of the League to Enforce Peace. By that time, considerable support had appeared. The French Chamber of Deputies endorsed an association in June of 1917, and a League of Nations Society, organized under Léon Bourgeois, presented a plan in November 1918.[8]

One of the most widely discussed and detailed proposals in France came from Paul Otlet, a Belgian who had spent most of the war in Paris. He included provisions for executive, legislative, and judicial bodies and called for an international army. A council would function as an executive; a bank

6. Charles S. Macfarland, *Across the Years*, pp. 114–115; "Brief Peace Notes," *Advocate of Peace*, LXXIX (August 1917), 244; "International Notes," *ibid.*, LXXX (October 1918), 282; Beales, *History of Peace*, pp. 296–297.

7. Stoddard Dewey, "The Dying of Internationalism," *The Nation*, CIII (September 14, 1916), 254–255; Jordan to John l'Homme, September 9, 1915, Jordan Papers; Beales, *History of Peace*, p. 297; "Ligue des Droits de l'Homme," *Advocate of Peace*, LXXIX (February 1917), 61.

8. Jong van Beek en Donk, "German and French Views of Peace," *Advocate of Peace*, LXXIX (April 1917), 106; "Current Forerunners of a League of Nations," *ibid.*, LXXX (January 1918), 21–22; "Ligue des Droits de l'Homme," *ibid.*, p. 29; "Among the Peace Organizations," *ibid.*, (March 1918), p. 93; Holt to Taft, November 16, 1916, Taft Papers. Marburg to Lowell, September 3, 1917, and Marburg to Holt, July 29, 1918, in Latané, *Development*, I, 334–339, II, 494–498, contain excellent summaries of activities and attitudes in Europe.

would transact the business of the union and issue a world currency; and members would be assessed for payments on the basis of one percent of their annual individual budgets. Otlet insisted that justice determine the affairs of states without much discussion on how this should be done. He provided for the enforcement of decrees and even the guaranteeing of national territories, but he did not elaborate extensively upon those points.[9] Otlet formulated a plan distinctly modern in concept but not in advance of what the world government advocates in the United States had been proposing for years.

French interest in a league mounted as Wilson became a spokesman for the ideal. Indeed, one Frenchman coined the word "wilsonism" to describe the goal. Eventually Premier Georges Clemenceau yielded reluctantly to the pressures of men like de Sillac in allowing the creation of a study commission. Its report in 1918 rejected proposals for a powerful agency. It suggested that any society be built upon a judicial and legal foundation.[10]

Elsewhere on the continent, except in Switzerland and Italy, men contributed little to the movement. Fourteen Swiss peace groups formed a *Comité d'Action des Sociétés Suisses de la Paix* by 1917, but discussions centered more upon mediation and the protection of neutrals and only in a limited way on a postwar league. By 1918, the Swiss president, Felix Calonder, who had written a plan of his own, named an official commission to draft one. In Italy, action came late. Not until 1918, when Holt and other League to Enforce Peace advocates began a campaign there, did any real movement begin.[11]

English concern and planning faced the same problems as elsewhere in the belligerent countries. Hence, discussions in the first years of the war remained private and discreet. Yet within certain circles considerable action occurred. It began with G. Lowes Dickinson, a publicist and scholar, who combined with Bryce and others in the study group which produced the Bryce-Dickinson "Proposals for the Avoidance of War." These circulated privately in February 1915 and, as noted, influenced the men at the Century Club dinners in March and April.[12]

9. Otlet, "A World Charter," *Advocate of Peace,* LXXIX (February 1917), 44–48.

10. "Kant and Wilson, on 'Peace Without Victory,' " *Review of Reviews,* LV (April 1917), 426–427; "Brief Peace Notes," *Advocate of Peace,* LXXX (March 1918), 85; "International Notes," *ibid.,* (July 1918), p. 217.

11. "Among the Peace Organizations," *Advocate of Peace,* LXXIX (August 1917), 247–248; *Progress Towards Internationalism,* leaflet, July 1918, Holt Papers. Calonder's scheme can be found in the House Papers. Marburg to Holt, July 29, 1918, in Latané, *Development,* II, 497.

12. Henry R. Winkler, *The League of Nations Movement in Great Britain, 1914–1919,* pp. 16–23; Forster, *Dickinson,* pp. 163–164.

The English showed much more interest in an international organization than did advocates elsewhere in Europe, and their ideas must be compared with those in the United States. Planners in both countries reflected common prewar internationalist goals; hence, their basic programs were quite similar. Their major differences appeared over the use of sanctions and the degree to which the association of nations should be formally organized.

Leaders in both bodies believed that a program acceptable to everyone could be found; therefore, they exchanged views for many months. This led to compromises and modifications in their respective plans, primarily on the subject of sanctions. The Americans moved more and more toward the Bryce "Proposals" when they began to emphasize economic pressure over that of military arms; the British, in April of 1917, accepted the League to Enforce Peace principle of automatic action against violators of the treaty.

In other ways, however, the two groups did not reach common accord. The Bryce-Dickinson men continued to insist that any organization use "diplomatic, economic or forcible" power against a nation which did not wait the full year of the cooling-off period or went to war within six months after a decision had been rendered. Such response, however, still had to be determined by the members in each instance. Conferences would also be held to decide upon a course of action against a government which ignored the suggestions of its Council of Conciliation or the decrees of courts. The Englishmen's desires in regard to sanctions eventually exceeded those of the Americans, but in another way, when they extended their initial program to include the use of force against states engaged in "hostile preparations" or against nonmembers if they attacked members. The major emphasis of the Bryce-Dickinson "Proposals," despite these clauses, remained on submission and delay.[13]

While this plan continued to be discussed and revised in England throughout 1916 and into 1917, many of the leaders of the Bryce-Dickinson group had united with other advocates in the spring of 1915 to form the League of Nations Society. Its plan differed in a few respects from that of the "Proposals." It called for the standard courts and council of inquiry and conciliation but insisted on the automatic use of sanctions against members who relied upon force before utilizing this machinery. It thus paralleled the League to Enforce Peace platform in its major points, except it, like the Bryce scheme, initially said nothing about its organization drafting international law. Its leaders later verbally indicated that conferences could be

13. Winkler, *League Movement,* pp. 20, 22. Evidence of the exchange of ideas can be found in Latané, *Development,* I, 57–67, 71–76, 83–85, 91–95, 302–306, II, 800–804.

held for this purpose, and such a provision finally appeared as part of the formal propositions. The League of Nations Society also departed from the American plan in calling for the defense of members under attack and also when it adopted amendments approving the enforcement of the judgments of the courts and council.[14]

The League of Nations Society advocates also maintained a close contact with Americans, which may explain some of the similarities in their programs. Where differences existed, the parties discussed them candidly. Extensive correspondence with both English groups plus exchanges of visitors resulted in agreements for co-operation despite variations in proposals. The Americans protested against the provisions for sanctions in the British schemes, for they feared that such clauses would never receive the endorsement of the Senate. A limited plan might gain acceptance; force to uphold decisions or to wage wars in defense of members went too far. Bryce and other Englishmen recognized the constitutional problem which the Americans faced in gaining senatorial approval, but they envisaged an essentially European union to which other nations might adhere; hence, they were never as concerned with the problem facing the Americans as were internationalists in the United States.[15]

Other groups also appeared in England. The Fabian Society Research Department organized a special committee under journalist Leonard Woolf, which issued a plan in July of 1915. It reflected the current emphasis on delaying or preventing wars by having disputes peacefully resolved. It differed in providing for a secretariat to function as a permanent administrative bureau, in inserting a clause on the formulation of law, and in its primary emphasis on economic sanctions. It also included more details than other contemporary proposals by discussing membership, representation, voting, methods of operation, and selection of judges. The most unusual provision dealt with the law-making power. Any nation could veto an act, but in so doing it had to indicate the specific clauses to which it objected. It then had to state what it would accept, and that part then applied to any dispute to which its government became a party. Theodore Marburg especially liked the Fabian plan even though it would uphold the decrees of its court. He found in its phrases and wording direct evidence that the League to Enforce

14. Winkler, *League Movement*, pp. 50–52, 65–70.
15. Bryce to Chandler P. Anderson, December 10, 1914, Anderson Papers, Library of Congress; Bryce to Root, December 15, 1915, Root Papers; Bryce to House, September 23, 1914, House Papers; Dickinson to Lowell, August 3, 1925 [1915]; *Minutes*, Executive Committee, February 16, 1916, Lowell Papers. Other evidence of contacts with English leaders can be found in Latané, *Development*, I, 19–20, 23–26, 32, 46, 94–105, 134–136, 156–160, 219–221, 227–228, 255, 276–281, 316–317.

Peace proposals and publications by Americans had influenced the Fabians.[16]

The Union of Democratic Control in England also presented a program. It had been founded in 1914, primarily by members of the British Labor Party. It insisted that, before any league could work, governments would have to alter their methods of diplomacy and allow greater democratic control. In this way, principles of right would have a chance to prevail. Then an organization with limited goals and machinery could resolve disputes peacefully. The UDC thus sought to inject international morality into the current discussions.[17]

Many individual Englishmen also drafted plans for some type of union. Most of their schemes fit the pattern established by the Bryce-Dickinson "Proposals," although considerable variation existed in their emphasis and on the degree to which sanctions should be applied.[18] Significant developments in England, however, came not from internationalists but from statesmen. As in the United States, it took political figures to give hopes a tinge of reality. Sir Edward Grey, the British Foreign Secretary until December 1916, as early as July 30, 1914, proposed a European system to reduce conflict. Subsequently, he raised the possibility that the United States might co-operate in a league in messages to Washington and in conversations with House. Grey's remarks had widespread influence in the United States where the League to Enforce Peace leaders interpreted them to be a challenge to greater activity. Prime Ministers Herbert Asquith and David Lloyd George also spoke on behalf of the ideal between 1914 and 1918. The Lloyd George ministry agreed early in 1917 that an official commission should begin to plan some of the details for an international organization, and on June 26, 1918, the House of Lords approved of the principle of co-operative action in settling disputes.[19] In their beliefs, these men also fit the prevailing pattern

16. Winkler, *League Movement*, pp. 7–16; Woolf, *International Government*, pp. 371–410; Marburg to Short, October 26, 1915, in Latané, *Development*, I, 78–79.

17. Winkler, *League Movement*, pp. 23, 26; Arthur Ponsonby, "International Morality," *International Journal of Ethics*, XXV (January 1915), 160–164; Norman Angell, "America and a New World State," *Current History*, II (April 1915), 78–80. The plan can be found in Bourne, *Enduring Peace*, p. 277.

18. Winkler, *League Movement*, pp. 84–110.

19. League to Enforce Peace, *A Reference Book for Speakers*, pp. 48–54; Marburg to William Phillips, April 28, 1915; Grey to Marburg, September 16, 1916, in Latané, *Development*, I, 40, 163–164; "The Plans for a Peace League," *The Survey*, XXXVII (November 4, 1916), 134; [Holt], "Europe Asks Our Help," *The Independent*, LXXXVIII (November 6, 1916), 214; "The League of Peace: Viscount Grey and Viscount Bryce," *The Outlook*, CXIV (November 8, 1916), 524–525; Winkler, *League Movement*, pp. 229–243.

of advocating an essentially European association built along the lines of the Bryce-Dickinson "Proposals."

One of the most notable features of English thought can be found in the obvious willingness to defer leadership to the United States. Discussions in England before April of 1917 had been largely private; hence, public agitation had to emanate elsewhere. Furthermore, advocates there realized how active the Americans were.[20] Journalist and publicist Norman Angell observed that a five-minute talk with any American pacifist would find him drawing "from his pocket a complete scheme for the federation of the world." English spokesmen often argued, too, that the United States, as a neutral, could propose such programs prior to 1917 without being accused of ulterior motives.[21] Once Congress declared war, these attitudes did not substantially change, especially in the light of Wilson's leadership.

By 1918, the co-operation between advocates in both countries reached a peak. The League to Enforce Peace had long considered whether to establish a branch in England, but in June of 1918 the Executive Committee ended that possibility when it approved a resolution inviting the League of Nations Society to associate with it. This did not materialize, but it did not hinder discussions as governments turned to drafting plans. Lord Bryce had often requested an official study by the United States government, and he had appealed to Root and the League to Enforce Peace to agitate for that goal. The Wilson administration, however, in its desire to keep discussions on a broad level, resisted such pressures until it had to act in the summer of 1918.[22]

20. "America's Part in the Settlement," *Living Age*, CCLXXXIII (December 5, 1914), 624–626; "America and the World-War," *ibid.*, CCXC (July 1, 1916), 56; J. G. Snead-Cox, "A Future Machinery of Peace," *ibid.*, CCXCII (March 31, 1917), 775, 779; "America and the Future," *ibid.*, CCXCIII (June 2, 1917), 555–559; James D. Whelply, "America at War," *ibid.*, (June 9, 1917), pp. 583–584; Sidney Low, "America and the Peace Settlement," *ibid.*, (June 16, 1917), pp. 644–645, 653–654.

21. Norman Angell, "America and the European War," *World Peace Foundation Pamphlets*, V (February 1915), 14; Angell, "American Neutrality After the War," *Yale Review*, VI (October 1916), 44–59; G. Lowes Dickinson, "Democratic Control of Foreign Policy," *Atlantic Monthly*, CXVIII (August 1916), 152; Sir Frederick Pollock, "The American Plan for Enforcing Peace," *ibid.*, CXIX (May 1917), 655; H. N. Brailsford, "The United States and the League of Peace," *ibid.*, (April 1917), pp. 437, 439–442; Bryce to House, August 26, 1916, House Papers.

22. *Minutes*, Executive Committee, June 29, 1918, Lowell Papers; Winkler, *League Movement*, pp. 17–18, 20–21; Bryce to House, December 17, 1917, March 15, May 24, 1918, House Papers; Taft to Bryce, January 25, 1918, Taft Papers; Bryce to Marburg, February 1, [April] 1918, in Latané, *Development*, I, 403–404, 436–437; Aneurin Williams to Marburg, July 5, 1918, *ibid.*, II, 486–487; Bryce to Root, December 21, 1917, in H. A. L. Fisher, *James Bryce*, II, 178.

It is remarkable that groups in both countries which formulated specific programs managed to maintain such cordial relations. They did agree on basic principles, notably those to obtain delay and gain investigation of disputes; but an analysis of the major English plans shows significant differences from the League to Enforce Peace platform on three points: The Americans emphasized an association with legislative powers; the English believed in a greater application of force; and the League to Enforce Peace hoped to create a court with the authority to determine its own jurisdiction or the justiciability of questions. The issue over sanctions, however, proved to be the big one. British schemes favored the enforcement of decisions of the court and the protection of members. Most Americans refused to go that far but wanted any enforcement to be automatic when it was applied. The British wished to proceed more cautiously and thus included provisions for consultation before action. In this respect, the more radical British suggestions on sanctions really meant less than the more modest goal of the League to Enforce Peace, since the latter's proposals left no doubt about the final outcome.

The League to Enforce Peace, in attempting to reconcile these differences and in seeking to spread its doctrines, created a Committee on Foreign Organization headed by Theodore Marburg. He conducted extensive correspondence, made one lengthy trip to Europe, and informed officials in governments of developments. When some of the League's study groups formulated tentative constitutions for an international organization in the winter and spring of 1918, Marburg sent their work through all the channels he had developed. American ideas thus reached those persons in Europe writing official proposals.[23]

Meanwhile, the League to Enforce Peace faced two major problems in pursuing its course at home. First, it had to convince the public after the declaration of war that it was not a pacifist society. To do this, it incorporated a "win the war" objective into its program. It also supported preparedness efforts, aided Liberty Loan drives, and emphasized the victory theme in its campaigns.[24] Thus it maintained a satisfactory public image.

---

23. Marburg to Lowell, September 3, 1917; to Lowell, May 6, 1918; to Holt, July 29, 1918, in Latané, *Development*, I, 334–339, 443, II, 494–498.

24. Bartlett, *League to Enforce Peace,* pp. 87–98; Resumé of Activities of Committee on Publications, *Report* to the Executive Committee, June 30, 1917, Lowell Papers; Theodore Marburg and H. E. Flack, eds., *Taft Papers on League of Nations,* pp. 81–98. Major publications of the League included the report of its annual meeting in May of 1918, *Win the War for Permanent Peace, A Reference Book for Speakers,* and Robert Goldsmith, *A League to Enforce Peace.*

Its second problem stemmed from success. Once the government through Wilson became the major spokesman for the cause, people paid less attention to the League to Enforce Peace. This affected its budget. Hard work, however, kept its machinery moving, and it even expanded its news bureau and mailing activity. Its leaders realized that such efforts had to be continued. It would be far easier, Marburg speculated, to win acceptance of the idea "abroad than at home." Traditional attitudes had to be modified; thus publications reiterated that the warnings of the founding fathers against alliances could no longer be taken literally. They did not bar membership in an international organization.[25]

The most important operation of the League to Enforce Peace took place away from the public eye. From December of 1916 until April of 1918, discussions on a detailed plan of union proceeded in study groups. The work began in an unofficial way when some of the more ambitious members decided that the basic statements of the League should be developed. They hoped through interpretive clauses to expand the platform into a draft proposal for an international organization. Pressures from abroad, demands at home for clarifications, and the ever-closer hour when a league might come into existence contributed to the need for action. One rule prevailed throughout all of the meetings. All discussions had to be based on the "present program as fixed and unalterable."[26]

Marburg presided over most of the meetings of the private study group, which held eight sessions. The participants emphasized that they had no official connection with the League to Enforce Peace, because some of the latter's officers had doubts about such work. No one wished to do anything which might adversely affect the parent organization or its operation.

The discussions covered a variety of topics, including the headquarters of the union, the obligations of the United States in relation to constitutional provisions on warmaking, membership, and that problem which had wrecked the hopes of the Second Hague Conference, the selection of judges for a court. Even more knotty questions, however, arose. The participants explored the nature of the executive agency, the power of any assembly to enact laws, and the touchy subject of sanctions. That almost insoluble query which John Bassett Moore had raised years before also prompted debate. How could any organization determine when a hostile act had occurred or

25. Marburg to Lowell, September 3, 1917, in Latané, *Development*, I, 334–339. Evidence of the reasoning and arguments employed can be found in Goldsmith, "The Foundations of a Lasting Peace," *Bookman*, XLVII (May 1918), 227–234.
26. Resumé of Discussions, December 15, 1916, in Latané, *Development*, II, 721.

where guilt or responsibility lay? Interestingly, in all of the discussions, the phrase League of Nations replaced that of League to Enforce Peace.[27]

The final draft of their program, "The United Nations," appeared in *The Independent* in January of 1918. The first article, entitled "Covenant," listed the obligations of nations to settle disputes peacefully, to utilize the machinery of a court or council of conciliation, and to employ economic and military force to uphold the objectives of the union. The second article contained the most significant contribution and departure from the League to Enforce Peace planks. It created an executive agency in the form of an International Council which would explore economic, social, and political "conditions affecting international relations." It could also propose laws and call periodic conferences to enact these, determine when a state of war or violations of the peace had occurred, establish the standards or fitness of governments to sit in the league, and create a bureau to function as a ministry or executive body. The latter could handle claims or grievances, administer the armed forces, and ask for injunctions against lawbreakers to compel them to appear before the judges or the council of conciliation.

Article three dealt in detailed fashion with a court of justice. It would consider all justiciable matters, determine the justiciability of a dispute, issue injunctions to prevent "objectionable acts," and decide cases. An elaborate electoral system sought to solve the problem of selecting judges. The fourth and fifth provisions dealt with operational details. These suggested a financial obligation, with payments according to wealth. They also revealed that statutes formulated by the periodic conferences would be in effect after one year if no signatory registered a protest.

The other revealing aspect of this draft appeared in statements which delegated many procedural matters to the new organization. Each branch of the government, whether judicial or executive, enjoyed wide leeway to determine its own procedures and operating rules. Thus, the proposed constitution called for a powerful agency. It could not, however, operate in arbitrary fashion because of two limitations. First, the league could never act beyond its peace-keeping function. It could only compel the submission of disputes to settlement, not stop wars after they had begun; neither could its forces be employed to uphold a decision of the court. Second, all of its authority rested upon principles of right, justice, and law.[28]

---

27. The minutes of these sessions with comments can be found *ibid.*, pp. 721–754.

28. "The United Nations," *The Independent*, XCIII (January 26, 1918), 141, 152–156. This document was a revised version by Marburg based on suggestions on the draft of the October 20 meeting. Marburg to Holt, December 19, 1917, in Latané, *Development*, I, 380–381.

The efforts of Marburg's study group did not please some of the leaders in the League to Enforce Peace, especially Lowell. The plan went too far; hence, the League did not adopt it. Instead, Lowell received authorization on October 2, 1917, to establish an official commission to formulate a program.[29] Only a few persons served on both study panels, which meant that the conclusions of the new body reflected views different from those of Marburg's draftsmen.

The Marburg men had reflected a faith in democracy. They believed that delegates to a league would represent people. The Lowell men argued that any international government would have to be built upon nations and that practical politics should be considered in determining the structure and operation of a union. Holt voiced the opposing view when he expressed his concern that legislative aspects should not be neglected and that democratic principles should be adopted which would protect men more than member-states.[30]

The "Tentative Draft" of the "official study committee" was formally accepted on April 11, 1918. It contained twenty points and far fewer words than that of the private group. More important, it revealed other significant differences. First, it avoided discussion of procedural matters even more than the unofficial plant did. It was primarily substantive, dealing with structure, machinery, and membership. Second, it created a special Court of Conflicts to determine the justiciability of disputes. Third, it conferred no specific power to issue injunctions on any organ of the league, although that right apparently existed. Fourth, it remained unusually vague on an executive branch, its powers, and its operation. Fifth, it based financial payments on each signatory's "contributions to the Universal Postal Union," with the proviso that if any member fell one year in arrears it lost its "right of representation." Finally, it allowed a state to withdraw on one year's notice if no legal action or penalty existed against the party.[31]

These discussions within the League to Enforce Peace disclose three significant factors, two of which should have been of concern to anyone eventually charged with drafting a covenant for an international organization. In the first place, the two plans revealed the current and widespread diversity of views upon what should be included, what structure seemed suitable, and what powers should be conferred. Considering the fact that

29. Lowell to Taft, July 5, 1917, Taft Papers; Short to Marburg, July 11, 1918, in Latané, *Development*, II, 488; Marburg to Lowell, October 3, 1917, Lowell Papers.

30. Lowell to Taft, July 5, 1917, Taft Papers; Holt to Short, January 2, 1918, Holt Papers.

31. "Tentative Draft of a Treaty for a League of Nations," Holt Papers. A copy appeared in the *Advocate of Peace*, LXXX (July 1918), 205–209.

everyone in both study groups agreed upon the basic terms of the League to Enforce Peace, the differences provided warning of the complexity of the task and the fact that many people would inevitably be dissatisfied when any constitution neglected points they considered essential. The varied plans of European associations and their inability to agree should have amplified that point even more.

In the second place, the discussions in both groups disclosed a tendency to become bogged down on details. Questions of membership, structure, courts and councils, selection of judges and even their rate of pay soon obscured the major aim of finding a workable formula. If the League to Enforce Peace could not avoid these pitfalls, could anyone else? Finally, the efforts of both committees revealed the low level to which arbitration had fallen. Little consideration was given to its development or its achievements under the Hague system. The "Tentative Draft" revealed that emphasis upon machinery rather than principles which characterized so many programs.

Even as the League to Enforce Peace began to consider specific plans, it did not abandon its basic aim of education so that the Senate would eventually act favorably upon any agreement to join an international body. Its important actions in this way can be seen in its co-operative efforts with other organizations, especially religious bodies. In 1917 and 1918, Protestant church leaders joined in the quest for a league, and from that point on, even in the 1920s and 1930s, they pursued it with almost missionary zeal.

Clergymen had always been close to the peace movement, whether as participants in pacifist groups or as individuals. They had been indoctrinated by the prewar internationalists at the Lake Mohonk Arbirtation Conferences and at peace congresses. They had read of developments in religious journals, most notably in Frederick Lynch's *Christian Work* and in Christian Endeavor publications, and they had been indoctrinated on a modest scale by the Federal Council of Churches of Christ before the war and by the Church Peace Union after 1914.

The Federal Council had established a Commission on Peace and Arbitration in 1911, which caused Lynch to ask how ministers in all lands might be aroused against war, and he prodded Carnegie for funds for such a project. When Carnegie founded the Church Peace Union, Lynch did not rest. He co-operated with European churchmen in organizing a meeting at Constance, Germany, in August of 1914, where they formed the World Alliance for International Friendship Through the Churches.[32]

32. Lynch, "A Church Peace League," *Mohonk Report, 1912*, pp. 198–199; Macfarland, *Pioneers for Peace*, pp. 46, 98–99.

Such internationalists as Lynch, Holt, and Charles S. Macfarland, who served as trustees of the Church Peace Union, soon had the Union committed to the work of the World Alliance. The latter formed committees in each nation, and the American branch's roster contained the names of all of the above men who directed it along their path. By May of 1917, the Alliance circulated "A Petition to the President and Congress" which combined an appeal for a wise immigration policy with one for a league of nations. It also suggested a "Pan-American Federation." Another publication urged greater education for the "New Internationalism" and outlined a study program for congregations and ministers.[33]

It took little imagination for these men to perceive another possibility. In November 1917 they persuaded the trustees of the Church Peace Union to establish a National Committee on the Churches and the Moral Aims of the War. It soon assumed much of the work of the American Branch of the World Alliance, of the Church Peace Union, and of the Commission on International Justice and Good Will of the Federal Council of Churches. It sought to convince the people "that out of this war must come some new international order."[34]

Even before the creation of the Committee on Churches and the Moral Aims of the War, the Church Peace Union had been exploring possible avenues of co-operation with the League to Enforce Peace. Now the new body solved all administrative problems since Holt, as a key figure in all three groups, co-ordinated plans which assumed ambitious proportions. The Church Peace Union agreed to underwrite a one-hundred-thousand-dollar educational campaign through the churches by sending the finest clergy- and lay-speakers on tours. While the aim appeared in an ambiguous announcement that they sought "to educate in a peace *program*," everyone knew it meant "the idea of a League of Nations and a World Court." A statement noted that any international organization created should seek "to promote justice and preserve peace through legislative, judicial, and executive functions supported by all available sanctions, moral, economic and physical." These words reveal that in essence the platform of the League to Enforce Peace had been adopted.[35]

33. Macfarland, *Pioneers for Peace*, pp. 47, 49. Copies of these documents can be found in the Holt Papers.

34. Lynch, *President Wilson and the Moral Aims of the War*, p. 7.

35. Report of the Committee of Five, October 19, November 7, 1917, *Minute Book, 1914–1918*, Church Peace Union Papers; *Minutes*, Executive Committee, League to Enforce Peace, November 24, 1917, Taft Papers; Macfarland, *Pioneers for Peace*, pp. 64–70; Kuehl, *Hamilton Holt*, p. 131.

The National Committee on the Moral Aims of the War blanketed the nation with speakers in 1918 and published a series of pamphlets. By December, Lynch reported that 711,000 persons had heard speakers at 1,259 meetings. Furthermore, 33,000 clergymen had been approached on the subject, and many had become converts.[36] In this way, the internationalists gained access to an extensive and influential forum which continued to advance their goals long after the campaign ended.

Meanwhile the Federal Council, through various agencies, had also been promoting the league idea. As early as 1915, its Christian Education Commission published a volume on *Selected Quotations on Peace and War*. It included extensive sections on "The Interdependence of the Nations" and "World Federation," in which the themes of justice, brotherhood, and law prevailed. By 1917 and 1918, its Commission on International Justice and Good Will had assumed the responsibility for educating the public. It sought, through public forums, debates, publications, and Chautauqua-type meetings, to encourage the study of "Christian Internationalism."[37]

The League to Enforce Peace also enjoyed the support of other groups in its campaign of education. The American School Peace League continued its work through Mrs. Andrews by sponsoring essay contests. Children could write on "How Should the World Be Organized so as to Prevent Wars in the Future?" and "The Teaching of Democracy as a Factor in a League of Nations." The World Peace Foundation continued to support the League to Enforce Peace through financial grants, and in October of 1917 it issued the first of a series of pamphlets under the heading *A League of Nations*. The announcement left no doubt of its purpose. It sought to deal "chiefly with plans and projects for the kind of international organization outlined by the advocates of a League to Enforce Peace."[38]

Not everyone in the United States concerned with the subject, however, agreed that the League to Enforce Peace offered the best formula for a successful association. A solid core of opposition continued to exist against

36. Kuehl, *Hamilton Holt*, p. 132. The committee's publications included one by Holt, *The Moral Values of a League of Nations*, one by Samuel Z. Batten, *The New World Order*, and *League of Nations*.

37. Commission on Christian Education, *Selected Quotations on Peace and War*, pp. 206–311, 509–511; "To Establish a Christian World Order," *Advocate of Peace*, LXXIX (November 1917), 293. A pamphlet, *A New Era in Human History*, contained a four-week study program built largely around scriptural references. Macfarland, *Pioneers for Peace*, p. 70.

38. "Among the Peace Organizations," *Advocate of Peace*, LXXX (May 1918), 156; "War Declarations of Peace Organizations," *World Court*, IV (March 1918), 189; "Announcement," *World Peace Foundation Pamphlets*, League of Nations Series, I (October 1917), iii.

the idea of sanctions, and a large block of conservatives continued to insist upon a judicially oriented union. Joseph H. Choate's remark that he could endorse the League to Enforce Peace if it left out its plank on force seemed to be a standard point among such men. The pacifist position remained unchanged in this respect, with the American Peace Society continuing to support the ideal of a congress of nations while at the same time denying it any power. The Society, however, continued to explore plans and to publish many views with which it did not agree.[39]

Neither did the men associated with the Carnegie Endowment alter their thinking as a result of their nation's commitment to war. The Endowment sought to build a public opinion favorable to an international court largely through publications designed to lay a foundation for peace through law. Under the editorship of J. B. Scott, it printed a series of "Classics of International Law," Ladd's *Essay on a Congress of Nations, James Madison's Notes of Debates . . . and Their Relation to a More Perfect Society of Nations*, and a two-volume study of the *Judicial Settlement of Controversies Between the States of the American Union*. These works leave no doubt that Scott believed in an international organization, but one with limited powers.

The other leaders of the Endowment, Root and Butler, presented their views in less voluminous fashion. In fact, Root remained relatively silent, continuing his policy of not speaking or writing for publication except on special occasions. Also, Root became involved for several months in an unhappy experience with the Wilson administration over problems with Russia. He continued to believe, however, in a judicial structure preferably modeled after the Central American Court of Justice. Such a body, Root believed, should have the authority to determine its own jurisdiction, but he had doubts about its deciding upon the justiciability of a dispute.[40]

Butler often referred to *The Basis of a Durable Peace* as an expression of his views. In general, he favored all the planks of the League to Enforce Peace except the one on force. A "League to Secure Peace" appealed to him more. He feared any imposed arrangement not based on law and justice. If the latter existed, there would be little need for sanctions. Thus Butler did not rule them out; but, like many of the English planners, he would apply

39. Edward S. Martin, *The Life of Joseph Hodges Choate*, II, 381; Levermore, *Samuel Train Dutton*, p. 231; Joseph Swain to Jordan, January 14, 1918, Jordan Papers; George W. Kirchwey, "Pax Americana," *Advocate of Peace*, LXXIX (May 1917), 145–146; "A Governed World," *ibid.*, p. 131; "The Rising Tide," *ibid.*, (October 1917), pp. 259–260; Harold G. Townsend, "The Opportunity of the American Peace Society," *ibid.*, LXXX (January 1918), 20; "Force and a League of Nations," *ibid.*, (July 1918), pp. 198–199.

40. Leopold, *Elihu Root*, pp. 103, 116–120; Memorandum of an interview with Root, October 15, 1917, Anderson Papers.

them only in accordance with clearly stated principles. Butler, too, often resorted to his prewar advocacy of an "international mind," and he called for greater education and co-operation in economic and social matters.[41]

The other major body supporting a judicial organization, the World's Court League, suffered from a limited budget after April of 1917. Nearly all of its funds went into its monthly *World Court* magazine. Efforts to affiliate with the League to Enforce Peace continued, but the issue of sanctions kept them apart. Samuel Dutton, as secretary-general of the World's Court League, insisted that his society's moderate views would prevail. After all, men had turned to the phrase "League of Nations." This seemed to indicate that they doubted the wisdom of sanctions as they dropped the word "enforced."[42]

The cautious internationalist viewpoint also appeared in discussions of the Hague system. William Hull proclaimed its advantages, and John Bassett Moore revived the subject of arbitration by recalling its successes prior to 1914 and by noting that its proceedings had always been marked by judicial process and hearing. William Blymer, a New York attorney, also enlarged upon a project he had originally conceived in 1892. Governments, he declared, would not accept the authority of an international organization, but they might agree upon some tribunal with limited powers. A system of compulsory arbitration combined with disarmament would go far to maintain peace, especially if the major governments agreed to an "isolation plan by which they would embargo economically and diplomatically any nation which refused to arbitrate a dispute."[43]

James M. Beck also looked back and wondered if men had not outpaced

41. Butler to Bryce, June 12, 1917; to Walter R. Gray, March 1, 1918; to Herbert S. Houston, May 14, 1918; to Short, June 13, 1918, CEIP Papers. Butler, "A Governed World," *Advocate of Peace*, LXXX (August 1918), 235–236; Butler, "The International Mind: How to Develop It," *Proceedings*, Academy of Political Science, VII (July 1917), 208–212.

42. "Annual Report of the General Secretary . . . ," May 1, 1917, World's Court League folder, SCPC; "Finance Committee Report," May 1, 1917; *Minutes*, Ways and Means Committee, November 27, 1917, *ibid*; Dutton, "The World's Court League . . . ," *World Court*, IV (July 1918), 395–398; Dutton to Scott, May 4, 1917; to Butler, February 18, 1918, CEIP Papers; Dutton, "The United States and the War," *Annals*, American Academy of Political and Social Science, LXXII (July 1917), 18–19; Levermore, *Samuel Train Dutton*, pp. 171, 184–186.

43. Hull, "A World Court," *Proceedings*, Academy of Political Science, VII (July 1917), 221–227; Moore, "International Arbitration," *World Court*, III (October 1917), 493–498; Blymer, *The Isolation (or non-intercourse) Plan With a Proposed Convention*, pp. 1–5, 11–23, 27–29. Blymer had presented a similar idea earlier. *Bulletins*, Fourth and Twelfth Universal Peace Congresses (1892), pp. 70, 208, (1903), pp. 113–114.

themselves in a wild search for new formulas. They had not tried the old ones. Arbitration had never been fully supported or applied. Beck recognized that rules of justice should prevail; he admitted that force might be needed; but he worried that countries could not agree upon even a simple set of standards. They could not even find an acceptable definition of the word "justiciable."[44]

References to the Hague system also revived the old problem of the selection of judges, and some writers explored that subject. Others argued whether international law really existed. If it did not, it would be an unreliable tool for an organization, since nations would never agree upon its codification or application. Some persons returned to the platitudes that true peace would have to depend upon right and justice, and such thinking resulted in the presentation of an idea which had an impact in the 1920s. Why not simply brand wars as unlawful? Pacifists had raised this question before, but in March 1918 a Chicago lawyer, Salmon O. Levinson, revived it. Armed conflict would continue, he argued, as long as men recognized that governments had a right to conduct them. Nations, therefore, should outlaw war, compel the submission of disputes for settlement and uphold by force "the decrees of the international tribunal."[45]

The conservative approach to world union also appeared in the thinking of other men. Historian George B. Adams decried the plethora of plans and argued that a successful association could never be fashioned around an administrative machine. The moral will of people provided the only foundation on which to build. This meant that any society would have to be based upon commonly accepted concepts of law and right and only in an English-Speaking Union could men agree upon these. Other democracies could join if they wished, said Adams, and George L. Beer echoed his sentiments.[46]

David Jayne Hill, as a former delegate to the Second Hague Conference, concurred with Adams and Beer. Hill had written many treatises on inter-

44. Beck, "A Yearning for World Peace," *Annals*, American Academy of Political and Social Science, LXXII (July 1917), 208–213.

45. Charles H. Levermore, "How Shall a World Court be Constituted?" *World Court*, III (June–July 1917), 276–291; E. D. Dickinson, "A League of Nations and International Law," American Political Science *Review*, XII (May 1918), 304–311; Munroe Smith, "The Nature and the Future of International Law," *ibid.*, (February 1918), pp. 1–16; E. S. Roscoe, "The Future of International Law," *North American Review*, CCVII (April 1918), 558–563; H. M. Chittenden, "Peace by Coercion," *The Forum*, LVII (May 1917), 553–566; Levinson, "The Legal Status of War," *New Republic*, XIV (March 9, 1918), 171–173.

46. Adams, "The British Empire and a League of Peace," *The Nation*, CVI (April 4, 1918), 392–394; Adams, "Alliance vs. Federation," *ibid.*, (June 15, 1918), p. 710;

national relations, and he published a work in 1918 which explored many plans from Crucé to Kant. He dismissed them as futile. They required a reorganization which nations would never accept because of the sentiments of sovereignty and nationalism. Only a plan built upon "mutually adaptable" principles and "expressions of a common life" could succeed. It would be best to begin with a nucleus of governments which held similar views of right and which accepted international law. They could sign an agreement and gradually develop administrative machinery, a code, and judicial procedures. No sanctions would be needed in such a union.[47]

Another newcomer, poet Sidney A. Witherbee, disagreed with this reasoning. He drafted an elaborate plan based on twenty-five "world statutes." Most of these referred to sovereignty, disarmament, open diplomacy, trade, and citizenship. They also required the submission of disputes to a judicial body with enforcement of decisions, the cost to be paid by the offender. Witherbee failed to mention any administrative machinery other than a court; hence his scheme left important questions untouched.[48]

The limited approach of judicially and legalistically inclined advocates was matched on the opposite extreme by the spokesmen for world government. The middle ground had been usurped by the proponents of a league-type organization with specified powers and duties, but some men did not think such an approach would work.[49] Indeed, they challenged the principles of the League to Enforce Peace. Darwin Kingsley, once an active supporter, had changed his mind by 1918. The sovereignty of nations had to be subordinated in any federation. Only a "new State, a new Power" deriving its authority from people rather than governments would succeed. Arbitration and councils of conciliation should give way to a court which would resolve all difficulties. Kingsley provided few details on the structure of his union, but he referred to the Constitution of the United States as a model.[50]

Beer, "Liberals in Alliance," *New Republic*, XIII (November 3, 1917), 20–21; Beer, "America's Place in the World," *Yale Review*, VII (January 1918), 239–248.

47. Hill, *The Rebuilding of Europe*, pp. 173–207, 226–227, 277, 281–282.

48. Witherbee, "World Law—Fixed by World Statutes," *The Forum*, LIX (February 1918), 183–186.

49. J. M. Mack to Jordan, August 20, 1917, Jordan Papers; A. Brodbeck to Endowment, July 6, 1917, CEIP Papers; J. R. Chapman to Taft, January 2, 1918, Taft Papers; George H. Boke, *Proposals for a Federal World Government*, pp. 1–4; Algernon S. Crapsey, *International Democratic Republic*, pp. 13–28; Milwaukee *Leader*, May 28, 1918; James H. Hanger to House, March 6, 1918 (copy), Mezes Papers, Library of Congress.

50. Kingsley to Short, April 18, 1918, LEP Papers; Kingsley, "A New Charter of Liberty," *North American Review*, CCVII (March 1918), 404–413.

Kingsley had adopted two ideas for a supranational government from earlier spokesmen, both of whom continued to ponder the subject. Raymond Bridgman kept insisting that only a completely established world body with a military force could maintain peace. Oscar Crosby's idea of a court-oriented society also appeared in Kingsley's scheme. Crosby remained relatively silent throughout 1918, for he was drafting a proposal for publication. Filled with details, it paralleled Bridgman's thinking because only an all-powerful agency could have performed the functions he listed.[51]

Three other early advocates of a strong organization also continued to promote their ideas. Harrison Gray Otis republished his plan in the Los Angeles *Times* in July 1917, just a few weeks before his death. His revisions reveal a growing reliance upon force and an even greater acceptance of a strong "World Government." George Shibley prepared a lengthy draft of a "world federation." It would make and administer laws, regulate members, attain disarmament, levy a tax, enforce the agreement, oversee backward areas, and establish an international capital. Although Shibley included guarantees to exclude the internal affairs of members and he believed that economic sanctions should precede military action, he wished to limit the sovereignty of nations. Charles Eliot insisted upon a "peace-preserving international force." He had never bothered about details, but in the spring of 1918 he grew concerned. He started an unsuccessful crusade to convince statesmen that any program required immediate planning. Governments should appoint commissions to draft jointly a feasible scheme.[52]

The young historian Samuel Eliot Morison, then a lecturer at Harvard, also perceived the need for a more powerful union than the one envisaged by the League to Enforce Peace. He called for "a United States of the World, a super-national government, with full control over the armed forces of the members." Laws had been ignored because nations controlled their own armies. This would change if an international organization could be created along the lines he outlined. Its popularly elected legislature would

---

51. Bridgman to Taft, January 15, 1918, Taft Papers; Bridgman, "A World-Unity Conference," *Bibliotheca Sacra*, LXXV (January 1918), 133–142; Crosby to House, June 10, 1918, House Papers. The Crosby Papers contain a draft of Crosby's work which was not published at that time because Wilson asked him to delay its appearance. Baker, *Wilson: Life and Letters*, VII, 427–428.

52. Los Angeles *Times*, July 22, 1917; Shibley, *The Road to Victory: It Lies Through the United States . . .* , pp. 28–38; Eliot to the editor, New York *Times*, August 5, 1917; Eliot, "Is An Informal Peace Conference Now Possible?," *Scientific Monthly*, V (October 1917), 317–322; Boston *Herald*, February 15, 1918; Eliot to Marburg, May 15, 1918, Marburg Papers; New York *Times*, April 27, 1918; Eliot to Butler, May 8, 1918, CEIP Papers.

uphold the decisions of a court, protect and oversee backward lands, and "guarantee equal access to raw materials."[53]

Other advocates of an extreme position came from the Middle West, the Pacific Coast, and the East, but their views did not vary on the point of power. Whatever league the nations established, it would need extensive authority to uphold laws and decrees, check aggression, and even tax. At least one congressional resolution reflected the desire for a strong union. In S.J. Res. 94 Senator Robert L. Owen of Oklahoma requested the President to invite other nations to a conference to discuss a league. They should create a government with a legislature, a court with jurisdiction limited to justiciable matters, and an executive in the form of a cabinet. An armed force would defend members against attack and uphold law. Secretary of the Navy Josephus Daniels did not think exactly as Owen did, but he called for an international navy, primarily to achieve disarmament.[54]

It is obvious from the number of plans in 1917 and 1918 that three major groups existed: the cautious legalists with their judicial approach, the venturesome internationalists who favored a supranational government, and the popular middle-ground spokesmen for a limited-type league. Not all persons, however, fit neatly into these categories.[55] A considerable number of proposals reflected the particular desires of the writers. Some, like Daniels, wished to achieve disarmament through an organization; some supported an association to uphold peace because it would promote military training.[56]

Still others hoped to see a union solve the most outstanding economic problems of the world, largely through free trade and the elimination of economic injustices which led to war. A few man believed that the maritime issues of neutral rights could be resolved if a federation could neutralize

53. Boston *Morning Globe*, May 12, 1918.

54. A. R. Foote, *The United Democratic Nations of the World*, pp. 7–13, 19–23; Carl H. P. Thurston, "Is the Pen Swifter Than the Sword?," *Bookman*, XLVI (November 1917), 291; Theodore Harris, *A Proposed Constitution for the United Nations of the World*, pp. 4–44; *Congressional Record*, 65 Cong., 1st sess., 55, pt. 6:6164–6165. Daniels included his suggestion in his annual report of 1917. "Police of the Sea," *The League Bulletin*, No. 65 (December 14, 1917), pp. 109–110.

55. An excellent summary of attitudes can be found in Stephen P. Duggan, "The Conference on the Foreign Relations of the United States," *International Conciliation*, No. 121 (December 1917), pp. 19–28.

56. E. S. Martin, "The Great World Movie: A Machine to Guard Machinery," *Good Housekeeping*, LXVI (March 1918), 42, 135–136; Luigi Carnovale, *How America Can Easily and Quickly Prevent Wars Forever*, pp. 1, 10–11; W. W. Core to Scott, May 12, 1917, CEIP Papers; Frank H. Short, *Peace or War? Which Shall It Be?*, pp. 2–3, 5–8.

waterways, guarantee access to important trade routes, and uphold the freedom of the seas.[57] The editors of the *New Republic* hoped to see a league built on "an economic basis," which would spread democracy, achieve disarmament, and regulate "those vital supplies on which human life depends." Thorstein Veblen, the economist and social theorist, also emphasized this theme. He provided little information on the workings of his organization other than to suggest a league to neutralize those conditions which contributed to war. He admitted that his society would have to enforce peace at times, but he provided no details on this important topic.[58]

One also finds continuing interest in a worldwide Monroe Doctrine system in which nations would agree not to tolerate certain disturbances. Another program centered around the idea of international commissions. Edward Krehbiel, a professor of history at Stanford, helped revive this concept by reviewing the work and action of nineteenth-century commissions. A number of these, he believed, operating in specified areas, could gradually formulate a set of procedures and rules to resolve conflicts.[59]

An interesting variation on the commission theme appeared in a plan by Arthur K. Kuhn, an attorney and professor at Columbia University. He accepted the platform of the League to Enforce Peace but suggested the creation of six regional agencies. They would act upon problems in their areas and if necessary refer them to the international council. Kuhn also favored the enforcement of decisions and the creation of a ministry.[60]

57. C. De Kalb, "The Formula for Peace," *Atlantic Monthly*, CXX (December 1917), 754; Roger W. Babson, "Drawing Together the Americas," *Proceedings*, Academy of Political Science, VII (July 1917), 448–451; J. Russell Smith, "Economic Access and Neutralization of Waterways," *ibid.*, pp. 272–278; Bruno Lasker, "The Way to Durable Peace," *Yale Review*, VII (October 1917), 24–42.

58. "The World in Revolution," *New Republic*, XI (May 5, 1917), 4–5; "The Necessary Step," *ibid.*, XII (September 1, 1917), 119–120; "Leaving Policy to the Government," *ibid.*, XIII (December 1, 1917), 108–110; "National Self-Determination," *ibid.*, XIV (March 16, 1918), 193; "Editorial Notes," *ibid.*, X (April 28, 1917), 357; Veblen, *An Inquiry Into the Nature of Peace and the Terms of Its Perpetuation*, pp. vi–viii, 205–220, 256, 258–263, 237–240, 296.

59. J. H. Latané, "The Monroe Doctrine and the American Policy of Isolation . . . ," *Annals*, American Academy of Political and Social Science, LXXII (July 1917), 100–109; George G. Wilson, "The Monroe Doctrine After the War," *Proceedings*, Academy of Political Science, VII (July 1917), 297–302; "The Responsibility of a Nation's Strength," *World's Work*, XXXVI (May 1918), 13; Charles M. Bakewell, "The Philosophy of War and Peace," *Bookman*, XLV (May 1917), 230; Krehbiel, "The European Commission of the Danube," *International Conciliation*, No. 131 (October 1918), pp. 543–565.

60. Oscar Straus to Taft, January 17, 1918, with enclosure of Kuhn plan, Taft Papers.

The most sophisticated proposal for commissions, however, came from attorney Alpheus H. Snow of Washington, D.C. The Hague structure needed a court as well as legislative and executive bodies which Snow preferred to call "directorates." One would act as an administrative arm, function as a conciliation commission, investigate disputes, and seek settlements through persuasion. The other would gather information and legislate "by laying down general rules." It would seek treaties to internationalize sea lanes, open trade channels, and tax governments. Since the powers of these directorates would be limited largely to conciliation and persuasion, the sovereignty of states would not be affected. Over the years, Snow believed, his administrative directorate would develop and gain experience in settling disputes.[61]

Another theme which appeared after 1917 called for a union based upon the wartime bodies established by the Allies to conduct the war. It reflected a concern that a peace conference at the end of the struggle might be too preoccupied with negotiations to formulate an intelligent plan. Hence, discussions should begin among those nations already united as brothers-in-arms, and the neutral states could be invited to join.[62]

Woodrow Wilson had his ideas, too, and he became the leader of the movement because nearly everyone looked to him for direction. Unfortunately, Wilson pursued a course which discouraged the internationalists. He supported the ideal with consistency, and he encouraged discussions as long as the subject-matter remained abstract. But he feared consideration of specific plans about the operation and powers of an organization. Acceptance of general principles by governments and people came first. Any attempt to formulate details would stimulate opposition and offend groups and statesmen.[63]

Wilson's position proved to be both sound and unsound. Too much discussion could excite men as they considered various alternatives. On the other hand, if no one explored the problems which might arise, statesmen

61. Snow, "International Legislation and Administration," *Proceedings*, Academy of Political Science, VII (July 1917), 228–245; Snow, "Cooperative Union of Nations," *World Court*, IV (April 1918), 202–210.

62. Frank F. Williams, "A Communication," *Advocate of Peace*, LXXX (July 1918), 220–221; Baker, *Wilson: Life and Letters*, VIII, 245, 327, 573; "Create a Political Council Now," *Equity*, XX (April 1918), 106–107; "New League for War: Why Not Also for Peace?," *ibid.*, pp. 107–108; "Two Leagues to Enforce Peace," *ibid.*, (July 1918), pp. 159–160; Edward L. Conn, "Can There Be Political Unity Among the Associated Governments?," *World Court*, IV (May 1918), 276–278.

63. Wilson to B. D. Gibson, May 5, 1917; Frank L. Polk to Jusserand, July 20, 1917, in Baker, *Wilson: Life and Letters*, VII, 53, 203.

would be left with an enormous task at the peace conference. The President also realized that any league would have to be created after consultation with other governments, a fact which prompted caution. He had other reasons, however, for moving slowly. His duties in conducting the war took so much of his time that he could not add to his burdens. He devoted so little attention to the currents about him that House recorded in his diary in September 1917 how startled he was at Wilson's lack of knowledge on the subject.[64]

Wilson's position left many internationalists in a quandary, especially those in the League to Enforce Peace. Marburg sent the President the plan of his informal study group, but when he and others sought Wilson's opinion they discovered an almost unreasonable attitude. When Vance McCormick, a loyal Democrat and chairman of the War Trade Board, approached Wilson about the League's work, the latter refused to approve any of its pending projects. Short suspected that such intransigence stemmed from Wilson's objections to any detailed program.[65] Early in 1918, when Lord Bryce inquired how the League to Enforce Peace planned to co-operate with the Wilson administration in formulating a practical program, Marburg transmitted the letter to the President. Wilson again insisted that no formal constitutions be written, and he expressed his irritation to House. He called the League to Enforce Peace men "butters-in" and referred to Marburg as "one of the principal woolgatherers." Later that month, Taft and Lowell had an interview with Wilson in which they delivered the revised draft of their official study. The haughtiness of the President discouraged and shocked them. He informed them, Taft reported, that he wished "to take back and give up everything he had been saying about" the League to Enforce Peace since his first reference to it.[66]

At almost the same time, the British government submitted one of its preliminary suggestions for a union, an event which only added to Wilson's vexation. He explained to House how important it was that any constitution had to "*grow* and not be made; that we must *begin* with solemn cove-

---

64. House Diary, September 10, 1917, House Papers.

65. Marburg to Wilson, January 23, 1917; Wilson to Marburg, January 25, 1917, in Latané, *Development,* I, 257–258, 262; Vance McCormick to Holt, August 15, 1917, Short to Taft, August 30, 1917 (copies), Holt Papers.

66. Wilson to Marburg, March 8, 1918; to House, March 20, 1918, in Baker, *Wilson: Life and Letters,* VIII, 17, 38; Wilson to Marburg, May 6, 1918; Bryce to Marburg, February 1 [April], 1918, in Latané, *Development,* I, 403–404, 436–437, 441–442; Taft to Mrs. Taft, March 29, 1918; Lowell to Taft, March 30, 1918, Taft Papers.

nants, covering mutual guarantees of political independence and territorial integrity" and that events should develop as cases arose. It would be wrong to place "executive authority in the hands of any particular group of powers." It would sow distrust and jealousy. Furthermore, the "Senate would never ratify any treaty which put the force of the United States at the disposal of any such group or body. Why begin at the impossible end when there is a possible end and it is feasible to plant a system which will slowly but surely ripen into fruition?"[67]

Wilson's refusal to consider detailed programs contributed to misunderstandings about his views. The judicial advocates on one occasion believed that Wilson had abandoned the League to Enforce Peace and assumed that he favored the more legalistic approach of the World's Court League. Other internationalists read into his broad remarks an endorsement of whatever plan they happened to be promoting, or they felt offended at some of his comments.[68]

Despite Wilson's attitude and his statements, he recognized that the subject could not be ignored. Thus, as early as September of 1917, he asked House to consider the problem of a postwar conference and the policies the United States might pursue. House interpreted this assignment broadly, for he approached the major internationalists for advice. These included Taft, Lowell, and Holt of the League to Enforce Peace, Mrs. Andrews of the Central Organization for a Durable Peace, and Butler and Root of the Carnegie Endowment. Furthermore, in the official group formed to consider a postwar settlement, The Inquiry, a few members began to explore the topic.[69]

Nearly everyone concerned about a league knew by 1918 that in House they had a sympathetic friend. He had been involved in Wilson's deliberations over a Pan-American organization, had injected the subject into his discussions with statesmen on his visits to Europe, and had kept informed of developments in the United States. In 1916, when Wilson spoke before the League to Enforce Peace, House not only served as intermediary but also supplied Wilson with data for the address. Until 1917, however, House

67. Wilson to House, March 22, 1918, in Baker, *Wilson: Life and Letters*, VIII, 43–44.
68. Frank Chapin Bray to Butler, September 24, 1917; Dutton to Butler, September 25, 1917, CEIP Papers; John R. Commons to Albert Shaw, January 12, 1918, Shaw Papers.
69. House Diary, September 4, 5, 7, 1917, January 13, 1918; Mrs. Andrews to Holt, January 18, 1918, Andrews Papers; Seymour, *Intimate Papers*, IV, 7–8; Lawrence E. Gelfand, *The Inquiry: American Preparations for Peace, 1917–1919*, pp. 119–121, 137, 149.

apparently agreed with Wilson that no constitutions should be drafted until governments could be persuaded to accept the idea. Thus until that time House had not carefully studied the plans of any group or individual.[70]

Thereafter House changed. He saw that no peace could be secure without an organization, and he developed close ties with the internationalists. He even aided the League to Enforce Peace in obtaining financial support and endorsements. House maintained a relationship which can only be described as frank. By the summer of 1917, he consistently advised advocates to avoid Wilson. He warned them that the President, in his desire to be independent, might not be cordial. With such forthrightness, House won their confidence. The League to Enforce Peace agreed to co-operate with him unofficially, and Lowell's study committee worked with House through Walter Lippmann, who served as an intermediary.[71]

House did not rely entirely upon established groups to keep him informed. He also utilized his brother-in-law, Sidney E. Mezes, the president of City College of New York. Mezes gathered data and in November 1917 presented House with a plan which Secretary of State Robert Lansing examined. It called for a league based upon a covenant in which the signatories would uphold and guarantee each other's territory and "political independence under republican forms of government." They would also agree to settle their disputes amicably or refer them to an arbitral court or comissions of inquiry. They did not, however, have to submit any question involving national honor, independence, or vital interest. Furthermore, each signer promised not to intervene in any way to upset the government of another member.[72]

Throughout 1918, House continued to solicit advice and to answer inquiries about what role the United States should subsequently play. On one occasion, he invited Taft, Root, Lowell, Mezes, and the visiting Archbishop of York to lunch where they agreed to have Root draft a memorandum on three points: the United States should be concerned with wars

70. Seymour, *Intimate Papers,* IV, 2–6; Kuehl, *Hamilton Holt,* p. 136; Short to Lowell, January 15, 1917, Lowell Papers; Short to George W. Kirchwey, January 19, 1917, Short Papers; Short to Taft, October 2, 1917, Taft Papers; House to Wilson, February 19, 1917, Wilson Papers; House Diary, November 13, 1917.

71. House Diary, July 17, 27, August 25, September 3, December 30, 1917; Short to Taft, October 2, 1917; Lowell to Taft, November 2, 1917, Taft Papers; Lowell to House, October 2, 1917, House Papers.

72. Mezes to Lansing, November 30, 1917, enclosing "A Simple Form of International Co-operation," Mezes Papers. The House Papers contain a "Tentative Draft of an Association of Nations" by Mezes, dated January 1, 1917.

everywhere; some machinery should be created; the world needed a court or arbitral bureau. He held such meetings, House noted, to control discussions and keep the President from being embarrassed by controversial suggestions.[73]

But outside pressures, especially from England, forced House and Wilson to move ahead. Lord Robert Cecil kept prodding House by letter and through Sir William Wiseman, chief of British military intelligence in the United States. Finally, in mid-June, House drafted a note to Cecil in which he briefly outlined his ideas. It revealed a cautious approach. House believed not in administrative and judicial machinery but in standards of honor. Nations, said House, should behave toward each other as men do, with their actions regulated by laws. He called for a league in which disputes should be referred to arbitration for settlement. If a government went to war, the other members would then resort to diplomatic and economic sanctions and, if necessary, "physical force." Thus House reflected in large measure the pacifist-legalist outlook, although his concepts of a court were highly limited. The core of his plan rested upon advances in arbitration since 1899. Yet House did add toward the end of his letter one point which placed him far ahead of most internationalists. He included the phrase which had appeared in Wilson's proposal for a Pan-American league. Members should agree to "guarantee each other's territorial integrity."[74]

After holding this letter for several days and gaining the advice of a number of men, House dated it June 25 and sent a copy to Wilson. The President did not find time to reply until July 8, and then his answer contained no hint of his views. Wilson had been preoccupied with the Russian question and had not been concerned with the mounting tempo of internationalist activity. He had received a copy of the Phillimore Report, the final draft of the British proposal, but he had not had time to read it. Nevertheless, he realized that if the United States held back any longer it would abdicate its leadership. Hence, he authorized House to prepare a constitution based upon the Phillimore plan. House assumed from this that Wilson had accepted the views in his letter of June 25. Wilson, however, had not changed his mind about allowing others to act. When the League to Enforce Peace

73. House Diary, March 7, April 11, June 11, 1918; Bryce to House, April 17, 1918, House Papers; Seymour, *Intimate Papers*, IV, 15–17.

74. Seymour, *Intimate Papers*, IV, 17–20; House Diary, June 20, 1918. Mezes insisted that conciliation would be a more effective method than arbitration and that the league should demand investigations where threats to peace existed. Mezes to House, June 29, 1918, Mezes Papers.

approved a resolution suggesting the advisability of an official commission to work with European governments, he insisted that it restrain its members. It could embarrass the administration if the League became involved in discussions with such groups in Europe.[75]

Wilson had reason to be concerned on this point, for the League to Enforce Peace men and other enthusiasts had already been in touch with European officials. Holt had been in Europe for three months, where he had interviews with Balfour, Cecil, and Bryce in England, with President Poincaré, Premier Clemenceau, and Léon Bourgeois in France, and with King Victor Emmanuel, Premier Vittorio Orlando, and Baron Sidney Sonnino in Italy. Everywhere, he reported to Wilson, these leaders and others had insisted upon action. Crosby and New York justice William Wadhams had also talked with many of these men, and they also reported on attitudes in Europe.[76]

Thus, by mid-July, the United States had agreed to move. House, following Wilson's instructions, began work on July 13 at his home in Magnolia, Massachusetts. After two days of labor he completed a draft which, after some minor revisions, he planned to send to Wilson.[77] The United States had only reluctantly entered the movement in an official capacity, but once it did there was no turning back. The leadership which American internationalists had held for decades and which Europeans continually insisted belonged in American hands at last began to assert itself.

75. House Diary, June 24, July 9, 1918; Lowell to House, July 5; Wilson to Lowell, July 11, 1918 (copy), House Papers; Seymour, *Intimate Papers*, IV, 21–22; Wilson to Lowell, July 18, 1918, in Baker, *Wilson: Life and Letters*, VIII, 275–276.

76. Holt to Wilson, July 12, 1918, Wilson Papers; Crosby to House, June 10, 1918, House Papers; Baker, *Wilson: Life and Letters*, VIII, 253; "Closer Relations Abroad," *The League Bulletin*, No. 94 (July 6, 1918), pp. 226–227.

77. Seymour, *Intimate Papers*, IV, 23–24.

The Stars
in their
Courses

To William Howard Taft and other internationalists, it seemed that by the latter half of 1918 "the stars in their courses" were struggling to achieve a league of nations.[1] Events seemed to augur an auspicious future. European statesmen had agreed upon its creation, and the Wilson administration was committed to it. Colonel House revealed this as he studiously drafted his proposal for the President.

House wrote this with the aid of David Hunter Miller, a law partner of House's son-in-law, Gordon Auchincloss. House did not consult the Phillimore Report until he had completed his work; then he compared the two and added a number of points from the English plan. He thought, in assessing his contribution, that it was much more effective than the British effort. It should have been, for House's contacts with internationalists had given him some awareness of current ideas. Miller, moreover, had investigated the subject quite fully. He came to his meeting with House armed with "voluminous notes."[2]

House called for a league of great powers in which honor, ethics, and open diplomacy would apply. His proposal reflected Wilsonian idealism and the judicialists' dream of justice and right. He called for a court but gave

1. Marburg and Flack, *Taft Papers*, p. 156.
2. Baker, *Wilson: Life and Letters*, VIII, 278–279; House Diary, July 13, August 11, 1918; Seymour, *Intimate Papers*, IV, 23–26. The House draft appears *ibid.*, pp. 28–36.

it limited authority. It could consider differences relating to treaty questions and to matters which governments submitted to it. All other issues unresolved by diplomacy should be arbitrated, with a right to appeal decisions by taking them to the league assembly. House called for special arbitral bodies in each instance, thus bypassing the existing machinery at The Hague. Here he reflected the disillusionment of many internationalists with the prewar structure. Most of these men, however, had substituted a council of conciliation to function with a court of justice. House did not include such. The omission is of interest since the Wilson administration, through the Bryan treaties, had sought to promote this method of settling disputes.

Other parts of the House plan contained more ambitious suggestions. The league would consider "any war or threat of war" as its concern, could assemble "in the interests of peace" whenever desirable, and, where a government refused to resort to the machinery or declared war prior to submitting its dispute for settlement, the other members would apply economic sanctions and even a blockade against it. These clauses reflected the English position more than that of the League to Enforce Peace advocates who included military pressures as well. House did incorporate into another article, however, a provision on force which few internationalists had espoused with enthusiasm, and in doing so he used words that Wilson had employed. The signatories would "unite in several guarantees to each other of their territorial integrity and political independence." House realized that a league should not be a repressive body, so he qualified this proviso by acknowledging that changes might be needed and by his refusal to add a section on how the article would be enforced.

The House plan included other current ideals, including ones on disarmament, the rights of nonmembers, the use of good offices, the appointment and removal of judges, and the selection of delegates. His clauses on finances, procedures, and voting remained as indefinite as those on force. Thus House revealed a cautious approach and outlook. Yet he went well beyond the Phillimore Report, which called for a treaty arrangement rather than a formal league, completely avoided a discussion of guarantees, and wished only a limited application of sanctions.

When House submitted his plan to Wilson, the President proceeded to redraft it. This resulted in changes in phraseology, in a rearrangement and condensation of the articles, and in two revealing alterations. First, he deleted the sections on a court and virtually all clauses relating to it. No evidence exists to explain this act. House had only recently embraced that concept, as he admitted in his covering letter to the President; Wilson had not yet been converted. He must have known of it, for it had been a core idea in nearly every internationalist proposal. Indeed, it was the one idea on which there had been more agreement than any other.

The suspicion that Wilson could not have been well informed about a court or the pacific settlement of disputes is amplified by his continuation of House's provisions for arbitration procedures which virtually discarded the Hague system. Neither House nor Wilson understood the complexity of this subject. They showed no awareness of the distinctions between justiciable and nonjusticiable matters or of the need to have councils of conciliation for questions which nations would not submit to courts or arbitration. The compulsory arbitration of all disputes had never been accepted by the Senate or generally by other major governments, yet this was essentially what the House-Wilson draft demanded.

Wilson's second major change appeared in House's clause providing for economic sanctions against those states which resorted to war without utilizing the machinery of arbitration. Wilson here inserted a phrase which called for the "use of any force" to uphold this proviso. His belief in a powerful league appeared elsewhere. If nations did not arbitrate, or if a nonmember attacked a member, or if a country resorted to war in disregard of an arbitral decision or a recommendation of the league, the powers should jointly assist the violated nation by "combining their armed forces in its behalf." Thus, Wilson revealed himself as a confirmed sanctionist ready to go as far as the most venturesome internationalist. Certainly, he went beyond the League to Enforce Peace policy of employing arms and economic pressures only to compel the submission of disputes.

Another phrase related to the subject of sanctions revealed Wilson's concept of a strong organization. He retained those words which had appeared in both the House and Miller plans. Members would "unite in guaranteeing to each other political and territorial integrity." Wilson had been fairly consistent in adhering to this idea since he had incorporated it into his suggestions for a Pan-American league in 1916.[3]

Wilson prefaced his draft with the word "Covenant," a term which has intrigued scholars and prompted speculation on what it revealed of Wilson's personality and background. While it may have been a word that Wilson favored, it was not new to the terminology of the internationalists. House had embodied it in his plan; it appeared in Miller's proposal dated June 28,

---

3. Baker, *Wilson and World,* I, 223, III, 88–93. Baker implies that House may not have been enthusiastic about a court and that he may have added a provision for one after a conversation with Root. *Ibid.,* I, 218, 222.

1918; and the League to Enforce Peace study group employed it as a heading for its first article.[4] It had an even more ancient lineage. William Ladd employed it in his scheme for a Congress of Nations, Mason used it in 1911, and so did Holt in his important editorial on "The Way to Disarm" in 1914. Even Theodore Roosevelt found it useful to describe his goals when he wrote on the subject in 1914.

As the internationalists learned of the work being done by House and Wilson, they tried to exert influence on them. Lowell sought House's support for the League to Enforce Peace program and expressed his concern over Wilson's hostility toward his organization. Holt made a pilgrimage to Magnolia on July 22. He reported to House on the strength of internationalist thought in Europe, which he had assessed on a recent trip. He examined House's draft and immediately thereafter expressed his concern that it did not include provisions for periodic conferences to formulate law. Holt had long argued for some legislative function by an association of nations, and he had finally succeeded in obtaining such in the platform of the League to Enforce Peace. Now he began again. In this instance, however, House ignored him. House gave other visitors that summer a chance to discuss the Covenant, including Lord Reading, the British special ambassador to the United States, journalist Carl Ackerman, William Wiseman, and Attorney General T. W. Gregory.[5]

On August 15, Wilson visited Magnolia. House had eagerly awaited his arrival, for by this time he had become intellectually and emotionally involved with the subject. He worried because Wilson did not give more thought to a league even though he knew the President had a full commitment to wartime problems. They discussed the Covenant but left it basically unchanged. They seemed more concerned about how to proceed and what public statements they should issue. They feared that publication of their plan might arouse opposition from opponents of the idea and from internationalists who disliked its provisions or scope. They did decide to insist at the peace table that a league be incorporated into the treaty and not left as a separate entity.[6]

On a few subjects House and Wilson disagreed. House especially protested against the elimination of a court but finally remained silent on the

4. Miller's draft contained a phrase, "A General Association of Nations Must be Formed under Specific Covenants . . . ," House Papers. Baker, *Wilson and World*, I, 222.

5. Lowell to House, July 15, 1918; Holt to House, July 23, 1918, House Papers; House Diary, July 23, 28, 30, August 11, 1918.

6. House Diary, July 30, August 15, 1918; Seymour, *Intimate Papers*, IV, 48–50.

assumption that the other delegates at the peace conference would reinsert it. House may have chafed at times, for he realized how little Wilson knew about the topic. On one occasion, when he showed the President a French plan, he recorded in his diary that he found Wilson "not at all up to date."[7]

After their meeting, Wilson devoted but little attention to the Covenant until he sailed for Paris. He apparently made a few minor revisions in the August draft, but he faced many problems concerning the war and the Armistice arrangements. He also had to appoint the members of the Peace Commission. Critics have charged that Wilson courted disaster when he failed to include prominent Republicans in his official group and when he ignored senators. He might have been hard pressed to find any internationalists in the upper chamber qualified for such work, but he could have found many in the Republican party. House recognized the importance of naming such men, for at the meeting on August 15 he had suggested Root and Taft as commissioners. After Wilson dismissed both men as "impossible," House concluded that they would never be considered since they seemed to antagonize Wilson. Certainly Root's emphasis upon a judicially oriented league would have conflicted with Wilson's views even if other political and personal obstacles had not existed. Taft seemed more acceptable, but he, too, would have found it hard to co-operate because of partisanship and in the light of Wilson's attitude toward the League to Enforce Peace.[8]

The delegates as announced on November 29 included Wilson, House, Secretary of State Robert Lansing, General Tasker H. Bliss, and Henry White. Of these, only White represented the Republicans, but he had little influence in the party save for his close friendship with Root, Lodge, and Roosevelt. He did have considerable diplomatic experience and had been aware of the developing prewar peace structure. Neither Lansing, Bliss, nor White had ever been active in the internationalist movement. Lansing had been involved in efforts to extend arbitration, but he had written Wilson a critical memorandum on the League to Enforce Peace. His views had paralleled those of J. B. Scott. Bliss fell into the moderate camp. In commenting upon a plan by Mezes, he expressed concern over the word "guarantee," argued against commitments, and noted that total disarmament might be the best solution. The internationalists, however, never openly

7. House Diary, August 15, September 24, 1918.

8. *Ibid.*, September 9, August 15, 18, 1918; David Hunter Miller, *My Diary at the Conference of Paris,* I, 48; House and Wilson had discussed Taft and Root as possible commissioners several months before. House Diary, January 27, 1918; Leopold, *Elihu Root,* pp. 131–133.

objected to the composition of the Commission. They trusted Wilson and realized they might have done worse. Indeed, some of them had warned Wilson away from such cautious thinkers as Scott.[9]

While Wilson concentrated upon wartime and diplomatic problems in the fall of 1918, his advisors continued their research on the league question. Both House and Miller gathered data in the form of proposals and published plans, but their collection remained quite incomplete. Holt had offered his services and his extensive library on the subject, but no one responded. Hence, the files of House and Miller reflected an unbalanced picture of internationalist thought. They obtained, for instance, many more European than American proposals because they had arrived in France late in October in anticipation of an armistice and gathered their data there.[10] In Europe, however, ideas had developed more slowly, and they did not correspond completely with those of Americans. House's inadequate files were the inevitable result of Wilson's delays.

Wilson left for the peace conference aboard the *George Washington* on December 4, 1918, and arrived in France on the thirteenth. Considerable debate over whether he should have made the trip occurred at the time, and scholars have subsequently argued over this decision. Two observations should be made. First, few internationalists in the United States raised objections to his going. Second, it placed in Paris the one statesman totally dedicated to the idea. It may have been a mistake to leave the country—it may have weakened Wilson's hand in negotiations during the conference—

9. George Curry, "Woodrow Wilson, Jan Smuts, and the Versailles Settlement," *American Historical Review,* LXVI (July 1961), 978–979; Lansing to Wilson, May 25, 1916; Holt to Wilson, November 16, 1918, Wilson Papers; Bliss to Miller, December 26, 1918, House Papers. Holt's letter was also signed by Marburg, Lowell, and R. H. Gadsden.

10. These conclusions are based upon a study of plans in the House and Miller Papers. The House files have no printed materials under the names Holt, Lynch, Andrews, Dutton, Lowell, or the League to Enforce Peace. They do have copies of Carnegie's *League of Peace* and Crosby's *International War* dated 1919. Many of the reports of the Central Organization for a Durable Peace reached House, but Europeans prepared most of these. Bliss sent a Captain H. C. Bell to England, who did a thorough job. His report summarized plans of Bluntschli and Levi and contemporary British and European writers. His only reference to American ideas appeared in a general summary of the League to Enforce Peace program and in excerpts from speeches by Wilson. Report of Capt. H. C. Bell, December 5, 1918, "A Review of the Schemes for a League of Nations and Disarmament." A more complete study by Bell and Lt. L. A. Crosby, dated December 22, does not reveal the sources for the composite views summarized. Miller Papers. Mrs. Andrews to Holt, November 1, 1918, Andrews Papers; "Statement of Hamilton Holt," enclosed with H. Morgenthau to Wilson, November 18, 1918, Wilson Papers.

but his presence at Paris more than that of any other individual insured the establishment of a league. He had been acclaimed for months as the leader of the movement and men everywhere sensed his importance as America's voice in the settlement.[11]

The *George Washington*'s passengers also included most of the Peace Commissioners and the major figures attached to the American delegation, including members of the Inquiry. Wilson did little on the voyage to enlighten these people on his plans for a league. He addressed them once on the subject, admitted he had but indefinite ideas, then spoke in generalities. A detailed organization which included a court and a police force, he did observe, could not be created at a single conference lasting a few weeks. It would be far better to seek accord through pledges or covenants which would outline desires "in *general form*" and then rely "on *experience to guide subsequent action.*" Periodic meetings could be held to resolve crises. Wilson thus disclosed, in part, his objections to a court. Efforts to include it would result in delays. His statement on this point, however, seemed partially to contradict another he made to his fellow passengers. The program of the League to Enforce Peace could not be accepted because an association should be able to resolve problems and rearrange boundaries. Another inconsistency appeared in his remarks that a grant of such sweeping authority would also stimulate debate. Wilson's words convinced Henry White, however, that his fellow Republicans could swallow any fears that the armed forces of the United States would ever be at a league's disposal. He reported that Wilson contemplated a "very slender organization . . . as a first start."[12]

If Wilson failed to formulate his ideas on the *George Washington*, he had no time after his arrival in Europe to do so. He lived a hectic life with

11. Sidney Brooks, "Mr. Wilson and the Treaty," *Nineteenth Century,* LXXXVI (December 1919), 1185; Lord Parmoor, "President Wilson and the Peace Settlement," *Contemporary Review,* CXV (January 1919), 10–11; E. J. Dillon, "The Empire and the World League," *Living Age,* CCXCIX (November 23, 1918), 453, 458; Grey of Fallodon, "A League of Nations," *ibid.,* pp. 472–480; Austin Harrison, "A World Declaration of Rights," *ibid.,* (December 7, 1918), pp. 594–597; H. H. Asquith, "President Wilson and the League of Nations," *Current History,* VIII (September 1918), part 2, 511–513; Winkler, *League Movement,* pp. 82, 261.

12. "Reminiscences of James W. Wadsworth," OHRO, II, 238–239; Gelfand, *The Inquiry,* pp. 170–173. Gelfand cites diaries of William C. Bullitt and George L. Beer. A memorandum by Isaiah Bowman appears in Seymour, *Intimate Papers,* IV, 280–283. White to Lodge, December 24, 1918, Lodge Papers. White gained his information in another meeting with Wilson, but his summary of the President's views coincided with reports of others. Allan Nevins, *Henry White: Thirty Years of American Diplomacy,* pp. 359, 362.

receptions, trips, and speeches. Moreover, he had to keep posted on developments at home and at the same time digest the information which poured in from his advisors on a variety of subjects which required attention as part of the peace settlement. House noted in his diary on December 19 that the President seemed vague in discussing a league and that he would have to refresh his mind about the points covered at Magnolia in August.[13]

House was the only person who could have succeeded in this task, for other persons in the American advisory group had little voice in writing the Covenant. Bliss, Lansing, and White did no more than comment on various drafts. Members of the Inquiry fared no better, even though some, like Manley Hudson, who was consulted at times, had prepared preliminary reports for Miller.[14]

A large number of unattached internationalists who appeared at Paris also gained only a limited hearing for their views. The League to Enforce Peace sent Holt and Oscar S. Straus as its official representatives. The latter, a veteran of Theodore Roosevelt's cabinet, had loyally supported the League to Enforce Peace. Holt, who planned to attend the conference to report activities for *The Independent*'s readers, had an ambitious plan which did not materialize. He hoped to found a daily newspaper, as W. T. Stead had done at the Second Hague Conference, to report on developments, to keep dangerous rumors at a minimum, and to influence the outcome. He failed, however, to find a patron for this project.[15]

The official instructions to Straus and Holt ordered them to support Wilson in his plan, to keep their society informed on how it could best support the President, and to find some means to co-ordinate the work of the League to Enforce Peace with similar societies in Europe. Since Straus did not arrive in Paris until February 9, Holt assumed charge of the mission. He had others to aid him, however, including Frederick Lynch and Fannie Fern Andrews.[16]

13. House Diary, December 19, 1918. At least one authority claims that Wilson was "much wrapped up in the League" for a month prior to the conference. While Wilson did refer to the idea often in speeches, there is little evidence of constructive thought on his part. Thomas A. Bailey, *Woodrow Wilson and the Lost Peace*, p. 186.

14. Frederick Palmer, *Bliss, Peacemaker: The Life and Letters of General Tasker Howard Bliss*, pp. 355–358. Nevins, *Henry White*, p. 357; House Diary, December 16, 1918, February 7, 1919; Gelfand, *The Inquiry*, pp. 149, 170, 176, 302–304, 308–312. Copies of Hudson's drafts and other plans can be found in the Miller Papers.

15. Kuehl, *Hamilton Holt*, pp. 139–140; Holt to Mrs. Andrews, November 4, 1918, Andrews Papers.

16. *Minutes*, Emergency Campaign Committee, December 16, 1918, LEP Papers. Holt left New York on December 28.

Holt followed his instructions in all three particulars, but the effort to unite the various societies proved to be the most time-consuming. Delegates from the associations met regularly from January 25 through February 3. Many of them from the Continent had been active only a short time. The *Ligue pour une Société des Nations* had been formed in France in 1917, but not until November 10, 1918, did a truly representative and live organization appear as the French Association for a Society of Nations. In the meantime, the French government had created a study group, and it had issued a report late in 1918. Léon Bourgeois, who had served as its director, headed the twenty-three Frenchmen at Paris who represented the various societies from their country.[17]

No delegates from Germany appeared, for internationalist thought there did not develop until the very eve of the war. Five Italians came even though organized groups had not developed well in their country. As late as October 1918, Holt found on a visit "less interest there" than anywhere else in Europe.[18] Men from Belgium, Serbia, Roumania, and China participated; but Great Britain sent the most prominent and dedicated men, including Lord Shaw of Dunfermline, Sir Willoughby Dickinson, and Aneurin Williams. Since the English had entered the ranks around 1914, only the Americans, Bourgeois, and the Baron d'Estournelles de Constant could boast a longer attachment to the cause.

The English, however, had been exceptionally active in the last year of the war. The older League of Nations Society and a younger organization, the League of Free Nations Association, had merged as the League of Nations Union. It rallied the major political figures to it—Herbert Asquith, Arthur Balfour, Lloyd George, Edward Grey, and Cecil. The British had an advantage at the meetings which the Americans lacked. They had a clearer idea of their government's thinking on the subject since the Phillimore Report had been published. It was not highly detailed, but it did express basic aims and ideas. Few private groups in their plans had done much more.[19]

The delegates at Paris from these organizations were exceedingly cau-

17. Edmund J. Steytler, "France and the Wilsonian Program," pp. 288–289, 362; Marburg, "The Movement for a League of Nations," *Unpopular Review,* XI (January–March 1919), 12–15.

18. "Germany Now for World-Wide Brotherhood," *Literary Digest,* LIX (November 16, 1918), 19–20; Holt to Marburg, October 15, 1918, in Latané, *Development,* II, 532.

19. Winkler, *League Movement,* pp. 70, 75–76, 233–247, 260–261.

tious. They did not wish to formulate a constitution; they hoped to find certain objectives and principles which could guide the statesmen drafting the Covenant. After studying various plans, they formulated a "Protocol." All nations should be equal in voting; an international court should be created to hear justiciable disputes and a committee of conciliation should determine whether questions should be referred to the court or to arbitration; and a representative council should develop international law and maintain order. The statement on sanctions was less definite. Holt had urged the use of military as well as economic force to execute decisions of the court, but the provision finally read, "economic, and, if necessary, military." The delegates also agreed that members should prevent or curtail "jointly, by the use of all means at their disposal" all disturbances of the peace, but they did not elaborate upon what this meant or how it should be applied. They also approved action by the league to control armaments, an idea which initially aroused opposition from the Americans who insisted that any direct regulation would be objectionable to governments. Special resolutions endorsed such ideals as an international labor bureau and Mrs. Andrews's dream of an international commission on education.[20]

The resolutions of the Conference of Delegates of the Allied Associations for a League of Nations reached the statesmen drafting the Covenant. Bourgeois handed them to Clemenceau, and they found their way to House and Wilson. David Hunter Miller had attended some of the sessions, and the American delegates had interviews with the President and House. Holt met with Wilson on January 30 and with House on January 31; he and Straus talked with House and other officials after February 10. What they learned in these conversations often disturbed them. In one instance, Holt wrote a lengthy memorandum to House protesting two omissions in the drafts of the Covenant he had seen. He liked many of the propositions, but a league, he insisted, should have the authority to "create and develop international law." He also questioned the creation of a council of nine powers vested with extensive authority. This made the league not one of peoples but of governments. He wished a genuine democratic deliberative assembly with a council functioning as an executive agency and conciliatory body.[21]

Even though these internationalists spoke their piece, they were little

20. *Proceedings of the Conferences of Delegates of Allied Societies for a League of Nations,* pp. 8–20.

21. Shaw of Dunfermline to Marburg, February 5, 1919, in Latané, *Development,* II, 605; Miller, *Diary,* I, 92, 95, 105; Straus, "Random Notes on 'My Mission to the Paris Peace Conference . . . ,' " Straus Papers, Library of Congress; Holt to House with memorandum, February 5, 1919, Holt Papers.

heeded. A handful of men assumed the task of drafting the Covenant. Nineteen persons officially served on the League of Nations Commission, and that number would have been smaller had not the lesser governments insisted upon increasing the size of their delegation. Wilson and House represented the United States; Cecil and General Jan Smuts, Great Britain; Bourgeois and Ferdinand Larnaude, France; and Premier Orlando, Italy. Wilson served as chairman. Most of the delegates, except the British, had reservations about a league. They may not have been as hostile as some observers have claimed, but Wilson's presence and position kept them from raising serious objections or from expressing opposition to the ideal.[22]

The commissioners had been selected at the Second Plenary Session of the Supreme Council on January 25, 1919. No action had been taken prior to that date because no decision had been reached whether a league would be an integral part of the treaty. Wilson had insisted on such a course and prevailed despite considerable doubts on the matter. Subsequently, questions arose over the wisdom of that decision but few internationalists challenged the idea at the time. They were too eager to see their dream materialize to question the form in which it should appear.

The delegates met ten times between February 3 and 13, often in the evenings, since all served on other commissions which demanded their attendance during the day. Since they had little time to devote to the subject, they sought to simplify their task by instructing the legal advisors of Great Britain and the United States, C. J. B. Hurst and David Hunter Miller, to write a composite work based on several plans which had been presented. These included one from the United States, a version of the scheme Wilson and House had drafted in August which Wilson had revised three times in Paris—on January 10, 20, and February 2. The British had circulated proposals by Cecil and Smuts along with their official one, and the French and Swiss had also presented programs. For a time, Wilson had hoped that one of his versions might be used as a basis for discussions, but he finally agreed to have Hurst and Miller proceed with their project.[23]

These men relied primarily upon the official British plan and what is known as Wilson's second Paris draft. Wilson had considerably reworked

22. Bailey, *Wilson and the Lost Peace*, p. 188; David Hunter Miller, *The Drafting of the Covenant*, I, 82–85. Baker presents the stereotyped portrait of the French as the enemies of the League in *Wilson and World*, I, 235–240.

23. Curry, "Wilson, Smuts, and the Versailles Settlement," pp. 968–986, presents a concise but conventional account of the predrafting developments. Various preliminary drafts can be found in Miller, *Drafting*, II, 23–116. He describes the process in I, 51–75.

the scheme he had brought to Europe. He had been impressed with Smuts's propositions and had relied upon them in a revision dated January 10. This resulted in a reorganization of articles, in the addition of a provision for a council of both large and small powers, in structural changes concerning arbitration and disarmament, and in proposals for what became sections on mandates, labor, and minority rights. Suggestions by Bliss, Miller, and possibly Lansing, led to improvements in phraseology and in clauses on religious equality, freedom of the seas, disarmament, nondiscrimination in trade, and the publication of treaties.[24]

Wilson subsequently revised this version to produce his second Paris draft of January 20. It incorporated certain ideas from the official British program. The latter, in turn, had sought to include provisions from the earlier plans of Wilson which had circulated among the delegates. But it still contained points on colonies, minorities, and a court of justice which had to be reconciled with Wilson's Covenant. Hurst and Miller had a difficult task in finding a compromise acceptable to everyone, and Wilson found undesirable features in their work which led him, for a time, to ask that a revised program of his be placed before the Commission. The British objected; hence, the Hurst-Miller document served as the basis for discussions between February 3 and 13.[25]

The meetings took place in House's quarters at the Hôtel de Crillon. Wilson presided most of the time and dominated the hearings. The other commissioners usually deferred to him on "final opinions" except the French who occasionally argued points. While these statesmen and a drafting committee made additions, rearranged sections, and revised words, the final proposals did not depart drastically from the Hurst-Miller version.[26]

On February 14, Wilson presented the Covenant to a plenary session of the peace conference and to the world. Advisors of the major powers, many of the delegates, and nearly all of the American internationalists in Paris crowded into the Salle de l'Horloge where Wilson read the draft and explained the aims of the League. "A living thing is born," he declared. "It is a definite guarantee of peace. It is a definite guarantee by word against aggression."[27]

---

24. Miller, *Drafting*, I, 34, 40, 48; Baker, *Wilson and World*, I, 224–231.
25. Miller, *Drafting*, I, 54–55, 72–75; Baker, *Wilson and World*, I, 231–232.
26. Miller, *Drafting*, I, 126, 351–353.
27. Baker, *Wilson and World*, I, 285. The Covenant was only presented to the plenary session on this date. It was not adopted until April 28, and then only after amendments. Those changes will be discussed in Chapter Thirteen.

The Covenant contained a preamble and twenty-six articles. Since it emerged as the result of an idea which had been discussed for decades, its provisions should be examined in the light of previous thought and advocacy. To what degree did the Covenant fulfill the dreams of the internationalists? In what measure did it present new ideas? What philosophy or school of internationalism did it mirror? There had been many views, innumerable differences of opinion, and even rivalry over conflicting programs. Where did the Covenant fit into the pattern of thought?

The first three articles outlined the basic structure of the League. The first two called for an assembly of delegates and essential administrative agencies. Article I fulfilled the goal of all internationalists because it realized Ladd's old dream of a congress meeting "at stated intervals" and whenever else needed. These sections also suggested the creation of a council and a permanent secretariat. Thus they met the desires of those moderate internationalists who wished to see executive agencies created which could function continuously and be available in times of crisis. Article II contained one clause of interest in the history of internationalism. It provided that each nation be given one vote regardless of its size or strength. There had been suggestions over the years for some system of proportional representation according to population, trade, wealth, or political power. Most advocates, however, had ruled these out, as did the delegates at Paris. The commissioners engaged in some debate over how many representatives governments should have but not over their voting strength. The doctrine of sovereignty was too strong. This incongruous idea could not be discarded even though it left the smaller countries as strong as the most powerful. No alternative existed in the world of 1919. Internationalists like Bridgman had failed in their propaganda efforts to destroy that concept which stood as the greatest single enemy of an international organization.

Article III compensated for this irrational voting power in the Assembly by creating a council in which the major nations dominated. In so doing, it helped destroy the dream of a democratic organization representing people rather than governments. The commissioners had decided after considerable debate to create a nine-member agency in which the five great powers would hold permanent positions and four lesser nations would be seated on a rotating basis. Considerable sentiment had existed for a council composed exclusively of the major countries, but arguments by Smuts that the League should be somewhat democratic resulted in a compromise. The idea for a council can also be traced to Smuts. Wilson had not considered it in his original plan, but he did add it at Paris.[28] It had, however, appeared in the schemes of many internationalists, and the Draft Proposal of the League to Enforce Peace had noted the necessity for such an administrative agency.

The Council, despite a semblance of authority, possessed little power. Although it could consider all matters "affecting the peace of the world," its considerations had to be "within the sphere of action of the League." Even the most cautious internationalists had agreed that an organization had a fundamental duty at least to discuss dangers to the peace irrespective of what other steps it might take.

Article IV dealt with the procedures of the Council. While not vital in itself, it could have become important if interpreted broadly. The Council could determine a course of action on any problem within its sphere of activity. A later revision calling for unanimous action, however, prevented the Council from ever becoming an effective agency.

Provisions for a secretariat appeared in Article V. While largely procedural in content, it included one point on financing. Members would pay "in accordance with the apportionment of the International Bureau of the Universal Postal Union." The absence of any statement on collection or on action where nations fell in arrears made it more dream than reality. Many internationalists had avoided this subject, too, although some had included elaborate provisions on how costs should be allocated and collected. Most observers had recognized, however, that the concept of sovereignty barred any clauses on enforcement.

Article VI provided for privileges and immunities for officials of the League and its delegates. Early planners had generally taken this point for granted.

Procedures for membership appeared in Article VII. Nations could join after a two-thirds vote of approval. Only three restrictions applied. Each nation had to be "fully self-governing"; it had to be ready to accept the decisions of the League regarding armaments; and it had to be willing to fulfill "its international obligations." While considerable discussion had ensued during the war over the membership of the Central Powers, most statesmen and internationalists realized that an effective league had to be a world organization. There had also been debate during the preliminary discussions over the admission of self-governing members of the British Empire, but this issue had been resolved before the final sessions.

The subject of disarmament in Articles VIII and IX had been an im-

28. Miller, *Drafting*, I, 226, 137, 157.

portant item in the thinking of most internationalists. They had envisioned a league as a defender of people, as an agency to prevent war, and as a body so effective in maintaining peace that it would allow nations to dismantle their arsenals. The inclusion of disarmament clauses in the Covenant, however, stemmed from no such lofty motives. The French wished security against another German attack. This could be gained if the League could limit armies. Smuts and Wilson had included clauses on disarmament in their early drafts, but these had been eliminated in the Hurst-Miller plan. Wilson insisted in discussions with the commissioners that they be reinserted, and he carried his point.[29]

The Council, therefore, could formulate plans to reduce armies and to curtail the manufacturing of armaments, and a "permanent commission" would be created to oversee these tasks. Member states would also agree to exchange information on the size of their forces. The effectiveness of these provisions, however, rested upon the assumption that governments could agree upon programs and that if they did so everyone would accept the recommendations of the commission. Some internationalists had faith in such a Utopian possibility, but the more militant among them had realized that a world organization would have to uphold these clauses. When the League failed to achieve disarmament in ensuing decades, it seemed to prove what the sanctionists had often said. As long as individual governments could retain national forces greater than the army of a league, the latter would have little chance to be an effective agency for peace.

Article X, which embodied the modern concept of collective security, prompted no heated discussion among the commissioners. It called for members "to respect and preserve as against external aggression the territorial integrity and existing political independence of all States members of the League." In case of aggression or danger of such, "the Executive Council shall advise upon the means by which this obligation shall be fulfilled."

The idea of an agreement to protect members of an international organization had gained considerable currency by 1919, largely because Wilson had publicized it in various speeches. It had appeared in the draft by House and in Wilson's first and second plans. Those documents, however, contained paragraphs which modified the statement to allow changes by orderly procedures. Wilson's third draft had incorporated an additional phrase, suggested by Bliss, which greatly qualified Wilson's usual terminology. He added the words, "as against external aggression." The Hurst-

29. *Ibid.,* pp. 171–172.

Miller proposal had then altered this article by dropping all modifying clauses except this one. It simply called upon members to protect and guarantee the territory and political independence of each other against external aggression.[30]

The reports of the sessions of the League of Nations Commission provide little evidence on the discussions which ensued on this article, but Cecil had objected to it as initially presented. Wilson agreed to an amendment that the Council consult on ways to fulfill the obligations under the article, and the Commission adopted it. Subsequently a drafting committee concerned with phraseology and intent revised the wording to cover threats of aggression as well as actual attacks.[31]

Article X must be considered the handiwork of Wilson. At Paris, the phrases in the various plans all paralleled those of the President. Furthermore, he resisted efforts to alter the basic intent of the article. Lansing, in particular, sought to convince Wilson that such guarantees should be negative rather than positive. He noted possible constitutional objections and prophetically warned that the Senate would either seek to defeat the treaty on this point or "at least render it impotent." He believed in a guarantee, he claimed, as "the heart of the League of Nations," and thought that objections could be overcome with the proper wording. He suggested that governments take a pledge that they would not "violate the territorial integrity or impair the political independence of" other members. Miller thought this sounded logical, but Wilson remained unconvinced.[32] The final wording in the Covenant, therefore, contained phrases similar to those Wilson had used in his discussion of a Pan-American pact in 1916.

In the light of the subsequent debate over Article X, it is important to examine this doctrine in relation to internationalist thought. While most of the sanctions had not gone so far in their proposals as to guarantee territory and independence, a few of them had suggested action along such lines. Holt's editorial, written for Theodore Roosevelt's benefit in 1910, contained the idea, and Roosevelt had hinted at it in his Nobel address. He returned to the theme in his speech in Rio de Janeiro on October 24, 1913, when he observed that the nations of the Western Hemisphere should find a formula

30. *Ibid.*, I, 48, II, 94, 233, 264.

31. *Ibid.*, II, 264, 305; I, 168–170.

32. Lansing to Wilson, December 23, 1918, Wilson Papers; Miller, *Drafting*, I, 29–30; *Papers Relating to the Foreign Relations of the United States, 1919: The Paris Peace Conference*, I, 515–519, 526–527.

to guarantee them "from molestation by others." Later, in his writings in 1914 after the outbreak of the war, he again raised the subject.[33]

At almost the same time, Slayden's resolution contained phrases virtually identical to those Wilson later used. The McCall resolution of May 16, 1911, had also revealed an awareness that a league should guarantee the safety of its members. Its words, however, paralleled those of Lansing. They called for a peace conference at which nations would agree to recognize their national independence, territorial integrity, and absolute sovereignty in domestic affairs, and that they will "not seek to increase their territory by conquest."[34] This phraseology of recognizing rather than guaranteeing became quite common in the years from 1912 to 1915, and it appeared often in the vocabulary of the internationalists.

No evidence exists to indicate where Wilson acquired his idea for Article X. The words he preferred had been printed a few times in 1914 in *The Independent*, first in Holt's discussion of a Latin-American league. He commented on a proposed treaty between Chile, Argentina, and Brazil in which the signatories would "guarantee the territorial integrity and political independence of the other countries concerned." A reprint of Holt's "Way to Disarm" essay of September 28 also contained the guarantee doctrine. In his original editorial, Holt had used the popular phrase on respecting territory and independence, but he altered the wording when the Church Peace Union published it as a pamphlet which stated that nations should "agree to respect and guarantee the territory and sovereignty of each other."[35] Holt had dropped this idea, however, when the founders of the League to Enforce Peace opposed it. Most internationalists refused to go that far. In retaining it, Wilson failed to realize that it did not typify internationalist thought either in the United States or elsewhere. Only the more radical thinkers, who represented a minority view, favored such action.

In the light of Wilson's remarks during the commissioners' debate over Article X and his later comments during the treaty fight, it is surprising that he insisted to the end that Article X remain intact. His philosophy seemed to require no rigid guarantee. He believed that nations under the Covenant had a moral obligation to uphold the principle of Article X even if un-

33. Roosevelt, "American Internationalism," *The Outlook,* CV (November 1, 1913), 474.

34. *Congressional Record,* 62 Cong., 1st sess., 47, 2:1260; Report No. 705, House Calendar No. 236, 62 Cong., 2d sess.

35. [Holt], "A Basis for a League of Peace," pp. 83–84; Kuehl, *Hamilton Holt,* pp. 146–147.

written. Miller expressed this view when he later observed that "any League of Nations must include Article X as a reality, whether or not it includes it in words. If you do not end aggressive war, there is no League of Nations. If there is a League of Nations you end aggressive war."[36]

Since Article X did seek to eliminate aggression between the signatories but did not include a provision for stopping conflicts between nonmembers, the planners added Article XI. It declared that "any war or threat of war" should also be the concern of the League. Members could "reserve the right to take any action" they "deemed wise and effectual to safeguard the peace of nations." Furthermore, governments could call to the attention of the Council any threatening situation. This provision reflected how far attitudes had advanced from the time of the First Hague Conference when the delegates there agreed that an offer of good offices should not be considered a hostile act. Article XI could not have satisfied many sanctionists. Its vague phraseology and the lack of any automatic obligation to act against breaches of the peace must have disappointed them.

Articles XII through XV dealt with the pacific settlement of disputes and outlined the machinery which governments could utilize. Nearly all internationalists before 1919 had seen this aspect of a league as the core of their program. Indeed, their philosophy ran in a different direction from that embodied in Articles X and XI. Most of them reflected the pacifist-judicialist belief that peace could best be attained by preventive action. Quarrels and differences should be resolved peacefully; then nations would have no reason to attack their neighbors. Wilson believed in placing the primary emphasis upon ending wars after they began, for aggressors should not be allowed to enjoy the fruits of their depredations. The Covenant, therefore, emphasized Wilson's belief, but it did contain sections which reflected the legalistic approach. According to Articles XII and XIII, states would agree not to engage in war until they had submitted their problems either to arbitration or to inquiry by the Council, and a cooling-off principle appeared in provisions for delay before and after hearing. Articles XIV and XV suggested the creation of a court and outlined the steps to be followed in submitting and deciding cases and in accepting recommendations.

The Covenant's clauses on these points, however, did not reflect the thinking of most contemporary internationalists. They had relegated arbitration, for instance, to an insignificant place by 1919. They realized its limitations despite some earlier success in resolving a number of minor disputes. Governments, however, referred only innocuous questions to agencies for

36. Miller, *Drafting,* I, 168, 31.

pacific settlement; differences involving national honor or vital interests, the very type which often resulted in war, would not be settled in this way. Furthermore, they had come to realize that arbitral procedures provided no firm foundation on which to build a rule of law. Decisions often compromised differences, with awards rendered, not according to fact or right, but simply to end a crisis.

Where the more conservative internationalists did include arbitration in their plans, they suggested the use of the Hague machinery. While the Covenant emphasized the method, it ignored the established tribunal. Most of the commissioners, especially Wilson, House, and Cecil, viewed the Hague system as a failure and refused to mention it. Article XIII referred to it only indirectly by noting that governments could utilize the court to be "agreed on by the parties or stipulated in any convention existing between them." The French delegates unsuccessfully sought a number of times to amend the Covenant to include a specific reference to the Hague Conferences. Bourgeois could not understand the desire to dismiss an existing agency in the rush to create something new. But Miller reflected the prevailing view when he observed that the arbitral structure of the Hague Conference "belongs to a past era."[37] Considering Wilson's training as a political scientist and his well-known emphasis upon evolutionary processes in government, this omission remains an enigmatic aspect of the Covenant.

Article XIII contained no reference to obligatory arbitration. This point had been dropped from Wilson's proposals on the insistence of the British. Wilson apparently accepted the optional or semivoluntary procedure outlined in the Smuts plan which in turn had been influenced by the highly conservative Phillimore Report.[38] Even here, the wording of this section robbed it of meaning. Disputes had to be those recognized as "suitable" for submission, an ambiguous proviso apparently left to individual governments to interpret.

In seeking a way to avert wars more effective than arbitration, the internationalists had turned to the ideal of a court of justice and a council of conciliation. The former could decide justiciable questions not resolved through diplomacy or referred to arbitration. The latter could hear those

37. *Ibid.*, I, 175, 189–190, 260–263, 326–328, II, 365–368, 449–450. Miller's commentary contains only a few sparse references to the Hague Conferences. Several of the preliminary plans did mention them, notably those of Cecil and Miller and the official British and French drafts. *Ibid.*, II, 62, 87, 310, 491–492, 459–460, 238–244. Stephen Bonsal, *Unfinished Business*, p. 151.

38. Curry, "Wilson, Smuts, and the Versailles Settlement," pp. 976–977; Miller, *Drafting*, I, 40, 37; Winkler, *League Movement*, pp. 237–238.

cases involving vital interests which governments would not entrust to a tribunal. Even if decisions were not enforced, a process of compulsory submission would cause delays during which tempers could cool. The Covenant did approach this goal, but these agencies did not become the heart of its structure as in the programs of the League to Enforce Peace and the League of Nations Society. Also, the Council became the conciliation body. Most internationalists before 1919 had thought in terms of a more democratic and representative agency than one dominated by the great powers.

The Covenant did recognize prevailing desires, however, in a few ways. A provision for compulsory action appeared in Article XVI, since it called for force to make nations resolve their disputes peacefully. The Covenant in these sections also paralleled internationalist thought in its refusal to enforce awards. It also followed the popular belief that a nation should still have the right to fight if it fulfilled all of the obligations outlined. Governments, under Article XIII, could "resort to war" after a hearing if none of the parties wished to accept the decision. While Article XIII gave the Council the authority to "propose" action where nations refused to honor awards, it could not compel nations to accept its recommendations. The League to Enforce Peace had recognized that the problems of enforcing judgments would be exceedingly difficult and that sufficient benefits might accrue if an international organization could at least compel hearing. British advocates had at first insisted that the work of the tribunals and conciliation bodies be upheld, but they had finally capitulated in the face of American attitudes and also because of the reluctance of their own government to stand behind any sanction.

The provision for a court of justice in Article XIV partially fulfilled a major goal of the prewar internationalists. The clauses in the Covenant, however, offer no evidence that the draftsmen at Paris fully comprehended the aims of the legalists. The court could hear arbitral cases, but not a word appeared about its jurisdiction or the scope of its power to determine its own authority. The article also ignored the widely discussed problem of justiciable and nonjusticiable disputes. This presumably meant that the judges could not determine whether a case should be referred to arbitration or to conciliation, a point which men like Lowell and Taft saw as an absolute necessity. A clause on justiciable questions had been expunged, which further reveals the lack of a judicial outlook on the part of the commissioners.[39]

39. Lowell to Root, August 18, 1915; Taft to Lowell, February 15, 1916, Lowell Papers; Miller, *Drafting,* II, 700.

The men at Paris who wrote Article XIV thus created a court system not far different from that already at The Hague. Governments would have considerable freedom to decide whether to use the new agency, whose decisions were advisory. The system envisaged by most internationalists went far beyond that, for they wished a genuine judicial body with power to decide according to law and then to have its verdicts recognized and applied as accepted doctrines. They later went beyond the articles in the Covenant, for the judicial statesmen who assembled in 1920 to plan a court created one in keeping with their dream and not one which might have been implied from the Covenant. It should also be noted that neither the delegates at Paris nor those later draftsmen established tribunals on a regional basis as some internationalists had suggested.

The provision for a court had finally been included over the objections of Wilson. All of the British drafts, including that of Smuts, had contained this feature, but Wilson had refused to incorporate such into his work. Until January 31, he resisted the British efforts, through the Cecil plan, to include it. The Hurst-Miller document contained clauses for a court, but Wilson sought again to eliminate them in his third Paris draft before finally agreeing to use the Hurst-Miller synthesis as the basis for discussions. House had been right when he surmised earlier that this idea had become too important to omit when Wilson first removed it from his plan and that the other powers would insist upon its incorporation. Again, however, the debates on this subject disclose Wilson's disregard of how vital this principle had become in internationalist thought by 1919.[40]

Article XV outlined the procedures to be followed by parties seeking to settle controversies where the arbitral system had been rejected. It called for the Council to use its good offices to investigate and issue reports on disputes. It could also recommend action where a government refused to abide by a unanimous decision of the Council and could, in certain instances, refer questions to the Assembly. The aims here represented no departure from established concepts save in a clause which called for the acceptance of Council decisions unanimously rendered. This idea reflected the belief that since governments felt compelled to abide by arbitral awards they should also respect other types of decisions, especially those which reflected

40. Miller, *Drafting*, I, 73. As least one authority has attributed the court idea to the British because they insisted upon it at Paris while Wilson resisted. Such a conclusion is valid only from the perspective of the conference. Historically, this ideal had been a core plank in American internationalist thought from the time of Ladd. Seth P. Tillman, *Anglo-American Relations at the Paris Peace Conference of 1919*, p. 129.

unanimity. Some discussion did ensue over whether the Council should act if a government refused to co-operate, but this proviso disappeared in revisions of the Covenant after February 14.[41]

Article XVI contained the clauses for sanctions under Article XII. The members of the League would compel the submission of disputes to pacific settlement. They would respond immediately with a commercial, financial, and personal embargo, and the Council would "recommend what effective military or naval forces the members of the League shall severally contribute to the armed forces to be used to protect the covenants of the League." The members would further co-operate by mutually supporting each other in any ventures.

This article incorporated the basic philosophy of the League to Enforce Peace for compulsory hearing and enforced delay. But where the League to Enforce Peace called for an automatic use of both economic and military force to compel the submission of a dispute, the Covenant did not. Only after Council action could arms be used. The Covenant thus reflected the program of the British government on this point. Furthermore, the wording of Article XVI had been altered during discussions so as to diminish its effectiveness. Wilson had included in his second draft an idea borrowed from Smuts. If any member violated the Covenant it would "thereby *ipso facto* become at war with all the members." The President, however, changed this in response to warnings by Miller and Lansing that such a clause would be judged unconstitutional. Wilson accordingly revised it to read that such a member would "thereby *ipso facto* be deemed to have committed an act of war against all the members."[42] This modification weakened the Article, and subsequent world events showed that governments felt no obligation regarding the proviso. Under Article XVI, and elsewhere in the Covenant, public opinion became the only genuine sanction. In nearly every instance where decisions required a military response, the members first had to decide upon their course of action. Article X provided the one exception. It protected from attack any member that followed the rules and utilized the machinery.

The concept of force embodied in Article XVI had been expressed periodically by Wilson and the more advanced internationalists before 1919, but the commissioners spent little time on the subject of sanctions. The only major debate arose over the best means to uphold the Covenant. The French wished a separate police force since it would provide the type of guarantee

41. Miller, *Drafting*, I, 193.
42. *Ibid.*, I, 48–49.

they wished against attack. They had included such a proposition replete with details in their official plan only to meet resistance from the British and Wilson. The President believed that any proviso which gave the League authority over American troops would be unconstitutional. The French argued that an international army could be used under Article VIII to inspect and control armaments as well as perform when needed. Until the last day of the sessions they sought to include it.[43]

In omitting such a provision, the Covenant reflected the desire of most internationalists. Most pacifists and judicially oriented advocates had opposed positive sanctions. Only a few persons had considered a police agency an essential part of an organization, and even those moderates who had endorsed this idea, like Holt, Bartholdt, Mrs. Mead, and Carnegie, had often changed their minds.

One other observation seems necessary regarding Articles X and XVI. The commissioners spent virtually no time exploring the problem of aggression.[44] Such legalists as John Bassett Moore and Root had often expressed concern over how to determine the aggressor in any particular instance. The limited debate on this subject may reveal further the lack of faith in judicial processes which characterized the men who wrote the Covenant.

Article XVII sought to provide an answer to two difficult questions. What should the League do if a member and a nonmember became involved in a dispute? What action should it take in the event of a war between two outsiders? In the first instance, the Covenant suggested that the nonmember be invited to join so that the machinery of the League could be applied to resolve the issue. If the outsider rejected the invitation and attacked a member, the governments would then consider this a violation of Article XII and act under Article XVI. In the second case, the Council would invite both outsiders to become members. If they did not respond, the Council could then recommend action or move to resolve the dispute and prevent war. Despite the importance of this subject, few internationalists had devoted much attention to it prior to 1919. Only the more outspoken sanctionists had suggested that wars, wherever they occurred, should be stopped.

Articles XVIII through XXVI of the Covenant of February 14 contained provisions on a variety of subjects. Article XVIII gave the League the power to control trade in armaments, a point which pacifist interna-

43. Baker, *Wilson: Life and Letters,* VI, 386; Short to G. W. Kirchwey, January 19, 1917, Short Papers; Baker, *Wilson and World,* III, 157–159; Miller, *Drafting,* I, 180, 209–210, 216, 244–260.
44. Miller, *Drafting,* I, 181.

tionalists had often advocated. Article XIX considered the delicate subject of mandates. The idea of giving a league the job of administering outlying or disputed territories or former colonies had appeared in Smuts's plans, and Wilson's early Paris drafts included it. They could have borrowed it from any number of sources. Nicholas Murray Butler suggested a system late in 1918, and Holt's *Independent* had long advocated such a program. That magazine had published an article on the subject by Theodore Marburg in 1912, and it had revived interest in 1917 with an editorial advancing the scheme. Where it originated would be difficult to determine, but it had been suggested as early as 1889.[45]

Article XX called for an International Labor Bureau and included a statement on "fair and humane conditions of labor." Few Americans had expressed an interest in this subject and it appeared largely because the British had included it.[46] Article XXI contained a vague statement on free trade. Liberal internationalists had often insisted upon such a clause, but the Covenant fell short of their ideal. It noted that nations should be provided freedom of access in their trade but said not a word about freedom of the seas. The representatives of England killed that point.

Article XXII recognized the evolutionary development which had resulted in international bureaus. These would henceforth operate under the aegis of the League. Thus a rather commonplace suggestion in internationalist thought became a reality. Article XXIII reflected the ideal of open diplomacy which had gained currency during the war when it called for the registration of all new treaties.

In Article XXIV, the draftsmen at Paris sought to provide the Covenant with an escape valve. Many persons had feared that a League might create a status quo, and the plans of House, Wilson, and the British had reflected this concern. This section emerged largely as a result of discussions on Article X.[47] Frontiers should be allowed to change, and no unfair conditions would be tolerated. The Assembly could correct inequities by recommending revision of treaties which became obsolete or inapplicable or which threatened the peace because of intolerable terms.

45. *Ibid.,* pp. 34, 101–107, 185; Curry, "Wilson, Smuts, and the Versailles Settlement," pp. 973–974; [Holt], "The German Colonies," *The Independent,* XCVI (November 9, 1918), 149; [Holt], "For a Holy War," *ibid.,* XCII (December 15, 1917), 497–498; Straus to Holt, December 18, 1917, Holt Papers; Marburg to Holt, December 19, 1917; to K. Colegrove, April 22, 1919, in Latané, *Development,* I, 379; II, 631; "Federation *versus* War," *Westminster Review,* CXXXI (January 1889), 1–7.

46. Miller, *Drafting,* I, 191.

47. *Ibid.,* pp. 202–203.

Articles XXV and XXVI stated that all agreements between members contrary to the provisions of the Covenant should be abrogated and that the Covenant could be amended when three fourths of the members ratified any change. The former proviso had been of little concern to internationalists, but the latter had been considered from the time of the earliest planners.

No analysis of the Covenant should fail to comment on the subjects which it did not mention and which had been of interest to American internationalists. Several liberal and humanitarian ideals on health, education, sanitation, religion, race, and economic equality did not appear in the draft of February 14. They had been explored by the commissioners, but they represented complex questions which defied simple statements.

More significantly, the Covenant omitted any reference to the Monroe Doctrine. It had been suggested as an item worthy of inclusion, and in internationalist thought it had been hailed as a regional policy which a league could borrow and extend to the world. Wilson had expressed an interest in including this point; indeed, he saw Article X as an extension of the Doctrine. Its omission soon prompted considerable criticism in the United States.[48] Various records of the discussions reveal a reluctance on the part of European powers to include some mention of the Doctrine, but the real reason for its omission is not clear.

The absence of a representative assembly with legislative authority also seems significant. Many internationalists had seen this goal as important for two reasons: it would diminish the power of governments and increase that of the people; and it would lay the foundation for a peace of justice built on law. The commissioners at Paris did discuss this subject because Smuts introduced it with a proposal that they create a congress of delegates elected by the domestic legislatures of the member-states. He received little support. It is not amazing that such a suggestion should have been ignored, but it is remarkable that at the Paris conference no one revived the old dream that the Interparliamentary Union act as an international assembly. Cecil had suggested this in his early draft, but the idea gained no supporters. This proposal, like that of the Hague system, seemed anathema to the commissioners.[49]

Finally, the Covenant of February 14 contained no provision for withdrawal. Most of the planners before 1919 had considered this an essential

48. *Ibid.*, pp. 444, 448, 458–459.
49. *Ibid.*, I, 220, 231–236, 226, 272–275, 38; II, 62; House Diary, February 12, 1919.

item affecting the very existence of a league. The right of withdrawal might encourage governments to join since they could leave if dissatisfied. On the other hand, a loose policy would enable nations to abandon a league and thus weaken its effectiveness. The commissioners may have sought to avoid this dilemma by ignoring the subject. Subsequent revisions which added clauses on withdrawal showed that men in 1919 still considered the matter of importance.

Where then did the Covenant fit into the patterns of internationalist thought? Not surprisingly, it reflected the extremes of the spectrum. On one end, it revealed views close to those of traditional peace spokesmen which most internationalists had adopted. The Preamble observed that the League would seek co-operation, peace, and security, "by the acceptance of obligations not to resort to war." The signatories would agree to maintain justice, respect treaties, and pursue "open, just and honourable relations" with their neighbors. The emphasis upon arbitration likewise mirrored a pacifist outlook. The Covenant also achieved a "Congress of Nations," the old "American plan" of Ladd and Burritt. It advanced that principle of conference which had been realized on a broad scale for the first time at the Hague meetings. It now made that system permanent insofar as an assembly was concerned.

On the opposite end of the spectrum, the Covenant's provisions on force and judicial procedures seemed far from the mainstream of internationalist thought. The clauses on force may have been qualified by such words as "advise," "propose," and "recommend," but they still represented ideas which most planners had rejected because they knew from experience how conventional-minded men were and how alarming bold ideas could be. The League to Enforce Peace reflected that knowledge when it initially called for a limited use of sanctions, and many people who would have opposed a more extensive use of force accepted its cautious step forward. The Covenant showed no such awareness of the admonitions of Root and Roosevelt not to move beyond what men might be willing to accept.

The drafters of the Covenant also revealed little awareness of the legalistic and procedural approach of the internationalists. The Covenant contained provisions on justice and right, but these could hardly develop in an organization which lacked machinery to create or determine international law. Likewise, such principles could scarcely thrive in an association dominated by the great powers. The lesser nations may have had a voice, and they could register complaints and gain a hearing, but they could do little to advance democracy or justice. The belief in an imposed peace seemed more important to the draftsmen at Paris than the vision of a world adjusting to new conditions under a system of justice and law.

Such a result might have been predicted. The European statesmen, with only a few exceptions, had no lofty concept of an idealistic international organization, and the American delegates and their advisors had little background or experience for their work. Despite their efforts to become informed, they remained neophytes on the subject, or they were in no position to argue persuasively with Wilson over the merits or shortcomings of his proposals. Since he became the key figure in the drafting and showed little awareness of what had been done in the United States and the world, the Covenant Wilson prepared could hardly have been fully in keeping with internationalist thought. Miller's massive twenty-one-volume diary mentions the League to Enforce Peace by name only two times and in neither instance in relation to discussions about articles.

Neither did the constructive endeavors of the prewar internationalists receive any consideration by the commissioners. When their Covenant ignored the evolutionary gains, especially those of the Hague Conferences, Bourgeois reminded them that those efforts should at least be acknowledged. The work

> done at The Hague has not been done in vain as the opponents of Right have claimed. They are the one who have piled up jokes and raillery on the work done at The Hague; they have tried to cast discredit on the first great enterprise for the organization of right in the world . . .
>
> I foresee, I announce and I want it to be written in the minutes that, against the work we are now undertaking, the same criticisms and the same raillery will be made, and that they will even try to say that this work is useless and ineffective. As for me, I am proud to have been with a few of those who are here, among the workers at The Hague. . . . We were 32 faithful free countries, having the sentiments of right.[50]

Bourgeois did not succeed in influencing the statesmen, and neither did other internationalists. They had not known that their ideas would receive so little consideration, and they continued to formulate plans even as the commissioners assembled. Many persons prepared proposals varying from

---

50. Miller, *Drafting,* I, 175, 225, 229–230, 260–263. Miller observed in the 1920s that "to intimate that the Covenant was a continuation of what was done at The Hague would have been a very misleading kind of half truth." *Ibid.,* I, 225.

vague endorsements to detailed projects.[51] They reveal, however, the prominence of the issue in the minds of citizens, who compiled their schemes for their own satisfaction or with the hope that their suggestions might contribute to official discussions on the matter.

Many of these writers, by their broad statements, revealed a limited knowledge of the subject. Some went a bit further by considering the arrangement between the Allied governments as the basis for a permanent league.[52] Other men of liberal views increasingly emphasized that an international organization could prevent an unjust peace: it could maintain equality of trade, guarantee minorities their rights, oversee colonies, abolish secret diplomacy, and establish rules of fair play between nations.[53]

A few of the newcomers sought aims which the older internationalists had long discussed. Some examined the problem of proper representation and pondered the complexities of establishing a court or of building a society upon principles of right.[54] A considerable number spoke boldly and in detail for a supranational agency. They wished a force capable of upholding decisions of tribunals, of defending justice, and of performing all duties necessary to prevent war. The most elaborate of these came from a professor of law at the University of Virginia, Raleigh C. Minor, who examined

51. Edwin B. Copeland to Jordan, October 20, 1918, Jordan Papers; Dallas Bondeman to Taft, February 13, 1919, with 27-page plan; F. D. Smith to Taft, February 12, 1919, with 12-page manuscript, Taft Papers; B. H. McFarland, "Constitution for a League of Nations," dated January 2, 1919, House Papers. The State Department received many suggestions. These were sent to Paris where they were boxed and returned without being read. *Foreign Relations, Paris Peace Conference,* XI, 113, 161.

52. William McClellan, "The Creation of a Supernational Mind," *North American Review,* CCVIII (December 1918), 874–880; "Is World Security Possible?," *The Forum,* LX (October 1918), 424–429; W. M. Sloane, "Napoleon and Hohenzollern," *The Nation,* CVII (November 2, 1918), 508–510; Herbert A. Gibbons, "The Armistices and Peace Negotiations," *Century Magazine,* XCVII (February 1919), 543; Vachel Lindsay, "A Word of Advice About Policy," *The Dial,* LXV (September 5, 1918), 176; Charles W. Eliot to Short, September 27, November 8, 1918, LEP Papers.

53. John Dewey, "A League of Nations and Economic Freedom," *The Dial,* LXV (December 14, 1918), 537–539; Dewey, "The League of Nations and the New Diplomacy," *ibid.,* (November 16, 1918), pp. 401–403; Harold Stearns, "Will Russia Defeat Us?," *ibid.,* pp. 397–399; "The Issue and Our Critics," *New Republic,* XVI (October 19, 1918), 340–342.

54. Arnold Bennett, "A Peace League Based on Population," *Current History,* VIII (August 1918) part 2, 355–357; Paul Kester, "International Legislative Representation," *North American Review,* CCVIII (September 1918), 401–409; Thomas W. Balch, *A World Court,* pp. 6, 97, 123–153; Thomas Raeburn White, "A League of Nations Now," *The Independent,* XCV (September 14, 1918), 354, 363, 367.

the structure and operation of a United Nations and included a thirty-eight-page constitution modeled after that of the United States. His union would have made every country subordinate to his government.[55]

Of the many and varied proposals, only a few contained unique ideas. A Chicago physician, Emil G. Beck, suggested a bonding system. Members should sign an agreement not to violate the laws drafted by an international assembly, and they should post a bond which they would forfeit if they broke the treaty. The parliament would also have a force available to uphold the covenant. Economist, theorist, and businessman I. C. Blandy of Greenwich, New York, called for "an International Reserve Bank" under a union to establish a world currency and to facilitate trade.[56]

Another economic theme came from a professor of geology, Thomas C. Chamberlin, of the University of Chicago. He argued that a league could succeed only where nations had something in common. The governments engaged in the war against Germany could find that bond in their economic interests. They should form a police force to control the seas and trade routes and regulate and administer commerce. Election of delegates as well as voting strength would depend upon each nation's trade, and the machinery would be financed by a tax on goods exchanged.[57]

The historian Frederick Jackson Turner also explored the subject of a league. As an authority on the impact of sectionalism on American history, Turner examined that subject in relation to an international organization. He saw a need for a legislative agency with powers "limited but real," a court, and a council, but he also saw that tremendous forces would continually threaten it. Political parties had served as a stabilizing and unifying factor in the United States. If they could be created to transcend boundaries and attract the loyalties of men, they could prevent the disruption of any

55. James E. Ely, *World Reconstruction and Permanent Peace,* pp. 7–8, 10–15; Dubuque *Times-Journal,* November 11, 1918; [C. R. Van Hise], "A League of Free Nations," *Review of Reviews,* LVIII (December 1918), 643; "An International Democracy," *Bellman,* XXV (November 16, 1918), 539–540; Howard H. Gross, *After the War, What?* pp. 5–8; George H. Hull to Taft, December 9, 1918, January 9, 1919, with enclosures; Henry K. Laud to Taft, December 11, 1918, with 34-page plan; Minor, *A Republic of Nations: A Study of the Organization of a Federal League of Nations,* pp. 257–295.

56. Beck to Jordan, January 25, 1919, Jordan Papers; Beck to Taft, December 18, 1918, Taft Papers; Blandy, "An Open Letter to the President," *The Dial,* LXV (November 30, 1918), 501.

57. Chamberlin, "World-Organization After the World-War—An Omninational Confederation," *Journal of Geology,* XXVI (November–December 1918), 701–721.

organization.[58] Turner provided no answers on how this difficult task could be achieved.

New societies as well as new thinkers appeared with suggestions. In Boston, a group of women under the leadership of Mrs. J. Malcolm Forbes formed a League for Permanent Peace which called for an association built upon principles of justice and law. The most significant new body, however, appeared in September 1918. It called itself the League of Free Nations Association, a name which a British group had recently adopted. A number of liberals, social workers, journalists, and attorneys had met that summer to seek a common accord. Such persons as John Dewey, Herbert Croly, Charles A. Beard, Felix Frankfurter, Stephen P. Duggan, and Norman Hapgood drafted a "Statement of Principles" they hoped would insure order by preventing war, establishing justice, and allowing change according to principles of right.[59]

These newcomers, whether as individuals or organizations, did not stand alone in their desire to influence events and statesmen. The older internationalists also sought to affect the outcome. The League to Enforce Peace and the National Committee on the Churches and the Moral Aims of the War launched a speaking crusade which took their advocates before hundreds of thousands of citizens. The League to Enforce Peace also measured favorable and unfavorable response to its idea. Wherever it found adverse opinion or doubt, it worked to change views.[60]

These groups faced a major problem, however, over what type of organization they should advocate. As long as Wilson insisted that no detailed plans be formulated prior to the conference, they faced a dilemma of what to do. At times, Taft and Lowell even doubted the President's commitment to the cause. Late in November, however, the League to Enforce Peace and the League of Free Nations Association decided to unite upon a program. They adopted the basic platform of the older organization but added other ideas. Liberal aims appeared in provisions to protect "backward regions" and in phrases on the "betterment of human relations." Also, no world union should inhibit "the forces of healthy growth and changes." Additional

58. William Diamond, ed., "American Sectionalism and World Organization, by Frederick Jackson Turner," *American Historical Review,* XLVII (April 1942), 545–551.

59. *Organize the World . . . ,* p. 1; Bartlett, *League to Enforce Peace,* p. 111; New York *Times,* December 2, 1918.

60. Kuehl, *Hamilton Holt,* pp. 131–132; Macfarland, *Pioneers for Peace,* pp. 76–77; Lynch, "Report to Trustees," November 12, December 5, 1918, Church Peace Union Papers; Bartlett, *League to Enforce Peace,* pp. 97–98.

clauses provided for the enforcement of court decisions, possible action by consultation to uphold recommendations by the Council of Conciliation, and a strong stand against war. Military and economic steps should be taken to prevent "resort to force by *any* nation."[61] These additions reflected a shift from the cautious stand of the League to Enforce Peace toward a broader and stronger international organization. Yet in structure and operation, the plan remained essentially judicial. In their move toward a greater reliance on force, the League to Enforce Peace advocates had experienced no real change of heart. They did little more than climb aboard the Wilson bandwagon. They knew his views, having seen copies of the early House and Wilson drafts of a Covenant, and House had advised Short that if his society really wanted to help it should support what House and Wilson had in mind.[62]

The proponents of this "Victory Program" further revealed their desire to co-operate with the President by still avoiding a detailed scheme. They simply proclaimed principles upon which an association should be built. By such phraseology, they hoped they would not alienate Wilson, but they did not succeed. When the Chicago *Tribune* published an item in its Paris edition on December 18 that the President had endorsed the program of the League to Enforce Peace, Wilson promptly issued a denial. Such officials as Short responded by noting the falsity of the report, by insisting that his society wished no fame or credit, and by reassuring Wilson that it only wanted to see a league in the treaty of peace. The episode, however, disrupted activities in the United States.[63] Throughout late December, January, and the first weeks of February, the League to Enforce Peace officials adopted a wait-and-see attitude until they could determine what the President had done at Paris.

Other groups followed the same philosophy. The World's Court League, the Carnegie Endowment for International Peace, and the American Peace Society did not modify their programs. They still hoped for a judicial system, for the development of law, and for some type of federation, but they began no new campaigns.[64]

---

61. Taft and Lowell to G. W. Wickersham, December 11, 1918; Taft to Lowell, September 30, 1918; Taft to W. A. Brown, November 19, 1918, Taft Papers; Lowell to Bryce, October 11, 25, 1918, Lowell Papers; Bartlett, *League to Enforce Peace,* pp. 111–112; Latané, *Development,* II, 798–799.

62. House Diary, September 21, 1918.

63. Latané, *Development,* II, 798; Press statement, December 18, 1918, Miller Papers; Short to House, December 31, 1918 (copy of cablegram), Holt Papers.

64. Samuel T. Dutton to Jordan, December 11, 1918, Jordan Papers; Butler, *The*

Perhaps no widespread propaganda effort had to be made. After nearly four years of concerted effort, the American people seemed to be highly in favor of a world organization. Every sign verified that fact. The League to Enforce Peace Committee on Information tallied newspaper opinion on the subject and reported a continuing and overwhelming endorsement. In June of 1917, it found only 8 of 100 editorials opposed; on August 18, it noted 2 of 200 against; on November 24, only 3 of 400 newspapers objected to a league. By December of 1918, an analysis of 833 editorials showed only 20 to be hostile.[65] Some of the editors recognized that the entire idea could be considered "an American one" in terms of "its present form and application." The movement and advocacy in the United States had spread to the world and when adopted would be "America's greatest contribution to the welfare of the human race."[66]

Other indexes of public attitudes provide additional evidence of the favorable response. Labor leaders endorsed the idea as did union members in their conventions. Religious denominations and dozens of national professional, agricultural, civic, business, and legal organizations also voted statements of approval. More significantly, a Committee on Memorials of the League to Enforce Peace had obtained resolutions from sixteen state legislatures by November 1918.[67]

Most of these testimonials, whether by private or public bodies, contained phrases which did not commit their authors to anything more than a broad principle. One survey available, however, provides insight into the more specific thought of citizens. A Council of the National Economic League circulated a questionnaire late in 1918 and received four hundred replies. The respondents approved of a union "to further develop a system of international law" (363 to 17), "to provide effective agencies for its enforcement" (331 to 27), and to guarantee peace by arbitration and public hearing (362 to 14). They voted against the creation of "an embryo state not a mere league" (102 to 208). Yet they approved of some sacrifice of

---

War and After the War, p. 5; New York *Times,* July 28, 1918. The American branch of the Central Organization for a Durable Peace had not developed. Doty, *Durable Peace,* pp. 85, 159, 161–164.

65. *The League Bulletin,* No. 37 (June 1, 1917); Report of Committee on Information, August 18, November 24, 1917, Lowell Papers; Hugh Chan, "American Agitation for a League of Nations, 1914–1922," pp. 69–70.

66. St. Louis *Globe Democrat,* November 17, 1918.

67. *The League Bulletin,* No. 121 (January 11, 1919), pp. 339–340; *The Fighting Program of the National Nonpartisan League;* "The American Labor War Platform," *The Outlook,* CXIX (May 29, 1918), 186; *Minutes,* Executive Committee, August 18, November 24, 1917, April 11, 1918, LEP Papers.

sovereignty (275 to 66), believed that "an international Congress" should fix "all national boundaries" (226 to 101), and favored a court and police along with disarmament and the abolition of protective tariffs as a means to achieve peace and democracy (173 to 136). When asked whether the right of armaments should be considered more essential than a league in maintaining peace, 34 replied yes and 292 said no.[68]

While this survey reveals specific views, it must be assumed that the average citizen remained unconcerned with details. The propaganda campaigns, including those of the League to Enforce Peace, had often noted that particular programs should be sacrificed for the attainment of the ideal. Hence, men had little trouble endorsing a goal which had much in common with motherhood. If an organization could eliminate war, who would oppose it? Wilson had been right on this point, and he had also guessed correctly in assuming that voices of opposition would increase as the moment came for specific proposals.[69]

Some expressions of doubt had appeared in England and in the United States even before the Armistice. Almost all of these, however, questioned not the ideal but the method. Pacifists opposed force; legalists feared an arbitrary structure which might act autocratically; liberals wished to add principles of right; adventurous internationalists objected to plans which did not go far enough.[70]

A few voices of dissent did reflect isolationist and nationalist philosophies. They referred to Washington's advice on alliances or worried about commitments which might involve their nation in war. Some statements can be found from the 1890s on, but they were isolated instances until 1918, and only late in that year did the pro-league advocates begin to worry about them.[71]

---

68. *A Vote of the National Council of the National Economic League on International Problems of Reconstruction,* in E. L. Philipp Papers, State Historical Society of Wisconsin.

69. Selig Adler, *The Isolationist Impulse: Its Twentieth-Century Reaction,* pp. 39–40; "The Defeatists," *New Republic,* XVI (October 19, 1918), 327–329.

70. Ellery C. Stowell, "A League of Nations," *The Nation,* CIII (December 7, 1916), 536–538; Lippmann, *Stakes of Diplomacy,* pp. 222, 140–145; Allaben, "The World's Need of International Government," pp. 417–436; H. M. Chittenden, "Questions for Pacifists," *Atlantic Monthly,* CXVI (August 1915), 158–159; H. Begbie, "Can Man Abolish War?," *North American Review,* CCV (June 1917), 886–894; Elsie Clews Parsons to Randolph S. Bourne, May 22, 1917; H. M. Kallen to Bourne, May 15, 1917, Bourne Papers, Columbia University; [O. G. Villard], "Critics of the League to Enforce Peace," *The Nation,* CIV (January 4, 1917), 5–6; "Will the United States Fight to Preserve the Peace of the World?," *Current Opinion,* LXII (February 1917), 82–85.

71. Paul Reinsch, *World Politics at the End of the Nineteenth Century,* pp. 23–24;

The potential opposition first appeared in threatening form in the political arena. The congressional election of 1918 contributed to it, for Wilson's call for support of Democratic candidates did inject partisanship into discussions on a league. Wilson correctly believed that members of his own party would receive his peace program more kindly, but he did not foresee the reaction. Republicans capitalized upon his words to deny an implied disloyalty, to demand vindication by the voters, and to warn the public about the dangers of an autocratic president. The election gave the Republicans control of the Senate, and thus Henry Cabot Lodge assumed the chairmanship of the key Committee on Foreign Relations. The Senate had been an almost overwhelming obstacle in the approval of arbitration treaties, a fact which most internationalists recognized. They worried about a threat to their dream, and even the President and his advisors recognized the role the Senate might play.[72]

Congressmen, however, had not revealed much hostility toward a league before the fall of 1918. A Hitchcock resolution in January 1917 had prompted the beginning of antagonistic remarks, but only a few men had spoken then. In ensuing months, only a small number of senators assumed an unfavorable position.[73] Indeed, as late as November 1918, polls by the League to Enforce Peace indicated that most senators could be counted on in any vote. Yet observers like Lowell remembered how easily they could be aroused. Certainly two men gave him reason for concern. Republican William E. Borah of Idaho had introduced a resolution in January of 1917 which endorsed the traditional policy of nonentanglement. He warned that an international organization would threaten the Monroe Doctrine and that danger existed where men planned to use force to abolish war. Philander C. Knox of Pennsylvania, Taft's former secretary of state, also revealed doubts. He had refused to join the League to Enforce Peace because he feared the obligations it entailed; by December of 1918 he, too, resorted to the device

---

G. W. Wickersham, "Our Compulsory Arbitration Treaties Should Be Amended," *Annals,* American Academy of Political and Social Science, LXXII (July 1917), 200; Henry Forster to Members, Committee on International Arbitration of New York City Bar Association, January 6, 1919, Forster Papers, New York Public Library; James W. Wadsworth to Taft, January 26, 1917, Taft Papers; David J. Hill to Marburg, August 21, 1915, Marburg Papers; Adler, *Isolationist Impulse,* pp. 40–42; F. F. Andrews to Holt, October 29, 1918, Andrews Papers; Charles B. Elliott to Taft, December 23, 1918; W. H. Cowles to Taft, January 10, 1919, Taft Papers.

72. Baker, *Wilson: Life and Letters,* VI, 431, VIII, 44; Short to Taft, December 26, 1917, Taft Papers; Wilson to George W. Anderson, November 18, 1918, Wilson Papers.

73. Baker, *Wilson: Life and Letters,* VI, 403–404, 418; Kendrick, "Republicans and the Treaty," pp. 19–21, 40.

of resolutions to record his views. He particularly objected to the incorporation of a league into the peace treaty.[74]

Lodge was the most influential senator to raise questions. His second
thoughts about a league had made him not an unbeliever but a doubter. He
noted the many difficulties involved and warned that great care had to be
taken in drafting any treaty. The peace settlement should not be entangled
with the ideal of extending the Monroe Doctrine to the world. The nation
should not submit "to control by an armed League." It might be proper,
Lodge conceded, to enforce the decisions of a court or to uphold provisions
on which countries might specifically agree. Even here, however, Lodge
seemed unwilling to have vital interests decided by any international agency.
If a code and arbitration could be developed along with a disarmament
plan and a healthy public opinion as the moral force behind all action, these
might be sufficient. Lodge had not developed significantly in his thinking
since 1911 when he had insisted upon exempting vital interests and national
honor from the Taft treaties. Thus he appeared to favor a league if its powers
could be clearly defined or established, if it could be kept separate from the
peace treaty, if the provisions would not unduly obligate the nation, and if
it did not intrude upon established policies like the Monroe Doctrine, the
tariff, and immigration.[75]

Two political figures outside the Senate resembled Lodge in supporting
an association, yet with qualifications that appeared hostile. Root continued
to cause the internationalists concern because of his reluctance to air his
views publicly. That he favored a world organization cannot be doubted,
but Root's internationalism had not increased. He wished all action to be
carefully and wisely decided, and he still insisted that nations should adopt
only those provisions they would honor. A court for judicial disputes, a
council of conciliation for nonjusticiable matters, a system to develop law,

74. Kendrick, "Republicans and the Treaty," pp. 23–36, 40, 52; "Report of National Campaign Manager," *Minutes,* Executive Committee, November 16, 1918, LEP
Papers; Lowell to Bryce, October 14, 1918, Lowell Papers; Baker, *Wilson: Life and
Letters,* VI, 432; Philander Knox to Marburg, August 17, 1915, in Latané, *Develop-
ment,* I, 63.
75. Kendrick, "Republicans and the Treaty," pp. 19–21, 37–39; Garraty, *Henry
Cabot Lodge,* pp. 346–347; Lodge to Lowell, February 3, 1917, Lowell Papers; Lodge
to James M. Beck, September 28, 1918; to A. J. Beveridge, November 23, 1918; to
George V. Crocker, December 24, 1918; to Lord Balfour, November 25, 1918; to
Courtenay Crocker, November 26, 1918; to Clarence W. Alvord, December 26, 1918,
Lodge Papers; Henry L. Stimson to Roosevelt, February 3, 1917, Stimson Papers, Yale
University.

and a moral regard for right would be sufficient. He particularly opposed a strong agency vested with sanctions.[76]

Theodore Roosevelt also worried the internationalists. His mercurial personality at times led them to think he had abandoned his once vigorous espousal of a union. He had certainly given them cause for alarm. He had refused to endorse the League to Enforce Peace, although it never became clear whether he refused from conviction or because of his quarrel with Taft. An examination of Roosevelt's stand on the arbitration treaties of 1911, however, should have indicated why he remained aloof. He had then objected to any agreement which the nation would not honor, and he had attacked the word "justiciable" as meaningless. Since consistency had never been one of Roosevelt's virtues, perhaps the internationalists hoped he had changed his mind on those points. Only rarely did they challenge him when he assaulted them with expletives which revealed his militaristic and nationalistic sentiments more than hostility toward their aim.[77]

Some change may have occurred shortly before his death in January of 1919. Roosevelt and Taft met in May of 1918 and effected a reconciliation which Taft subsequently exploited in trying to woo the colonel into the League to Enforce Peace. Roosevelt proved to be receptive but cautious. Then, on August 15, he informed Taft he had "found a modus vivendi!" He would support the society "as an *addition to,* but not as *a substitute for,* our preparing our own strength for our own defense."[78] His writings after that date reflected that theme. An international organization might be useful; but since he had no great faith in its effectiveness, he insisted that his nation rely on its own defenses. He favored a union based on the platform of the League to Enforce Peace, but Roosevelt added some significant qualifications. The court should have the right to determine justiciable questions but not its own jurisdiction. The council of conciliation could hear non-justiciable disputes, but the governments should clearly define these, and the United States should reserve certain matters from consideration, espe-

76. Root to House, August 16, 1918; to L. Ward Bannister, December 9, 1918, Root Papers; Memoranda of conferences with Root by Chandler Anderson, November 18, December 12, 1918, Anderson Papers; Henry L. Stimson Diary, December 22, 29, 1918, Stimson Papers; Leopold, *Elihu Root,* pp. 123–124, 128, 130, 133–134.

77. New York *Times,* December 2, 1915; Roosevelt to John St. L. Strachey, December 5, 1916; to Lodge, February 5, 1917, Roosevelt Papers; "An International League for Peace," *The Outlook,* CXV (January 31, 1917), 189; "Questions for American Conservatives," *New Republic,* XVI (September 21, 1918), 213–216.

78. Roosevelt to Taft, August 15, 1918; Taft to Horace Taft, November 6, 1918; Taft to Bryce, December 5, 1918, Taft Papers.

cially the tariff, immigration, and "spheres of interest" like the Monroe
Doctrine. Court decisions should be upheld, but Roosevelt seemed unwilling to obligate the armed forces of the United States for this task.[79] Thus,
except for a difference of views on armaments, Roosevelt's desires paralleled
those of Lodge. He reflected a philosophy which more aptly fitted his position
during debates on the Taft treaties than his Nobel speech or writings of
1914 and 1915.

While Roosevelt may have been shifting in late 1918, other doubters
moved in the opposite direction. Evidence of opposition increased substantially in the winter of 1918–1919. Some of this stemmed from concern
about Wilson's attending the conference; some arose after Wilson announced
the composition of the peace commission. A few men worried that the
President would not achieve the kind of settlement they wanted. Wilson's
selection of the peace commissioners, however, did more than anything else
to harden political opposition. His refusal to name any senators and his
choice of only one nominal Republican alienated the leaders of that party.
Partisanship had not been apparent because most of the active internationalists had been Republicans, but that fact soon carried little weight. Although
Taft warned that his party should not oppose the popular league cause,
resistance imperceptibly hardened.[80]

Although the leaders may have been cautious, some Republicans revealed their partisanship. Senator Lawrence Y. Sherman of Illinois announced that congressmen would examine the treaty carefully. "We shall
have our spectacles on, we shall look for every dot on the i, for every comma
and we shall put the periods in ourselves." Senators Warren G. Harding of
Ohio, Eugene Hale of Maine, and Frank B. Kellogg of Minnesota likewise
believed that they should test carefully any Wilsonian agreements. Lodge
seemed determined to raise more questions than could be answered, and
he sought to undercut Wilson's efforts in Europe by revealing to English
statesmen the increasing opposition.[81]

79. Ralph Stout, ed., *Roosevelt in the Kansas City Star,* pp. 188–196, 229–231,
246, 261–265, 277–281, 292–295.

80. Taft to Lowell, October 17, 1918, Lowell Papers; Taft to Straus, January 19,
1919, Straus Papers.

81. Sherman, "The Aims of the Republican Congress," *The Forum,* LX (December
1918), 743; "Memorandum prepared by N.M.B. in December 1918, following conversation in Washington with Senators Harding, Hale, and Kellogg," Butler Papers; Kendrick, "Republicans and the Treaty," pp. 40, 43–50, 61–72; Lodge to Lord Balfour,
November 25, 1918; to Bryce, December 14, 1918; to George Trevelyan, December 27,
1918, Lodge Papers.

By February 1919, according to Taft, the situation in the Senate had reached "a state of explosion." He sensed an uneasiness on the part of "intense Republicans." Their blind views, Taft believed, would not prevent ratification of "a treaty worth having, a league with any 'bite' in it, containing covenants of real cooperation." Theodore Marburg, however, felt less certain. A struggle would have to be made to gain approval of an agreement "without qualifications."[82]

Thus, the actors in the ensuing drama were taking their positions. Taft had been right about the inevitability of a league, but an important question remained unanswered. How would the people of the United States and their senators respond to the Covenant when they read it? Only time could indicate whether the "stars in their courses" had also predetermined membership for the United States.

82. Taft to Horace D. Taft, February 5, 1919; to Robert Taft, February 10, 1919, Taft Papers; Marburg to Henry Goudy, January 27, 1919, in Latané, *Development,* II, 602.

Hollow
Victory

The story of the debate over the Treaty of Versailles and the refusal
of the Senate to endorse American membership in the League of
Nations has been retold many times. Little could be gained by another extensive account, but one aspect of the episode has not been fully explored.
What role did the internationalists play? What did the discussions and debates reveal of their thought and attitudes?

The struggle began on February 15, 1919, when newspapers first printed
the Covenant, and ended on March 19, 1920, when the Senate for a second
time failed to approve the treaty. In interpreting this battle, scholars have
concentrated upon the participants, notably Wilson and Lodge. One portrait reveals the President as an idealist who because of zeal or illness stub-
bornly refused to compromise. Thus he blocked membership and weakened
his own creation. The more traditional view casts Lodge as a villain. He
was, it has long been argued, an irreconcilable at heart. He opposed membership, resorted to subterfuge, and thus avoided a direct confrontation because such a course would alienate voters and adversely affect his party's
chances at the polls. Other writers have explained the outcome by noting
the presence of partisanship, of personal hatreds, and of the constitutional
obstacle which makes treaty-making difficult. They have also explored the
traditional policy of isolationism, but the ideological ingredient of interna-

tionalism must be added to the picture to clarify it and provide insight into the events between February 15, 1919, and March 19, 1920.[1]

The internationalists did not anticipate an adverse outcome in February of 1919. They found evidence of an initial public sentiment highly favorable to League membership. Newspapers which summarized polls of readers confirmed this fact. Of 1,377 editors queried on whether they favored joining, 718 responded with "yes" and 181 with "no." The remaining replies indicated approval but with qualifications. Sixteen other newspapers with a circulation of two million readers printed a questionnaire in the form of a ballot in which they inquired, "Do you wish the United States to enter a League of Nations to preserve peace?" Over 107,700 respondents answered in the affirmative, as opposed to 33,427 in the negative. Other reports from religious, agricultural, business, and labor bodies reflected a similar preponderance of sentiment for membership. Another survey, early in March, showed that from a sample of 4,712 letters received by senators, 1,628 favored ratification without change, 1,240 qualified their approval, and 1,580 could not endorse the Covenant "in its present form."[2]

Other evidence of enthusiasm for the League can be found in the attendance figures at public meetings. When Lowell and Lodge met to discuss the Covenant on March 19 in Symphony Hall in Boston, more than forty thousand people sought admission. When Taft and Wilson spoke at the Metropolitan Opera House on March 4, nearly one hundred thousand persons applied for the four thousand tickets available.[3]

While such indexes of opinion disclose a predominant pro-League senti-

1. The fuller scholarly works are Thomas A. Bailey, *Woodrow Wilson and the Great Betrayal*; Denna F. Fleming, *The United States and the League of Nations, 1918–1920*; Kendrick, "Republicans and the Treaty;" Ralph A. Stone, "The Irreconcilables and the Fight Against the League of Nations"; John C. Vinson, *Referendum for Isolation*; Arthur Walworth, *Woodrow Wilson: American Prophet*; *World Prophet*; Baker, *Woodrow Wilson and World Settlement*; Leopold, *Elihu Root*; Garraty, *Henry Cabot Lodge*; and Bartlett, *League to Enforce Peace*. Only Bartlett concentrates upon the internationalists.

2. Boston *Herald,* March 8, 11, 12, 13, 1919; "Educators and the League," *Advocate of Peace,* LXXXI (April 1919), 111–112; "Home and Foreign News," *ibid.*, p. 122; "Public Opinion and the League," *ibid.*, p. 102; "Will the Peace League Prevent War?" *Literary Digest,* LX (March 1, 1919), 11–13; "Nation-Wide Press-Poll on the League of Nations," *ibid.*, LXI (April 5, 1919), 14–16, 120–128; St. Louis *Globe-Democrat,* March 12, 1919; Clifford J. Reutter, "St. Louis Reaction to United States Foreign Policy," p. 132; New York *Evening Post,* April 18, 1919.

3. "The Lodge-Lowell Debate," *The Independent,* XCVII (March 29, 1919), 428; "President Wilson Lauds the League," *ibid.,* (March 15, 1919), p. 358.

ment, they also reveal a questioning attitude in the minds of citizens. These doubts may have been instinctive, but they were probably stimulated by public figures who detected flaws in the Covenant and suggested revisions. Even the internationalists engaged in that exercise. Some endorsed the Covenant but proposed changes which reflected their particular desires. Others believed it might be wise to accept amendments in order to weaken any opposition.

They can be divided into three groups: those with advanced views, those more moderate in their outlook, and those very cautious in their attitudes. The advanced thinkers wished to strengthen and improve the League. They also favored changes to make the Covenant more acceptable to critics, provided those alterations did not impair the effectiveness of the organization. Holt reflected such views as he publicly called for a stronger League and for revisions to clarify certain articles. Privately, he marked some fifty-five "improvements" on his copy of the Covenant. Most of these were minor, but a few touched upon fundamental principles of internationalist thought. He decried the omission of any clauses that would make the League a legislative agency. He worried lest the body of delegates play a secondary role in relation to the Council and suspected that the former would represent governments rather than people. He believed that an international police force would have been a wise creation, especially to uphold disarmament agreements. Finally, he wished action to be automatic whenever nations violated provisions of the Covenant.[4]

Other advanced thinkers added their criticisms. Marburg considered the unanimity rule in the Council and Assembly to be "deadening." George H. Boke believed that the League would never function effectively because of its limited powers. The world needed a "Supreme International Government." William Blymer called the Covenant a delusion. It would never function properly under the unanimity provision. Its powers should be increased, the articles on a court should be clarified and developed, and it should adopt his "isolation plan."[5]

William Crozier agreed with these men as he speculated on the effectiveness of the League if it had existed earlier in history and been confronted with wars. It would have failed, for only a world federation with executive,

4. New York *Sun,* March 26, 1919; New York *Times,* March 30, 1919; Marked copy of Covenant, Holt Papers.

5. Marburg to Wilson, March 28, 1919 (cablegram), in Latané, *Development,* II, 622; Boke, *The Federal Inter-Nation,* pp. 1–16; Blymer, *Memorandum on the Draft of the Constitution of the League of Nations,* pp. 1–10.

legislative, and judicial authority could maintain peace. Crozier recognized, however, that nations would not yet embark upon a "common government"; hence, he called for a thorough revision of the Covenant. It should be condensed and emphasis placed on a judicial system that would not intrude upon any country's sovereignty but still lead to a "collective assumption of responsibility," judgment, and enforcement. Crozier remembered his service at the First Hague Conference when he criticized Articles XII and XIII for virtually ignoring the established arbitral system. William Dudley Foulke, the Indiana publicist and attorney who had been active in the League to Enforce Peace, also looked at the settlement with a doubtful eye. "The final covenant included in the Versailles treaty," he concluded, "differed widely from any of the previous plans."[6]

Some of the newer converts to internationalism also wondered about the planned organization. George Nasmyth of the League of Free Nations Association in Massachusetts believed in a more democratic system in which delegates would be elected by popular vote, and he called for an easier amending process. Professor of political science Charles W. Fenwick of Bryn Mawr noted that the Covenant made it easy for governments to evade the machinery created. He, too, seized upon the limited judicial system as a point of criticism.[7] Indeed, this weakness came to be the one point upon which nearly all of the commentators could agree.

The moderate internationalists who wished a revised Covenant favored the League but feared that isolationist forces would block American membership. Thus, while they defended the Covenant, they readily agreed that some changes might be necessary. The shortcomings, the omissions, could be corrected. In particular, they saw a need to protect traditional policies like the Monroe Doctrine. They also acknowledged that revisions should be made where the wording in the Covenant left any doubt about its meaning.

Taft and Lowell best illustrate this type of internationalist. Their position is of interest since the Covenant went far beyond anything they had favored prior to 1919. Taft's desire for an organization, however, led him to praise Wilson's work. When critics appeared in the Senate, Taft spiritedly

---

6. Crozier, *A Discussion of the Proposed Constitution for the League of Nations,* pp. 2–16. A similar argument appears in Amos J. Peaslee, *Proposed Amendment to the Judiciary Articles of the Constitution of the League of Nations,* pp. 1–10; William Dudley Foulke, *A Hoosier Autobiography,* p. 186.

7. Nasmyth to Wilson, March 4, 1919, Miller Papers; Fenwick, "The Constitution of the League of Nations," *Catholic World,* CIX (April 1919), 38–41.

defended the Covenant and developed rational arguments in support of nearly all of its provisions.

Yet Taft readily assented to certain alterations. He saw no harm in adding an exemption for the Monroe Doctrine. He agreed that if decisions of the Council were to be unanimous, this should be clearly stated. The Covenant should also indicate how long the League would operate, and he felt that domestic policies should not be included under the terms of Article XV. When asked why he proposed changes at the same time he defended Wilson's labors, Taft replied that he did "it for the purpose of removing objections to it created in the minds of conscientious Americans." Words could be subject to varying interpretations, and any clarifying provisions would resolve doubts and gain senatorial approval. He opposed, however, any "revision of the form of the League so as to change its nature."[8]

Lowell, too, accepted the Covenant but indicated that he preferred amendments. While he thus qualified his endorsement, Lowell spent an amazing amount of time defending various articles against critics. On March 31, he suggested that the supporters of the League compile a series of essays modeled after the *Federalist Papers*, which had answered objections to the Constitution when it first appeared. Like Taft, he rationalized his inconsistent position by arguing that alterations would help gain adoption. He asked only for changes "that would make the Covenant acceptable to the American people, not for what would make it thoroughly satisfactory." The pro-League advocates had "to drive a wedge between the men, like Lodge, who believe in some league of nations, and will be forced to accept the Covenant, and those few senators who do not want any league at all." Lowell favored revisions to allow for withdrawal, to exclude from the League's jurisdiction such domestic questions as the tariff and immigration, and to see that principles like the Monroe Doctrine remained intact. Lowell did not view Article X very warmly. This was remarkable since he had been largely responsible for the platform on sanctions of the League to Enforce Peace, but Lowell believed that Article XVI adequately covered that subject.[9]

Other moderates joined the critics. David Starr Jordan liked the Covenant but discovered weaknesses. William Jennings Bryan announced his support on March 12, 1919, but included suggestions for changes. He wished to

8. Marburg and Flack, *Taft Papers,* pp. 230, 234, 238–239, 244, 276, 291–294.
9. "The Lodge-Lowell Debate," p. 429; Lowell to Root, April 2, 1919, Root Papers; Lowell to Taft, March 28, 31, 1919, Taft Papers; Short to Straus, March 29, 1919 (cablegram) in Miller, *Diary,* VII, 332; Lowell to Allan P. Ames, April 24, 1919; to Kenneth Colgrove, April 28, 1919, Lowell Papers; Bartlett, *League to Enforce Peace,* pp. 123–124.

protect the Monroe Doctrine, gain a greater voting right for the United States, have a broader qualification for membership, and allow each member to decide whether it would accept a mandate or support the decisions of the Council. Bryan concluded that since the Covenant had been drafted in so brief a time, it could not be perfect. A more recent convert to the internationalist cause, George W. Wickersham, also joined the moderates. Wickersham, who had been attorney general under Taft, had one unusual suggestion regarding Article X. Where practical, any action by the League should "be intrusted to that member state which, by reason of the territorial proximity and national interest, is most vitally and directly affected by the threat or danger." He also favored extending the sanction under Article XVI to breaches of Articles XIII, XIV, and XV, in addition to breaches under XII.[10]

The third group of internationalists who supported membership did so with considerable reluctance. Such Republicans as Root and Lodge and Taft's secretary of war, Henry L. Stimson, reflected a cautious attitude. They raised objections to the Covenant because of provisions which disturbed them or because it did not include clauses to safeguard the sovereignty of the United States. They moved warily, however, because the League issue threatened to disrupt their party. Thus they hoped to find a proper formula which most Republicans could accept.

Root emerged as the intellectual leader of this group. The absence of extensive provisions on a court and some of the unqualified references to force disturbed him. In the first place, he did not even like the word "league." Even more, he mistrusted "covenants," which bound future generations to provisions they might not wish to honor. Root did believe by 1919 in some accord to combine nations in a quest for peace, and he even conceded that a proper use of force might be included as part of any union's function. Governments, though, should be left free to determine in each emergency what they wished to do to compel other countries to respect the law.[11]

Root had been consulted by a number of senators even before the Covenant appeared. They wished his views; so too did Wilson and the Republican National Committee. Root responded after February 15, 1919,

10. Jordan to Albert L. Guerard, March 4, 1919, Jordan Papers; Miller, *Drafting,* I, 374–377; Henry W. Taft to Taft, March 18, 1919, Taft Papers.

11. Philip C. Jessup, *Elihu Root,* II, 383–384; Leopold, *Elihu Root,* pp. 133–134; Chandler P. Anderson interview with Root dated December 12, 1918, Anderson Papers; Stimson Diary, December 29, 1918, and March 1, 1919, addenda; Kent G. Redmond, "Henry L. Stimson and the Question of League Membership," *The Historian,* XXV (February 1963), 203–204.

with six "judicious amendments." They would make the treaty acceptable and yet "ensure the development of the rudimentary provisions of this paper into a real League of Peace" in which law and judicial machinery would play a major role. Root suggested to the State Department on March 28 that exclusively domestic matters and the Monroe Doctrine be exempt from the League's authority, that it be authorized to establish an inspection system on armaments, that governments be given a right to withdraw, that the Covenant be subject to revision after five years, and that Article X be considered applicable for a similar period and then dropped or renewed.

Root's most revealing recommendation appeared in his request for a complete rewriting of Article XIII to include detailed provisions for arbitration. He suggested that all disputes including those of vital interest and national honor be referred to the Hague tribunal or, if justiciable, to an international court. He then offered a definition of "justiciable" issues. Any subject involving the "interpretation of a treaty," questions of fact or international law, and the amount of reparations for breaches of the peace would be included. The bodies established to hear cases could decide whether the disputes were justiciable or not. Root's program also included provision for the development of law. He did not agree with men like Taft and Lowell that the articles on the pacific settlement of disputes would work. Nations would not always resort to arbitration, and the Covenant then left them but one recourse. They could ask the Council for a hearing. But the decision would have to be unanimous according to Article XIII. Since Root saw such an outcome as a rarity, he had little confidence in the League's ability to maintain peace.[12]

The chairman of the Republican National Committee, Will H. Hays, believed that Root's amendments provided him with a formula which his party could endorse, and he announced that the Covenant would be approved if Wilson would but heed such suggestions. Root, however, had doubts about the President's response in the light of Root's belief that Wilson had disregarded senators and others who wished to express opinions. Yet despite such a pessimistic outlook, Root hoped that all "friends of a League of Nations" would remain united.[13]

As an admirer of Root and as an attorney, Stimson expressed similar views. He realized that members of his party had a responsibility to suggest changes and that they must be constructive. Stimson felt strongly about the

12. Jessup, *Elihu Root,* II, 385–396; Leopold, *Elihu Root,* pp. 134–136; Root to Charles H. Strong, April 28, 1919, Root Papers; *Drafting,* I, 377–379.
13. Jessup, *Elihu Root,* II, 394; Root to Lowell, April 29, 1919; to Lodge, April 4, 1919, Root Papers.

absence of any mention of the Monroe Doctrine, but Article X alarmed him. He could not see how it could ever be effective. Like Root, he believed in an evolutionary process which would bring a consultative and legal system. With such a philosophy, Stimson could not comprehend why the Covenant failed to mention the Hague Conference of 1907.[14]

Charles Evans Hughes and Henry Cabot Lodge joined their fellow Republicans in their cautious attitudes. Hughes had committed his party to the ideal of a world organization in the campaign of 1916, and he still believed in 1919 that nations should unite. The Covenant would serve the desired purpose if it could be amended. He suggested seven changes, including ones on Article X, the right of withdrawal, the Monroe Doctrine, and domestic questions. Article X, however, troubled him most. He wished a more flexible arrangement which would give each government the right to determine what action it would take in time of crisis. He hoped for revisions to meet his objections because he wished to see the United States in the League.[15]

Lodge did not move as quickly or speak as openly as most Republicans. His belief in a limited type of association and his conviction that the United States should not ratify any treaty which it would not support explain his reluctance to endorse the Covenant. He found it "loose, involved, and full of dangers"; he worried that Article X might lead to the creation of an international army; and he wished guarantees for the Monroe Doctrine and safeguards for vital interests. He reflected his fears of 1911 when he protested against the League's assuming jurisdiction over all questions.[16]

These concerns motivated Lodge when he introduced the famous "Round Robin" statement into the Senate on March 3. Based on a proposal by Senators Frank B. Brandegee of Connecticut and Philander C. Knox, it contained the signatures of thirty-nine Republican senators and senators-elect who thus declared that they could not accept the Covenant in its present form and that they desired a treaty which separated the peace terms from the proposition for a League. This type of challenge, which revealed that the required two-thirds vote would not be possible, simply inspired the internationalists to continue their campaigns for a revised treaty.

14. Henry L. Stimson and McGeorge Bundy, *On Active Service in Peace and War,* pp. 102–104; Stimson to Hays, February 18, 1919 (copy); to Taft, February 20, March 6, 12, 1919, Taft Papers.

15. Merlo J. Pusey, *Charles Evans Hughes,* I, pp. 395–397; Dexter Perkins, *Charles Evans Hughes and American Democratic Statesmanship,* pp. 75–78; Miller, *Drafting,* I, 382–384.

16. Garraty, *Henry Cabot Lodge,* pp. 300, 318, 345–346, 350–352; Lodge to Lowell, February 3, 1917, Lowell Papers; Lodge to A. J. Beveridge, February 18, 1919, Lodge Papers.

Lodge watched closely as Wilson sought revisions in subsequent negotiations at Paris, and he corresponded with Root and other cautious thinkers who proclaimed the need for a revised Covenant. He discreetly refrained, however, from sending Wilson the exact changes he would accept. He may have been naturally cautious, but more probably he resented Wilson's failure to consult the Senate. He believed that the President should have officially requested a slate of amendments from the Senate rather than fish for ideas from individuals. When Henry White cabled from Paris to solicit a detailed statement from Lodge, the latter wrongly suspected a Wilsonian plot. He would not reply because he feared that he might be committed to any changes. Thus, he insisted in vague fashion that domestic issues and the Monroe Doctrine should be protected and that the treaty should be separated from the Covenant. In all his remarks, however, he emphasized again and again that he favored an international organization in which the United States would participate.[17]

Lodge reflected but one view in the Senate. Even on the Democratic side suggestions for revisions appeared. Hitchcock, the retiring chairman of the Foreign Relations Committee, informed Wilson that judicious amendments could influence votes. A reservation on domestic matters, protection of the Monroe Doctrine, a clause on withdrawal, a provision to reject mandates if the United States did not wish any, and minor improvements would allay concerns.[18]

Societies, like individuals, also proclaimed the need for revisions in the Covenant. The League to Enforce Peace circulated the proposed amendments of Taft and Lowell, but its leaders could not agree upon an official slate of changes. Hence, they initially adopted a resolution which asked only for "a more specific reservation of the Monroe Doctrine."[19] The World's Court League did not become involved in the discussions because in February it merged with the New York Peace Society to form the League of Nations Union. The latter took a vague stand by supporting the Covenant while "not irrevocably committed to any particular detail." Since the World's

17. Garraty, *Henry Cabot Lodge,* pp. 353–362; Lodge to Root, March 14, 1919; Lowell to Root, April 2, 1919, Root Papers; L. Ward Bannister to Lowell, April 10, 1919, Lowell Papers; "Joint Debate on the Covenant of Paris [by] Henry Cabot Lodge, A. Lawrence Lowell," *World Peace Foundation Pamphlets* (League of Nations Series), II, (April 1919), 50–51, 55–62, 91–94.

18. Miller, *Drafting,* I, 276–277.

19. Bartlett, *League to Enforce Peace,* p. 124; Allan P. Ames to Taft, March 18, 1919, Taft Papers; *The League Bulletin,* No. 136 (April 26, 1919), p. 399; *Minutes,* Executive Committee, April 10, 1919, Lowell Papers.

Court League had already changed the name of its journal to the *League of Nations Magazine*, the new association actually endorsed the Wilsonian program more than its official statement would imply. It is significant that while the periodical campaigned for acceptance of the League, most of the leaders of the Union did not participate fully in the crusade for ratification in 1919. Such men as Theodore E. Burton, Charles Levermore, Albert Shaw, and John Bates Clark were too dedicated to the judicial concept to be enthusiastic about the Covenant. Two other societies, the League of Free Nations Association and the New York City Bar Association, endorsed a slate of revisions similar to those of Root.[20]

The most interesting proposals for amendments in the weeks after February 15 came from Europe where American internationalists joined with other Delegates of Allied Societies for a League of Nations. They had offered their suggestions to the diplomats at Paris during the drafting of the Covenant, and they reassembled in London on March 11 to seek agreement on a slate of changes. Straus, Holt, Mrs. Andrews, Samuel Gompers, Lynch, and several other Americans participated. Actually, these Americans offered only two resolutions. One called for a clause on freedom of religion; the other sought the protection of properties within nations held by nonnationals. The Americans approved of the other proposals by delegates, however, since most of them received a unanimous vote. These suggested an assembly with greater authority, a court with more power, a relaxation of the unanimity provisions, and a clarification of the disarmament sections. The most ambitious revision appeared in a call for a League with clearly established "legislative, judicial and executive powers."

The greatest controversy arose over Article XVI when the English delegates suggested a change to make it apparent that violators of the Covenant would automatically be at war with all members. The Americans objected. They could accept such only if an additional clause provided that no action could be taken "except in cases where the constitution of any nation is inconsistent with such an undertaking." The issue prompted such heated debate that it was abandoned.[21]

This evidence in the form of actions and statements by individuals and groups indicates that between February 15 and the end of April few internationalists gave the Covenant their unqualified endorsement. Their response

---

20. *Minutes,* Organizational Meetings, February 20, 24, April 23, 1919, SCPC; solicitation letter for members, April 20, 1919, Holt Papers; Root to Frank Polk, April 6, 1919, Root Papers.

21. *Proceedings of the Conferences,* pp. 21–36.

can be readily explained. The statesmen at Paris had not kept them informed; hence, they had been unprepared for what they read. Furthermore, the Covenant contained many provisions which did not reflect internationalist thought. Its limited references to a court system, its neglect of law, and its advocacy of sanctions without safeguards in the form of democratic or judicial processes came as a surprise. It is remarkable that men accepted the Covenant to the degree they did.

Their qualified approval, however, soon became little better than no endorsement at all. The flood of proposed changes created an impression of an improperly conceived instrument. The internationlists might have been able to check such a notion had they agreed upon a slate of amendments, but they seemed unaware of the need for such a step. Root reflected their attitude when he observed that it meant little for them to unite. The statesmen at Paris and subsequently the Senate would decide the matter; the views of citizens would carry little weight whether expressed as individuals or as groups.[22] But Root lost sight of the essential point. The lack of agreement made it appear that the Covenant had more shortcomings than it actually did. The diverse suggestions of the internationalists thus contributed to doubts and strengthened the hands of opponents. In making their proposals for change, they encouraged, if they did not initiate, the strategy which eventually resulted in the Senate's rejection of the treaty.

Not all internationalists approved of the Covenant even with amendments. Emil Beck believed that his original plan far surpassed that of the Paris commissioners because it avoided the subjects in the Covenant which aroused objections and it included safer guarantees. Homer Moore, a New York attorney, prepared a constitution which he considered far better and which contained one distinctive idea: the court, legislature, and members should arrive at a definition of justiciable disputes by a three-fourths vote.[23]

Philander Knox, who had explored the basis of a judicial league in 1910, also opposed the Covenant and, as a senator, fought ratification. Late in 1918, he had called for an organization to be formed after the governments negotiated peace treaties. They should agree to the compulsory arbitration of disputes, erect a court with power to uphold its decrees by military and economic force, and declare that wars should be considered a crime. John Bassett Moore, with his judicially oriented mind, believed the Covenant would perpetuate inequities and be dominated by the major nations. It

22. Root to Charles C. Hyde, April 29, 1919, Root Papers.
23. Beck to Jordan, March 11, 1919, Jordan Papers; Moore to Taft, June 16, 1919, Taft Papers.

would subordinate principles of law and justice to power politics. Furthermore, every violation of the peace would become a world war, and it would destroy traditional policies of the United States, especially the Monroe Doctrine and neutrality.[24]

Another legalist also raised objections. David Jayne Hill feared that the League would lead to the abandonment of Washington's advice on alliances and of constitutional principles. In referring to the plans of Crucé and Sully, Hill noted the need for popular support for any international organization and concluded that the League would never gain this. It had been built upon concepts of power, not on law and justice. Indeed, the Covenant had abandoned those principles.[25]

The American Peace Society and some of the nation's leading liberals also expressed doubts which kept them from fully endorsing the League of Nations. The Society noted a lack of "judicial processes" in the Covenant which made the League "Prussian in its conception and in its dangers." Therefore, the Society continued to support the "Recommendations of Havana."[26] A large number of individual pacifists likewise hesitated despite their earlier advocacy of an international organization. In nearly every instance, they, too, expressed concern over the neglect of law and courts and of the League's essentially undemocratic character. The liberals, best illustrated by the editors of the *New Republic*, labeled the Covenant unjust. With its authoritarian overtones and emphasis on coercion, they found the price of membership too high and turned away.[27]

The vast number of criticisms and suggestions for changes left Wilson little choice but to seek revisions.[28] This was possible since the League of Nations Commission had not yet asked the plenary session to approve its work. In fact, it had solicited the opinions of governments and peoples in

24. Fleming, *United States and the League,* pp. 68–69, 142–146; Megargee, "John Bassett Moore," pp. 299–303.

25. Boston *Herald,* June 21, 1919; Hill, *Present Problems in Foreign Policy,* pp. 1–37, 104–105, 122–129.

26. Edson L. Whitney, *The American Peace Society: A Centennial History,* p. 298; A. D. Call, "American Peace Society's Memoranda," *Advocate of Peace,* LXXXI (March 1919), 100.

27. A. D. Call to Scott, May 14, 1919, CEIP Papers; George A. Finch, "The American Society of International Law," *AJIL,* L (April 1956), 307–308; Charles Forcey, *The Crossroads of Liberalism: Croly, Weyl, Lippmann, and the Progressive Era, 1900–1925,* pp. 289–291.

28. Miller, *Drafting,* I, 354–389, contains summaries of proposals. Miller may have revealed a hostile frame of mind when he entitled this chapter "Further Criticisms." His papers contain penned remarks: "File in Criticisms."

anticipation of amendments. Even so, Wilson faced a difficult situation when he arrived in Paris on March 14 after a brief visit to the United States. Controversial questions were reopened and resolved only after compromises which did not please everyone. Some governments insisted upon additional qualifications, additions, or privileges, all of which taxed Wilson as he faced the demands both of Europeans and critics at home.[29]

By mid-March, the commissioners had assembled the texts of proposed amendments. House, Miller, and Cecil reviewed many of these on March 18, and that evening Wilson joined the group. The results of their decisions appeared on March 20 in a printed draft which contained the changes to be presented. On March 20–21, a subcommittee considered these and other possible improvements sent from neutral governments; the commissioners discussed them March 22–24. A large number of suggestions thus received consideration, and a committee finally tried to compile the ones which the commissioners had liked.[30]

On March 26, the commissioners sought to clarify and approve some of these, and they then sent them to a Committee on Revision. Its members had considerable authority to recast the Covenant in the light of the decisions, and they incorporated new points, changed words, and added a few additional articles. This task and minor alterations and translations took several days; hence, the final version did not gain the approval of the plenary session until April 28. Then, for the first time, the Covenant became an integral part of the Treaty of Versailles.[31]

Did the revised work meet the objections raised in the United States? While perhaps forty substantive changes had been recommended by Americans, only seven of these could be classified as important. The major figures in the episode—Taft, Root, Lodge, Hitchcock, and Hughes—had agreed upon some need for revision on four of these. They included protection for the Monroe Doctrine, the exemption of domestic questions from the League's jurisdiction, a provision for withdrawal, and clarification of the voting procedure in the Council and the Assembly. Article X had disturbed Lodge, Hughes, Root, and others, but not Taft or Hitchcock. Root also wanted some clause to provide for periodic conferences to develop interna-

29. Bonsal, *Unfinished Business*, pp. 144–217; Bailey, *Wilson and the Lost Peace*, pp. 216–218. Bailey cogently observes that if Wilson had allowed more public comment before 1919, he could have been more fully informed at Paris in January. He would then not have had so great a problem in incorporating revisions into a revised draft. *Ibid.*, p. 217.

30. Miller, *Drafting*, I, 276, 279–335.

31. *Ibid.*, I, 336–472.

tional law, while Lodge and Hitchcock had expressed concern over ambiguities.[32]

The revised Covenant revealed that an effort had been made to meet many of the objections. It contained a reference to the Monroe Doctrine in a new Article XXI. Wilson had supported revision on the Doctrine for a reason far different from those of most of the men who had raised the point. They feared that the League might intrude upon what had been an American policy; but Wilson saw the Covenant as an extension of an American principle and wished to include it by name to make nations more aware of that fact. Article X, to Wilson, would assure governments of the same guarantees for independence and territorial integrity that the Doctrine had always provided for Latin American countries.[33] This change, however, still did not satisfy some critics who wished a clearer wording.

A new paragraph in Article XIII provided for the exemption of domestic questions by defining justiciable disputes. Only questions involving "the interpretation of a treaty, as to any question of international law, as to the existence of any fact which if established would constitute a breach of any international obligation" or matters involving reparations could be arbitrated.[34] An additional clause in Article XV noted that where the Council considered issues not settled by arbitration, it would determine if the question, according to international law, lay within the domestic jurisdiction of a nation. Where it so decided, it would refuse to act. If the quarrel endangered the peace, it could refer it to the Assembly which could formulate a report. These clauses, however, did not specifically mention such troublesome points as the tariff and immigration. Critics, therefore, still worried lest the League consider them, especially since the Council and possibly the Assembly could decide what constituted a judicial question. The Senate had objected to delegating such authority to a Council of Conciliation during the debates over the Taft treaties, and that attitude remained alive in 1919.

Provisions for withdrawal appeared in Article I. It allowed a nation to leave after a notice of two years if it had fulfilled its international obligations. This change met some of the objections but left an important point unanswered. Who would decide, the League or the individual government, whether the member withdrawing had fulfilled its obligations?

32. The major changes can be found *ibid.,* I, 393–395, 410–418, 469–472, 495–497.
33. *Ibid.,* I, 322, 325, 336, 338, 442–450, 453–454, 457–460; Baker, *Wilson and World,* I, 326.
34. Miller, *Drafting,* I, 327.

Articles IV and V resolved the issue over voting procedure. They provided for one vote for each government, for one representative on the Council for each nation, and for unanimous decisions on almost all substantive matters. Article XXII indicated that no government had to accept a mandate against its will. Article XVI contained a clause which allowed for the expulsion of members who violated agreements; it also made the amending process easier. Article X remained untouched although partially qualified by the provision on the Monroe Doctrine. No major changes appeared in the sections on the pacific settlement of disputes. The proposed international court did receive a grant of power to render advisory opinions on matters referred to it by the Council or Assembly, a definition of justiciable disputes appeared, and a slightly altered wording in Article XIV clearly established that arbitration would not be compulsory.

The revised Covenant, however, still did not reflect those legal and procedural ideas which most internationalists held. They wanted a court, not in the future, but as an integral part of the League and as its major agency. They wished separate but clearly established bodies to hear different types of controversies, and they wanted a league with power to formulate and codify law. The delegates at Paris, especially the Americans and their advisors, persisted in their exceptionally cautious attitude on these subjects.[35]

The revisions not only continued to subordinate law to sanctions; they actually strengthened the principle of force. Article XI had originally provided that members would "reserve the right to take any action that may be deemed wise and effectual to safeguard the peace of nations." As revised, the first words read that they "shall take" such action.[36] The sanctionists among the internationalists must have been happy with the revised Covenant when they read it for the first time on April 29, but the judicial thinkers could only have been displeased.

Response to the revised Covenant thus varied greatly. Nearly everyone agreed that it had been improved even though individuals persisted in criticizing certain provisions. Even before it appeared in print, reports had indicated what it would contain, and it seemed for a time as if resistance to it in the Senate would not be strong enough to block approval. Observers

35. *Ibid.,* I, 290–292, 300, 328–333, 379–380, 391, 404–406. Miller showed no awareness of the distinction between obligatory and compulsory arbitration. He used the two words interchangeably although he referred to the latter.

36. *Ibid.,* I, 289–290. Efforts by the French to insert a provision for a military staff again met with failure. *Ibid.,* I, 324–325.

in Washington reported that only fifteen votes would be cast against it.[37]

But opposition did continue among the senators, who had legitimate reasons for being critical. Wilson had ignored them in filling the Peace Commission; he had failed to consult them during the drafting of the Covenant. Then, when he did invite members of the relevant Senate and House Committees to the White House on February 26, 1919, he did little to woo doubtful men or allay their concerns. His remarks suggested that he had little regard for their views.[38] By June 1919, a state of belligerency existed between the President and many senators. It reached a climax when Wilson refused to transmit the final version of the Treaty of Versailles to the Senate despite the fact that copies had been printed in Europe and the United States. Wilson, however, felt bound by a Paris agreement that it not be published until signed.

On the other hand, the Senate's opposition cannot be entirely explained in terms of an uncompromising President. Wilson had obtained reasonable changes, and he had conferred with those senators most concerned with the treaty process. But partisanship appeared when Republicans successfully delayed a vote on appropriations in the spring of 1919, thus forcing Wilson to call a special session of Congress which assembled on May 19. Since the results of the election of 1918 determined the composition of this body, it meant that the Republicans controlled the Senate. In organizing the Committee on Foreign Relations, Lodge, now chairman, carefully screened the new members. Most were hostile to the Covenant. They included some men of irreconcilable temperament, like Republicans Hiram Johnson of California and George H. Moses of New Hampshire and Democrat John K. Shields of Tennessee, who opposed membership in any international organization. Since irreconcilables Frank B. Brandegee of Connecticut, William E. Borah of Idaho, Albert B. Fall of New Mexico, and Philander Knox were already on the committee, it meant that seven of the seventeen members were "bitter-enders." Other new additions included men closer to Lodge in their thinking, for Harding and Harry S. New of Indiana wished changes to make the League acceptable. Of the total membership, over half were thus ready to challenge the President's work.

The Senate's attitude toward the Treaty of Versailles was influenced by

37. Bartlett, *League to Enforce Peace*, pp. 126–127; Holt, "The New Covenant," *The Independent*, XCVIII (May 10, 1919), 199–200; Horace Taft to Taft, April 23, 1919; Gus Karger to Taft, April 16, 1919, Taft Papers; Jordan to W. P. Briggs, June 18, 1919, Jordan Papers; Henry Haskell to Edoardo Giretti, April 29, 1919, CEIP Papers.

38. Bailey, *Wilson and the Great Betrayal*, pp. 3–4, 9–15, 49–52, 76, 83–84.

factors other than the provisions of the Covenant. Some men opposed the territorial, economic, and political settlements. Others feared the French Security Treaty, which Wilson had negotiated to placate the French when they failed to obtain positive guarantees in the Covenant for their protection. Also, personal feelings amounting to hatred made it difficult for the participants in the struggle to view the League issue rationally.[39]

The internationalists knew this opposition could thwart their desires. Hence most of them labored with unremitting zeal to maintain opinion favorable to the League. The League to Enforce Peace held a number of "State Ratification Conventions" between May 21 and June 7, sending a special railroad car with Taft, Lowell, and other notables on tour. Additional speakers delivered an average of twelve thousand addresses a day in May. These men believed that the "hour of fate" had struck. They did not question their duty. They abandoned jobs, families, and other commitments, and where they could not contribute their time, they gave their money. Bankers J. P. Morgan and Jacob Schiff and businessmen Charles M. Schwab, Bernard Baruch, Cleveland Dodge, and Edsel Ford each sent checks for five thousand dollars. Edward A. Filene donated five times that amount.[40]

Other propaganda efforts appeared in publications programs. One of these took the form of the "Covenanter" articles by Lowell, George W. Wickersham, and the Taft brothers, William Howard and Henry. In detailed fashion, these men analyzed the provisions of the Covenant as earlier statesmen had explored the Constitution in the *Federalist Papers*. Hundreds of newspapers carried their comments, and the series appeared in pamphlet form on July 1. Another publication presented Taft's speeches and writings on a league.[41]

The League to Enforce Peace also enrolled members in increasing numbers. By the spring of 1919, over three hundred thousand persons, some of them prominent, had joined. They included Wickersham, who had been converted after a trip to Europe in the winter of 1918–1919, and Herbert Parsons, a member of the Republican National Committee, who became vice chairman of the New York State Branch after his release from the army. As early as May 13, he threatened to bolt his party if partisan opposi-

39. *Ibid.*, pp. 7–8, 77–83, 169; Fleming, *The United States and the League*, pp. 205–218.

40. Bartlett, *League to Enforce Peace*, pp. 127–128; Short to Holt, June 19, 1919, Holt Papers; Morgan to Lowell, July 3, 1919, Lowell Papers; *Minutes*, Executive Committee, June 13, 1919, and pledges, LEP Papers.

41. "The Covenanter," *World Peace Foundation Pamphlets* (League of Nations Series), II (June 1919); Marburg and Flack, *Taft Papers*.

tion did not cease. Another member of prominence represented the Democrats. Senator Hitchcock joined the speakers in their ratifying conventions in 1919.[42] He too had been a slow convert. He had opposed the Taft arbitration treaties in 1912, largely because of the provision for a special commission to determine the justiciability of questions. He considered it a "trap" which would embroil the nation "in innumerable international difficulties." He called the agreement un-American and recorded his opposition to any departure "from the old American idea of isolation." By August of 1918, Hitchcock had shifted significantly, and he subsequently played a key role during the treaty fight as Senate minority leader.[43]

The efforts of the League to Enforce Peace helped maintain opinion highly favorable to membership. Support for Wilson may have been waning, but no marked decline occurred concerning the League of Nations. Speakers who reported upon their experiences found, without exception, friendly sentiment. Educational, farm, labor, and religious groups, plus newspapers, women, and Democrats seemed allied on one side. On the other, only Republicans and, to a lesser degree, businessmen appeared to be opposed.[44]

Public attitudes, however, did not determine the course of events in the Senate where the treaty faced a series of delays. A small core of irreconcilables wanted time to warn the people of the dangers involved. A group of "reservationists," nearly all of them Republicans, also endorsed this tactic but for another reason. They wished to make changes or at least add interpretive clauses to clarify certain provisions of the Covenant. Here they could not agree, however, because some of them wished statements to be "strong," and they sometimes spoke in terms of amendments. Another faction wished modifications that would be "mild" and not crippling in their effect. The old issue of prerogative also determined the Senate's response. It wished to act carefully before approving such an important matter.

As chairman of the Foreign Relations Committee and majority leader, Lodge largely determined events. He faced three factions in his party in the form of the irreconcilables and the two reservationist groups. He also considered the political benefits to the Democrats if they could gain approval

42. New York *World*, March 23, 1919; Parsons to W. M. Calder, May 13, 19, 1919; Parsons Papers.

43. *Congressional Record*, 62 Cong., 2d sess., 48, pt. 1:646–648; Hitchcock, "Our New Internationalism," *The Forum*, LX (August 1918), 139–140.

44. Holt, "The People and the President," *The Independent*, XCVIII (June 28, 1919), 476–477; Bailey, *Wilson and the Great Betrayal*, pp. 10, 46–47, 401; Fleming, *The United States and the League*, pp. 218–220; Holt to House, May 2, 1919, House Papers; Arnold B. Hall to E. L. Philipp, May 2, 1919, Philipp Papers.

of the treaty without change. In order to keep the irreconcilables content, Lodge first sought to placate them by insisting on strong reservations, which he preferred. But the moderate Republicans would not support him in sufficient numbers to gain this end. The only answer, therefore, lay in finding some middle ground.[45]

Discussions and debates led in this direction. Root had pointed the way when he suggested the need for changes in the Covenant after the revised version appeared in April. He realized that amendments would not attract much support; therefore, he came forward on June 19 with a proposal to Lodge which outlined four points on which reservations should be demanded. These included the right of withdrawal after two years with no clause requiring the fulfillment of all obligations, statements on the Monroe Doctrine and domestic questions, and a disallowance of Article X. On the last point, Root retreated from his earlier suggestion that Article X be accepted for a five-year period and then reconsidered.[46]

Wilson helped the reservationists on June 27 when he announced from Paris that he opposed amendments since they would require action by the other signatories. He aided Lodge at the same time when he also voiced an objection to reservations. This forced the various factions in the Senate to consider a course of action. Such moderate Republican senators as Charles L. McNary of Oregon, Frank Kellogg, LeBaron B. Colt of Rhode Island, and Porter J. McCumber of North Dakota discussed their dilemma with Lodge, and the latter encouraged them to submit a slate of proposed changes, which they did late in July.[47]

Another factor also contributed to the movement for reservations. As the Senate considered the Covenant and criticisms mounted, some of the advocates outside that body began to worry. Taft, Parsons, Lowell, Wickersham, and other internationalists concluded that, while they preferred acceptance without further revision, they might have to compromise. If the treaty could not be ratified without some qualifications, then they should work for acceptable ones and co-operate with those senators who preferred

---

45. Garraty, *Henry Cabot Lodge*, pp. 361–377; Kendrick, "Republicans and the Treaty," pp. 132–133, 141–143, 145, 173–177, 299.

46. Jessup, *Elihu Root*, II, 397–403; Kendrick, "Republicans and the Treaty," pp. 131–134.

47. Kendrick, "Republicans and the Treaty," pp. 164–170, 182–187; Karger to Taft, July 1, 1919; Charles D. Hilles to Taft, July 11, 1919, Taft Papers; Reed Smoot to Jordan, July 5, 1919, Jordan Papers; Lodge to Root, July 7, 1919, Root Papers; R. M. Boeckel, "The Treaty's Chance in the Senate," *The Independent*, XCIX (July 12, 1919), 39–40, 42.

that course. Taft, Lowell, and other leaders within the League to Enforce Peace first spoke privately about accepting reservations. Then, in the middle of July, Taft drafted a set of conditions which he sent to Will Hays. He also circulated his views to several senators; the press printed them; and the other members of the League to Enforce Peace found themselves in an embarrassing situation. Their organization had taken an unqualified stand against reservations after April 29; now their president seemed to undercut that position. The society insisted that Taft's remarks reflected a personal view, but considerable damage had been done. Men like Holt continued to rail publicly against any alterations, but even he conceded privately that the treaty could not pass without changes.[48]

The reservationists also received encouragement on August 19, 1919, by a statement from Wilson that he would be willing to consider modest interpretive statements if these were added as a separate resolution by the Senate and not included in the vote on the treaty. He had met with twenty-three Republican senators between July 17 and August 1, and many of these men had sensed no great objection to some form of conditional approval. Wilson might not have been willing to compromise to any substantial degree, but his attitude encouraged the moderate Republicans and even led some Democrats, including Claude A. Swanson of Virginia, to confer with the mild reservationists. Sometime in August, however, Wilson became intransigent. Thereafter, he refused to negotiate and thus lost any sympathy the moderates might have had for him or any support they might have given him.[49]

While discussions on reservations proceeded, the Foreign Relations Committee had been considering the treaty. It began its hearings on July 14, and weeks passed as it perused the lengthy document and heard witnesses, many of whom were distinctly hostile. Wilson watched uneasily as this testimony and criticisms of the Covenant raised doubts in the minds of citizens. Therefore, he planned a speaking tour to stimulate popular support. Some of the internationalists had urged such a course upon him for a

48. Bartlett, *League to Enforce Peace,* pp. 143–152; Taft to Hitchcock, July 21, 1919, Hitchcock Papers, Library of Congress; Parsons to Taft, July 1, 1919; Short to Taft, July 15, 1919; Henry Taft to Taft, July 9, 1919; to Hays, July 13, 1919; Lowell to LeBaron Colt, August 1, 1919 (copy), Taft Papers; Kuehl, *Hamilton Holt,* pp. 141–143.

49. Kendrick, "Republicans and the Treaty," pp. 203–205; Stone, "Irreconcilables and the League," p. 204; Karger to Taft, August 11, 1919; Arthur Capper to Taft, July 29, 1919; Francis E. Warren to Taft, November 17, 1919; T. Williams to Taft, October 1, 1919, Taft Papers.

considerable time, but the President had not heeded their advice until necessity demanded action. On September 3, he began the trip on which he covered eight thousand miles before his physical collapse on September 25 in Colorado. In his speeches, he argued that the League would not intrude upon American sovereignty or continually involve the country in wars as some opponents had charged. Article X, he insisted, had to be retained without alteration if the machinery of peace was to work. The League provided the only effective way to prevent war, and membership by the United States was essential to its success.[50]

While Wilson was on tour, the Foreign Relations Committee concluded its work. Three reports appeared on September 10. The majority statement recommended approval, but only after extensive changes, including forty-five amendments and four reservations. A minority declaration by the Democrats suggested consent without any revision. In a separate pronouncement, Senator McCumber castigated the majority recommendation for its hostile and critical attitude and called for ratification with only modest interpretive reservations.

These reports reflected the alignment which had developed. On one extreme, the Wilsonians supported the President in demanding no change. They numbered around forty, with only one Republican, McCumber, openly sympathetic to their position. On the other extreme, a small group of irreconcilables wished rejection. Between them lay the rest of the Senators who favored alterations but who still could not agree upon what they would accept.

The Senate sought to resolve these differences by first considering the amendments and reservations of the Foreign Relations Committee and others introduced during the debates. These touched upon provisions of the peace settlement more than on the Covenant, and the senators rejected them one by one. They failed because it was commonly believed that amendments would require action by the other signatories, and few senators wished to complicate the peacemaking process. Moreover, many of them did not agree with the drastic nature of the proposals. Thus, a bloc of mild reservationists united with the Democrats to kill the amendments. The Senate then turned to a slate of more moderate qualifications presented by Lodge. He had faced a difficult task in obtaining these because he had to keep his Republican factions pacified. He had supported amendments to keep the irreconcilables happy and to force the mild reservationists toward a middle ground where

50. New York *Sun,* March 26, 1919; Holt to House, May 2, 1919, House Papers; Baker and Dodd, *Public Papers, War and Peace,* II, 1–416; Link, *Wilson the Diplomatist,* pp. 140–150.

they would accept provisions stronger than they desired. His fourteen reservations thus represented a compromise between the various groups.[51] They included ideas which Wilson and many internationalists did not like, but they reflected concerns which had been neglected or inadequately expressed in the Covenant.

They covered the subject of withdrawal, noted that the United States should be the sole judge of what action it would take in every instance, and provided that disputes involving purely domestic legislation could not be considered by the League. Others exempted the United States from disarmament agreements under certain conditions and clearly placed the Monroe Doctrine outside the League's jurisdiction. Five indicated that only Congress could determine such matters as mandates, membership in the International Labor Organization, appropriations for the League's expense, and the appointment of representatives and their duties. Two touched on treaty provisions totally unrelated to the Covenant. Of these, the one giving Congress rather than the President the sole power to determine the activities of American representatives was of major import since it challenged the traditional right of the executive department to formulate foreign policy.

Three other reservations also had meaning. One noted no obligation to preserve anyone's territory or political independence. Another further weakened the principle of sanctions by claiming a right to disregard Article XVI insofar as it related to specified "nationals of a covenant-breaking state." A third removed the United States from any responsibility to abide by League decisions where any member through colonies or dependencies had more than one vote. The preamble also contained a highly restrictive item. It called for the approval of all reservations by three out of four of the major powers which had drafted the Covenant.

On November 19, the senators finally voted on the treaty. By a margin of 39 to 55, they rejected membership on the basis of the Lodge reservations. Four Democrats and thirty-five reservationists stood on one side; thirteen irreconcilables and forty-two Democrats cast negative votes. The latter had been told by Wilson to stand firm, and they did. On a vote on the treaty without any changes thirty-seven Democrats and McCumber voted favorably; fifty-three reservationists and irreconcilables opposed membership on that basis. Some eighty percent of the senators had voted to join an interna-

---

51. Fleming, *The United States and the League,* pp. 382–393; Kendrick, "Republicans and the Treaty," pp. 225–227, 252–254; Bailey, *Wilson and the Great Betrayal,* pp. 153–154; Karger to Taft, November 6, 1919; Charles L. McNary to Taft, September 26, 1919; Porter J. McCumber to Taft, October 24, 1919; Taft to Lowell, October 5, 1919, Taft Papers.

tional organization; they could not agree upon the formula on which they would base their participation.

The role of the internationalists in influencing this outcome is not easily analyzed. In the first place, they never coalesced into one group with a consistent statement of aims. This was not surprising; they had never been of one mind upon a program. In 1919, they divided into various groups. If a man's allegiance lay with the Democratic party or if he held advanced views, he favored the treaty without revision. Likewise, anyone internationally inclined who happened to be a Republican or who favored some qualified membership had little recourse save to follow whatever faction expressed his views. A third factor also restricted individual internationalists. By 1919, most had affiliated with an organization. Thus they had little recourse but to support the stated position of their society.

It is interesting to note the efforts of some of the persons long associated with the crusade for a world organization. Despite advancing age, Charles Eliot endorsed the League and, in keeping with his early views on sanctions, wholeheartedly approved the commitments that membership involved. Fannie Fern Andrews devoted all of her energy to writing and lecturing in support of the League without reservations.[52] Lucia Mead had to restrict her activities in order to care for her invalid husband; nevertheless, she campaigned for ratification.

Nicholas Murray Butler acted in a somewhat unexpected fashion. He had always been a generalist who tended toward the judicial approach, and his prewar statements as well as his reluctance to join the League to Enforce Peace should have dictated a cautious attitude toward the Covenant. But Butler endorsed it, albeit with a call for changes, and he aided the mild reservationists in developing their program. Perhaps Butler feared that the Republican party would be accused of defeating the treaty.[53]

Bryan followed a similar path. As an old foe of force, he should have been opposed to Article X. Yet he favored the League, although with "improvements." He believed in "free and frank discussion to perfect" it and added the usual qualifications on the Monroe Doctrine, mandates, and domestic matters.[54]

52. Eliot to Jordan, May 24, 1919, Jordan Papers; to Marburg, June 11, 1919, in Latané, *Development,* II, 643; Mrs. Andrews to Marburg, September 10, 1919, Andrews Papers.

53. Butler, *Across the Busy Years,* II, 197–200.

54. Lawrence W. Levine, *Defender of the Faith: William Jennings Bryan; The Last Decade, 1915–1925,* pp. 134–138.

David Starr Jordan supported the League wholeheartedly. He accepted it with the practical observation that the world could not turn back. He found nothing in the Covenant which violated the Constitution or the Monroe Doctrine. At first he suggested that the Senate approve and then seek what changes it thought would be needed to make the League acceptable and workable; later he agreed to reservations if they would insure the participation of the United States.[55]

Of all the pioneer internationalists, Hamilton Holt labored the most. He lent energy to the League to Enforce Peace, moved across the nation on the lecture trail, and made *The Independent* the most active general periodical favoring the League. Holt had not been pleased with the final Covenant because it still lacked the democratic qualities he desired in an international organization. Moreover, it had still no provision for the codification of law. Holt also preferred an agency with more extensive powers. Yet he publicly defended the Covenant and in discussions in the League to Enforce Peace called for the rejection of all amendments and reservations.[56]

A few pioneers did not rally to the cause. Hayne Davis remained silent until after the vote in November; then he again worked with Holt early in 1920. Raymond Bridgman likewise did not participate actively in the campaign for the League. His health may have been a factor, since he was over seventy years of age. Ginn, Trueblood, and Dutton had died. Poor health kept both Mead and Carnegie from the fray. Bartholdt and McDowell said little as the Senate debated the Covenant, and Oscar Crosby's study appeared too late to influence the debates.

Other early advocates also failed to join the struggle. John Bassett Moore remained hostile, and William I. Hull likewise viewed the Covenant with suspicion. He objected to the way it had been drafted, and he found serious weaknesses in it. As a pacifist, he protested against its emphasis on sanctions, condemned it for failing to take immediate action on disarmament, and found other shortcomings in its undemocratic structure and its limited provisions for a court system. Hull also questioned clauses on the Monroe Doctrine

55. Jordan to H. B. Hawley, March 8, 1919; to C. A. Eggert, May 22, 1919; to Hiram Johnson, June 24, 1919, Jordan Papers; Jordan, *The League of Nations*, pp. 1–4.
56. Kuehl, *Hamilton Holt*, pp. 142–143; New York *Sun*, March 26, 1919. Holt wrote an editorial noting the role he and *The Independent* had played in the development of the League: "The Independent and the Covenant," *The Independent*, XCVIII (May 17, 1919), 235–236.

and mandates, but he essentially feared that the Covenant would foster international instability rather than encourage peace.[57]

One other pioneer did not participate in the debates, yet his name often appeared as various factions claimed that he would have stood with them had he been alive. But had Theodore Roosevelt been living, he would have supported neither extreme faction—the internationalists who wished approval without change or the irreconcilables. His closest friends became reservationists in 1919, and he would have been influenced by Root, Lodge, and Taft. He would have supported reservations on the Monroe Doctrine, on immigration, and quite likely on Article X. It seems unlikely that Roosevelt would have approved of the principle of an armed force as he did in 1910 at Christiania, for he had often expressed the philosophy which made Root an adamant foe of Article X. Nations should not commit themselves to any agreement that they might not be willing to honor in time of crisis. Roosevelt had objected to the Taft treaties on this ground, and he had not changed his views on this point in 1918. Finally, Roosevelt's hostile attitude toward Wilson would have kept him from endorsing membership without some reservations.[58]

The internationalists, as individuals, had little influence in the Senate during the debates, and their organizations likewise failed despite widespread activity, especially in Washington. Divisions over reservations within the League to Enforce Peace nullified its effectiveness. From the time that Taft publicly endorsed ratification with changes, the society faced a split membership. No matter how much Taft argued that the treaty could never be approved without modifications, men like Short and Holt dissented. They had little chance to win, however, for Taft threatened to resign if they repudiated his stand. At a meeting of the Executive Committee on November 13, when Holt moved that they stand for rejection of the treaty rather than accept reservations, the proposal lost by a vote of five to ten.[59]

Hitchcock begged Taft and Lowell to withold any announcement of this vote, but shortly thereafter, the League to Enforce Peace endorsed

---

57. Hull, "The Proposed League of Nations," *Advocate of Peace*, LXXXI (November 1919), 321–323; Megargee, "John Bassett Moore," 300–304.

58. Olson, "Roosevelt's Conception of an International League," pp. 351–353; William H. Harbaugh, *Power and Responsibility: The Life and Times of Theodore Roosevelt*, pp. 516–518.

59. Taft to H. Houston, September 17, 1919; to Karger, September 20, 21, 1919; to A. H. Vandenberg, October 21, 1919; Lowell to Taft, September 20, 1919; *Minutes, Executive Committee*, November 13, 1919, Taft Papers; Lowell to T. Williams, November 7, 1919, Lowell Papers; Bartlett, *League to Enforce Peace*, pp. 148–154.

the Lodge reservations except for the preamble. The society asked that the latter be dropped since it required approval by the major signatories to the treaty.[60] The weakness of the League to Enforce Peace position can be seen in the fact that the senators ignored the recommendation. They had nothing to fear from a body decimated by internal division.

If the major organization of the time proved ineffective, so too did others. Because of inadequate resources the League of Nations Union had to suspend publication of its magazine in July 1919. It had sought unsuccessfully to merge with the League to Enforce Peace, a failure which further illustrates the weaknesses of the internationalists. The League of Free Nations Association did not inject itself into the struggle with great zeal. It endorsed the Covenant but favored reservations. It criticized provisions of the Treaty of Versailles because its liberal and democratically inclined members judged many of its terms to be unfair and unjust. They suggested ratification with a resolution listing specific objections and called for a more democratic league which would not interfere in internal revolutions.[61]

Other groups took an even less active part. The American Peace Society continued its destructive criticism while supporting reservations in ambiguous fashion. It objected most to the provisions for the use of force and to the inadequate judicial machinery. Even as the Senate tallied its votes, the Society suggested that a third Hague Conference convene to create a peace structure based upon principles of justice.[62] The Carnegie Endowment for International Peace took no official stand, but it did publish much literature on internationalism and the peace treaty. The World Peace Foundation likewise operated indirectly through its subsidy and publication program. The English-Speaking Union and the American Rights League took advantage of the popular mood to advance the goal of Anglo-American unity as they supported the Covenant.[63]

---

60. Bartlett, *League to Enforce Peace,* p. 164; Hitchcock to Taft, November 12, 1919; Taft to Karger, November 5, 1919, Taft Papers; Hitchcock to Lowell, November 15, 1919, Lowell Papers; Taft to Hitchcock, November 15, 1919, Hitchcock Papers.

61. Charles H. Levermore to M. Alice Mathews, November 24, 1919 (copy), CEIP Papers; League of Free Nations Association to Wilson, June 9 (copy of cablegram); James G. McDonald to Jordan, August 6, 1919, Jordan Papers; printed statements and form letter to members, June 30, September 17, November 11, 1919, SCPC.

62. "The Popular Control of the League," *Advocate of Peace,* LXXXI (August 1919), 239–240; "As to Reservations," *ibid.,* (July 1919), pp. 208–209; "Our Course as to the Treaty," *ibid.,* (September and October 1919), pp. 275–276; "Our Way Out— A Conference of the Nations," *ibid.,* (November 1919), pp. 307–309.

63. George Finch to Jonathan Bourne, July 23, 1919, CEIP Papers; Conference Number 16, Council on Foreign Relations, July 25, 1919, Shaw Papers; Septimus, "A

Religious bodies played a more prominent role during the ratification controversy than did the older peace organizations. The Church Peace Union continued to support the work of the World Alliance for International Friendship and of the Committee on the Churches and the Moral Aims of the War. Their concern was not so much over how the United States should join as to see that it did join. The Federal Council of Churches also participated. It sponsored meetings, underwrote speaking tours, and flooded ministers with pamphlets. The results appeared in an almost universal endorsement of the League by the major Protestant denominations, their clergymen, and their journals.[64]

The most interesting aspect of the work of these League supporters, whether as individuals or organizations, can be found in the arguments they developed and the methods they employed to gain a hearing. They relied primarily upon the spoken and written word, and they passed through three phases. At first, they sought to explain and clarify the provisions of the Covenant; later they tried to defend it against the onslaughts of the irreconcilables and other critics; finally, they had to take a stand and either defend or reject reservations.

In the first two periods, the internationalists employed logic and common sense. They noted the need for some world organization and warned that the nation should no longer heed George Washington's advice about permanent alliances. Times and conditions had changed, and no amount of wishful thinking or blind attachment to the past would change that reality. They also defended the Covenant. The League would be no "super-state"; membership would involve no great sacrifice of basic powers; reservations should be considered only to the degree that they did not cripple the League.[65]

The internationalists also praised the Covenant as an outstanding achievement of mankind with a minimum number of shortcomings. Further-

---

Sound League of Nations," *English-Speaking World* (June 1919); Roosevelt and George Haven Putnam, "An Alliance of the English-Speaking Peoples of the World," and Putnam and L. F. Abbott, "The Treaty of Peace and the League of Nations," *American Rights League Bulletins,* No. 44 (July 1919), and 47 (August 1919).

64. Robert Moats Miller, "The Attitudes of the Major Protestant Churches in America Toward War and Peace, 1919–1929," *The Historian,* XIX (November 1956), pp. 15–23.

65. [Holt], "Reductio ad Absurdum," *The Independent,* XCVIII (May 31, 1919), 308; Holt, "What Is This Treaty of Peace?," *ibid.,* XCIX (July 12, 1919), 49–50; Henry Holt, "The Scheme Proposed," *Unpopular Review,* XI (April–June 1919), 268–270; Dwight W. Morrow, "The Relation of the Covenant to Recent International Cooperation," *Proceedings,* Academy of Political Science, VIII (July 1919), 361, 369–371.

more, it reflected American aims. They reminded people that plans and organizations had been developing for nearly a century. They noted that Republicans had been far more active than Democrats in advancing internationalist thought. Such men as Roosevelt and Taft, with their work on behalf of the Second Hague Conference and arbitration, had contributed as much to the movement as Wilson and his party. Shortly before the Senate began its debates, some discussion ensued over the possibility of a Republican's rising to remind members of his party that they had a tradition and responsibility to support the League of Nations.[66]

Perhaps the most rational case, however, lay in the claim that the American people wanted membership in the League. The internationalists had sufficient evidence on this point, but they relied primarily upon the resolutions by state legislatures. By the middle of 1919, thirty-two had recorded their endorsement.[67] While most of these, in wording, approved an ideal rather than the specific provisions of the Covenant, they did reflect an overwhelming sentiment which kept senators aware of their responsibilities.

Among other rational arguments, the pro-League spokesmen resorted to a historical comparison between discussions over accepting the Covenant with those over the ratification of the Constitution. They noted that in 1789 the "people" had triumphed over obfuscation and the tactics of delay. The internationalists also sought to expose inconsistencies in the arguments of men who raised objections to the Covenant. They found Root an inviting target because of his great reputation. When he shifted on Article X and called for its elimination, they quickly noted that he had originally endorsed it with a reservation restricting its application to a specified time period.[68]

As the struggle moved into the later phases of the debate and the assault on the Covenant increased, the internationalists injected irrational and emotional arguments into their discussions. They branded their opponents as immoral and dishonest men. Blind partisanship, they claimed, had determined the course of certain Republicans. Many of the reservationists, they charged, did not wish to correct weaknesses but to destroy the Covenant. They also played upon patriotic sentiments by suggesting that the League would fulfill the wartime goal of a warless world. American soldiers

66. John F. Moors, "The President at the Peace Conference," *The Public*, XXII (July 26, 1919), 796–797; Holt, "The League or Bolshevism," *The Independent*, XCVIII (April 5, 1919), 3–4; [Holt], "Republican Contribution to the Covenant," *ibid.*, (May 24, 1919), p. 275; Frederick Lynch to Taft, April 25, 1919, Taft Papers; Lowell to W. Murray Crane, April 22, 1919, Lowell Papers.

67. Bartlett, *League to Enforce Peace*, p. 130.

68. *The Constitution Weathered the Storm*; Oscar Straus, *Mr. Root and Article X.*

had died for this dream, and the Senate should not repudiate them or the nation's aims. They further cautioned that if the United States refused to join the League, Europe and the world would turn again to armaments, alliances, anarchy, and secret diplomacy which would bring war in another generation. In seeking support for this last claim, some of the internationalists flagrantly appealed to European political leaders for statements to support their catastrophic prediction.[69]

The most emotional argument, however, centered around the growing fear of bolshevism. Following the Russian revolution of 1917, the threat of communism seemed real to many people. The advocates of the League took advantage of this hysteria to present Wilson's creation as a bulwark against the spread of unorthodox ideas. It would stabilize Europe, strengthen governments there, and thus block the bolshevists from achieving their avowed aim of world domination. The United States would have to be a member to make the League strong enough to achieve this end.[70]

These arguments, logical and emotional, had some effect on public opinion during the League fight, even though they did not influence the vote in the Senate. The American people continued to favor membership despite doubts raised by reservationists and irreconcilables. The internationalists may have been neophytes in the political arena, but in the field of winning converts they had had considerable experience.

One can imagine the disappointment which the internationalists felt at the Senate's failure to approve the treaty. Some of them vented their ire upon Wilson. Taft and Root believed that had the President accepted reservations, the Senate would have voted favorably and the nation would have joined the League. Taft also reflected the disdain many men felt toward Lodge. If he as well as Wilson had not been so vain, selfish, egotistical, and "lacking in real, broad, tolerant patriotism, and self-sacrifice" the results would have been different. Jordan considered Lodge to be "the most detestable character in public life." Most of the advocates, however, looked

---

69. [Henry Holt], "En Casserole: The League of Nations," *Unpartizan Review,* XII (July–September 1919), 200; Moorfield Storey, "Why the Treaty Should be Ratified," Boston *Herald,* July 2, 1919; Holt, "What Is This Treaty of Peace?" pp. 49–50; E. Venizelos, "Why We Need the League of Nations," *The Independent,* XCVII (March 22, 1919), 404–405; Holt, "Burning Down the House to Roast the Pig," *ibid.,* XCVIII (June 21, 1919), 436–437; Samuel M. Lindsay to Straus, August 13, 1919, Straus Papers.

70. Holt, "The League or Bolshevism," pp. 3–4; Gilbert Hitchcock, "The League or Bolshevism? We Must Choose," *The Independent,* CIII (August 28, 1920), 235, 259; Marburg and Flack, *Taft Papers,* p. 273. All of these devious arguments can be found in the speeches of senators supporting the League. Wilson also used some of them.

beyond personalities. They found the answer in a narrowness of mind which had prevented compromise. Forty-five of them, including Eliot, Holt, Lowell, Marburg, Short, Taft, Wickersham, and William A. White, signed a full-page advertisement, which appeared in many newspapers, appealing for a new outlook. Senators should forget their intransigence, reject partisanship, and try again.[71]

This statement reflected the desire and strategy of most internationalists. They wished to see the Senate reconsider the subject, and they embarked upon a campaign to obtain ratification with a set of acceptable reservations. There seemed to be widespread popular agreement after November 19 that only on that basis could the treaty be approved. But the spirit of compromise had not as yet appeared in Washington. Wilson and his loyal bloc of senators held firm, and most reservationists and irreconcilables felt no need for genuine compromise.

The League to Enforce Peace, the League of Free Nations Association, and other societies thus embarked upon a new campaign. First, they sought to arouse the American people and in this way compel the Senate to reconsider the treaty. They launched appeals in the form of broadsides, articles, editorials, speeches, and prayers, all of which called for agreement. Second, they approached senatorial leaders on both sides. They particularly sought the elimination of the irreconcilables from discussions, since the latter had helped write the Lodge reservations. Only the true friends of the League should draft the qualifications, for only they could arrive at a reasonable formula acceptable to all supporters of the Covenant. The President would then be forced to accept their handiwork.[72]

For a few weeks it appeared that an agreement could be reached. Hitchcock sounded out the leading Republican reservationists, reported to Wilson, and drafted a slate of revisions. Finding the President agreeable at first, he began to negotiate for provisions which represented a "reasonable compromise." He insisted, however, that the Republicans initiate proposals, for

---

71. Taft to Horace Taft, November 26, 1919; to Casper Yost, November 27, 1919; to M. S. Sherman, November 27, 1919, Taft Papers; Jordan to Lucia Mead, December 8, 1919, Jordan Papers; Root to George Gray, December 1, 1919, Root Papers; Frederick Hale to Raymond Calkins, December 2, 1919, Lowell Papers; Springfield (Mass.) *Republican,* December 5, 1919.

72. Bailey, *Wilson and the Great Betrayal,* pp. 225–226; Bartlett, *League to Enforce Peace,* p. 172; Macfarland, *Pioneers for Peace,* pp. 73–76; Holt, "Compromize," *The Independent,* CI (January 10, 1920), 59, 74; Hayne Davis, "A Solution Of Our Treaty Tangle," *ibid.,* (January 24, 1920), pp. 127–129, 153–154; "Is There A Way Out?" *Advocate of Peace,* LXXXII (February 1920), 40–42.

Wilson believed it would be a strategic mistake for the Democrats to say what they would accept.[73]

There is doubt concerning the degree to which Wilson knew of these compromise efforts or the spirit with which he entered into them. He still felt the effects of his illness and was shielded from unnecessary business. Hence, the success of the internationalists to reach and influence him is not fully known. Many prominent persons sought to persuade him to accept reservations. Colonel House and such Republicans as Senator Atlee Pomerene of Ohio sent pleas to him, but Wilson did not heed such messages if he saw them. The initial hope that he would co-operate faded when a statement from the White House on December 14 announced that the opposition should formulate the reservations, that the Democratic senators should stand firm, and that under no circumstance could there be a compromise on Article X. On January 8, Wilson blamed the Senate for the deadlock and insisted that the United States accept the treaty "without changes which alter its meaning." If it did not do so, the election of 1920 would be a "great and solemn referendum" on the issue.[74]

Meanwhile, Lodge, too, held a precarious position as he felt pressures from the pro-League factions. He still faced a divided party since the mild reservationists would not allow him to forget the treaty and the irreconcilables wished to avoid any reconsideration. Both sides issued ultimatums which placed Lodge between them. He had initially agreed to a bipartisan conference after the Senate reconvened on December 1, and from January 15 to 30, 1920, discussions were held off the floor. The senators reached accord on several points; but when they came to Article X, negotiations collapsed. Various reasons have been ascribed for the failure, including statements by Lord Grey that Britain would accept reservations and the threat of the irreconcilables to bolt their party if Lodge compromised. Also, both sides had utilized the negotiations to strengthen their own position. The Democrats hoped to divide the Republicans by finding reservations acceptable to some senators but not to others. The Republicans thought

73. Hitchcock to Wilson, November 22, 24, 1919, Wilson Papers; to E. Cummings, December 17, 1919 (copy), Lowell Papers; Hitchcock, "The Administration and The Treaty," *The Independent*, C (December 20, 1919), 233; Bailey, *Wilson and the Great Betrayal*, pp. 226–229.

74. House to Wilson, November 24, 27, 1919, Seymour, *Intimate Papers*, IV, 509–511; Pomerene to Wilson, November 28, 1919; Mrs. Wilson to Hitchcock, December 19, 1919, Wilson Papers; House to Lowell, January 1, 1920, House Papers; "The President, the Senate, the People, and the Treaty," *Advocate of Peace*, LXXXII (January 1920), 28–29.

that by being co-operative they could erase any public impression that they had followed obstructionist tactics during the League fight. If they could find a new slate of reservations which Wilson would not accept, then the onus of rejection would fall on him.[75]

While Wilson may have been willing to accept many of the agreements drafted during the bipartisan discussions, he would have balked at any statement that qualified Article X. It is doubtful that he would have agreed to any change on that point which Lodge would have accepted. The effort to compromise, therefore, had no chance of success.

It is notable that during these efforts, the internationalists united for the first time during the treaty fight. Representatives of twenty-six societies favoring membership in the League sought to co-ordinate their work by sending delegates to conferences in Washington on January 13 and February 9. Labor, educational, religious, farm, and women's groups joined with the established agencies to plan a course of action. Their delegates discussed the situation with Lodge and Hitchcock and other key figures and later issued an open letter to the President and the Senate urging ratification with compromise reservations. They claimed to represent fifty million people who wanted the United States in the League and who could not understand why a few fine points in wording in the proposed reservations should abort that desire.[76]

Individuals also continued their efforts as new advocates and groups appeared. Fannie Fern Andrews formed a Massachusetts Non-Partisan Save-the-Treaty Committee, and the National Council of Women created a Committee on Permanent Peace. Friends and foes of the treaty found their mails flooded with literature and letters from such organizations and from the New York realtor Samuel Colcord, who conducted an almost one-man crusade on behalf of the League.[77]

Many of these persons again embarked upon lengthy speaking tours and conducted polls to measure the depth of public opinion early in 1920. Their samples revealed a strong sentiment favorable to membership but

75. Bailey, *Wilson and the Great Betrayal,* pp. 228–239, 401–402; Stone, "Irreconcilables and the League," pp. 267–271, 290–291; Lodge to J. T. Williams, February 2, 1920, Lodge Papers; Garraty, *Henry Cabot Lodge,* pp. 383–389; Fleming, *The United States and the League,* pp. 405–412.

76. *Minutes,* Conferences of January 13, February 9, 1920, Lowell Papers.

77. Anna G. Spencer, "Women and the Peace Treaty," *Advocate of Peace,* LXXXI (December 1919), 359–360; Mrs. Andrews to Lucy S. Patrick, December 12, 1919, Andrews Papers; Colcord to Parsons, December 17, 1919, Parsons Papers; New York *World,* December 30, 1919; Philadelphia *Public Ledger,* November 21, 1919.

considerable diversity on how such should be effected. A referendum on 410 college campuses showed that of 158,078 students and faculty members, 61,494 approved of some compromise and 48,232 wished to accept the treaty without change. The Lodge reservations received the support of 27,970, 13,943 hoped to see the League rejected, and 6,449 thought that a new treaty should be drafted. Another group polled showed 11,096 ministers in favor of the Covenant and 816 opposed. Several newspapers surveyed their readers. The returns from fourteen dailies in ten states showed 48 percent for membership without alterations, 35 percent for some compromise, "10 per cent. for the Lodge reservations, and 7 per cent." for rejection. Holt recorded the opinion of audiences he addressed in the winter of 1919–1920 and reported that less than 10 percent supported the irreconcilable or strong reservationist position. Robert Ely, the director of the League for Political Education in New York City, queried one of his audiences and discovered 765 persons in favor of compromise, 109 for ratification with the Lodge qualifications, 31 supporting membership without change, and 16 against joining the League.[78]

Despite their obvious shortcomings, these polls indicate that the people wished the Senate to vote again, and the public mood influenced events after January. The Republicans carefully weighed the impact of another rejection or of inaction on the electorate and concluded that it would be best to move and perhaps avoid the issue in the presidential campaign that fall. A spirit of moderation prevailed in the Republican camp early in February, and on the ninth of that month the Senate voted to reconsider the Treaty of Versailles.[79]

On the other hand, the work of the internationalists in showing a strong current of public opinion favorable to the League possibly backfired. It may have convinced Wilson that he should not compromise and moved him to consider a popular referendum on the issue. Late in 1919 and early in 1920, he pondered whether to challenge those senators who had opposed the treaty without reservations to resign and seek re-election. If most of them returned, he would appoint a Republican as secretary of state, he and

78. New York *Times,* January 17, 24, 1920; Short to Holt, January 23, 1920, Holt Papers; W. O. Hart to Mrs. Andrews, December 29, 1919, Andrews Papers; Waterbury (Conn.) *American,* March 9, 1920; New York *Evening Mail,* February 16, 1920; Bailey, *Wilson and the Great Betrayal,* p. 401.

79. Henry W. Rose to Parsons, January 26, 1920 (form letter of Republican National News Service Bureau), Parsons Papers; Taft to Karger, February 7, 1920, Taft Papers.

his Vice President would resign, and the new cabinet officer would then assume the presidency.[80]

Certainly in the ensuing weeks no new spirit of compromise appeared either from the White House or from Lodge. A feeling of hopelessness descended upon the internationalists as they again watched a stalemate develop. It had appeared at one point as if Democratic senators might drift to the reservationist position, but that dream disintegrated when Wilson summarily discharged Robert Lansing as secretary of state. This assertion of leadership, not directly related to the treaty fight, convinced Hitchcock that approval with reservations would be futile. Why send Wilson a qualified treaty if he would not accept it?[81]

Thus, even before the final vote, the internationalists lost hope. Enough Democrats stood with Wilson to block approval with reservations, and the reservationists held sufficient votes with those of the irreconcilables to prevent favorable action on the unaltered treaty. The senators first accepted fifteen reservations of the Foreign Relations Committee; then, on March 19, with these added, they cast their ballots. The two-thirds rule required the support of fifty-six senators. Forty-nine stood for the proposition; twenty-three stalwart Democrats upheld their President and voted with twelve irreconcilables against acceptance with reservations. Several Democrats deserted Wilson but not enough.

The internationalists surveyed their defeat with despair. The League of Nations had begun that January without the United States, and chances seemed slim that the Senate would again consider the matter. The internationalists had seen their dream come true, but it was a hollow victory as long as their nation refused to participate in the agency they had done so much to create.

---

80. The Wilson Papers contain mounted newspaper clippings reporting results of polls which Wilson followed. Kurt Wimer, "Woodrow Wilson's Plan for a Vote of Confidence," *Pennsylvania History,* XXVIII (July 1961), 279–293, contains a full analysis of the plan.

81. Karger to Taft, February 5, 20, 1920, Taft Papers; Report of "Conference with Senator Hitchcock," February 29, 1920, Holt Papers; R. M. Boeckel, "Congress, the People and the President," *The Independent,* CI (February 28, 1920), 316; Bailey, *Wilson and the Great Betrayal,* pp. 245–260.

Utopia
or Hell

Since the internationalists did not like the verdict of the Senate on March 19, 1920, they immediately adopted a "Utopia or Hell" philosophy. They argued that the League with the United States as a member would succeed and peace would reign; without the United States it would fail and wars would plague mankind. Their claim eventually influenced the thinking of generations of Americans and even permeated historical writing. Few if any scholars have applauded the defeat of the treaty; they have generally assumed, as did the internationalists, that the Senate's action did irreparable harm to the world.

Historians, therefore, have asked what went wrong, and most of them have concentrated on individuals in trying to discover an answer. Here, those internationalists who castigated Lodge and viewed him as the arch-villain of the episode subsequently saw their interpretation adopted by many historians. They assumed that Lodge was at heart an irreconcilable, that he resorted to subterfuge because a direct challenge to the Covenant would have alienated voters and harmed the Republican party, that he succeeded remarkably well in clouding the issues by insisting upon reservations, and that he thus divided the Senate into factions which immobilized it. Lodge, they also presumed, hated Wilson and knew his temperament. He realized that the President would not compromise and accept certain reservations, and he could, therefore, count upon Wilson's intransigence to contribute to the defeat.[1]

Members of the League to Enforce Peace suspected early in 1917 that Lodge would never be friendly to any plan which came from Wilson. When the proposition to separate the treaty and the Covenant, largely fathered by Knox but supported by Lodge, appeared, the *New Republic* branded this postponement as "a proposal to kill the project forthright. That Senator Lodge understands very well." Later, as Lodge became more reluctant to endorse a postwar organization, the League to Enforce Peace leaders grew concerned. Taft feared that Lodge, with his vanity, conservatism, partisanship, and hatred of Wilson, would block ratification. Holt charged that the entire purpose of adding reservations was "not to change, but to defeat the treaty." By December of 1919, Short concluded on the basis of his conversations and correspondence that people everywhere were blaming Lodge as "the great obstructionist, the center of opposition, the mobilizer of the enemies of the treaty."[2]

Even some of Lodge's Republican colleagues in the Senate who favored ratification came to suspect his motives. Kellogg observed as early as July of 1919 that Lodge's "sympathies are with the insurgents, who wish to beat everything." And Kellogg in August perceived one element of the strategy which eventually appeared. He surmised that many Republican senators might kill the proposed reservations "in the hope that enough will vote against the treaty without amendments or reservations and defeat it." Senator Colt also deduced that the Republican leaders seemed "to be determined to kill the whole Treaty." The Wilsonians, of course, also referred to senators who "favor or pretend to favor" the League and noted a "concealed purpose" on their part.[3]

Many observers outside the Senate came to believe that Lodge hoped "to defeat the treaty entirely," and that he was "bent on killing it by indirec-

---

1. Bartlett, *League to Enforce Peace*, pp. 146, 161, 210–214; Fleming, *The United States and the League*, pp. 307, 475–476, 481; Holt, *Treaties Defeated*, pp. 260–266.

2. W. H. Mischler to G. Nasmyth, February 3, 1917 (copy), Taft Papers; "The War Against Peace," *New Republic*, XVII (December 28, 1918), 241; Taft to Horace Taft, February 18, May 5, 1919, January 2, 1920; to Marquis Eaton and to Sidney Shepard, September 14, 1919; Short to Taft, December 8, 1919, Taft Papers; Holt, "Defeat the Reservations," *The Independent*, XCIX (September 27, 1919), 442.

3. Kellogg to Butler, July 29, 1919, Butler Papers; to Taft, August 20, 1919, Taft Papers; Colt to Root, September 2, 1919, Root Papers; Hitchcock to Wilson, November 22, 1920 [1919], Wilson Papers; J. S. Williams to Hitchcock, January 9, 1920, Hitchcock Papers.

tion."[4] The Washington correspondent of *The Independent* even reported that during the final negotiations over reservations Lodge ended the discussions when he "arranged a new 'ultimatum' from the Irreconcilables." Before the March vote, Root became alarmed over the popular impression that the reservationists were "not sincere in their purpose to ratify the Treaty." Voters were quite familiar with the strategy of killing measures by indirection, and he feared the impact upon his party.[5]

The reaction of many internationalists in blaming Lodge, however, may well reveal their own frustration rather than an ulterior motive on his part. As a man of conviction and principle, Lodge often let issues determine his decisions. He had supported many Wilsonian policies prior to 1919, including the declaration of war and most of the subsequent wartime measures. Personal hatred may have existed, but it did not affect his actions then. Moreover, Lodge's record as a senator and statements during the treaty debates indicate that partisanship did not always determine his stand on foreign policy issues. He had been a man of conviction first and a Republican second when he opposed treaties by Republican presidents, including the first Hay-Pauncefote agreement in 1900 and when he had insisted upon changes in the Roosevelt and Taft arbitration accords in 1904–1905 and 1911–1912. Lodge often observed that he considered the League question to be a matter of such momentous import that he would never "for reasons of party expediency modify the honest views which I have upon it." Partisanship did exist; Lodge realized that Wilson and his party could be discredited on the League issue; but he did not plot his course solely because of those factors.[6]

Lodge's statements clearly reveal his "honest views," and he uttered them often both publicly and privately. He was not an irreconcilable but a conservative internationalist. He should be ranked as a legalist, but even here he assumed a cautious stand. He endorsed the prewar voluntary system of co-operation and raised no objection to it if "as well put as it can be." A

4. Moorfield Storey to Lowell, September 12, 1919, Lowell Papers; M. E. Driscoll to Parsons, February 24, 1920, Parsons Papers; F. P. Powers to editor, *Unpartizan Review*, XIII (January–February 1920), 204.

5. R. M. Boeckel, "Playing Politics," *The Independent,* CI (March 13, 1920), 396; Root to Kellogg, March 13, 1920, Root Papers. Lodge later defended his actions in *The Senate and the League of Nations.*

6. Garraty, *Henry Cabot Lodge,* documents Lodge's views toward Wilson, pp. 296–297, 300, 312–313, 336–340; Holt, *Treaties Defeated,* pp. 206n, 233–234; Lodge to Lowell, November 29, 1918, Lowell Papers; to Calvin Coolidge, February 24, 1919, Lodge Papers.

reconstructed Hague arrangement "if properly guarded and in exact accord with our feelings" would be acceptable. The Covenant came nowhere near

what many of us had in mind when we talked of Leagues of Peace where international law was to be developed and the great feature was to be a strong international court to interpret and lay down the law and behind which the nations were to stand. The court has almost disappeared; international law, I think, is hardly mentioned; and the thing has turned into a plain political alliance.[7]

Despite his nation's involvement in war and the enlargement of its international responsibilities, Lodge had not progressed in his thinking. He may have referred to an effective court, but he still wished in 1919 to exempt domestic questions from its jurisdiction, which placed him in a position comparable to the one he held during the debates over the Taft treaties.[8]

With such beliefs, Lodge found "great dangers" in the League. He feared it as an armed alliance which could control the forces of the United States and interfere in domestic affairs. It would breed misunderstandings and possibly wars. The revised Covenant, he concluded, remained as loosely worded as the first draft despite some improvements.[9] While he initially preferred amendments to correct those weaknesses, he finally accepted the reservation method when he became convinced that it would safeguard the interests and independence of his nation just as well.

Again and again, he reiterated one basic point. "All I want to do is to save the United States. If we can take the United States out by reservations my purposes are fulfilled." The reservations "will simply take us out and make the United States safe."[10] They should "take the United States out of the treaty entirely on all the points where we wish to refuse obligations." "I am seeking to . . . release us from the obligations which might not be kept and preserve rights which ought not to be infringed."[11] Lodge thus not only insisted upon specific reservations but also added the preamble which required the assent of other governments to all changes.

7. Lodge to W. Sturgis Bigelow, January 29, 1919; to A. J. Beveridge, December 3, 1918, January 30, February 18, March 8, 21, 1919, Lodge Papers.
8. Lodge to Henry White, May 10, 1919; to John T. Morse, June 7, 1919, Lodge Papers.
9. Lodge to Beveridge, July 16, 1918, January 30, 1919; to John T. Morse, February 20, 1919; to Bryce, March 4, 25, 30, May 27, 1919; to Root, April 29, 1919, Lodge Papers.
10. Lodge to Root, July 7, September 3, 29, 1919, Root Papers; to W. S. Bigelow, July 19, 1919.
11. Lodge to L. A. Coolidge, August 7, 1919; to John T. Morse, August 18, 1919, Lodge Papers.

While Lodge did not have perfect control over the situation in the Senate during the drafting of the revisions, the final results satisfied him. The internationalists in the Senate and those outside like Taft may have softened the reservations, but Lodge did not complain. He accepted them because he believed they still protected those interests he wished to uphold.[12] His comments on the reservation on Article X reveal his conviction that the obligations involved had been effectively nullified. He refused to accept any change during the compromise sessions which would alter its intent; and he had the assurance of Hughes, Root, and other authorities that the wording "cut out every possibility of obligation."[13]

Thus Lodge, while hostile to the Covenant, did not wish to see the treaty defeated, especially through a frontal assault. He realized that such tactics would not succeed, that the Republicans should not inherit the blame for any rejection, and that membership could be assumed with proper safeguards. Recent scholars have moved far enough away from the stereotyped portrait of Lodge drawn by the internationalists that they have more recently acquitted him of the most devastating charges leveled against him.[14]

But in reassessing Lodge, historians have inevitably turned to examine his opponent in the struggle. Wilson, too, had aroused the ire of the internationalists, but they tended to be more forgiving in his case because he had adopted their cause. He had certainly been a frustrating factor, however.

In the first place, he had greatly hindered their work between 1915 and 1919 by insisting that they restrict their activities and planning. Secondly, he virtually ignored them. The Wilson Papers disclose only a cursory correspondence with them; hence, none of them influenced him directly, and he refused to approach them. He did acknowledge on rare occasions their support in the struggle, but he still chose his own path.[15]

Wilson also contributed greatly to the division in the ranks of the internationalists because they rarely knew whether to follow him or their own convictions. He never assumed charge of the organized forces favoring ratification, nor did he co-operate with them in any united campaign. This would have been a more logical approach to the people in 1919 rather than his speaking tour. He could have had the strength of several societies behind

12. Lodge to Bryce, December 2, 1919, Lodge Papers; to Root, March 6, 13, 1920; Kellogg to Root, March 12, 1920, Root Papers.

13. Lodge to L. A. Coolidge, February 11, March 17, 1920; to Root, March 6, 1920, Lodge Papers.

14. Bailey, *Wilson and the Great Betrayal,* pp. 278–279; Garraty, *Henry Cabot Lodge,* pp. 377–390.

15. Chan, "American Agitation," p. 104.

him to keep enthusiasm high in communities after he had departed. The League to Enforce Peace specials went one way; Wilson's train went another. Furthermore, Wilson's lack of co-operation with the internationalists, combined with his uncompromising position during the Senate debates, eventually antagonized many of the pro-League advocates. Ratification, Taft complained, would come "in spite of Wilson and not by reason of his aid." He referred to the President as that "mulish man in the White House." Wilson, Kellogg plaintively observed, "is doing more to defeat this treaty than any other man in the United States."[16]

A number of recent scholars have echoed those sentiments. Indeed, they have shifted much of the blame from Lodge's shoulders to Wilson's. They have emphasized his intransigence, possibly aggravated by illness and isolation, his hatred for Lodge, and his natural temperament to stand and fight. Had he compromised, they declare, had he accepted the Lodge reservations or released the Democratic senators to vote according to their convictions, the treaty would have been ratified and the United States would have joined the League.[17]

Such conclusions, however, are based upon precarious assumptions, most of which the internationalists helped mold. The first one implies that it was far better to have a League with the United States as a member even if limited in its actions than to have an association weakened by the absence of the nation. This "Utopia or Hell" attitude presumes that the League would have been more effective with the United States as a member and that history might have been different, at best a questionable conclusion.

A more important assumption by certain scholars is that the reservations had little meaning—that if Wilson had let the Senate have its way the qualifications would have had only limited effect on the government's policies toward the League.[18] This was a doubtful claim in 1920, and it remains so. In the first place, certain reservations specifically designated Congress as

16. David H. Jennings, "President Wilson's Tour in September, 1919: A Study of Forces Operating During the League of Nations Fight," p. 202; Henry W. Taft to Taft, June 9, 1919; Taft to Mrs. W. A. Edwards, September 16, 1919; Kellogg to Taft, September 25, 1919; Taft to Horace Taft, March 8, 1920, Taft Papers; Lowell to Lodge, February 1, 1917, Lowell Papers.

17. John M. Blum, *Woodrow Wilson and the Politics of Morality,* pp. 170–171, 179–180, 183, 186, 189, 191–193, 196–197; Link, *Wilson the Diplomatist,* pp. 129–133; Bailey, *Wilson and the Great Betrayal,* pp. 275–280; Robert E. Osgood, *Ideals and Self-Interest in America's Foreign Relations,* pp. 294–295, 302–303; Walworth, *Wilson,* II, 393–394.

18. Osgood, *Ideals and Self-Interest,* p. 294; Blum, *Wilson,* p. 186; Bailey, *Wilson and the Great Betrayal,* pp. 166–167, 383–384.

the only agency to act on a number of important matters, thus restricting any president or his secretary of state. Secondly, reservations did have meaning. Lodge thought they had; so, too, did Wilson. Those international-ists and supporters of the League in 1919 and 1920 who dismissed them as unimportant were merely trying to rationalize away their own com-promises. The very word "mild" often associated with the reservations has also led to an incorrect conclusion that they were relatively innocuous.

A third assumption rests upon a belief that Wilson could have com-promised. Older defenders of the President argued that had he accepted one slate of changes, the opponents would have appeared with more until the entire peace structure had been decimated. This interpretation has been effectively negated, however, by the argument that no time remained during the voting procedures for such to have occurred. Had Wilson released his supporters on either November 19 or March 19, they could have voted for the treaty with the mild reservations.[19]

But whether Wilson could have made such a compromise is exceedingly doubtful. He argued correctly that approval with the Lodge reservations "does not provide for ratification, but rather for the nullification of the treaty." The preceding assumption that the reservations were innocuous has led scholars to dismiss them almost totally as a real issue. But Lodge said that his slate of changes effectively did nullify every provision and every obligation of the Covenant which he feared. Wilson recognized that fact, stated it clearly, and had more insight into the nature of the reservations than most of his contemporaries or many observers since. It was not un-reasoning obstinacy or illness which determined his course. He refused to accept membership under the conditions specified because they would have destroyed what he considered as the salient features of the League of Nations. This was especially true in regard to Article X, the heart of the Covenant, for the Senate's proviso would have nullified even a moral obliga-tion to act.[20]

Wilson might have refused to compromise for yet another reason. Every concession on a reservation stimulated doubts about the Covenant. Every change seemed to be an acknowledgment of error. The members of the League to Enforce Peace learned that truth much to their embarrass-ment. When they admitted weaknesses by agreeing to revisions, they often destroyed confidence in the very instrument they defended.

19. Bailey, *Wilson and the Great Betrayal*, pp. 279–280.
20. Wilson to Hitchcock, November 18, 1919, Hitchcock Papers; Vinson, *Referen-dum for Isolation*, pp. 3–4, 103–104, 108.

The issue to Wilson may also have been pride of authorship, but on that point he had little support from the internationalists. By March of 1920, nearly all of them favored reservations. Wilson's lonely position accents again the individual route, so far removed from prevailing thought, he had chosen. It also discloses how important provisions and wording of the Covenant became in the treaty fight. The issues of personality, partisanship, or prerogative cannot be dismissed, but it is imperative to realize that ideas also played an essential role.[21] The struggle became not so much one between those for and against the League as it was between those who could not agree upon the nature of the League they wanted.

Wilson asked the American people to join an international organization based upon the Covenant. But the widespread discontent with the Articles reveals that they did not match the desires of many persons. No extensive opposition to the ideal of a league had appeared in years of agitation. As the world moved close to the creation of one, men inevitably raised objections as they read the provisions in various plans; but the widespread dissatisfaction with the Covenant indicates serious shortcomings on its part. Indeed, it may disclose that Wilson's real error lay not in his refusal to compromise on Article X but in his inclusion of it at all. Thus Wilson may have been wrong about many things—his individualistic course, his failure to heed the internationalists who had spent years exploring a league, and his inadequate knowledge of the prevailing ideas and ideals of American thought on the subject.

To see the extent to which this was true it is necessary to examine the broad ideologies and basic principles which had become doctrine to those men who had labored for a world organization. Americans had come to accept six essential beliefs or principles: a league should be open to all governments but limited in its powers, disputes should be settled peacefully through procedural action, a system for world order should evolve gradually, the use of force should be limited under legal safeguards, an international organization should be established along democratic lines, and it should be a continually functioning body.

The internationalists in the United States had been highly consistent in their belief in a universal league with limited powers in which their coun-

21. Roland N. Stromberg, *Collective Security and American Foreign Policy: From the League of Nations to NATO*, p. 34; Stromberg,"The Riddle of Collective Security," *Issues and Conflicts: Studies in Twentieth Century American Diplomacy*, George L. Anderson, ed., pp. 148, 156–164; Richard N. Current, "The United States and 'Collective Security,' " *Isolation and Security*, Alexander DeConde, ed., p. 38; Link, *Wilson the Diplomatist*, pp. 128, 134–138, 154–155.

try should participate. A few Americans had flirted with the idea of a European association and with plans for an English-Speaking Union or a Latin American type of regional grouping, but such were exceptions. The internationalists had also abandoned dreams of a federation of the world with a government vested with extensive powers. The Covenant thus reflected their desire for a universal confederation which they had often referred to as a "league of peace," but it went beyond most planners in its provisions on force.

The second basic principle appeared in a belief in the pacific settlement of disputes. Three commonly accepted formulas had emerged: arbitration with conciliation and the Hague system; faith in international law and a court of justice; and an agency to formulate the rules to be followed. Americans had become converts to these methods to such a degree that nearly every internationalist after 1900 believed in such procedural machinery to resolve disputes.

The position of the Covenant on these matters can be explained only in terms of Wilson's disregard for them except for arbitration. Virtually every plan at Paris save his had provisions for a court and the development of law, and they appeared in the Covenant only because of the insistence of other statesmen. Even then, they did not constitute the core of the League's structure but seemed additions, with a separate court outside as first suggested by Ladd. Internationalists of the twentieth century wished a world body with the court as an integral part of its machinery. They did so because concepts of justice and law lay at the very heart of their thinking.

Taft revealed their feelings when he accused Wilson of "studiously" omitting the plan for "an international court and the settlement of justiciable questions." The President's "prejudice against courts," Taft concluded, "is well known." Root complained of the omission of "the rule of law and provision for the development and application of law," and one can find many similar remarks in 1919 and 1920.[22] In his testimony to the Senate Foreign Relations Committee, Lansing made that point and later expressed it in speeches and writings. But the *Advocate of Peace* voiced its objection in even more poignant terms.

When one remembers that the covenant for the League of Nations provides for the abrogation of the long line of arbitration treaties set up especially through the last hundred years, for the abrogation of the Wilson-Bryan treaties, for the dis-

22. Taft to W. Hays, July 20, 1919, Taft Papers; Root to George Gray, December 1, 1919, Root Papers.

establishment of existing international law, and when one recalls the importance of law especially in democracies, the smudge that is Paris does not lighten, it deepens.[23]

The distinction between the Covenant and internationalist thought on this topic can be seen in other ways. Most league advocates had declared that no world body should have the authority to act in arbitrary fashion, to intervene in internal affairs, or to do much more than avert war or delay it. In other words, it should operate in just fashion with its primary function the pacific settlement of disputes. Jordan expressed that idea perfectly when he suggested "the interposition of a series of obstacles to prevent a declaration of war" and the League to Enforce Peace program reflected this same philosophy.[24] Men should resolve controversies before they led to war, not wait for a conflict to develop and then move against the lawbreakers.

In subordinating concepts of law and justice, Wilson established the League upon a political foundation rather than a legal one. This may be what Root meant when he observed that the Wilsonian policy involved "a radical change in the settled foreign policy always pursued before Mr. Wilson's time." Professor Sterling E. Edmunds of the St. Louis University Law School left his meaning clear. "From the standpoint of International Law," he declared, "it may be affirmed that no modern treaty of peace has done this system such violence."[25]

The concepts of law and justice, furthermore, may have received a setback by the Covenant from which they did not recover in ensuing decades. In its subsequent history, the League relied upon political machinery to resolve disputes and compiled a notable record of failure. The Charter of the United Nations likewise left judicial features on the periphery rather than placing them at the heart of its structure as most internationalists before 1919 would have done.

The third principle of the internationalists' thought reflected their philosophy of gradualism. The path of evolution and the policy of building upon previous experiences and achievements would result inevitably, they be-

---

23. Lansing, *The Peace Negotiations: A Personal Narrative,* pp. 68, 74, 82, 169, 126–130; "The Blur That Is Paris," *Advocate of Peace,* LXXXI (May 1919), 137.

24. Jordan to Marjorie Brewster, April 10, 1919, Jordan Papers.

25. Root to John F. Bass, December 24, 1920, Root Papers; Edmunds, *International Law Applied to the Treaty of Peace,* pp. 1–2. In a lengthy treatise, Edmunds compared the Articles of the Covenant and provisions of the Treaty of Versailles to "Applicable Principles of the Law of Nations" and found both did great harm to the latter.

lieved, in a world union. While some of them had presented extreme proposals, they often described even these as "next steps." Few of them ever suggested abandoning established ideas or machinery as they sought to push on.

The Covenant reflected little of their work of previous years. Its deliberate and almost cynical failure to mention the Hague system provides glaring evidence on this point and further emphasizes its neglect of the slowly developed structure for the settlement of disputes. One could argue that the Covenant represented a more realistic view of international life when it gave less emphasis to some of these established principles. The Hague tribunal had never settled any dispute of major import; a code and a court remained more of a dream than a reality; and the internationalists had used the words "right" and "justice" so loosely as to make them lose all meaning.

But one should not conclude that they were not realists. Indeed, the entire evolutionary concept was based upon the belief that nations could move only as fast as the principles they would accept. When such men as Butler spoke of the importance of developing an "international mind," or when Root insisted again and again that laws and treaties should include only provisions which nations would uphold, they were being realistic. When the internationalists advocated the codification and formulation of law, they did not think in terms of what would be right or wrong but in the practical realm of what governments would accept. The League to Enforce Peace program recognized that all wars could not be abolished. It realistically argued that the proper machinery might avert most conflicts. Its program lay well within the evolutionary development of the league of peace idea which had gained such currency before 1914. It merely added refinements on the traditional ideas of arbitration, conciliation, and courts. Only two additions seemed to be a significant advance over what had been generally accepted—the application of a restricted sanction and the provision for an assembly to formulate laws. Both of these aims, however, had certainly been made popular and did not seem unrealistic to men in 1915.

Articles X and XVI moved far ahead of what most internationalists had come to see as the proper "next steps" along their evolutionary highway.[26] They had come to believe in what might be called a "half-way Covenant," not in a full and complete bridge built to save the world in a single operation. Had the commissioners in Paris created a league in keeping

26. Vinson, *Referendum for Isolation,* pp. 22–23, 34.

with prevailing thought, it might have been a more effective agency than the world had in the 1920s and 1930s.

The fourth principle of internationalist thought by 1919 involved the subject of force. A considerable diversity of views had existed. Some men rejected it completely, a few believed that no restriction should be placed on any organization's might, but the great majority had come to accept the idea of a limited application of power.

The concept in Article X that a league should defend the territory and independence of its members had appeared only a few times prior to 1919, notably in the plans of Bartholdt, Davis, Holt, Roosevelt, and Crosby. But most of these men modified or dropped their endorsement of such action in the face of protests and arguments from their co-workers. Even more important, nearly all of them qualified their advocacy of sanctions by insisting that any arms be applied according to procedures involving law and justice; hence, they had usually included provisions for a judicial system to prevent any autocratic action on the part of the organization.

Article X showed no awareness of this, and the opposition to it indicates how far Wilson was from prevailing thought. As Root remarked about Article X, "No nation in Europe would have had the effrontery to propose such an agreement to the United States."[27] Had Wilson been alert regarding the movement for an international organization, he would have realized that those advanced advocates of force represented a minority view. He would have known how often they had retreated from their statements or coupled their suggestions with plans for a judicial system.

Furthermore, if the American proponents of sanctions could not agree, how could anyone have hoped that senators and people less familiar with developing ideas could have supported advanced proposals for force? The fear of obligations and even limited commitments had been amply demonstrated in the Senate, especially in its refusal to accept the arbitration of all disputes. New conditions might have altered responses on that subject; people might have been willing to take some step forward; but they were not prepared to assume the responsibilities under Article X. Had a court system been tied to it, attitudes might have been different, and Article X might not have been so vigorously opposed. Men had increasingly accepted the idea that force might be applied after legal and mechanical processes had been followed. The application of arms under Article X, however,

27. Root to Adelbert Moot, July 19, 1919, Root Papers.

contained no such guarantees, and it thus aroused fears about the arbitrary nature of the League.

This point leads to the fifth principle of American internationalist thought. Any organization should be built along democratic lines. Few advocates had carried this concept to the extreme where they called for a union which exclusively represented people rather than governments, for the principle of sovereignty was too strong for that. But they did have faith in a federative society, in the development of a structure which paralleled the growth of the United States, and in a system in which nations voluntarily relinquished certain powers under guarantees of rights in return for the benefits of a peaceful world. They believed in a "declaration of interdependence," to borrow the phrase which B. O. Flower, the editor of the *Arena*, first used in 1900 and which Holt subsequently popularized. They wished, according to W. T. Stead, the "Americanization of the World."[28]

The disillusionment of most liberals with the Covenant and the Treaty of Versailles indicates how far the League fell short on this point. Requirements for unanimity rather than majority rule, the emphasis upon the Council in which the major powers dominated, and a lack of legislative power in the Assembly left the Covenant far removed from democratic ideals.

The sixth principle in internationalist thought was partially achieved by the Covenant. The old dream of a periodic congress had grown until men hoped to see an association in continuous operation. This did appear in 1920. It did not possess the one function, however, which most advocates wished it to have—some authority to pass laws or at least to codify them. In the light of the Covenant's limited interest in a legal system, this aim had not been considered at Paris.

In sum, the Covenant did not reflect prevailing patterns of internationalist thought which had emerged in the United States. It created an organization which men hoped could establish a system under which peace could be maintained. The internationalists had thought largely in terms of creating a system which in time would evolve into an international organization.

The internationalists, of course, never formulated any catalogue of beliefs, and this was their failing. That they were too individualistic in their ideas and actions is understandable, since in their age it took an independent thinker to become a practicing internationalist. As long as they sought

28. Flower, "The World's Unity League," *The Arena*, XXIV (November 1900), 535; Stead, "Internationalism as an Ideal for the Youth of America," *The Chautauquan*, LIV (May 1909), 336.

to propagandize or educate, their diverse and at times opposing views did not matter. But once the issue entered the realm of political action they failed. Even the largest and best organized of their agencies, the League to Enforce Peace, floundered during the treaty fight because of the disparate views of its members. Such a result might have been predicted, since the League had never attracted all of them. The inability to rally such men as Davis, Crosby, Butler, McDowell, Bartholdt, Root, and Roosevelt under the League to Enforce Peace standard should explain why the internationalists never worked in unified fashion during the debates of 1919–1920.

Their unbounded spirit of optimism also explains their failure. Only idealists could have lived with their hopes; only dreamers could have devoted the time they did to their cause; and thus in 1919 they lacked those practical qualities which would have enabled them to mount an effective campaign. Perhaps they believed so strongly in the inevitability of their success that they thought it unnecessary to combine in more than a temporary organization.

Their movement had grown, however, for many reasons. They were effective propagandists; they possessed leadership qualities as gadflies; and they had the experience of their own nation as an example. Its steps toward unification and its federal system inspired them to believe that such processes could be applied more broadly. Also, the democratic institutions of the United States stimulated that belief in justice and right which they hoped could be applied to the world. The continental distance which kept their land apart from other countries and stimulated isolationist concepts also encouraged internationalist thought. In an environment free from autocratic militarism, in a nation which did not fear aggressors, men could afford the luxury of speculating upon an ideal that could affect every nation. Thus, in large measure because of their efforts, the world had moved toward the "Utopia" of the internationalists. The League of Nations failed to do what they hoped such an organization might, in part because it did not reflect the experience of their endeavors. They believed, however, that the main factor was the absence of the United States; hence, when mankind later faced a major war, the internationalists again appeared with their plea and warning: "Utopia or Hell."[29]

29. Robert A. Divine, *Second Chance: The Triumph of Internationalism in America During World War II,* pp. 29–74.

Abrams, Irwin M. "A History of European Peace Societies, 1867–1899." Unpublished doctoral dissertation, Harvard University, 1938.

Addams, Jane. *Peace and Bread in Time of War*. New York: Kings Crown Press, 1945.

Addresses Given at the Organization Conference of the Woman's Peace Party, Washington, D.C., January 10, 1915 (pamphlet). Chicago: Woman's Peace Party, 1915.

Adler, Selig. *The Isolationist Impulse: Its Twentieth-Century Reaction*. New York: Abelard-Schuman, Inc., 1957.

Allen, Devere. *The Fight for Peace*. New York: Macmillan, 1930.

American School Peace League. *American School Peace League, 1909* (pamphlet). N.p., n.d.

———. *Program, American School Peace League* (pamphlet). N.p., [1909].

Anderson, George L., ed. *Issues and Conflicts: Studies in Twentieth Century American Diplomacy*. Lawrence: University of Kansas Press, 1959.

Anderson, Helen. "International Peace," *International Peace, Winning Essays* (pamphlet). Mohonk Lake, N.Y.: Lake Mohonk Conference on International Arbitration, 1913.

Angell, Norman. "America and the European War," *World Peace Foundation Pamphlets*, V (February 1915).

"Arbitration and the United States: A Summary of the Development of Pacific Settlement of International Disputes with Special Reference to American Policy," *League of Nations*, (pamphlet), IX (1926).

Ashbee, Charles R. *The American League to Enforce Peace: An English Interpretation*. London: George Allen and Unwin Ltd., 1917.

Atkinson, Henry A. *Theodore Marburg: The Man and His Work.* New York: Morton Littman Printing Co., 1951.

Babson, Roger W. *The Future of World Peace: A Book of Charts Showing Facts Which Must Be Recognized in Future Plans for Peace.* Boston: Babson's Statistical Organization, 1915.

Bacon, Robert, and James Brown Scott, eds. *Addresses on International Subjects by Elihu Root.* Cambridge, Mass.: Harvard University Press, 1916.

Bailey, Thomas A. *Woodrow Wilson and the Lost Peace.* New York: Macmillan, 1944.

————. *Woodrow Wilson and the Great Betrayal.* New York: Macmillan, 1945.

Baker, Ray Stannard, and William E. Dodd, eds. *Public Papers of Woodrow Wilson.* 6 vols. New York: Harper and Bros., 1925–27.

Baker, Ray Stannard. *Woodrow Wilson and World Settlement.* 3 vols. Garden City, N.Y.: Doubleday, Page and Co., 1922–23.

————. *Woodrow Wilson: Life and Letters.* 8 vols. Garden City, N.Y.: Doubleday, Page and Co., 1927–39.

Balch, Thomas W. *A World Court in the Light of the United States Supreme Court.* Philadelphia: Allan, Lane and Scott, 1918.

Barcus, James S. *First President of the World: A Prophecy* (pamphlet). New York: J. S. Barcus Co., 1910.

Bartholdt, Richard. *Address of Hon. Richard Bartholdt, President of the American Group at the XIII Conference of the Interparliamentary Union at Brussels, August 29, 1905* (pamphlet). Schleiz: R. Giegling, 1905.

————. *From Steerage to Congress: Reminiscences and Reflections.* Philadelphia: Dorrance and Co., 1930.

Bartlett, Ruhl J. *The League to Enforce Peace.* Chapel Hill: University of North Carolina Press, 1944.

Bartnett, Walter John. *The Federation of the World* (pamphlet). 2d ed. San Francisco: Dettner-Travers Press, 1906.

Batten, Samuel Z. *The New World Order* (pamphlet). New York: National Committee on the Churches and the Moral Aims of the War, [1918].

Beale, Howard K. *Theodore Roosevelt and the Rise of America to World Power.* Baltimore: Johns Hopkins University Press, 1956.

Beales, A. C. F. *The History of Peace: A Short Account of the Organised Movements for International Peace.* New York: Dial Press, 1931.

Beck, Emil G. *Reciprocal Representation in a World's Court and International Bonding: Remedies Against Recurrence of War* (pamphlet). Chicago: n.p., 1917.

Beckwith, George C. *The Peace Manual: or War and Its Remedies.* Boston: American Peace Society, 1868.

Bentham, Jeremy. *The Works of Jeremy Bentham. Published under the Superintendence of his Executor, John Bowring.* 11 vols. Edinburgh: W. Tait, 1843.

Béthune, Maxmilien de, duc de Sully. *The Great Design of Henry IV.* Introduction by Edwin D. Mead. Boston: Ginn and Co., 1909.

Bigelow, John. *World Peace: How War Cannot be Abolished, How It May be Abolished.* New York: M. Kennerley, 1916.

Blake, Nelson M. "The Olney-Pauncefote Treaty of 1897," *American Historical Review*, L (January 1945), 228–243.

Blum, John M. *Woodrow Wilson and the Politics of Morality.* Boston: Little, Brown and Co., 1956.

Bluntschli, J. C. *Gesammelte kleine Schriften: Aufsätz über Recht und Staat.* 2 vols. Nördlingen: C. H. Beck, 1879–81.

Blymer, William H. *The Isolation (or non-intercourse) Plan With a Proposed Convention* (pamphlet). [New York]: n.p., 1917.

———. *Memorandum on the Draft of the Constitution of the League of Nations* (pamphlet). New York: n.p., 1919.

———. *Observations on Compulsory Arbitration and Disarmament under Penalty of Non-Intercourse* (pamphlet). New York: n.p., 1905.

Boardman, George Dana. *Disarmament of Nations* (pamphlet). Philadelphia: Times Printing House, 1890.

Boas, Frank. "An Anthropologist's View of War," *International Conciliation* (pamphlet), No. 52 (March 1912).

Boke, George H. *The Federal Inter-Nation: The Federal Principle—the True Solution of the League of Nations Aims and Problems* (pamphlet). N.p., 1919.

———. *Proposals for a Federal World Government* (pamphlet). N.p., n.d.

Bolce, Harold. *The New Internationalism.* New York: D. Appleton and Co., 1907.

Bonsal, Stephen. *Unfinished Business.* Garden City, N.Y.: Doubleday, Doran and Co., 1944.

Bourne, Randolph S., comp. *Towards an Enduring Peace: A Symposium of Peace Proposals and Programs, 1914–1916.* New York: American Association for International Conciliation, [1916].

Bridgman, Burt N. and J. C., comps. *A Genealogy of the Bridgman Family.* Hyde Park, Mass.: n.p., 1894.

Bridgman, Raymond L. *The First Book of World Law: A Compilation of the International Conventions to Which the Principal Nations are Signatory, . . .* Boston: Ginn and Co., 1911.

———. *World Organization.* Boston: Ginn and Co., 1905.

Brinkerhoff, Edgar D. *Constitution for the United Nations Of The Earth* (pamphlet). 3d ed. Fall River, Mass.: Pamphlet Publishing Co., 1916.

Brown, Philip Marshall. *International Realities.* New York: Charles Scribner's Sons, 1917.

Brown, Robert. "International Arbitration: Looking Toward a World-State by a Political Dreamer," *International Peace, Winning Essays* (pamphlet). Mohonk Lake, N.Y.: Lake Mohonk Conference on International Arbitration, 1915.

Bryan, William J. "The Proposal for a League to Enforce Peace," *International Conciliation* (pamphlet), No. 106 (September 1916).

Burritt, Elihu. "A Congress of Nations," *Old South Leaflets,* VI (No. 146).

Butler, Nicholas Murray. *Across the Busy Years: Recollections and Reflections.* 2 vols. New York: Charles Scribner's Sons, 1939–40.

————. *The Basis of Durable Peace, Written at the Invitation of the New York Times by Cosmos.* New York: Charles Scribner's Sons, 1918.

————. *The Changed Outlook* (pamphlet). New York: n.p., 1915.

————. *The International Mind: An Argument for the Judicial Settlement of International Disputes.* New York: Charles Scribner's Sons, 1912.

————. *The War and After the War* (pamphlet). N.p., 1918.

————. *A World in Ferment.* New York: Charles Scribner's Sons, 1917.

Campbell, John P. "Taft, Roosevelt, and the Arbitration Treaties of 1911," *Journal of American History,* LIII (September 1966), 279–298.

Carnegie, Andrew. *A League of Peace: A Rectorial Address Delivered to the Students in the University of St. Andrews, 17th October, 1905* (pamphlet). Boston: Ginn and Co., 1906.

————. *Triumphant Democracy: or Fifty Years' March on the Republic.* New York: Charles Scribner's Sons, 1886.

Carnovale, Luigi. *How America Can Easily and Quickly Prevent Wars Forever* (pamphlet). 6th ed. Chicago: n.p., 1924.

Cassano, Prince de. *La Fedération européene* (pamphlet). Rome: Forzani and Co., 1909.

Chan, Hugh. "American Agitation for a League of Nations, 1914–1922." Unpublished doctoral dissertation, State University of Iowa, 1934.

Clayton, Joseph C. *Pax Nobiscum: A Plan for a Tentative Constitution of The United Nations to be Submitted to the First National Arbitration and Peace Congress of America, to the Second Hague Conference, and to the Interparliamentary Union* (pamphlet). New York: n.p., 1907.

Cole, E. W., comp. *Cyclopaedia of Short Prize Essays on the Federation of the Whole World.* Melbourne, Australia: E. W. Cole, n.d.

Collin, Christen C. *The War Against War and the Enforcement of Peace.* New York: Macmillan, 1917.

Commission on Christian Education. *Selected Quotations on Peace and War of Federal Council of Churches of Christ in America.* New York: Federal Council, 1915.

The Constitution Weathered the Storm (pamphlet). New York: League to Enforce Peace, n.d.

Cory, Helen M. *Compulsory Arbitration of International Disputes.* New York: Columbia University Press, 1932.

"The Covenanter." *League of Nations* (pamphlet), II (June 1919).

Crafts, Wilbur F. *Internationalism* (pamphlet). Washington, D.C.: International Reform Bureau, 1908.

Crane, Frank. *The War and World Government.* New York: John Lane Co., 1915.

Crapsey, Algernon S. *International Democratic Republic* (pamphlet). N.p., n.d.

Crosby, Oscar T. *The Armed International Tribunal Association: Its Purposes and Methods* (pamphlet). Washington, D.C.: Armed International Association, 1915.

————. *The Constitution of the United States of the World* (pamphlet). Warrenton, Va.: n.p., 1909.

———. *The Constitution of an International Court of Decree and Enforcement or A Plea for the Poor of all Lands* (pamphlet). Tokyo: n.p., 1914.

———. *International War: Its Causes and Its Cure*. New York: Macmillan, 1919.

Crozier, Alfred O. *Nation of Nations; the Way to Permanent Peace; A Supreme Constitution of Governments*. Cincinnati: Stewart and Kidd Co., 1915.

Crozier, William. *A Discussion of the Proposed Constitution for the League of Nations* (pamphlet). Washington, D.C.: National Publishing Co., 1919.

Crucé, Émeric. *The New Cyneas*, trans. and ed. Thomas W. Balch. Philadelphia: Allen, Lane and Scott, 1909.

Curry, George. "Woodrow Wilson, Jan Smuts, and the Versailles Settlement," *American Historical Review*, LXVI (July 1961), 968–986.

Curti, Merle. *The American Peace Crusade, 1815–1860*. Durham, N.C.: Duke University Press, 1929.

———. "Bryan and World Peace," *Smith College Studies in History*, XVI (April–July 1931).

———, ed. *The Learned Blacksmith: The Letters and Journals of Elihu Burritt*. New York: Wilson-Erikson, 1937.

———. *Peace or War: The American Struggle, 1636–1936*. New York: W. W. Norton and Co., 1936.

Darby, W. Evans. *International Tribunals: A Collection of the Various Schemes Which Have Been Propounded; and of Instances Since 1815*. 3d ed. London: J. M. Dent and Co., 1900.

Davies, David. *The Problem of the Twentieth Century: A Study of International Relationships*. London: Ernest Benn Ltd., 1930.

Davis, Calvin D. *The United States and the First Hague Peace Conference*. Ithaca, N.Y.: Cornell University Press, 1962.

Davis, George B. *Outlines of International Law*. New York: Harper and Bros., 1887.

Davis, Hayne, ed. *Among the World's Peacemakers*. New York: Progressive Publishing Co., 1907.

DeConde, Alexander, ed. *Isolation and Security: Ideas and Interests in Twentieth Century American Foreign Policy*. Durham, N.C.: Duke University Press, 1957.

Diamond, William, ed. "American Sectionalism and World Organization, by Frederick Jackson Turner," *American Historical Review*, XLVII (April 1942), 545–551.

Divine, Robert A. *Second Chance: The Triumph of Internationalism in America During World War II*. New York: Atheneum, 1967.

Dodge, David Low. *War Inconsistent with the Religion of Jesus Christ*. Introduction by Edwin D. Mead. Boston: Ginn and Co., 1905.

Donald, David. *Charles Sumner and the Coming of the Civil War*. New York: Alfred A. Knopf, 1960.

Doty, Madeleine Z. *The Central Organisation for a Durable Peace (1915–1919): Its History, Work and Ideas*. Geneva: Institute Universitaire de hautes études internationales, 1945.

Drysdale, George R. *Home Rule and Federation: With Remarks on Law and Government and International Anarchy; and with a Proposal for the Federal Union of France and England, as the Most Important Step to the Federation of the World* (pamphlet). London: E. Truelove, 1889.

Dubin, Martin D. "The Development of the Concept of Collective Security in the American Peace Movement, 1899–1917." Unpublished doctoral dissertation, Indiana University, 1960.

————. "Elihu Root and the Advocacy of a League of Nations, 1914–1917," *The Western Political Quarterly*, XIX (September 1966), 439–455.

Duggan, Stephen P. "The Conference on the Foreign Relations of the United States," *International Conciliation* (pamphlet), No. 121 (December 1917).

Dulles, Foster Rhea. *America's Rise to World Power, 1898–1954*. New York: Harper and Bros., 1954.

Duras, Victor. *Universal Peace*. New York: Broadway Publishing Co., 1908.

Eddy, George S. *A Project of Universal and Perpetual Peace* (pamphlet). New York: George Simpson Eddy, 1922.

Edmunds, Sterling E. *International Law Applied to the Treaty of Peace* (pamphlet). N.p., n.d.

Eliot, Charles W. *The Road Toward Peace*. Boston: Houghton Mifflin Co., 1915.

Ely, James E. *World Reconstruction and Permanent Peace* (pamphlet). 2d ed. Garden City, Kans.: n.p., 1919.

Faries, John C. *The Rise of Internationalism*. New York: W. D. Gray, 1915.

Fenwick, Charles G. *International Law*. 3d ed. New York: Appleton-Century-Crofts, 1948.

Field, David Dudley. *Outlines of an International Code*. 2d ed. New York: Baker, Voorhis and Co., 1876.

The Fighting Program of the National Nonpartisan League (pamphlet). N.p., [1918].

Filene, Peter. "The World Peace Foundation and Progressivism, 1910–1918," *New England Quarterly*, XXXVI (December 1963), 478–501.

Fiore, Pasquale. *International Law Codified and Its Legal Sanction*, trans. Edwin M. Borchard. New York: Baker, Voorhis and Co., 1918.

Fisher, H. A. L. *James Bryce (Viscount Bryce of Dechmont, O.M.)*. 2 vols. New York: Macmillan, 1927.

Fisher, Irving. *After the War, What? A Plea for a League of Peace* (pamphlet). New York: Church Peace Union, 1914.

Fleming, Denna F. *The United States and the League of Nations, 1918–1920*. New York: G. P. Putnam's Sons, 1932.

Foote, Allen R. *The United Democratic Nations of the World* (pamphlet). Washington, D.C.: American Progress, 1917.

Forcey, Charles. *The Crossroads of Liberalism: Croly, Weyl, Lippmann, and the Progressive Era, 1900–1925*. New York: Oxford University Press, 1961.

Forster, E. M. *Goldsworthy Lowes Dickinson*. New York: Harcourt, Brace and Co., 1934.

Foulke, William Dudley. *A Hoosier Autobiography*. New York: Oxford University Press, 1922.

Franklin, Benjamin. "On War and Peace," *Old South Leaflets*, VII (No. 162).

Fridenberg, S. L. *An Appeal for International Union* (pamphlet). Philadelphia: S. L. Fridenberg, 1915.

Friedrich, Carl J. *Inevitable Peace*. Cambridge, Mass.: Harvard University Press, 1948.

Gannett, William C. "International Good-Will as a Substitute for Armies and Navies," *World Peace Foundation Pamphlets*, II (January 1912).

Garraty, John A. *Henry Cabot Lodge: A Biography*. New York: Alfred A. Knopf, 1953.

Gelfand, Lawrence E. *The Inquiry: American Preparations for Peace, 1917–1919*. New Haven, Conn.: Yale University Press, 1963.

Giddings, Franklin H. "The Relation of Social Theory to Public Policy," *International Conciliation* (pamphlet), No. 58 (September 1912).

Ginn, Edwin. *The International Library* (pamphlet). [Boston: International School of Peace, 1910].

———. "Organizing the Peace Work," *World Peace Foundation Pamphlets*, III (July 1913).

———. "The World Peace Foundation," *World Peace Foundation Pamphlets*, I (April 1911).

Goldsmith, Robert. *A League to Enforce Peace*. New York: Macmillan, 1917.

"The Grange and Peace," *World Peace Foundation Pamphlets*, I (1913).

Grosch, G. "Die Friedensorganisation der Staaten," *Internationale Organisation* (pamphlet), No. 9/10. Berlin: Verlag der "Friedens-warte," 1914.

Gross, Howard H. *After the War, What?* (pamphlet). Chicago: n.p., 1918.

Grossmann, Kurt R. "Peace Movements in Germany," *South Atlantic Quarterly*, XLIX (July 1950), 293–302.

Grotius, Hugo. *De Jure Belli ac Pacis Libri Tres*, trans. F. W. Kelsey. 2 vols. Oxford: Clarendon Press, 1925.

Grunsky, Clotilde, and C. Ewald. *The Next Step: Published in the Interest of World's Peace* (pamphlet). San Francisco: Walter N. Brunt Press, 1915.

Hale, Edward Everett. *A Permanent Tribunal: The Emperor of Russia and his Circular Regarding Permanent Peace* (pamphlet). Boston: H. G. Ellis, 1899.

Harbaugh, William H. *Power and Responsibility: The Life and Times of Theodore Roosevelt*. New York: Farrar, Straus and Cudahy, 1961.

Harris, Theodore. *A Proposed Constitution for the United Nations of the World* (pamphlet). New York: C. E. Ruckstuhl, Inc., 1918.

Hart, Albert B. "Washington as an Internationalist," *Bulletin of the Pan American Union*, LXVI (July 1932), 475–491.

Hemleben, Sylvester J. *Plans for World Peace through Six Centuries*. Chicago: University of Chicago Press, 1943.

Hendrick, Burton J. *The Life of Andrew Carnegie*. 2 vols. Garden City, N.Y.: Doubleday, Doran and Co., 1932.

Heymans, G. "To the Citizens of the Belligerent States," *Towards an International Understanding* (pamphlet), No. 10. London: Union of Democratic Control, n.d.

Hicks, Frederick C. *The New World Order: International Organization, Inter-*

national Law, International Cooperations. Garden City, N.Y.: Doubleday, Page and Co., 1920.

Hill, David Jayne. *Present Problems in Foreign Policy.* New York: D. Appleton and Co., 1919.

————. *The Rebuilding of Europe.* New York: Century Co., 1917.

————. *World Organization as Affected by the Nature of the Modern State.* New York: Columbia University Press, 1911.

Hirst, F. W. *The Arbiter in Council.* London: Macmillan, 1906.

————. "The Logic of International Co-operation," *International Conciliation* (pamphlet), No. 14 (January 1909).

"Historical Light on the League to Enforce Peace," *World Peace Foundation Pamphlets,* VI (December 1916).

Hodges, Charles. *The Background of International Relations: Our World Horizons, National and International.* New York: J. Wiley and Sons, 1931.

Holt, Hamilton. *The Federation of the World* (pamphlet). New York: World Federation Committee of New York Peace Society, 1910.

————. *The Moral Values of a League of Nations* (pamphlet). New York: National Committee on the Churches and the Moral Aims of the War, [1918].

————. *The United States Peace Commission* (pamphlet). New York: New York Peace Society, 1910.

————. *The Way to Disarm: A Practical Proposal* (pamphlet). New York: Church Peace Union, 1914.

Holt, W. Stull. *Treaties Defeated by the Senate: A Study of the Struggle between President and Senate over the Conduct of Foreign Relations.* Baltimore: Johns Hopkins University Press, 1933.

Hughan, Jessie W. *A Study of International Government.* New York: Thomas Y. Crowell, 1923.

Hugo, Victor. "The United States of Europe," *World Peace Foundation Pamphlets,* IV (October 1914).

Hull, William I. "International Police, but Not National Armaments," Swarthmore College *Bulletin,* VII (September 1909), 16–25.

————. *The New Peace Movement.* Boston: World Peace Foundation, 1912.

————. *Preparedness: The American Versus the Military Programme.* New York: Fleming H. Revell Co., 1916.

————. "Six Sanctions of the International Court," *Judicial Settlement of International Disputes* (pamphlet), No. 25 (May 1916).

————. *The Two Hague Conferences and Their Contributions to International Law.* Boston: Ginn and Co., 1908.

Jay, William. *War and Peace: The Evils of the First and a Plan for Preserving the Last.* New York: Oxford University Press, 1919.

Jennings, David H. "President Wilson's Tour in September, 1919: A Study of Forces Operating During the League of Nations Fight." Unpublished doctoral dissertation, Ohio State University, 1958.

Jessup, Philip C. *Elihu Root.* 2 vols. New York: Dodd, Mead and Co., 1938.

Johnson, Joseph E., and Bernard Bush, eds. *Perspectives on Peace, 1910–1960.* New York: Frederick A. Praeger, 1960.

"Joint Debate on the Covenant of Paris: Henry Cabot Lodge, A. Lawrence Lowell," *League of Nations* (pamphlet), II (April 1919).

Jones, Robert, and S. S. Sherman. *The League of Nations from Idea to Reality* . . . . New York: G. P. Putnam's Sons, 1927.

Jong van Beek en Donk, B. *History of the Peace Movement in the Netherlands, 1870–1915* (pamphlet). The Hague: n.p., 1915.

————. "The Movement in Neutral Countries," *The Project of a League of Nations* (pamphlet), No. 15 (August 1917).

————, ed. *Recueil de Rapports.* 4 vols., The Hague: Martinus Nijhoff, 1916–18.

Jordan, David Starr. *The Days of a Man.* 2 vols. Yonkers-on-Hudson, N.Y.: World Book Co., 1922.

————. *The League of Nations* (pamphlet). San Francisco: James H. Barry Co., n.d.

Kant, Immanuel. *Perpetual Peace.* New York: Columbia University Press, 1939.

Kendrick, Jack E. "The League of Nations and the Republican Senate." Unpublished doctoral dissertation, University of North Carolina, 1953.

Kingsley, Darwin. *The United English Nations* (pamphlet). Burlington, Vt.: n.p., 1916.

Knox, Philander C. "International Unity," *International Conciliation* (pamphlet), No. 28 (March 1910).

————. *The Spirit and Purpose of American Diplomacy* (pamphlet). Philadelphia: University of Pennsylvania Press, 1910.

Krehbiel, Edward. "The European Commission of the Danube," *International Conciliation* (pamphlet), No. 131 (October 1918).

————. *Nationalism, War and Society.* New York: Macmillan, 1916.

Krey, August C. "The International State of the Middle Ages: Some Reasons for Its Failure," *American Historical Review*, XXVIII (October 1922), 1–12.

Kuehl, Warren F. *Hamilton Holt: Journalist, Internationalist, Educator.* Gainesville: University of Florida Press, 1960.

Kuiper, J. *De geheele wereld één Republiek* (pamphlet). Leeuwarden: Meijer and Schaafsma, 1916.

Ladd, William (Philanthropos). *A Dissertation on a Congress of Nations* (pamphlet). Boston: J. Loring Press, 1832.

Ladd, William. *An Essay on a Congress of Nations for the Adjustment of International Disputes Without Resort to Arms*, [1840]. Reprinted, with an Introduction by James Brown Scott. New York: Oxford University Press, 1916.

Ladd, William, and George C. Beckwith, eds. *Prize Essays on a Congress of Nations, for the Adjustment of International Disputes* . . . . Boston: Whipple and Damrell, 1840.

Lange, Christian L. *The Conditions of A Lasting Peace: A Statement of the Work of the Union* (pamphlet). Christiania, Sweden: Interparliamentary Bureau, 1917.

Lansing, Robert. *The Peace Negotiations: A Personal Narrative.* Boston: Houghton Mifflin Co., 1921.

Latané, John H., ed. *Development of the League of Nations Idea: Documents and Correspondence of Theodore Marburg.* 2 vols. New York: Macmillan, 1932.

Laveleye, Émile de. "On the Causes of War and the Means of Reducing their Number," *Cobden Club Essays, Second Series, 1871–72.* London: Cassell, Petter, and Galpin, 1872.

League of Nations: Outlines for Discussion (pamphlet). New York: National Committee on the Churches and the Moral Aims of the War, 1918.

League to Enforce Peace, American Branch: Independence Hall Conference . . . . New York: League to Enforce Peace, 1915.

League to Enforce Peace. *Enforced Peace: Proceedings of the First Annual National Assemblage . . . .* New York: League to Enforce Peace, 1916.

———. *A Reference Book for Speakers* (pamphlet). New York: League to Enforce Peace, [1918].

———. *Win the War for Permanent Peace. Addresses. . . .* New York: League to Enforce Peace, 1918.

Leopold, Richard W. *Elihu Root and the Conservative Tradition.* Boston: Little, Brown and Co., 1954.

Levermore, Charles H. *Samuel Train Dutton.* New York: Macmillan, 1922.

Levine, Lawrence W. *Defender of the Faith: William Jennings Bryan; The Last Decade, 1915–1925.* New York: Oxford University Press, 1965.

The Life of E. W. Cole. Melbourne, Australia: Book Arcade Printing Department, n.d.

Lindsey, Edward. *The International Court.* New York: Thomas Y. Crowell Co., 1931.

Link, Arthur S. *Wilson: Campaigns for Progressivism and Peace, 1916–1917.* Princeton, N. J.: Princeton University Press, 1965.

———. *Wilson the Diplomatist: A Look at his Major Foreign Policies.* Baltimore: Johns Hopkins University Press, 1957.

Linn, James W. *Jane Addams: A Biography.* New York: D. Appleton-Century Co., 1938.

Lippmann, Walter. *The Stakes of Diplomacy.* New York: Henry Holt and Co., 1915.

Lodge, Henry Cabot. *The Senate and the League of Nations.* New York: Charles Scribner's Sons, 1925.

———. *War Addresses, 1915–1917.* Boston: Houghton Mifflin Co., 1917.

Lorimer, James. *The Institutes of the Law of Nations: A Treatise of the Jural Relations of Separate Political Communities.* 2 vols. London: William Blackwood and Sons, 1884.

Lynch, Frederick. *The Last War: A Study of Things Present and Things to Come.* New York: Fleming H. Revell Co., 1915.

———. *The Peace Problem: The Task of the Twentieth Century.* New York: Fleming H. Revell Co., 1911.

———. *Personal Recollections of Andrew Carnegie.* New York: Fleming H. Revell Co., 1920.

——. *President Wilson and the Moral Aims of the War.* New York: Fleming H. Revell Co., 1918.

Lyons, F. S. L. *Internationalism in Europe, 1815–1914.* Leyden: A. W. Sythoff, 1963.

MacCauley, Clay. *Krause's League for Human Right and Thereby World Peace* (pamphlet). Tokyo: Fukuin Printing Co., 1917.

Macdonald, James A. "William T. Stead and his Peace Message," *World Peace Foundation Pamphlets,* II (July 1912).

Macfarland, Charles S. *Across the Years.* New York: Macmillan, 1936.

——. *Pioneers for Peace Through Religion: Based on the Records of the Church Peace Union, 1914–1945.* New York: Fleming H. Revell Co., 1946.

Malloy, William M., comp. *Treaties, Conventions, International Acts, Protocols, and Agreements between the United States of America and other Powers, 1776–1923.* 3 vols. Washington, D.C.: Government Printing Office, 1910–1923.

Marburg, Theodore. *League of Nations: A Chapter in the History of the Movement and Its Principles Examined.* 2 vols. New York: Macmillan, 1917–18.

——. "World Court and League of Peace," *Judicial Settlement of International Disputes* (pamphlet), No. 20 (February 1915).

Marburg, Theodore, and Horace E. Flack, eds. *Taft Papers on League of Nations.* New York: Macmillan, 1920.

Margrave, Robert N. "The Policy of the United States Respecting the Development of International Adjudication." Unpublished doctoral dissertation, American University, 1950.

Marriott, John A. R. *Commonwealth or Anarchy? A Survey of Projects of Peace from the Sixteenth to the Twentieth Century.* New York: Columbia University Press, 1939.

Martin, Edward S. *The Life of Joseph Hodges Choate as Gathered Chiefly from His Letters.* 2 vols. New York: Charles Scribner's Sons, 1920–21.

Mason, Robert W. *A Constitution for World-Wide Federation, Based upon the Constitution of the United States of America, Amplified and Adjusted for the "United Nations of the World"* (pamphlet). 2d ed. New York: n.p., 1911.

Massachusetts House Journal, 1915.

Massachusetts Senate Journal, 1915.

Maxim, Hudson. *Defenseless America.* New York: Hearst's International Library Co., 1915.

Maynard, Douglas. "Reform and Origin of the International Organization Movement," *Proceedings of the American Philosophical Society,* CVII (June 1963), 220–231.

Mead, Edwin D. "The American Peace Party and Its Present Aims and Duties," *World Peace Foundation Pamphlets,* III (April 1913).

——. "Annual Report," *World Peace Foundation Pamphlets,* IV (December 1914).

——. "Heroes of Peace," *World Peace Foundation Pamphlets,* II (January 1912).

——. *Horace Bushnell, the Citizen* (pamphlet). Boston: n.p., 1900.

————. "The International Duty of the United States and Great Britain," *World Peace Foundation Pamphlets*, I (April 1911).

————. *Organize the World* (pamphlet). Boston: International School of Peace, 1898.

————. *The Principles of the Founders* (pamphlet). Boston: American Unitarian Association, 1903.

————. "The World Peace Foundation: Its Present Activities," *World Peace Foundation Pamphlets*, II (July 1912).

Mead, Lucia Ames. *Educational Organizations Promoting International Friendship* (pamphlet). Boston: International School of Peace, 1910.

————. *Patriotism and the New Internationalism*. Boston: Ginn and Co., 1906.

————. *A Primer of the Peace Movement* (pamphlet). Boston: American Peace Society, 1907.

Megargee, Richard. "The Diplomacy of John Bassett Moore: Realism in American Foreign Policy." Unpublished doctoral dissertation, Northwestern University, 1963.

Merk, Frederick. *The Oregon Question: Essays in Anglo-American Diplomacy and Politics*. Cambridge, Mass.: Harvard University Press, 1967.

Meulen, Jacob ter. *Der Gedanke der internationalen Organisation in seiner entwicklung*. 2 vols. The Hague: Martinus Nijhoff, 1917–29.

Mez, John. "Jacques Novicow," *World Unity Magazine*, XIII (January 1934), 43–49.

Miller, David Hunter. *The Drafting of the Covenant*. 2 vols. New York: G. P. Putnam's Sons, 1928.

————. *My Diary at the Conference of Paris*. 21 vols. New York: Appeal Printing Co., 1924.

Miller, Robert Moats. "The Attitudes of the Major Protestant Churches in America Toward War and Peace, 1919–1929," *The Historian*, XIX (November 1956), 13–38.

Minor, Raleigh C. *A Republic of Nations: A Study of the Organization of a Federal League of Nations*. New York: Oxford University Press, 1918.

Moore, John Bassett. *History and Digest of the International Arbitrations to Which the United States Has Been a Party*. 6 vols. (53 Cong., 2d sess.; H.R. Misc. Doc. 212.) Washington, D.C.: Government Printing Office, 1898.

————. "International Cooperation," *International Conciliation* (pamphlet), No. 100 (March 1916).

Morison, Elting E., *et al.*, eds. *The Letters of Theodore Roosevelt*. 8 vols. Cambridge, Mass.: Harvard University Press, 1951–54.

Mower, Edmund C. *International Government*. Boston: D. C. Heath and Co., 1931.

Muzzey, David S. *James G. Blaine: A Political Idol of Other Days*. New York: Dodd, Mead and Co., 1934.

Myers, Denys P., comp. "Revised List of Arbitration Treaties," *World Peace Foundation Pamphlets*, II (July 1912).

Myers, Philip Van Ness. *Outlines of Nineteenth Century History*. Boston: Ginn and Co., 1906.

National Nonpartisan League. *The Fighting Program of the National Non-partisan League* (pamphlet). St. Paul, Minn.: n.p., 1918.

Nevins, Allan. *Henry White: Thirty Years of American Diplomacy.* New York: Harper and Bros., 1930.

A New Era in Human History: A Four Weeks Study in the Outlines of World Constructive Statesmanship (pamphlet). New York: World Alliance . . . and Commission on International Justice and Goodwill of the Federal Council of Churches of Christ in America, 1917.

Notter, Harley. *The Origins of the Foreign Policy of Woodrow Wilson.* Baltimore: Johns Hopkins University Press, 1937.

Nussbaum, Arthur. *A Concise History of the Law of Nations.* Rev. ed. New York: Macmillan, 1954.

Olson, William C. "Theodore Roosevelt's Conception of an International League," *World Affairs Quarterly,* XXIX (January 1959), 329–353.

Osgood, Robert E. *Ideals and Self-Interest in America's Foreign Relations.* Chicago: University of Chicago Press, 1953.

Paine, Thomas. *Rights of Man* (reprint). New York: Heritage Press, 1961.

Palmer, Frederick. *Bliss, Peacemaker: The Life and Letters of General Tasker Howard Bliss.* New York: Dodd, Mead and Co., 1934.

Papers Relating to the Foreign Relations of the United States, 1904. Washington, D.C.: United States Government Printing Office, 1904.

Papers Relating to the Foreign Relations of the United States, 1914. Washington, D.C.: United States Government Printing Office, 1922.

Papers Relating to the Foreign Relations of the United States, Paris Peace Conference, 1919. 13 vols. Washington, D.C.: United States Government Printing Office, 1942–47.

Patterson, David S. "The Travail of the American Peace Movement, 1887–1914." Unpublished doctoral dissertation, University of California, Berkeley, 1968.

The Peace Negotiations of the Nations: Suggestions for Adequate Guarantees for Lasting Peace, A Message to Christians of all Lands from Christians in America (pamphlet). N.p., 1917.

Peaslee, Amos J. *Proposed Amendment to the Judiciary Articles of the Constitution of the League of Nations* (pamphlet). [Paris: n.p., 1919].

Penn, William. "An Essay Towards the Present and Future Peace of Europe," *The Fruits of Solitude and Other Writings.* New York: E. P. Dutton and Co., 1915.

Perkins, Dexter. *Charles Evans Hughes and American Democratic Statesmanship.* Boston: Little, Brown and Co., 1956.

————. *Hands Off! A History of the Monroe Doctrine.* Boston: Little, Brown and Co., 1948.

Peter, Eunice B. "Democracy and the Cure for War," *International Peace: Winning Essays* (pamphlet). Lake Mohonk, N.Y.: Lake Mohonk Conference on International Arbitration, 1912.

A Petition to the President and Congress (pamphlet). New York: n.p., 1917.

Phelps, Christina. *The Anglo-American Peace Movement in the Mid-Nineteenth Century.* New York: Columbia University Press, 1930.

Phillips, Walter A. *The Confederation of Europe: A Study of the European Alliance, 1813–1823, as an Experiment in the International Organization of Peace.* New York: Longmans, Green and Co., 1914.

Pollard, Albert F. *The League of Nations in History.* London: Oxford University Press, 1918.

Proceedings of the Conferences of Delegates of Allied Societies for a League of Nations (pamphlet). New York: League to Enforce Peace, [1919].

Pusey, Merlo J. *Charles Evans Hughes.* 2 vols. New York: Macmillan, 1951.

Putnam, George Haven, and L. F. Abbott. "The Treaty of Peace and the League of Nations," *American Rights League Bulletin* (pamphlet), No. 47, n.p.

Ralston, Jackson H. *International Arbitration from Athens to Locarno.* Stanford, Calif.: Stanford University Press, 1929.

Randall, Mercedes M. *Improper Bostonian: Emily Greene Balch.* New York: Twayne Publishers, 1964.

Redmond, Kent G. "Henry L. Stimson and the Question of League Membership," *The Historian,* XXV (February 1963), 200–212.

Reiman, J. D. Jr. *The Solution of the International Crisis* (pamphlet). N.p., n.d.

Reinsch, Paul S. *Public International Unions: Their Work and Organization.* Boston: Ginn and Co., 1911.

―――. *World Politics at the End of the Nineteenth Century.* New York: Macmillan, 1904.

Republican Club of the City of New York. *Universal Peace by Conciliation and Arbitration Through an International Court of Arbitral Justice with Arbitration Treaties Between all Nations and Efficient Armament for National Security* (pamphlet). New York: n.p., 1910.

Reutter, Clifford J. "St. Louis Reaction to United States Foreign Policy: A Study of Opinion on Key International Events, As Reflected in Local Press and Congressional Expression, with Special Attention to the Isolationist Tendency." Unpublished doctoral dissertation, St. Louis University, 1950.

Richardson, James D., comp. *Messages and Papers of the Presidents.* 20 vols. New York: Bureau of National Literature, 1897–1917.

Rippy, J. Fred. *America and the Strife of Europe.* Chicago: University of Chicago Press, 1938.

Rivas, R. "Bolívar as Internationalist," *Bulletin of the Pan American Union,* LXIV (December 1930), 1266–1311.

Robinson, Margaret. *Arbitration and the Hague Peace Conferences, 1899 and 1907.* Philadelphia: n.p., n.d.

Roosevelt, Theodore, and George Haven Putnam. "An Alliance of the English-Speaking Peoples of the World," *American Rights League Bulletin* (pamphlet), No. 44, n.p.

Roosevelt, Theodore. *Works of Theodore Roosevelt.* 24 vols. New York: Charles Scribner's Sons, 1923–26.

Root, Elihu. "Address by the Honorable Elihu Root, . . ." *International Conciliation* (pamphlet), No. 18 (May 1909).

Schlesinger, Arthur M. *The Rise of the City.* New York: Macmillan, 1933.

Schwarzenberger, Georg. *William Ladd: An Examination of an American Proposal for an International Equity Tribunal.* London: Constable and Co., 1935.

Scott, James Brown. "America and the New Diplomacy," *International Conciliation* (pamphlet), No. 16 (March 1909).

————. *The Hague Peace Conferences of 1899 and 1907.* 2 vols. Baltimore: Johns Hopkins University Press, 1909.

————. *Peace Through Justice: Three Papers on International Justice and the Means of Attaining It.* New York: Oxford University Press, 1917.

————. "The Work of the Second Hague Conference," *International Conciliation* (pamphlet), No. 5 (January 1908).

Sells, Elijah W. *A Plan for International Peace* (pamphlet). New York: n.p., 1915.

Septimus. "A Sound League of Nations," *English-Speaking World* (pamphlet), June 1919.

Seymour, Charles. *The Intimate Papers of Colonel House.* 4 vols. Boston: Houghton Mifflin Co., 1926–28.

Shibley, George H. *The Allies Pledged to a United States of Europe* (pamphlet). Washington, D.C.: League for World Peace, 1915.

————. *The Road to Victory: It Lies Through the United States Program for World Liberation* (pamphlet). Washington, D.C.: League for World Federation, 1918.

Short, Frank B. *Peace or War? Which Shall It Be?* (pamphlet). N.p., n.d.

Short, William H. "How the League of Nations Came To Be." Mimeographed copy of speech delivered in 1926. Short Papers.

Sidgwick, Rose. "The League of Nations," *Rice Institute Pamphlets,* VI (April 1919).

Skinner, Hubert M. *The Federation of the World* (pamphlet). N.p., 1910.

Smialovzky, V. and T. *Through Darkest Imperialism: A Memorial of a Hundred Years' Peace, Suggestions for the San Francisco Exhibition* (pamphlet). Budapest: Pest Printing Co., 1914.

Smith, Roderick H. *A Constitution for World-Wide Federation* (pamphlet). N.p., [1911].

————. *Proposed Platform for the American Party* (pamphlet). Rev. ed. Buffalo, N.Y.: n.p., 1907.

————. *One of the Assets of the American Money Enterprise: Proposed Joint Resolution Inviting the Powers to Join the United States of America in Establishing a Court of Nations and to Provide for an International Army and Navy* (pamphlet). 3d ed. Buffalo, N.Y.: Roderick H. Smith, 1913.

Souleyman, Elizabeth V. *The Vision of World Peace in Seventeenth and Eighteenth-Century France.* New York: G. P. Putnam's Sons, 1941.

Stead, W. T. "To the Picked Half Million," *World Peace Foundation Pamphlets,* III (September 1913).

————. *The United States of Europe on the Eve of the Parliament of Peace.* New York: Doubleday and MacClure Co., 1899.

Stein, Robert. *An International Police to Guarantee the World's Peace* (pamphlet). Washington, D.C.: Judd and Detweiler, Inc., 1912.

Steytler, Edmund J. "France and the Wilsonian Program." Unpublished doctoral dissertation, University of North Carolina, 1956.

Stimson, Henry L., and McGeorge Bundy. *On Active Service in Peace and War.* New York: Harper and Bros., 1947.

Stone, Ralph A. "The Irreconcilables and the Fight Against the League of Nations." Unpublished doctoral dissertation, University of Illinois, 1961.

Stourzh, Gerald. *Benjamin Franklin and American Foreign Policy.* Chicago: University of Chicago Press, 1954.

Stout, Ralph, ed. *Roosevelt in the Kansas City Star.* Boston: Houghton Mifflin Co., 1921.

Stratton, George M. "The Double Standard in Regard to Fighting," *International Conciliation* (pamphlet), No. 59 (October 1912).

Straus, Oscar. *Mr. Root and Article X: His Conflicting Views* (pamphlet). N.p., n.d.

Stromberg, Roland N. *Collective Security and American Foreign Policy: From the League of Nations to NATO.* New York: Frederick A. Praeger, 1963.

Stuyt, M. *Survey of International Arbitrations, 1794–1938.* The Hague: Martinus Nijhoff, 1939.

Suchtelen, Nico Van. *The Only Solution—A European Federation* (pamphlet). N.p., n.d.

Sumner, Charles. *Works of Charles Sumner.* 15 vols. Boston: Lee and Shepard, 1870–83.

Suttner, Bertha von. *Memoirs of Bertha von Suttner: The Records of an Eventful Life.* 2 vols. Boston: Ginn and Co., 1910.

Taft, Philip. *The A.F. of L. in the Time of Gompers.* New York: Harper and Bros., 1957.

Taft, William Howard. "The Dawn of World Peace," *International Conciliation* (pamphlet), Special Bulletin, November 1911.

———. *The United States and Peace.* New York: Charles Scribner's Sons, 1914.

Tate, Merze. *The Disarmament Illusion: The Movement for a Limitation of Armaments to 1907.* New York: Macmillan, 1942.

Tillman, Seth P. *Anglo-American Relations at the Paris Peace Conference of 1919.* Princeton, N.J.: Princeton University Press, 1961.

Towne, Charles A. *Universal Peace Movement.* (62 Cong., 2d sess.; Sen. Doc. No. 289.) Washington, D.C.: Government Printing Office, 1912.

Trueblood, Benjamin. *The Federation of the World.* New York: Houghton Mifflin Co., 1899.

Tryon, James L. *The Interparliamentary Union and its Work* (pamphlet). Boston: American Peace Society, 1910.

United States, Congress. *Congressional Globe.* 42 Cong., 2d sess., vol. 45. Washington, D.C.: Government Printing Office, 1871–72.

———. *Congressional Record.* 43 Cong., 1st sess., vol. 2; 51 Cong., 1st sess., vol. 21; 2d sess., vol. 21; 58 Cong., 3d sess., vol. 39; 60–65 Cong., vols. 42–55.

Washington, D.C.: Government Printing Office, 1890–91, 1904–05, 1907–19.

The United States of Europe (pamphlet). N.p., n.d.

United States, House. *Report on Increase of Territory by Conquest.* Committee on Foreign Affairs. (62 Cong., 2d sess.; House Doc. No. 705.) Washington, D.C.: Government Printing Office, 1912.

———. *Hearing on International Federation for the Maintenance of Peace.* Committee on Foreign Affairs, May 7, 1910. (61 Cong., 2d sess.) Washington, D.C.: Government Printing Office, 1910.

———. *Hearing on Joint Assembly and Meeting of the Parliaments and National Legislative Bodies of the World in the United States.* Committee on Foreign Affairs, January 19, 1911. (61 Cong., 3d sess.) Washington, D.C.: Government Printing Office, 1911.

———. *Report on Universal Peace.* Committee on Foreign Affairs. (61 Cong., 2d sess.; House Doc. No. 1440.) Washington, D.C.: Government Printing Office, 1910.

United States, Senate. "International Arbitration." (63 Cong., 3d sess.; Sen. Doc. No. 987.) Washington, D.C.: Government Printing Office, 1915.

———. "International Peace Tribunal, Letter Addressed to John F. Shafroth by Oscar T. Crosby." (64 Cong., 1st sess.; Sen. Doc. No. 378.) Washington, D.C.: Government Printing Office, 1916.

———. "International Peace Tribunal, Letter Addressed to John F. Shafroth by Oscar T. Crosby." (64 Cong., 1st sess.; Sen. Doc. No. 245.) Washington, D.C.: Government Printing Office, 1916.

———. *Report of the Committee on Foreign Relations . . . upon the General Arbitration Treaties Signed on August 3, 1911. . . .* (62 Cong., 1st sess.; Sen. Doc. No. 98.) Washington, D.C.: Government Printing Office, 1911.

———. "Tribunal for International Disputes. Letter from Oscar T. Crosby to Senator John F. Shafroth." (64 Cong., 1st sess.; Sen. Doc. No. 535.) Washington, D.C.: Government Printing Office, 1916.

Vance, William R. "The Vision of a World Court," *Judicial Settlement of International Disputes* (pamphlet), No. 28 (February 1917).

Van Doren, Carl. *The Great Rehearsal: The Story of the Making and Ratifying of the Constitution of the United States.* New York: Viking Press, 1948.

Van Kirk, J. W. *Worldism* (pamphlet). Youngstown, Ohio: n.p., 1914.

Veblen, Thorstein. *An Inquiry Into the Nature of Peace and the Terms of Its Perpetuation.* New York: Macmillan, 1917.

Vincent, Francis. *Essay Recommending the Union of Great Britain and her Colonies and the United States, and the Final Union of the World into One Great Nation* (pamphlet). Wilmington, Del.: G. W. Vernon, 1870.

Vinson, John Chalmers. *Referendum for Isolation: Defeat of Article Ten of the League of Nations Covenant.* Athens: University of Georgia Press, 1961.

A Vote of the National Council of the National Economic League on International Problems of Reconstruction (pamphlet). N.p., n.d.

Walworth, Arthur. *Woodrow Wilson: American Prophet; World Prophet.* 2 vols. New York: Longman's, Green & Co., 1958.

Warren, Katherine. *International Peace: Winning Essays* (pamphlet). Lake Mohonk, N.Y.: Lake Mohonk Conference on International Arbitration, 1912.

Westermann, W. L. "Interstate Arbitration in Antiquity," *Classical Journal*, II (March 1907), 197–211.

Wheeler, Everett P. "A World Court and International Police," *Judicial Settlement of International Disputes* (pamphlet), No. 26 (August 1916).

White, Andrew D. *Autobiography of Andrew Dickson White*. 2 vols. New York: Century Co., 1905–07.

————. *Seven Great Statesmen*. New York: Century Co., 1910.

Whitney, Edson L. *The American Peace Society: A Centennial History*. Washington, D.C.: American Peace Society, 1928.

Wilson, George G., and George F. Tucker. *International Law*. 5th ed. New York: Silver, Burdett and Co., 1910.

Wimer, Kurt. "Woodrow Wilson's Plan for a Vote of Confidence," *Pennsylvania History*, XXVIII (July 1961), 279–293.

Winkler, Henry R. *The League of Nations Movement in Great Britain, 1914– 1919*. New Brunswick, N.J.: Rutgers University Press, 1952.

Woolf, Leonard S. *International Government: Two Reports*. New York: Brentanos, 1916.

Worcester, Noah A. *Solemn Review of the Customs of War* (pamphlet). London: n.p., 1917.

World-Federation League. *The Peace Movement: The American Peace Commission* (pamphlet). New York: World-Federation League, 1910.

————. *The Peace Movement: The Federation of the World* (pamphlet). New York: World-Federation League, 1910.

World Peace Foundation. "Annual Report, 1915," *World Peace Foundation Pamphlets*, V (December 1915).

————. "World Peace Foundation Work in 1914," *World Peace Foundation Pamphlets*, IV (December 1914).

Wylie, F. J. "Cecil Rhodes and His Scholars as Factors in International Conciliation," *International Conciliation* (pamphlet), No. 25 (December 1909).

Wynner, Edith, and Georgia Lloyd. *Searchlights on Peace Plans: Choose Your Road to World Government*. New York: E. P. Dutton and Co., 1944.

York, Elizabeth. *Leagues of Nations: Ancient, Mediaeval, and Modern*. London: Swarthmore Press Ltd., 1919.

Manuscript Collections

Chandler P. Anderson, Library of Congress
Fannie Fern Andrews, Radcliffe College
Emily G. Balch, Swarthmore College Peace Collection
Randolph S. Bourne, Columbia University
Nicholas Murray Butler, Columbia University
Andrew Carnegie, Library of Congress
Carnegie Endowment for International Peace, Columbia University and Endowment Papers, New York City

Church Peace Union, New York City
Oscar T. Crosby, Library of Congress
Hayne Davis, Southern Historical Collection, Chapel Hill, North Carolina
Henry Forster, New York Public Library
Gilbert Hitchcock, Library of Congress
Frederick W. Holls, Columbia University
Hamilton Holt, Rollins College
Edward M. House, Yale University
William I. Hull, Friends' Historical Society, Swarthmore College
David Starr Jordan, Hoover Institution on War and Peace, Stanford University
Lake Mohonk Arbitration Conferences, Swarthmore College Peace Collection
League to Enforce Peace, Harvard University
Henry Cabot Lodge, Massachusetts Historical Society
A. Lawrence Lowell, Harvard College Archives
William O. McDowell, New York Public Library
Theodore Marburg, Library of Congress
S. C. Mitchell, Southern Historical Collection
Sidney E. Mezes, Library of Congress
David Hunter Miller, Library of Congress
George Nasmyth, Swarthmore College Peace Collection
New York Peace Society, Swarthmore College Peace Collection
Oral History Collection, Columbia University
Herbert Parsons, Columbia University
Pennsylvania Arbitration and Peace Society, Swarthmore College Peace Collection
E. L. Philipp, Wisconsin State Historical Society
Theodore Roosevelt, Library of Congress
Elihu Root, Library of Congress
Albert Shaw, New York Public Library
William H. Short, Rollins College
Oscar S. Straus, Library of Congress
Henry L. Stimson, Yale University
William Howard Taft, Library of Congress
Benjamin F. Trueblood, Swarthmore College Peace Collection
United States Department of State, National Archives
Woodrow Wilson, Library of Congress
World's Court League, Swarthmore College Peace Collection

Series Publications and Proceedings of Conferences

American Conference on International Arbitration held in Washington, D.C., April 22 and 23, 1896. New York: [1896].
Second American Conference on International Arbitration held in Washington, D.C., January 12, 1904. Washington, D.C.: 1904.
American Association for International Conciliation. *International Conciliation.* New York: Nos. 1–135, 1907–1919.

American Friends' Peace Conference. Philadelphia: 1902.

American School Citizenship League. *Yearbook.* Boston: 1911–1919.

American Society of International Law. *Proceedings.* New York and Washington, D.C., 1907–1920.

American Society for Judicial Settlement of International Disputes. *Proceedings,* 1910–1916. Baltimore: 1911–1917.

Lake Mohonk Conferences on International Arbitration. *Report of First to Twenty-Second Annual Lake Mohonk Conferences, 1895–1916.* Mohonk Lake, N.Y.: 1895–1916.

League to Enforce Peace. *The League Bulletin.* New York: Nos. 38–167, 1917–1920.

Maryland Quarterly. Baltimore: Nos. 1–12, 1910–1912.

National Peace and Arbitration Congresses. *Proceedings* (titles and places of publication vary). 1907, 1909, 1911, 1913, 1915.

New England Arbitration and Peace Congress. *Report of the Proceedings.* Boston: 1910.

New York Peace Society. *Yearbooks* (titles vary). New York: 1906–1914.

Universal Peace Congress. *Proceedings* of the Fourth to Seventeenth.

World Peace Foundation. *Pamphlet* series, 1911–1917; *League of Nations* series, 1917–1918. Boston: 1911–1923.

Periodicals

Advocate of Peace, 1903–1920

American Journal of International Law, 1907–1919

American Political Science Review, 1907–1919

Annals of the American Academy of Political and Social Science, 1915–1919

Atlantic Monthly, 1915–1919

Bookman, 1914–1918

Current History, 1914–1919

Current Opinion, 1915–1918

The Forum, 1914–1919

Harper's Weekly, 1900–1916

The Independent, 1896–1920

League of Nations Magazine, 1919

Literary Digest, 1909–1920

Living Age, 1915–1919

The Nation, 1902–1919

New England Magazine, 1892–1897

New Republic, 1914–1919

North American Review, 1915–1919

The Outlook, 1902–1919

Peace Forum, 1912–1915

The Peace Movement, 1912–1914

Review of Internationalism, 1907

Review of Reviews, 1902–1919

The Survey, 1907–1919
War and Peace, 1913–1915
The World Court, 1916–1918
World's Work, 1910–1919
World Unity Magazine, 1927–1935
Yale Review, 1915–1919

INDEX